A HISTORY OF DEVIZES

RALPH B. PUGH

with contributions by
H. F. CHETTLE, ELIZABETH CRITTALL,
and D. A. CROWLEY

WILTSHIRE COUNTY COUNCIL
AND
KENNET DISTRICT COUNCIL
2001

The text, some of the illustrations, and the maps in this volume have been reset and reprinted from A History of Wiltshire, volume III, *edited by R. B. Pugh and Elizabeth Crittall, 1956, and* A History of Wiltshire, *volume X, edited by Elizabeth Crittall, 1975 (The Victoria History of the Counties of England; Oxford University Press for the University of London Institute of Historical Research).*

© *University of London, 1956, 1975, 2001*

All rights reserved. No part of this publication may be reproduced, stored in a retrieval system, or transmitted, in any form or by any means, electronic, mechanical, photocopying, recording, or otherwise, without the prior permission of Oxford University Press.

First published in this edition in 2001 by
Wiltshire County Council, Libraries and Heritage,
Bythesea Road, Trowbridge, Wiltshire BA14 8BS,
in conjunction with Kennet District Council

ISBN 0 86080 450 X

Typeset in 11/12.5 Bembo
Typesetting and design by John Chandler
Printed by Wiltshire County Council

CONTENTS

	PAGE
Contents	iii
List of Illustrations and Maps	v
Editorial Note	vii

Devizes   by RALPH B. PUGH

Introduction	1
Growth of the Town	13
Castle and Lordship to c. 1550	36
Castle Buildings	51
Parks	57
Castle Estate since c. 1550	60
Lesser Estates	67
The Town as a County Centre	73
Trade and Industry	80
Inns	103
Agriculture	109
Markets and Fairs	112
Borough Government	126
Municipal Buildings	149
Seals, Insignia, Records, and Chief Officers	155
Parish Government	158
Public Services	161
The Constituency	170
Churches	172
Roman Catholicism	199
Protestant Nonconformity	200
Social and Cultural Activities	215
Education	219
Charities for the Poor and Highways	234

Hospitals   by H. F. CHETTLE and ELIZABETH CRITTALL

The Hospital of St. John the Baptist	254
The Hospital of St. James and St. Denis, Southbroom	255

Index   by D. A. CROWLEY   257

LIST OF ILLUSTRATIONS AND MAPS

ILLUSTRATIONS   PAGE

Devizes: air view from the north-west. Aerofilms Ltd., 1955	viii
Dunkirk toll-house in 1958. Photograph by Margaret Tomlinson	6
Great Porch in 1998. Photograph, Wiltshire Libraries and Heritage	17
Greystone House. Photograph, Wiltshire Libraries and Heritage	25
Long Street. Photograph, Wiltshire Libraries and Heritage	26
The Brittox. Photograph of c. 1860 in the Town Hall	28
Bath Road, showing Dunkirk toll-house, Trafalgar Place, and, in the distance, Devizes prison, c. 1840. Drawing by W. Mudy, lithograph by Ackermann & Co., P11920, Wiltshire Libraries and Heritage	31
Cottages in Commercial Road (formerly Gains Lane), built after 1900. Photograph by John Chandler, 2001	34
The castle from the south. Photograph, 1972	64
Brownston House in the 1960s. Photograph, P910, Wiltshire Libraries and Heritage	68
Plan of Devizes Prison. Wiltshire and Swindon Record Office, A 1/509/4	76
Devizes Prison in 1889. Photograph, P18049, Wiltshire Libraries and Heritage	77
The Assize Court c. 1840. Drawing by T. H. Wyatt, lithograph by Ackermann & Co., P11922, Wiltshire Libraries and Heritage	78
The arms of the Devizes Guilds. Drawn by H. Ellis Tomlinson	85
Eighteenth-century trade labels from (i) photograph in Anstie Papers, (ii) British Museum	95
Anstie's snuff factory, formerly a cloth factory. Photograph, Wiltshire Libraries and Heritage	96
Wadworth's brewery c. 1968. Photograph, P765, Wiltshire Libraries and Heritage	98
The Bear Inn and the Corn Exchange. Photograph, Wiltshire Libraries and Heritage	117
Market Place. Photograph, Wiltshire Libraries and Heritage	118
The Market Place in 1798. From a pen-and-wash drawing by Robert Noyes in the possession (1974) of Appleby Bros., Fine Art Dealers, London	120

The Green c. 1840. Drawing by W. Mudy, lithograph by Ackermann
   & Co., P11926, Wiltshire Libraries and Heritage   125
St. John's Street in the earlier 18th century, showing the Wool or 'Old'
   Hall, rebuilt between 1806 and 1808. From an oil painting in the
   Town Hall   151
Town Hall, as rebuilt 1806–8. Lithograph of c. 1840 by Ackermann
   & Co., P11925, Wiltshire Libraries and Heritage   153
The arms of the Borough of Devizes. Drawn by H. Ellis Tomlinson   156
The church of St. John the Baptist in the early 19th century. Water-
   colour by John Buckler in Devizes Museum   184
The church of St. Mary in the early 19th century. Water-colour by
   John Buckler in Devizes Museum   189
The church of St. James, Southbroom, in 1803. Water-colour by John
   Buckler in Devizes Museum   195
The Crammer, with St. James's church and churchyard beyond, in the
   early 20th century. Photograph, P2611, Wiltshire Libraries and
   Heritage   197
The Old Alms-house in St. John's churchyard in 1998. Photograph,
   Wiltshire Libraries and Heritage   238

MAPS

Devizes Boundary Extensions   2
Part of Edward Dore's Plan of Devizes, 1759 (British Museum)   14–15
Devizes Street Plan, 1973   18

EDITORIAL NOTE

The text presented here, including the numbering of the footnotes, remains unchanged from when it was first published in the *Victoria History of Wiltshire* series in 1956 (Hospitals) and 1975 (Devizes). The format and pagination, however, are different, and in consequence a new index has been prepared based on the original indexes. The maps and illustrations which accompanied the text when first published are all included here, and they have been supplemented by others from the *Victoria History of Wiltshire* and from the collection held by Wiltshire County Council, Libraries and Heritage. A few footnotes have been amended to take account of the new pagination and the placing of maps and illustrations in the present edition. The footnotes and, to a lesser extent, the text include abbreviations employed according to the *Victoria History's* editorial conventions. While the meaning of most will be self-evident, some abbreviated references to documentary sources may cause difficulty, and readers are advised to consult the detailed lists of abbreviations and classes of public records used, which are prefaced to the original 1956 and 1975 publications. Among the most frequently used abbreviations are the following: B.L. (British Library); P.R.O. (Public Record Office); *V.C.H.* (*Victoria County History*); *W.A.M.* (*Wiltshire Archaeological and Natural History Magazine*); W.A.S. (Wiltshire Archaeological and Natural History Society); W.R.O. (Wiltshire and Swindon Record Office); W.R.S. (Wiltshire Record Society).

Devizes: air view from the north-west in 1955. St. Mary's church is on the left, the Market Place in the centre, and the site of the castle, partly obscured by trees, on the extreme right

THE BOROUGH OF DEVIZES

DEVIZES, a borough by prescription, lies almost exactly in the centre of the county.[1] Deemed a hundred in itself in Richard I's reign,[2] a part of Cannings hundred in 1280,[3] and a part of Bishop's Rowborough hundred in 1316,[4] it has since 1592 been claimed as a liberty within the hundred of Potterne and Cannings.[5] Speed, however, marked it (1610)[6] within Swanborough hundred and the boundary of that hundred, as he traced it, was considered to have some authority even in 1839.[7]

Today the boundaries of the borough enclose an irregular area of 1,420 a.[8] The town lies on a shelf at the point where an outlier of the Lower Chalk, which forms Roundway Hill, falls gradually to the Upper Greensand plain, and where, below Devizes, that plain yields to the Gault. A small projection from this shelf with steeply sloping sides forms a fitting base for Devizes castle and to the north and west of the castle the town grew up. The old town area contains many wells but there is hardly any running water apart from trickling streams in the old park, one of which, following its southern edge, was known in 1654 as Black Water.[9] In the 16th century, however, there was a town watering place to the south-east of St. John's church[10] and in the next century a stream to the north of the castle was said to possess the power of petrifaction.[11]

Until the early 19th century the borough was made up of the parishes of St. John (643 a.) and St. Mary (34 a.). The first, also called the

1 Though started much earlier this article was revised and completed between 1970 and 1973.
2 *Cur. Reg. R.* 1194–5 (Pipe R. Soc. xiv), 109.
3 J.I. 3/71 m. 18.
4 *V.C.H. Wilts.* vii. 175.
5 *W.N. & Q.* ii. 142; Cunnington, *Annals*, i (2nd pagin.), 93–4.
6 *Theatre of the Empire of Gt. Britain*.
7 Waylen, *Chrons.* 73.
8 *Census*, 1971.
9 Soc. Antiq., Jackson MSS. v, f. 151, Map. W.R.O. 943 gives information about the watercourses, then canalized, as they were in 1715.
10 See p. 23.
11 Aubrey, *Nat. Hist. Wilts.* ed. Britton, 24; cf. ibid. 26.

I

DEVIZES BOUNDARY EXTENSIONS

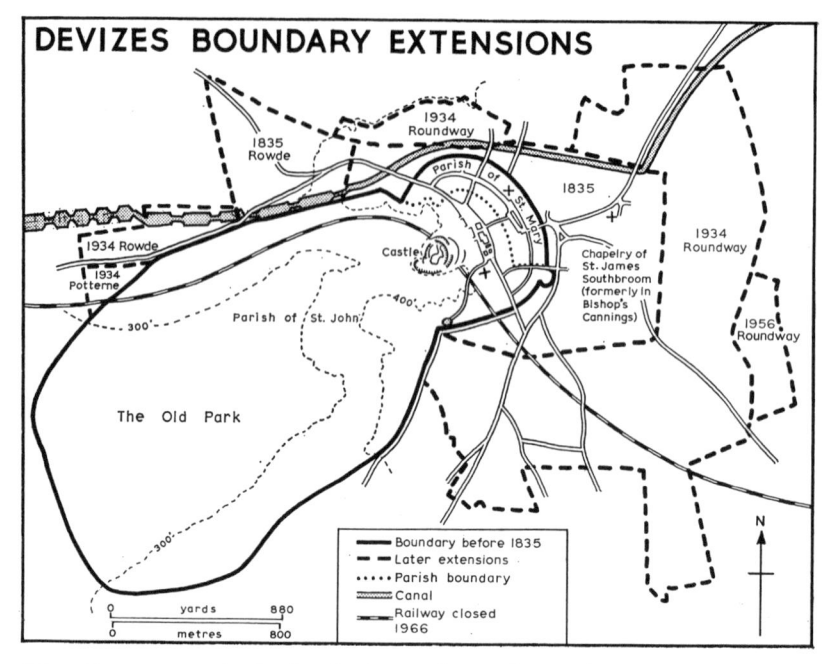

Map showing:
- 1934 Roundway
- 1835 Rowde
- 1934 Rowde
- 1934 Potterne
- Castle
- Chapelry of St. James Southbroom (formerly in Bishop's Cannings)
- 1835
- 1934 Roundway
- 1956 Roundway
- Parish of St. John
- The Old Park

Key:
- —— Boundary before 1835
- – – Later extensions
- ••• Parish boundary
- ≡≡ Canal
- — Railway closed 1966

New Port, comprised what had once been the castle precincts, with the old park stretching away beyond it; the second, also called the Old Port, what had been in the earlier Middle Ages the commercial area northeast of the castle.[12] In 1614 a part of St. John's parish lay outside the borough.[13] The extra-burghal area is not defined but it was perhaps the old park. If so, the exclusion did not remain unchallenged for much longer, for in 1646–7[14] the borough magistrates successfully asserted their authority over the park, and claimed in 1831 that they had exercised it throughout living memory.[15]

As the plan on this page shows, St. Mary's parish forms an arc bounded at most points by the outer and inner town ditches. The boundary, however, left the inner town ditch in Morris's Lane and turned eastward until it reached the outer town ditch towards the end of Hare and Hounds Street. It seems, too, that to the west of Maryport Street it ran somewhat to the west of the inner ditch.[16] St. John's parish lies to

12 The parochial areas are taken from *Census*, 1891.
13 W.R.O. 632/107, acct. of Apr. 12 Jas. I.
14 Cunnington, *Annals* (2nd pagin.), 115.
15 *Rep. Bdy. Coms.* iii (i), H.C. 141, p. 103 (1831–2), xl.
16 Thanks are due to Mr. Michael May, Devizes, for some help at this point.

the south-west of St. Mary's. The boundaries are so plotted in 1759[17] but in 1831 the boundary of the borough, and of St. John's parish, is extended on the east by an unexplained beak-shaped excrescence taking in the houses between Hare and Hounds Court[18] and Southbroom Road. By the Representation of the People Act, 1832,[19] and the Municipal Corporations Act, 1835,[20] the areas of the parliamentary and municipal boroughs were respectively extended by the addition of a small part of Rowde parish (mainly Dunkirk) and a part of the chapelry of St. James or Southbroom (in Bishop's Cannings 'ancient' parish). These extensions, designed to make the urban area and the borough coincide, enlarged the borough from 677 a. to 907 a.[21] In 1894 those parts of Rowde and Southbroom which lay within the borough were made separate civil parishes under the names of Rowde Within and Southbroom or St. James's. At the same time that part of Southbroom which lay outside the borough was formed into a new parish called Roundway. In 1934 11 a. of Potterne parish, 32 a. of Rowde parish, and 442 a. of Roundway parish were added to the borough and in 1956 29 a. more of Roundway parish.[22] Thus at the present time the borough is made up of the two 'ancient' parishes of Devizes, and parts of the 'ancient' parishes of Bishop's Cannings, Potterne, and Rowde. The history of Potterne and Rowde has already been narrated.[23] So in the main has that of Bishop's Cannings, including the modern parish of Roundway.[24] The history, however, of that part of the former chapelry of Southbroom that now lies within the borough is dealt with below as is that of Wick Green, formerly a tithing in that chapelry.[25]

Southbroom, lying on the east of the ancient borough, is first mentioned in 1227.[26] It was probably then part of a broom-clad area,[27]

17 Edw. Dore, *Plan of Ancient Borough of Devizes* (1759).
18 For map of the old borough with boundary extensions proposed 1831 and adopted 1832, see *Rep. Bdy. Coms.* (1831–2), xl, facing p. 103.
19 2 & 3 Wm. IV, c. 64.
20 5 & 6 Wm. IV, c. 76.
21 Second figure, from *Census*, 1861, is that for the urban sanitary district, which coincided with the borough.
22 *V.C.H. Wilts.* iv. 346; *Census*. The statements in *V.C.H. Wilts.* vii. 187 about the changes of 1894 are not completely accurate.
23 *V.C.H. Wilts.* vii. 207, 217.
24 Ibid. 187.
25 Ibid.
26 *Cal. Chart. R.* 1226–57, 51, 93.
27 *P.N. Wilts.* (E.P.N.S.), 243.

which seems still traceable in 1360, when a cottage stood 'super Southbrom'.[28] Indeed there is nothing to show that a distinguishable settlement ever bore its name. As a chapelry, however, it was distinct from its parent, and was a township (*villata*) in 1280.[29] In 1736–7 it was reputed a manor.[30] Its status as a chapelry was terminated in 1832 when it became a perpetual curacy.[31] Its most conspicuous characteristic is the Green, no doubt the remnants of the broom-covered tract of earlier times. Destined for inclosure in 1819, it survived that fate and in 1899 was bought by the corporation from the Estcourts, allottees under the award.[32]

The tithing of Wick lies due south of the old borough. There was a Roman settlement here apparently from the 2nd to the 4th century around the area once occupied by Pans Lane halt. There are also faint indications of another settlement on the green,[33] and a cemetery on the site of Southbroom junior school.[34] Wick is first mentioned in 1249[35] and is called 'the Weke' in 1542.[36] 'Netherwike' bears that name in 1593.[37] In 1736–7 the settlement consisted of Upper Wick and Wick.[38] In 1759 the former is no longer given any special name.[39] In 1773 the larger settlement is called Devizes Wick, the prefix being doubtless added to distinguish it from Potterne Wick and Wick in Rowde.[40] In 1795–6 the hamlet contained between 30 and 33 assessable houses.[41] The town has gradually encroached upon the tithing, which is now a residential suburb.

The earliest population estimate, that of 1548, is best expressed in comparative terms. Devizes then had fewer communicants than Marlborough and far fewer than St. Edmund's, Salisbury.[42] In 1696 the

28 B.M. Add. Ch. 37471.
29 J.I. 3/71 m. 18.
30 W.A.S. Libr., Devizes, Map, 1736–7.
31 See p. 194.
32 W.R.O., Inclosure Map, Bishop's Cannings, Southbroom, etc. 1819; Gillman, *Annals*, 68.
33 *V.C.H. Wilts.* i (1), 62–3.
34 *W.A.M.* lviii. 222–3.
35 *W.R.S.* xvi, p. 175, where, however, the place is indexed under Rowde.
36 Prob. 11/29 (P.C.C. 4 Spert, will of Wm. Page).
37 Soc. Antiq., Jackson MSS. v, f. 191.
38 W.A.S. Libr., Devizes, Map, 1647.
39 Dore, Map, 1759.
40 *W.R.S.* viii, pl. 11.
41 W.R.O., Q. Sess. Admin., Navy Act, 1795; Army and Navy Acts, 1796–7.
42 *W.A.M.* xxiii. 256.

roles of Devizes and Marlborough were reversed, many more men subscribing to the Association from the first than from the second. Salisbury, however, was still far ahead of both.[43] In 1655 the two Devizes parishes were said to contain 485 families.[44] In 1761 their population was 3,121, of whom 1,767 lived in St. Mary's.[45] In 1801 their population was 3,547. Southbroom then numbered 1,200. Both totals rose gradually over the next three decades. What the total population was immediately after the boundary changes of 1832–5 cannot be readily determined, but by 1851, when the census takes those changes into account, it was over 6,500. The number fluctuated slightly in the next 80 years, reaching its peak in 1871 and its trough in 1921. It then rose substantially after the boundary changes of 1934,[46] and in 1971 stood at 9,755.[47]

The road through Devizes from Marlborough to Trowbridge and thence westwards into Somerset is marked on Ogilby's map of 1675.[48] It was therefore an ancient and important thoroughfare. That section of it that ran into the town from Shepherd's Shore was turnpiked in 1706–7. So was the Salisbury road from the foot of Etchilhampton Hill near Stert, and the Chippenham road as far as Rowde Ford.[49] The alternative, southern, road to Salisbury was turnpiked as far as West Lavington in 1750–1 and the Melksham road as far as Seend at the same time.[50] Thus by the mid 18th century Devizes was approached by good roads on every side. The Improvement Commissioners, set up in 1825,[51] made them, as they approached the town, better still.[52]

The Melksham and Chippenham roads, which now part company at the former toll-house at the top of Dunkirk hill have not always done so. Until at least 1759 they diverged at an acute angle at a point now marked by the Bath Road bridge over the canal. The Melksham road ran along the line of the present St. Joseph's Road, or perhaps of the canal, to Prison bridge on the canal. Thence it descended by Caen Hill.

43 *W.N. & Q.* vi. 199–201, 350–1, 485–92.
44 *W.A.M.* ii. 330 n.
45 Ibid. xxvii. 314.
46 *V.C.H. Wilts.* iv. 343, 346.
47 *Census*, 1971.
48 *V.C.H. Wilts.* iv. 256.
49 Ibid.; 6 Anne, c. 26.
50 *V.C.H. Wilts.* iv. 259. What seems to be its present course is marked on *W.R.S.* viii, pl. 11.
51 See p. 146.
52 Cunnington, *Annals*, ii. 184.

The Chippenham road followed the course of the present Bath Road until it reached a point now marked by 'Braeside'. Thence two roads fell steeply to the plain. The easternmost, now called Little Lane, bore off northwards to Iron Peartree farm (in Rowde). To the west of it what is now called Big Lane descended north-westwards in a cutting to join the present Chippenham road near the Ox House.[53] Big Lane was abandoned presumably by 1773 in favour of the easier descent via Dunkirk.[54]

Dunkirk toll-house in 1958

Until the road to West Lavington was turnpiked the exits on the south were also somewhat different from what they are today. The present Potterne Road was primarily an approach to the hamlet of Wick which was itself fairly well connected with Crookwood and Urchfont by roads which have now largely lost their old significance.[55] Beyond Wick the present Potterne Road was 'only a sack and pack road'.[56] What is now Hillworth Road then as now ran westwards out of Long Street.[57] It then

53 Dore, Map, 1759.
54 *W.R.S.* viii, pl. 11; O.S. Map 6", ST 96 SE (1961 edn.).
55 W.A.S. Libr., Devizes, Map, 1647; *W.R.S.* viii, pl. 11.
56 Waylen, *Chrons.* 350, quoting letter of 1771.
57 W.A.S. Libr., Devizes, Map, 1647; Dore, Map, 1759.

took a sharp turn southwards and thereupon assumed the name of 'Devizes Sand Way' (1654) or 'The Sands Lane' (1736–7).[58] This is now Hartmoor Road (formerly Hartmoor), a name apparently taken from a small settlement in Potterne, recorded in 1424–5.[59] It runs along the side of the old park, and was in the earlier 20th century no better than a bridle path. In 1654, however, it is clearly marked[60] and seems even in 1773 to have been nearly as important as the Potterne road.[61] It led to Whistley (in Potterne) and beyond, and from it other roads gave access to Whistley and Jordon's mills. No doubt when those mills declined the Potterne road took its place. By 1970 Hartmoor Road, as it was then called, had once again been made up.

The exits on the north were more numerous than they are today. In 1736–7 a road of some substance led out of New Park Street to New Park, later Roundway House.[62] At that time it seems to have ended there, but by 1773 it continued northwards to debouch at Roundway mill.[63] Although in 1736–7 a road to the east of this one led direct to Roundway,[64] the straight avenue called Quakers Walk does not seem to have been then made. It existed, however, by 1759.[65] The stretch of the more westerly road that connected New Park house with the town was later abandoned.

Carriers were sending vans from London to Devizes by 1637, and by 1690 there was a weekly wagon service, which by 1722 had become twice weekly. A 'flying chaise' service for passengers, covering the London–Bath journey in a single day, was advertised in 1749, and by 1762 a coach service of equal speed seems to have been regularly available. By this time there were two direct routes from London to Bath, by Chippenham and by Devizes. The Chippenham route seems at first to have been preferred.[66]

The Kennet & Avon Canal, work on which began in 1796,[67] was diverted to the town from its original course through the efforts of the

58 Ibid. Maps, 1654, 1736–7.
59 Herkemour: D. & C. Sar. reeve's acct. Potterne prebend, 3–4 Hen.VI.
60 W.A.S. Libr., Devizes, Map, 1654.   61 W.R.S. viii, pl. 11.
62 W.A.S. Libr., Devizes, Map, 1736–7.
63 W.R.S. viii, pl. 11.
64 W.A.S. Libr., Devizes, Map, 1736–7.
65 Dore, Map, 1759.
66 W. A. Webb, *Early Years of Stage Coaching on Bath Rd.* (priv. print. 1922).
67 V.C.H. Wilts. iv. 275. The Kennet, from Newbury to Reading, had already been navigable for some time: ibid. 272.

three borough M.P.s.[68] It had reached Foxhangers (in Rowde) by about 1802 when a horse tramway connecting that place with the town was opened. The stretch to Foxhangers from the west was open for traffic in 1804 and the section from Devizes to Pewsey by 1807. The series of 29 locks from Foxhangers to Devizes was opened in 1810 and with it the whole canal from Bath to Newbury.[69]

The railway was brought to Devizes in 1857 when a branch was opened to connect the town with the Wilts., Somerset & Weymouth Railway at the point once occupied by Holt station. In 1862 the Berks. & Hants Extension Railway was built to connect it on the east side with Hungerford.[70] The station was built in 1856.[71] A halt was opened at Pans Lane in 1929[72] in anticipation of the traffic that might have been expected if the new county offices had been built beside the Green.[73] The station was closed for goods traffic in 1964 and for all purposes in 1966, the halt in 1964.[74] Both had been demolished by 1970.

The word 'Devizes' is the corruption of a pure Latin word,[75] a somewhat unusual origin for an English place-name. By 1330 the first syllable was beginning to be dropped and forms such as 'Vises' and 'Vies' remained common for a very long time. The addition of the English definite article was also common. 'The Devise' is found in 1519,[76] 'the Vyse' by 1480–3.[77] In 1839 Waylen said that prefixing the article in 'public documents' had 'become totally laid aside, only within a few years'.[78] Even in 1907, however, it could be said that 'country people' still spoke of 'the Vize'.[79]

The visits of early kings, their consorts, kin, and prisoners are set out below.[80] Later sovereigns naturally travelled the Bath road and so could enter the town with ease. Visits by James I are recorded in 1613,[81] 1618,[82] and 1624.[83]

68 K. R. Clew, *Kennet and Avon Canal*, 58.
69 *V.C.H. Wilts.* iv. 275.
70 Ibid. 284, 286–7.
71 Plans *penes* P.R. Dept., British Rail, W.R.
72 *V.C.H. Wilts.* iv. 291.
73 Ex inf. the late B. H. Cunnington; and see p. 74.
74 Ex inf. P.R. Dept., British Rail, W.R.
75 See p. 36.
76 *P.N. Cambs.* (E.P.N.S.), p. lvi.
77 *P.N. Wilts.* (E.P.N.S.), 243.
78 Waylen, *Chrons.* 11.
79 A. G. Bradley, *Round about Wilts.* (1907), 196.
80 See pp. 36–8, 43–5, 48.
81 Cunnington, *Annals*, i (2nd pagin.), 49.
82 Ibid. 57; *W.A.M.* ii. 319.
83 *W.A.M.* ii. 320.

Devizes, with Malmesbury, became in 1642, naturally enough, a centre for the North Wiltshire Militia,[84] and despite some local Royalist sentiment, including the mayor's (Richard Pierce), slipped readily into Parliamentary hands. This was the more easily achieved since Sir Edward Baynton, a deputy lieutenant who became in October commander-in-chief for the county, lived near by at Bromham House.[85] Warlike stores were brought in from other Wiltshire towns, ordnance was disposed so as to defend the town and its approaches, and perhaps some outworks were thrown up.[86] No attempt was made to fortify the castle.

In February 1643 the Royalist forces took Cirencester (Glos.) by storm and occupied Malmesbury. Their propinquity demoralized the Devizes garrison which was withdrawn on 20 February by Sir Edward Hungerford, who had succeeded Baynton. The Royalists took control next day. Though Hungerford returned briefly in March the town was from that month to remain in Royalist hands for nearly 2½ years. The garrison was strengthened about 9 July by some of the forces withdrawing from the indecisive battle of Lansdown (Som.), and Sir Ralph Hopton, who, though wounded, assumed command, requisitioned bedcords, as a substitute for match which was in short supply,[87] and lead from the church roofs. Waller drew up his forces on the east of the town, which he bombarded from the Jump, and his troops even reached 'the very streets'. Their way, however, was barred by barricades and it is doubtful whether they penetrated far.[88] Certainly the town did not fall and the battle of Roundway Down, fought on 13 July, which resulted in a decisive defeat for Waller, removed every threat for the time being.

During the course of 1644, however, the Parliamentarians strengthened their position in the neighbourhood. They recaptured Malmesbury, and, pressing right up to Devizes, charged the people round

84 Unless otherwise stated these three paragraphs are based on G.A. Harrison, 'Royalist Organisation in Wilts.' (Lond. Univ. Ph.D. thesis, 1963), and Waylen, *Hist.*
85 *V.C.H. Wilts.* vii. 181.
86 It seems clear that there were earthworks at the time of the siege of July 1643 (see below): Waylen, *Hist.* 163; *W.A.M.* liii. 280. There could hardly have been time to raise these between the arrival of the army from Lansdown and the inception of Waller's bombardment. The suggestion that the earthworks were no more than the remains of the town ditches (*W.A.M.* liii. 284) seems doubtful.
87 It has been said that a piece of hempen cord, worn as a hat–band, became a Royalist 'emblem of triumph', recalling the victory of Roundway Down (see below): Waylen, *Hist.* 172.
88 Waylen (*Hist.* 167) thought that they almost reached St. John's ch., but this seems unlikely (*W.A.M.* liii. 281).

about to destroy its earthworks. In the autumn the tables began to be turned. The Royalists planned to rebuild their strength in the west, centring their defences on Bristol and selecting Devizes as an outpost. Col. Charles Lloyd,[89] knighted soon after, became governor. He was an expert in fortification, and, in the first months of 1645, leaning perhaps on Hopton's aid, made Devizes castle the strongest fortress in the county. In March, while these preparations were in progress, the Prince of Wales (later Charles II) passed through the town to assume his post of 'General of the West' at Bristol. On 14 June, however, the New Model Army was victorious at Naseby and entering Wiltshire two weeks later and capturing Bristol on 11 September, dashed any hope that Lloyd may have cherished. On or about 21 September Cromwell appeared before the castle in person and on 23 September Lloyd capitulated. Although the Royalists made some forays in the ensuing winter, Devizes was permanently lost to them. It was in Devizes that Sir Edward Massey's brigade was disbanded in June 1646.

Lord Feversham's artillery passed through the town on 28 June 1685 and returned there after about ten days.[90] The Hampshire Militia followed hard upon the cannon[91] and the Wiltshire Militia entered on 10 July after the Sedgmoor campaign was over.[92] The story, however, that James II stayed a fortnight in the town after the battle cannot be verified.[93] George III passed through in 1789[94] and Pitt was demonstratively greeted in 1798.[95] A visit by Queen Charlotte in 1817 was matched by one paid by the Duchess of Kent and her daughter in 1830.[96] Edward VII, as Prince of Wales, was splendidly received in 1893 when he inspected the Yeomanry.[97]

From the 18th century some local disturbances are recorded. A riot, connected, it has been thought, with smuggling, occurred in 1765,[98] another in 1795 was averted by the arrival of the Yeomanry,[99] and a third of no great proportions a year later.[1] The last two were provoked by

---

89 *D.N.B.*
90 Hist. MSS. Com. 20, 11th Rep.V, *Dartmouth*, p. 126; ibid. 49, *Stopford-Sackville*, i, pp. 15, 21.
91 Hist. MSS. Com. 49, *Stopford-Sackville*, i, p. 11.
92 Waylen, *Hist.* 319.
93 Ibid. 319–21.
94 See p. 106.
95 Waylen, *Chrons.* 273.
96 See p. 106.
97 Gillman, *Annals*, 64–5.
98 Waylen, *Hist.* 406.
99 H. Graham, *Yeomanry Cavalry of Wilts.* 11.
1 Waylen, *Hist.* 470.

high food prices. A Militia riot in 1810, in which some townsmen and canal workers seemed disposed to participate, was quelled by the Yeomanry.[2] In 1817 a county meeting convened to congratulate the Prince Regent on his escape from assassination ended in disorder owing to hostility to 'Orator' Hunt who was in the crowd.[3] In November 1830 many townsmen were enrolled as special constables to withstand the current wave of agrarian sabotage, some Yeomanry units moved into the town, and a fair-sized group of suspects was imprisoned in the gaols.[4] A Working Men's Association existed in 1839 and for the next decade the town was never without some Chartists. The only disorder, however, occurred in March and April 1839 when two meetings were broken up, the second with violence.[5]

Devizes was the putative birthplace of Richard of Devizes, the 12th-century chronicler, Philip Stevens (d. c. 1660), botanist, Joseph Alleine (1634–68), Puritan divine, G. D. Bonner (1796–1836), wood engraver, F. E. Anstie (1833–74), physician, and Stephen Reynolds (1881–1919), author and expert on the inshore fishing industry. Thomas Pierce (1622–91), dean of Salisbury, Sir Edward Hannes (d. 1710), physician, and J. N. Tayler (1785–1864), rear-admiral, were the sons of Devizes men and probably natives. For about seven years from 1772 Sir Thomas Lawrence (1769–1830), the painter, lived at the Bear. Other residents were Charles Lucas (1769–1854), miscellaneous writer and divine, Elizabeth O. Benger (1778–1827), poet, novelist, and historian, and John Thurnam (1810–73), craniologist. The first was assistant curate, apparently from 1816, the second lived in the town only from 1797 to 1800, the third was medical superintendent at the county lunatic asylum from the time of its opening in 1851 until his death.[6] In 1843 George Eliot stayed with R. H. Brabant, a physician and prominent figure in town life, at his home at Sandcliffe, Northgate Street. Her host is said to have suggested 'Mr. Casaubon' in *Middlemarch*.[7]

---

2 Ibid. 493; Graham, op. cit. 56–8; W.R.O. 9, yeomanry letters, 1810.
3 Waylen, *Hist.* 508–13.
4 H.O. 52/11, Smith to Freeling, 22, 23 Nov. 1830, from Mair 27 Nov. 1830, from Devizes post office, 27 Nov. 1830, from Brotherton, 7 Dec. 1830.
5 *Chartist Studies*, ed. Asa Briggs, 178, 182–4, 198, 202, 212–13, 216.
6 *D.N.B.*; J Stratford, *Wilts. and its Worthies*, 128. For Reynolds, see *W.A.M.* xl. 371–2; xli. 74–8. For Pierce see also p. 86, for Tayler p. 30, and Lawrence pp. 105–6.
7 G. S. Haight, *George Eliot* (1968), 49–50, 449–50; *Leisure in Wilts.* (Wilts. Co. Council, 1969), 40.

The many notabilities connected with the castle are referred to below.[8] An unusually distinguished list of borough M.P.s includes the names of Sir Robert Long (d. 1673), Sir Francis Child the elder (1642–1713), John Methuen (?1650–1706), Henry Addington, later Viscount Sidmouth (1757–1844), Sir Philip C. H. Durham (1763–1845), Montagu Gore (1800–64), T. H. S. Sotheron Estcourt (1801–76), and James Bucknall Estcourt (1802–55).[9]

Since the time of James Davis (d. 1755), a Welsh physician resident in the borough, Devizes has been the nursing-mother of antiquaries. Davis's antiquarian interests seem to have been serious, but his only published work, the anonymous *Origines Divisianae* (1754), was at least in part a satire upon fantastic etymological theories then current.[10] John Collins (living 1771) was still remembered in 1839 as 'an antiquary in mind, manners, and dress'.[11] James Waylen (1810–94), the son of a cloth manufacturer, was born in Devizes, and, after spending some years as an engineer and a painter, settled at Etchilhampton in 1842, and later in London. He was the author of *Chronicles of the Devizes* (1839), the anonymous *History, Military and Municipal of ... Devizes* (1859), and other historical works.[12] His work on Devizes, strongest from the 17th century onwards, has not as yet been superseded. Edward Kite (1832–1930), the son of a small grocer in the Brittox, began writing antiquarian articles in the fifties and published his *Monumental Brasses of Wiltshire* in 1860. He was for a time assistant secretary of the Wiltshire Archaeological Society, but lost his connexion with it and ceased publishing in the *Wiltshire Magazine*. He often wrote, however, for *Wiltshire Notes and Queries* and the *Wiltshire Gazette*. When he died it was claimed that he 'could have written the history of central Wilts better than anyone of this or the previous generation'.[13] In 1829 William Cunnington II, nephew of William Cunnington I of Heytesbury, Sir Richard Colt Hoare's coadjutor, moved with his family to Devizes. The son, William Cunnington III (1813–1906), managed his father's business from his father's death in 1846 until his own retirement and departure from Devizes in 1874. He was well known as an amateur geologist, and many of the specimens that he collected have since passed to the Devizes and other museums. His interest in the Wiltshire Archaeological Society was keen and at the age of 82 he published the catalogue of its Stourhead

8 See pp. 36 sqq.
10 Ibid.
12 *W.A.M.* xxvii. 301–8.

9 *D.N.B.*
11 Waylen, *Chrons.* 346.
13 Ibid. xlv. 94–9.

Collection.[14] His brother Henry (1820–87) was curator of the Devizes museum from 1875 until his death and an excavator of Wiltshire prehistoric monuments.[15] Henry's son, Benjamin Howard (1861–1950), was born in Devizes, whither he returned in 1883 after a stay in London. He passed the rest of his life in the borough and was curator of the museum from 1888 until his death. He published two volumes of extracts from the borough records, called *Some Annals of the Borough of Devizes* (1925, 1926), edited other Wiltshire documents, and wrote many articles on Devizes antiquities.[16] With his wife, Maud Edith Pegge, as senior partner, he excavated several prehistoric sites.[17] Alfred Cunnington, another of Henry's sons, with his brothers' collaboration, installed perhaps the earliest private telephone connexion in England, linking Southgate House, the Cunnington home, with the wineshop.[18]

GROWTH OF THE TOWN. Devizes is a distinguished example of a medieval town whose defences were integral with those of the castle abutting it. Usually such towns are rectangular, but Devizes, like Launceston (Corn.) and Pleshey (Essex), is oval. The castle itself was encompassed by two ditches, an inner one, more or less round, tightly gripping the motte, and an outer one, approximately oval. Beyond these were a middle and an outer ditch. They are here called respectively the inner and outer castle ditches and the inner and outer town ditches.

The castle ditches are treated elsewhere.[19] The course of the two town ditches has aroused some local speculation.[20] The inner one originally bounded the outer bailey of the castle. Beside it there was in places a pathway, called Perambulation Walk in 1808 and Procession Walk in 1836.[21] On the inner side of the outer ditch within the urban

14 Ibid. xxxiv. 324–5; lv. 226–7. For the Cunningtons see also p. 93.
15 *W.A.M.* lv. 227; *W.A.S. Centenary Hist.* (1953), 23.
16 *W.A.M.* liii. 498–500; *The Times*, 30 Nov., 14 Dec. 1950; *Wilts. Gaz.* 30 Nov. 1950.
17 *W.A.M.* liv. 104–6; *The Times*, 2 Mar. 1951.
18 *W.A.M.* xlvii. 279
19 See pp. 51–2.
20 The argument about the course of these ditches advanced by H. G. Barry in *Devizes and Wilts. Gaz.* 21 Mar., 4 Apr. 1895 is in general here accepted. The inner one was visible in the late 19th cent. from the N. arm of Station Rd.: ibid. 29 Nov. 1894. It was also visible behind no. 40 Mrkt. Pl. in 1955 (*Ruth Pierce Panels*, n.d. priv. print.) but not behind Lloyds Bank, close by, in 1970 (ex inf. Mr. R. E. Sandell). Its course beside Hillworth Rd. was observed during excavations in 1944: *W.A.M.* li. 40.
21 W.A.S. Libr., Devizes, Kite's Notes, iv. 20, 29. For good cartographical representations see W.R.O. 844, Corp. Lease Bk., corp. lands, no. 53.

Part of Edward Dore's Plan of Devizes, 1759. Scale of original 1:1650, of reproduction 1:2946

Key according to Dore: 1 St. John's Church, 5 Baptist Meeting, 6 Quaker Meeting, 8 The Old Hall, 9 The New Hall, 10 The Measuring House, 11 Butchers' Shambles, 13 Bridewell, 14 Charity School, 15 Market Cross, 16 Old Market Place, 17 The Cross Tree, 18 St. John's Hospital, 19 An Alms House.

area, there is said to have been a bank, formed of soil dug from the ditch and surmounted by a stockade, doubtless the 'town walls' as they were grandiloquently called in 1642.[22] Beneath the bank was a pathway,[23] similar to the foregoing, which had been formed by 1724,[24] if not by 1563.[25] Some vestiges remained in 1832 when a broad elm-flanked promenade, running between St. Mary's churchyard and Commercial Road, enabled walkers to breathe the 'pure air' from Roundway Hill.[26] The stretch from Sidmouth Street to Hare and Hounds Court was called Procession Walk in 1779 and 1792.[27] Further to the south-east it was called Keeper's Walk in 1832.[28] At the point where the ditch passed through the gasworks it was 7 ft. deep, 25 ft. wide at the top, and 4 ft. wide at the bottom.[29]

The road pattern implies that the original entrances to the town were from the north and south only. The eastern approach by Sidmouth Street is irregular and narrow and the properties, compared with those on the north–south roads, have little depth. Access to the town was gained by a north gate, mentioned in 1416[30] and still in being in 1451.[31] Of other gates there is no evidence. The region called Southgate is probably named after an entrance to the park, made in 1494–5.[32]

The narrow space between the outer and inner town ditches was the site of the original urban area, equipped with a market-place.[33] This was the Old Port, so called by 1305,[34] and corresponded approximately with St. Mary's parish. The rest of the ancient borough constituted the New Port, first named in 1309,[35] which coincided with St. John's parish. The New Port presumably did not arise until the castle had ceased to be defensive and in 1561 could still be described as no more than a street.[36]

22 Waylen, *Chrons.* 153 (2nd pagin.).
23 *W.A.M.* li. 39.
24 W. Stukeley, *Itinerarium Curiosum* (1776 edn.), Cent. i. 145.
25 The 'town ditch or highway' in the Old Port: W.R.O. 212A/36/2, deed, mayor to Haynes, 16 Sept. 1563.
26 Wilts. Cuttings, v. 151.
27 W.R.O. 844, Corp. Lease Bk., corp. lands, nos. 10, 28.
28 Ibid. no. 113.
29 *W.A.M.* li. 39.
30 W.R.O. 212B/23/1/3, deed, 18 Feb. 1415.
31 Ibid. 844, Skippet deeds, no. 12.
32 S.C. 6/Hen VII/1136.
33 See p. 115.
34 W.A.S. Libr., Devizes, Devizes ch. property deeds, transcribed Kite.
35 Ibid.   36 B.M. Add. Ch. 37542.

Great Porch in 1998

On the other hand market-places had been established in the New Port by 1378,[37] so it is clear that by the later 14th century the urban area was no longer limited to St. Mary's parish.

Presumably the roads that now pass through the Market Place and connect the brewery corner with Bridewell Street originally gave access to the outer bailey of the castle only. The town itself was reached by New Park Street on one side and Bridewell Street on the other. The way from the town to the castle was across the inner town ditch, probably spanned by a bridge,[38] along the line of the Brittox. The word 'brittox', which first occurs c. 1300, has long been assumed to mean a brattice or stockade which flanked the roadway or some part of it.[39] It seems to have been a street of sorts by 1356,[40] and to have possessed a shop by 1420.[41]

Only two or three medieval houses survive to show the then pattern and character of domestic buildings. Nos. 6–8 Monday Market

37 See p. 115.
38 Deduced from fact that in 1240 there were 2 bridges outside the gate: E 372/84 m. 3.
39 *P.N. Wilts.* (E.P.N.S.), 243.
40 Westminster Abbey Mun. 1932, quitclaim of a tenement in 'la Bridasch'.
41 *W.A.M.* ii. 305.

A HISTORY OF DEVIZES

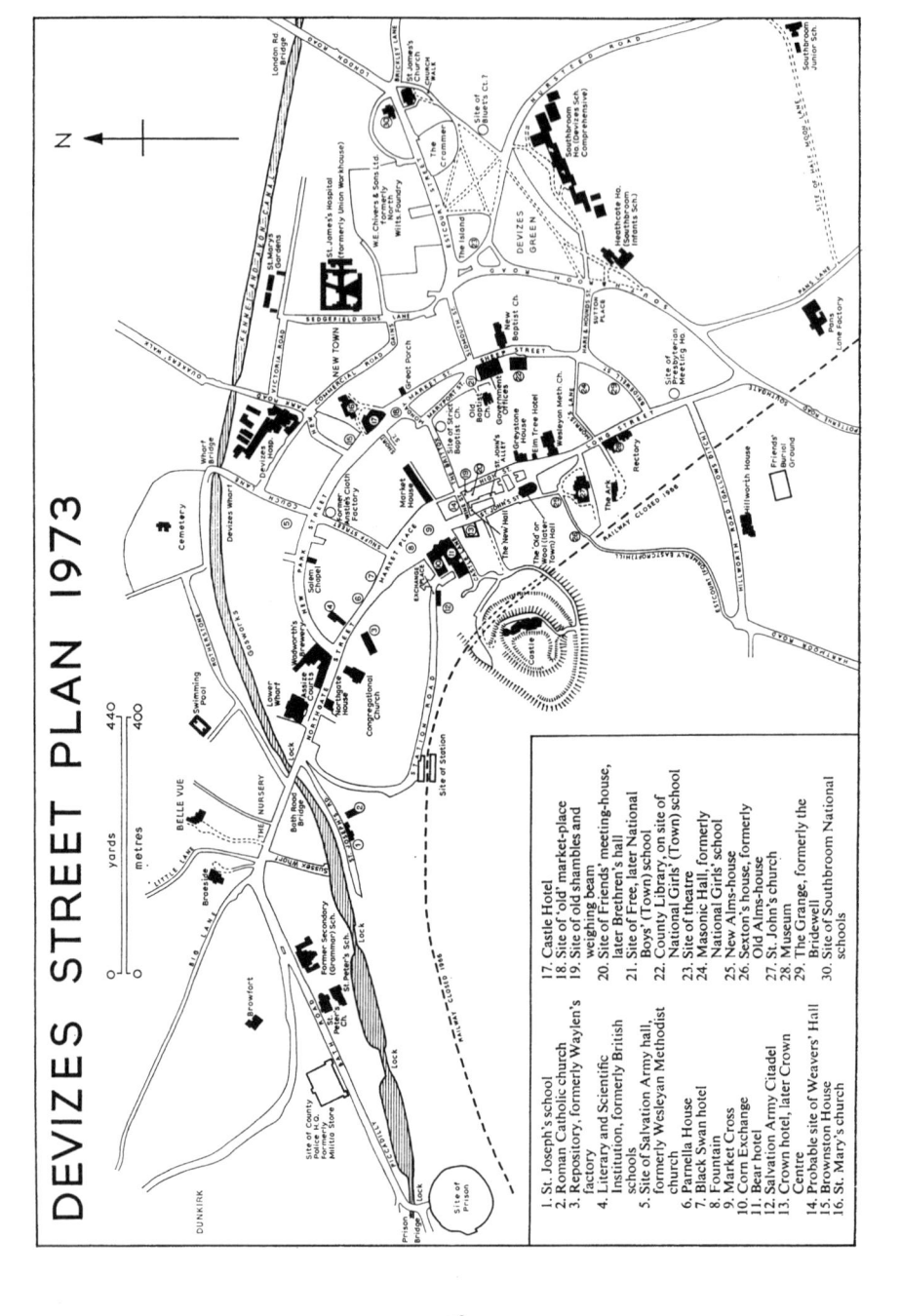

DEVIZES STREET PLAN 1973

1. St. Joseph's school
2. Roman Catholic church
3. Repository, formerly Waylen's factory
4. Literary and Scientific Institution, formerly British schools
5. Site of Salvation Army hall, formerly Wesleyan Methodist church
6. Parnella House
7. Black Swan hotel
8. Fountain
9. Market Cross
10. Corn Exchange
11. Bear hotel
12. Salvation Army Citadel
13. Crown hotel, later Crown Centre
14. Probable site of Weavers' Hall
15. Brownston House
16. St. Mary's church
17. Castle Hotel
18. Site of 'old' market-place
19. Site of old shambles and weighing beam
20. Site of Friends' meeting-house, later Brethren's hall
21. Site of Free, later National Boys' (Town) school
22. County Library, on site of National Girls' (Town) school
23. Site of theatre
24. Masonic Hall, formerly National Girls' school
25. New Alms-house
26. Sexton's house, formerly Old Alms-house
27. St. John's church
28. Museum
29. The Grange, formerly the Bridewell
30. Site of Southbroom National schools

18

Street, of which no. 8 is called Great Porch, are the greater part of a mid-15th-century house with a hall parallel to the street and a cross-wing at its east end. The scale and quality of the timberwork, and in particular the use of moulding and carving in the roof suggest that it was the house of a prosperous inhabitant. No. 4 St. John's Court with part of the adjoining property northwards formed a stone-walled four-bay hall of one storey with attics. It is of late-medieval date. Nos. 23 and 24 St. John's Street was originally one house and formed a timber-framed structure on a stone plinth. In 1954 no. 24 exhibited internal features, since destroyed, which might indicate a late-15th- or early-16th-century house.[42] Such generalizations as so small a sample permits suggest that, as in other towns of central southern England, the medieval building plots were relatively wide, permitting the use of a standard type of house plan arranged along the street with only ancillary rooms accommodated in rear wings.

Few street names precede the 16th century. The 'Wolstrate' (1289)[43] and East Street (1378, 1470)[44] are no longer identifiable. Outside the walls there was from 1207[45] to 1309[46] a street called 'reawe', the row, probably representing a small urban development on the western edge of the Green.[47] In the 16th century the situation changes. Northgate Street, named in 1547,[48] was then probably built up. By the mid century houses of good quality, as their names and (when in being) their architecture, testified, had begun to spring up on both sides of New Park Street. The gardens of those on the north side ran up to the outer town ditch[49] which perhaps was then partly filled in although some parts of ditch and bank were still visible in 1724.[50] Couch Lane, branching from New Park Street, is as old as 1547.[51] It originally led to a cow meadow, 'le cowasche', first named in 1371.[52] Short Street first occurs in

42 For some information about the former interior appearance see Wilts. Cuttings, xvi. 199.
43 P.N. Wilts. (E.P.N.S.), 243.
44 W.A.S. Libr., Devizes, Annexe 33, no. 10, abstracts of St. Mary's deeds; W.R.O. 212B/23/1/11, deed, 24 July 1470.
45 Rot. Chart. (Rec. Com.), 170.
46 Cal. Pat. 1307–13, 157.
47 The suggested identification with Wick (W.A.M. xliii. 503) is improbable.
48 P.N. Wilts. (E.P.N.S.), 243.
49 W.A.M. li. 40.
50 Stukeley, Itinerarium Curiosum (1776 edn.), Cent. i. 145 and pl. 69.
51 P.N. Wilts. (E.P.N.S.), 243.
52 In W.R.O. 189/34, lease of 1370–1.

1586.[53] Morris's Lane may be as old, for, though not expressly named until 1675–6,[54] it is probably the 'lane' in which the clothier Henry Morris kept a loom and owned property in 1572.[55] 'Paynter's Mead Lane' (1567), not strictly identifiable, was in the Old Port and seems to have led out of Northgate Street south-westward.[56] By the end of the century St. John's Alley had been built and doubtless also many of the houses, including the civic buildings[57] around the Market Place, in St. John's Street, and on the north-west side of Long Street. When Leland observed (c. 1540) that the 'beauty' of the town was 'all in one strete'[58] he was probably referring to the highway that under various names ran from the north gate to St. John's church and beyond, although the chain of streets from New Park Street to Bridewell Street is another possibility. By the end of the century the present Market Place, whose name occurs from 1603,[59] probably began to be used as the chief trading area, while the old market-place was reduced in size by filling up the island site bounded by Monday Market Street and Maryport Street. These, together with High Street, seem to have been prosperous streets in the 16th and early 17th centuries. In the latter century the Market Place also became a good residential quarter; John Kent[60] had his home there (no. 16, 1619).[61]

Few new street names appear in the 17th and earlier 18th centuries. Wine Street occurs first in 1632 and it and the Brittox were then undoubted thoroughfares.[62] North Street (1670)[63] is probably the same as Northgate Street. At Chapel Corner (1655–6), where Sidmouth and Monday Market Streets connect, there was a horse pool.[64] The chapel was that of St. John's hospital,[65] still extant in some form in 1666.[66]

Turning from the central streets we find that by 1647 there were houses from Potterne Road railway bridge to the corner of Hillworth

53 E 178/2429.
54 Cunnington, *Annals*, i (2nd pagin.), 162.
55 Prob. 11/55 (P.C.C. 2 Peter, will of Hen. Morris).
56 W.A.S. Libr., Devizes, Annexe 33, no. 117, abstracts of St. Mary's deeds.
57 See pp. 149–50.
58 *Itin.* ed. Toulmin Smith, v. 82.
59 *P.N. Wilts.* (E.P.N.S.), 243.
60 See p. 135.
61 *W.N. & Q.* iii. 36 n.
62 Cunnington, *Annals*, i (2nd pagin.), 89.
63 W.R.O. 130/58A, deed, 2 Nov. 1670.
64 Cunnington, op. cit. 125, cf. ibid. 143 and W.R.O. 844, town deeds, box 9 (1689).
65 *V.C.H. Wilts.* iii. 337.
66 In W.R.O. 402/1, proceedings of feoffees.

Road, which was then in being; they were mostly on the west side but also on the east where now is none.[67] The Green had assumed much its present shape, the more northerly part being parcel of Roundway township, the more southerly of Wick. A road ran from Heathcote House to join the Salisbury road and houses skirted the Green on the other side along the line of Southbroom Road from a point opposite Heathcote House to Sidmouth Street. The course of Pans Lane, not so called until 1819,[68] is marked as Wick Lane. Estcourt Street was then called Bedbury Street from the tithing of that name. Its present name was adopted in 1871.[69] Just about where the Breach leaves the Potterne road an irregular open space called Ashlers Green (Ashmoor Green in 1773,[70] Ashman's Green in 1819[71]) lay on either side of that road, which, as has been said,[72] did not then lead to Potterne. Wick consisted of two small groups of houses, one on the east side of Pans Lane and the other on either side of the present Wick Lane.

Surviving buildings indicate that by the 17th century most of the street frontages within the town were probably complete. The domestic building style of the late 16th and the 17th centuries may be deduced from the thirty or so timber-framed houses, not demonstrably medieval, that still survive. They seem to have had a uniform street elevation with a jettied upper floor, like those on the west side of St. John's Alley, which seems to have been a street of good quality when erected. In the later 17th century rows of contiguous dormers, rising off the eaves and producing a serrated roof-line, appear to have become fashionable. The Elm Tree, though much restored, is so designed. By the same period, too, the concealment of the timber framing behind plaster was probably general. When Stukeley came in 1724 he found the houses 'old' and mostly of timber. Since, however, they were of a good 'model', they struck him as 'tolerable'.[73] Before this time thatch had begun to be restricted. After 1655 corporation houses when reroofed were ordered to be tiled and not thatched.[74] St. Mary's feoffees had begun to require

67 W.A.S. Libr., Devizes, Map, 1647.
68 W.R.O., Inclosure Map, Bishop's Cannings, Southbroom, etc., 1819, where it is spelt Pann's.
69 Ibid. 844, Min. Bk. Local Bd. 22 Sept. 1871.
70 *W.R.S.* viii, pl. 11.
71 W.R.O., Inclosure Map, Bishop's Cannings, Southbroom, etc. 1819.
72 See p. 6.
73 *Itinerarium Curiosum* (1776 edn.), Cent. i. 145.
74 Cunnington, *Annals*, i (2nd pagin.), 122.

this in their leases five years before and continued to do so. They also insisted upon brick chimneys.[75]

The first town plan, 1737–8,[76] reveals an oval town, built up from Northgate Street to Southgate. Long, Bridewell ('Bridle'), Sheep, Castle, and St. John's Streets now for the first time appear by name. Maryport Street, often later St. Mary Port Street,[77] is first named a few years earlier.[78] Long Street, a name of obscure meaning,[79] then extended only from what is now Hillworth Road to Morris's Lane. Its continuation was St. John's Street which ran to the present Town Hall. In 1743 some part of that section of the street which lies in St. Mary's parish was called South Gate Street.[80] What is now St. John's Street is called in 1737–8 Castle Street. High Street is called 'Wine Street' probably in error, and New Park Street 'Back Street', a name which it still seems to have borne in 1843.[81] It was known by its present name in 1740.[82] The Chequer is called Half Moon Alley. Down the middle of the present Hartmoor Road runs 'Gallows Ditch', mentioned in 1601[83] and presumably the site of the town gallows, traceable from 1596.[84] From the north-east side of the present Hillworth Road a narrow road, called Nestcot (now Estcourt) Hill, runs in a semicircle to the north end of Hartmoor Road giving access to 'The Mint' and other houses. One of these may be on the site of 'The Ark' which still stood in 1973 and is mentioned by that name in 1783.[85] The course of Hare and Hounds Street is marked but not named. Known as Kilberry's Row in 1642–3[86] it seems to have been regarded as part of Bridewell Street in 1759.[87] Sidmouth Street is solidly built up on the north and partly so on the south. So is the north side of Estcourt Street, perhaps the 'reawe' of the distant past. Beyond the outer

75 W.A.S. Libr., Devizes, Annexe 30, no. 28, abstracts of St. Mary's deeds; cf. ibid. nos. 126–7, 129.
76 In W.A.S. Libr., Devizes.
77 e.g. Dore, Map, 1759.
78 Cunnington, *Annals*, i (2nd pagin.), 206.
79 For a discussion see *W.A.M.* li. 180.
80 W.R.O. 844, town deeds, box 9, 7 June 1743.
81 Cunnington, *Annals*, ii. 199.
82 W.R.O. 130/58B, deed, corp. to Phillips.
83 Cunnington, *Annals*, i (2nd pagin.), 37.
84 Ibid. 32.
85 Sar. Dioc. R.O., Glebe Terrier, 1783.
86 Cunnington, *Annals*, i (2nd pagin.), 107; *W.A.M.* li. 180. To clinch the identification see W.R.O. 844, Corp. Lease Bk., corp. lands, no. 28.
87 Dore, Map, 1759.

town ditch in Northgate Street there is hardly any building. There was an exit from the Market Place at what is now Castle Lane and a road is marked traversing the course of Commercial Road and Gains Lane. A narrow lane already connects them with New Park Street. These streets are not then named. Outside the town Half Moon Lane, closed as a thoroughfare by 1819 but then still so named,[88] connects Nursteed Road with Pans Lane which itself connects the eastern part of Wick with Upper Wick. The latter was the equivalent of Southgate. Wick, a larger settlement than Upper Wick, is grouped round a green, the Lower Wick green of 1819,[89] now represented by the point where Wick and Green Lanes connect.

The next plan, 1759,[90] shows few changes. The main one is that meanwhile Snuff Street, long so called popularly[91] but officially entitled New Street until 1965,[92] had been cut to connect the Market Place with New Park Street. Gallows Ditch has now become the name of Hillworth Road and not a mere kennel in its midst. While what was once Nestcot Hill, but which has come to be called Eastcroft Hill, retains its course, there is now an adit from the south-west corner of St. John's churchyard by steps, which seem to have existed by 1752.[93] The steps started at Worm Cliff, a declivity first mentioned in 1517.[94] In 1556 this was declared to be 'the common playing place of the town', and also a common watering place, for there a spring gushed forth. From it a right of way or 'law path' descended into the park.[95] Long Street now extends throughout its present course. The road running through the Market Place, south-eastwards from Northgate Street, is called Castle Street, still an alternative title in 1821.[96] The street so called in 1737–8 has adopted its present name of St. John's Street. High Street appears for the first time *eo nomine* and Wine Street occupies its present position. New Park Street has acquired its present name. Bridewell Street distinctly

88 W.R.O., Inclosure Map, Bishop's Cannings, Southbroom, etc. 1819.
89 Ibid.
90 Dore, Map, 1759.
91 *W.A.M.* li. 181.
92 Ex inf. Town Clerk.
93 W.R.O. 130/58B, deed, Beavan to Burrough. Nestcroft was still an *alias* for Estcourt Hill in 1841; Cunnington, *Annals*, ii. 198.
94 W.R.O. 212B/23/1/19, deed, 9 Sept. 1517.
95 Cunnington, *Annals*, i (1st pagin.), 8, 10, 15; cf. Prob. 11/28 (P.C.C. 10 Alenger) (1540).
96 W.R.O. 844, Corp. Lease Bk., corp. lands, no. 77.

turns the corner into Hare and Hounds Street. St. John's Alley is called Wine Street Alley. It had formerly been called Back Lane.[97] Monday Market Street, called Monday's Market Street, Leg of Mutton Street, and Mortimer's Court are named for the first time. The first must, of course, be a much older name, recalling the market in St. Mary's parish granted in 1567.[98] William Mortimer lived at the corner of the third in 1740.[99] Budge Row, also called Magpie Alley in 1776–7,[1] Magpie Alley alone in 1791,[2] and Hare and Hounds Court by 1885,[3] leads off Hare and Hounds Street to the south. The pond on the Green is first marked as the Crammer.

The plan of Devizes was significantly changed by the construction from 1750–1 of turnpike roads to West Lavington and to Seend. The first created a direct exit on the south in continuation of Long Street and caused the old routes via Hartmoor and Pans Lane to be abandoned. The second led ultimately though not immediately to the abandonment of Big Lane as the exit towards Chippenham.[4] On the north side of the new Bath Road a small knot of houses had sprung up by 1773.[5] By 1749 their site already bore its present name, Piccadilly.[6]

The change in architectural fashion that occurred at the beginning of the 18th century coincided in Devizes with a rapid rise in the use of brick for external walling. Brick earth was locally plentiful. In many of the larger 18th-century houses brick is associated with quoins, window architraves, and doorways of a fine limestone ashlar. Such stone would have been expensive in Devizes and it is used only occasionally for walling, notably at no. 23 Market Place and Greystone House, High Street, both of which have distinguished main elevations. Judging by style alone, the substantial 18th-century houses in the town were predominantly built in the first half of the century, mostly in brick, to good designs. During most of the second half less seems to have been built, although there was a revival at the very end. Besides completely new buildings many old timber buildings were faced with vertical plaster

97 W.R.O. 844, Corp. Lease Bk., St. John's leases, no. 15.
98 See p. 113.
99 W.R.O. 844, town deeds, box 9, 23 Aug. 1740.
 1 Ibid. Corp. Lease Bk., corp. lands, nos. 4–5.
 2 Cunnington, *Annals*, ii. 175.
 3 O.S. Map 1/2,500, Wilts. XXXIV. 14. 11 (1886 edn.).
 4 See p. 6.
 5 *W.R.S.* viii, pl. 11.
 6 W.R.O. 727, Wyndham Accts.

Greystone House

fronts, given new sash windows, and had the dormers joined together to make a full attic storey. A notable feature of the earlier-18th-century houses is the quality of the wood-work and plaster ceilings in some of the larger ones, especially no. 17 Market Place and Greystone House. This is paralleled in contemporary houses in neighbouring villages. The main area of 18th-century building activity was centred on the Market Place, St. John's Street, and Long Street with an extension along the Brittox to Brownston House. The most fashionable part of the town was probably Long Street and the area to the north of the Town Hall.

Apart from nos. 31 and 32 and no. 40 (part of the Museum), all the houses on the west side of Long Street as far north as St. John's churchyard were rebuilt in the 18th or early 19th centuries. They were of substantial size, double-fronted, with large gardens, and in two cases possessed side carriage entrances. The houses on the opposite side, as far north as Bridewell Street, are similar, though only no. 30, the home of the clothier family of Sutton,[7] has a large garden, and impressive houses, like no. 8 (1737), Joseph Needham's house,[8] begin again at Morris's Lane and run to the High Street. The intervening stretch on this side,

7 *W.A.M.* xliii. 374.
8 Ibid. xliv. 387.

and that from the churchyard to the Town Hall on the other, consists of older houses, altered but not rebuilt. The cramped nature of the sites with the lack of gardens and rear access may explain the failure to rebuild and so provide more sumptuous dwellings. Several houses on the west side of St. John's Street, notably nos. 28, 30, 37–8, and the Police Station, are as impressive as the best houses in Long Street with long five-bay frontages and gardens running down to the outer castle ditch and nos. 31–2 before rebuilding were the home of a prosperous man.[9] The northeast side of the Market Place continued to attract substantial houses, e.g. the Black Swan (1737),[10] Parnella House,[11] and a third house, now demolished, on the site of the Cooperative Furniture Store.[12] Such houses benefited from long gardens running back to the inner town ditch.

Long Street

The 18th-century features of houses on the east side of St. John's Street are less impressive than those on the west and cannot then have been so fashionable. Likewise New Park Street, judging from the style of the buildings then erected in it, had become a street of traders and small manufacturers in that century, though Brownston House[13] is of a

9 W.A.M. xliii. 235.
10 See p. 104.
11 See pp. 68, 233.
12 W.A.S. Libr., Devizes, sale cat. xx, no. 30.
13 See p. 67.

better order. Nor was High Street at this time any longer a street of distinction.

In 1795 there were 188 assessed houses in St. John's parish and 139 in St. Mary's.[14] The next year's assessment gives slightly lower figures but in the same proportion.[15] In 1821 the enumerated houses in St. John's were about 60 per cent of the total for the then borough.[16]

The building of the canal, completed at Devizes in 1807–10,[17] affected the town's appearance in various ways. First it enabled stone to be brought easily from Bath and greatly promoted its use. Secondly it altered the urban landscape. The canal mainly ran through open country, but notwithstanding changed the landscape by causing Prison,[18] Bath Road (called Nursery in 1885), Wharf, Quakers' Walk (called Park in 1885),[19] and London Road bridges to be constructed. It must also have broken the continuity of Dumb Post Passage which between 1759 and 1798 ran from New Park Street out into the country.[20] The first wharf, on a site leased by the corporation and hence called Corporation Wharf, was built in 1809–10 and enlarged later.[21] It forced the cutting of Wharf Street to give access from New Park Street. Beside the wharf was a bonded warehouse, not closed until 1946.[22] Other wharves followed from c. 1823 when the canal company began to prosper.[23] Hazeland's New Wharf, New Park Street, occurs by 1839,[24] New Wharf (perhaps the same) in 1851,[25] Maryport Wharf in 1844,[26] Station Wharf between 1869 and 1873,[27] and Sussex Wharf between 1878[28] and 1894.[29] Either

14 W.R.O., Q. Sess. Admin., Navy Act, 1795.
15 Ibid. Army and Navy Acts, 1796–7.
16 *Census*, 1821.
17 See pp. 7–8.
18 Tablet erected on bridge in 1840 commemorates John Blackwell for 30 yrs. the canal co's. engineer. This bridge was chosen for the tablet because of its proximity to the flight of locks, deemed to be Blackwell's greatest work: K. R. Clew, *Kennet and Avon Canal*, 95.
19 O.S. Map 1/2,500, Wilts. XXXIV. 14 (1886 edn.).
20 Wilts. Cuttings. ii. 171. The passage is not marked on Dore's Map (1759). The most southerly part of the passage was still discernible in 1885: O.S. Map 1/500, Wilts. XXXIV. 15. 3 (1886 edn.).
21 Cunnington, *Annals*, ii. 37, 39, 41–2; Wilts. Cuttings, iii. 5.
22 Wilts. Co. Council, *Leisure in Wilts.* (1969), 40.
23 K. R. Clew, *Kennet and Avon Canal*, 84.
24 Robson, *Com. Dir.* (1839), ii.   25 Slater, *Dir.* (1851).
26 Pigot, *Nat. Com. Dir.* (1844).   27 Gillman, *Dirs.* (1869 and later edns.).
28 Ibid. (1878 and later edns.).
29 W.A.S. Libr., Devizes, sale cat. viii, no. 60.

The Brittox, c. 1860. The position of the inner town ditch is indicated by the indentation in the line of the street

of the last two might have been the Lower Wharf of 1884 and 1899.[30] Sussex Wharf, although not named before, must have existed by 1839,[31] for there was then a group of cottages along the present (1973) lane running south from Bath Road. J. Romain, a builder, moved there c. 1898[32] and may have used the present warehouse for storing and the near-by wharf for transporting his materials. T. G. B. Estcourt and two others took the lease of a wharf in 1835.[33]

Shortly before the canal was opened two small streets were named or rechristened. The Little Brittox, marked in 1737–8 and called Exchequer Alley in 1740,[34] had acquired its present name by 1791.[35] The old name, however, was still intelligible in 1825, though the Short

30 W.R.O. 844, Corp. Min. Bk. 1882–9, 2 May 1884; *Kelly's Dirs. Wilts.* (1884, 1889).
31 W.R.O., Tithe Map, Devizes, St. John's Par.
32 Gillman, *Dir.*
33 W.R.O. 844, Corp. Lease Bk., corp. lands, no. 131.
34 Ibid. town deeds, box 9, 23 Aug. 1740.
35 Cunnington, *Annals*, ii. 175.

Brittox was an *alias*.[36] The Chequer, called by another name in 1737–8,[37] had become the Little Chequer by 1791[38] but had acquired its modern name by 1821.[39]

The Improvement Commissioners of 1825[40] did not alter the plan except to secure in 1832 the stopping-up of the northern end of St. John's Alley.[41] They thus probably secured the preservation of its houses by making the street so inconvenient to live in that it was not worth rebuilding. They arranged in 1826 for Chapel Corner Street (*alias* Leg of Mutton Street) to be renamed Sidmouth Street[42] and by ordering in 1835, as statute enjoined,[43] that street name-plates be erected[44] helped to stabilize nomenclature. The area at the south end of the Town Hall, vaguely called 'the road round the Town Hall' in 1791,[45] was known as Church Street in 1830.[46] That name, however, has not survived. Castle Lane is named by 1835.[47]

Though they left the plan virtually intact, the commissioners shaved off the corner of Maryport Street and the Brittox[48] and broadened the Brittox and Wine Street.[49] They also improved the street surfaces,[50] and, beginning in 1826, increased the safety and longevity of the houses by prohibiting the renewal of thatched roofs.[51] Nevertheless, even in 1847 thatch was not uncommon[52] and not unknown in 1868.[53] By these and other means Devizes began to be transformed. A resident said that before 1825 it was 'the most dirty and uninviting' town 'that can well be imagined',[54] and Crabb Robinson, returning after nearly 40

36 W.R.O. 844, Corp. Lease Bk., corp. lands, no. 88.
37 See above.
38 Cunnington, *Annals*, ii. 175.
39 W.R.O. 844, Corp. Lease Bk., corp. lands, no. 76.
40 See p. 146.
41 Cunnington, *Annals*, ii. 194.
42 Ibid. 187. The phrase 'Chapel Corner' was, however, still in use in 1851: Slater, *Dir.*
43 6 Geo. IV, c. 162, s. 31 (Priv. Act).
44 Cunnington, *Annals*, ii. 196.
45 Ibid. 175.
46 The then Borough Arms, now the Lamb, was then here: Pigot, *Nat. Com. Dir.* (1830).
47 *Lond. Gaz.* 8 Dec. 1835, p. 2429.
48 W.R.O. 844, Corp. Lease Bk., alms–ho. lands, no. 9.
49 Cunnington, *Annals*, ii. 192.
50 See p. 163.
51 Cunnington, *Annals*, ii. 185.
52 *Devizes Advertiser*, 20 May 1897.
53 W.R.O. 844, Min. Bk. Local Bd. 3 Apr. 1868.   54 Waylen, *Chrons.* 167.

years' absence, remarked upon the 'meanness of the streets'.[55] By 1839, however, 'handsome modern dwellings' were 'fast displacing' the timber buildings, which had characterized the town about half a century before.[56] In 1836 there were 1,213 houses.[57] This is over 300 more than were reported in 1816[58] but the smaller figure may refer only to the old borough area.

A significant part in the improvements was played by Joseph Needham Tayler, then Captain R.N.,[59] who, returning home after the wars, dived into the real estate market, apparently to his own ultimate detriment. He built after 1830[60] new shops on the south-east side of the Brittox, new houses on the south side of Wine Street and in Long Street, a middle-class terrace in Bath Road, called Trafalgar Place in 1844,[61] and, at the other end of the town, Southgate House and Villas.[62] To the same period, though not necessarily to Tayler's personal initiative, can be ascribed Handel House and Albion Terrace (formerly Place), both in Sidmouth Street, Melbourne Place and Farleigh Place, both in Bath Road, Sidmouth Terrace, once part of Southbroom Place and now of Southbroom Road,[63] and Lansdowne Grove and Terrace in Morris's Lane. Albion, Melbourne, and Farleigh Places, Lansdowne Grove, and Sidmouth Terrace, are first so called in 1844,[64] Lansdowne Terrace in 1885.[65] By 1841 both sides of Bath Road from the canal bridge to Little Lane were fringed with houses[66] forming on the north side the Nursery of brick and stone. There was also a line of small houses, called in 1871 Avon Row[67] and since 1885 Avon Terrace,[68] between Bath Road and Rotherstone House.[69] The Nursery first bears that name in 1839[70] and

55 Diary... Hen. Crabb Robinson, ed. T. Sadler, ii. 331–2.
56 Robson, Com. Dir. (1839).
57 Waylen, Chrons. 197.
58 T. B. Oldfield, Rep. Hist. of Gt. Britain (1816), v. 158.
59 D.N.B.
60 This is the yr. in which Locke, Hughes & Co.'s bank, compulsorily acquired, was sold: Cunnington, Annals, ii. 192. See also p. 103.
61 Pigot, Nat. Com. Dir. (1844).
62 Devizes and Wilts. Gaz. 23 Nov. 1893. Southgate Ho. had been built by 1828: W.R.O. 844, Corp. Lease Bk., corp. lands, no. 104.
63 The name Southbroom Rd. for the whole line of building from Estcourt St. to Long St. was adopted in 1969: ex inf. Town Clerk.
64 Pigot, Nat. Com. Dir. (1844).
65 O.S. Map 1/500, Wilts. XXXIV. 14. 11 (1886 edn.).
66 W.R.O., Tithe Map, Southbroom.
67 Ibid. Min. Bk. Local Bd. 22 Sept. 1871.
68 O.S. Map 1/500, Wilts. XXXIV. 13. 5 (1886 edn.).
69 W.R.O., Tithe Map, Southbroom.
70 Robson, Com. Dir. (1839). But this seems to have been forgotten by 1871 when that name was decreed de novo: W.R.O. 844, Min. Bk. Local Bd. 22 Sept. 1871.

Bath Road, showing Dunkirk toll-house, Trafalgar Place, and, in the distance, Devizes prison, c. 1840

derives it from a nursery garden.[71] The complex called Belle Vue, north of Bath Road, may well be contemporary with the Bath Road developments. It is first mentioned in 1839,[72] and, when plotted in 1885,[73] consisted of Belle Vue House, Villas, and Terrace, with 'The Laurels' in the middle. It was approached by Belle Vue Road.

The arrival of the canal and the development of tobacco manufacture increased the chances of local employment and in the early 19th century many small houses were built. Many were fitted into the courts and gardens behind existing houses; there is a noticeable concentration close to New Park, Sheep, and Bridewell Streets. Consequently those streets must then have ceased to be fashionable, although a substantial new house (no. 28 Bridewell Street) had been built early in the century.

These working-class houses were mostly of brick or timber-framed with panels in-filled with brick and poorly built and serviced. They

71 See p. 112.
72 Robson, *Com. Dir.* (1839).
73 O.S. Map 1/500, Wilts. XXXIV. 13. 5 (1886 edn.).

were usually in short terraces with a common yard but no garden and some had only a small single bedroom above a living room. Victoria Court, Bridewell Street, demolished c. 1970 was an example.

The boundary adjustments of 1832–5 had brought within the town not only Belle Vue and the Bath Road villas but also Dunkirk, with an inn and cottages, probably designed to serve and house the workers at the brick-works.[74] Dunkirk is first named in 1839[75] and at the same time Hare and Hounds Street, known by that name in 1829,[76] begins to be called South End.[77] It retained that name in 1885[78] but resumed its present one in 1869 and from 1903.[79] Outside the ancient borough there are also some changes to record. The roadway running from Couch Lane to the east end of St. Mary's church, known as Back Lane from 1792[80] to 1835[81] was said in 1827 to have been at least in part stopped up.[82] The Improvement Commissioners investigated the liability for its repair in 1833.[83] Evidently the road was in some way new made, for in 1839 the carriageway had been raised[84] and the road officially christened Commercial Road by 1851.[85] The name Back Lane was, however, still in use in 1867.[86] Gains Lane, which continues Commercial Road, was first so called c. 1834,[87] and the lane which joins the two of them to New Park Street begins to be known as New Park Road in 1828.[88] About 1834[89] and still in 1867[90] this region is called New Town. By 1831 a road, called from 1871 Church Walk, had been cut between St. James's church and Nursteed Road, and by 1841 there was a mass of small houses round Southgate, so called likewise from 1871.[91]

74 See pp. 101–2.
75 Robson. *Com. Dir.* (1839), ii.
76 Cunnington, *Annals*, ii, 190.
77 Robson, *Com. Dir.* (1839), ii.
78 O.S. Map 1/500, Wilts. XXXIV. 14. 11 (1886 edn.).
79 *Kelly's Dir. Wilts.* (1903); Weaver, Map, 1869.
80 W.R.O. 844, Corp. Lease Bk., corp. lands, no. 23.
81 *Lond. Gaz.* 8 Dec. 1835, p. 2429.
82 W.R.O. 844, Corp. Lease Bk., corp. lands, no. 93.
83 Cunnington, *Annals*, ii. 194.
84 Waylen, *Chrons.* 296.
85 Slater, *Dir.* (1851).
86 W.R.O., Min. Bk. Local Bd. 1 Nov. 1867.
87 *Endowed Char. Wilts.* (1908), lxxx, p. 398.
88 W.R.O. 844, Corp. Lease Bk., corp. lands, no. 96.
89 *Endowed Char. Wilts.* (1908), lxxx, p. 405.   90 *Kelly's Dir. Wilts.* (1867).
91 *Rep. Bdy. Coms.* H.C. 238 (1837), xxvi, Map; W.R.O., Tithe Map, Southbroom; ibid. 844, Min. Bk. Local Bd. 22 Sept. 1871.

As has already become apparent, most of the mid-19th-century residential building for all classes took place in the suburb of Southbroom and along the Bath and Chippenham roads. In the commercial centre older buildings continued to be replaced and shop fronts were inserted in many former houses especially in the Brittox. That street seems to have been largely commercial since the 17th century and many of its shops show successive builds. At various stages during the same century Estcourt Street was rebuilt unpretentiously.

The former railway station was built in 1856 and the Corn Exchange opened in 1857.[92] Their construction led to the creation of Exchange Place and of Station Road, so named by 1867,[93] running downhill to the station and up again in a cutting to Bath Road canal bridge. The north–south course of the railway approach was opened before the other, which dates from 1857.[94] The railway itself somewhat changed the direction of Estcourt Hill which had assumed its present course by 1885.[95] In 1865 the Roman Catholic church was opened[96] and the road in which it stood christened St. Joseph's Place (now Road).[97] The villas which adjoined the church were so placed as to give a good view northwards over the canal. Near contemporaries are the middle-class houses in London Road, e.g. Ormond Villas (recorded from 1867),[98] which lay upon the canal bank. Estcourt Terrace was built in 1874,[99] and Rotherstone Buildings, extending Avon Terrace on the east, by 1875.[1] To them Eastcourt Crescent, of the same character, had been added by 1885.[2] All these were streets of working-class houses. By 1869 Gallows Ditch, called Gallows Acre Lane in 1831[3] and Folly Lane in 1851,[4] acquired the name Hillworth or Hillworth Road.[5] At the same time a line of small houses faced the militia stores in Bath Road.[6] By 1896

92 See pp. 8, 117.
93 *Kelly's Dir. Wilts.* (1867).
94 E. H. Stone, *Devizes Castle*, 139 and n.
95 O.S. Map 1/500, Wilts. XXXIV. 13. 15 (1886 edn.).
96 See p. 200.
97 St. Joseph's Convent, Llantarnam Abbey, Cwmbran (Mon.): 'The Missionaries of St. Francis de Sales in England' (TS. diary of Fr. Larive).
98 *Kelly's Dir. Wilts.* (1867).
99 Date stone.
1 *Kelly's Dir. Wilts.* (1875).
2 O.S. Map 1/500, Wilts. XXXIV. 14. 7 (1886 edn.).
3 *Rep. Bdy. Coms.* (1837), xxvi, Map.
4 Slater, *Dir.* (1851). Hillworth Ho. was once called the Folly. See p. 70.
5 Weaver, Map, 1869
6 Ibid.

Cottages in Commercial Road (formerly Gains Lane), built after 1900

three small streets, of which the chief was Avon Road, had been built between the prison and the former bacon factory on the south side of Bath Road.[7] They covered Park Field, Old Park, which as far back as 1871 the owners had tried to develop for building.[8] By 1900, however, there were still vacant plots.[9] By the same time houses along Wick Green Road had also increased in number.[10] Shortly afterwards some cottages, under the Housing of the Working Classes Act, on the stretch of Commercial Road (then part of Gains Lane) which runs eastwards,[11] and Victoria Road were constructed.[12] By 1890 attempts to urbanize the area east of Nursteed Road had begun.[13] By 1914 Longcroft Road had been created here. It ran along the western part of the present Roseland Avenue and then turned southward. The sale of the residue of

7 O.S. Map 6", Wilts. XXXIV. SW. (1901 edn.); W.R.O., Tithe Award, Devizes, St. John's par., altered apportionment. Avon Rd. existed in 1895: W.R.O. 844, Corp. Min. Bk. 1889–95, 15 Mar. 1895.
8 W.A.S. Libr., Devizes, sale cat. xxviii, no. 53.
9 Ibid. no. 161.
10 O.S. Map 6", Wilts. XXXIV. SW. (1901 edn.).
11 Gillman, *Annals*, 68.
12 Decision to provide building plots taken by Town Council in 1900: ibid. 70. Road in being by 1922: O.S. Map 6", Wilts. XXXIV. SW. (1926 edn.).
13 W.A.S. Libr., Devizes, sale cat. viii, no. 35.

the Southbroom estate promoted this development.[14] A few building plots along London Road and Brickley Lane and taken out of the Spitalcroft estate seem to have been covered c. 1903.[15] Roughly south of Southbroom House a house called the Breach, connected in 1885 by a short road from Potterne Road,[16] had been pulled down and Breach Road (later the Breach) built to connect Potterne Road with Pans Lane. In 1899 the Breachfield building estate, named after a field so called in 1819,[17] was sold in plots by the Estcourt family for development,[18] but it was a while before it was filled up. Some time after 1895 some timber-framed houses 'of poor quality' and some plastered timber houses in Mortimer's Court were pulled down.[19]

Two amenities date from these years. In 1891 the Market Place was planted with trees[20] and more were planted in other streets in the next fifteen years.[21] Secondly in 1898 the Revd. Mills Robbins, of Chobham (Surr.), settled in trust a small plot, since maintained by the corporation, at the point where London Road joins Brickley Lane.[22]

After the First World War the town grew outwards on the east side of Nursteed Road[23] and by 1930 nearly 200 new houses had been built within the borough mostly near Brickley Lane.[24] To a lesser extent new building occurred on and around the site of the prison, demolished c. 1927,[25] on the opposite side of Bath Road,[26] in the Breach, and in the Wick and Pans Lane areas. After 1927 Sedgefield Gardens, which had until then been gardens in fact,[27] began to be built into a street.

After 1945 the town grew further. The Brickley Lane area had been completely filled up by 1967, and shops had appeared in it by 1952.[28] Hillworth Road was extended in 1951–2 along the course of

14 Ibid. x, no. 9.
15 Ibid. iv, no. 22.
16 O.S. Map 1/500, Wilts. XXXIV. 14. 16 (1886 edn.).
17 W.R.O., Inclosure Map, Bishop's Cannings, Southbroom, etc. 1819.
18 W.A.S. Libr., Devizes, sale cat. ii, no. 21.
19 *W.N. & Q.* i. 387.
20 W.R.O. 844, Corp. Min. Bk. 1889–95, 16 Feb. 1891.
21 R. D. Gillman, *Popular Guide to Devizes*, 23.
22 *Endowed Char. Wilts.* (1908), lxxx, p. 467.
23 Unless otherwise stated this and the next paragraph are based on information supplied by Mr. S. O'Brien, Dep. Town Clerk (1970).
24 Wilts. Cuttings, ii. 49.   25 See p. 77.
26 Wilts. Cuttings, xi. 260.
27 W.A.S. Libr., Devizes, sale cat. xx, no. 42.
28 Wilts. Cuttings, xxi. 33.

Gillott's Lane, as it was called in 1839,[29] and West View Crescent built near by. The break-up of the Old Park[30] and Broadleas estates on the south of the town led to the creation of new streets, and the grounds of Hartmoor House (called Park Cottage in 1885)[31] and Moorlands (traceable from 1830 and known as Old Park Cottage before c. 1890)[32] in the same area were likewise used for housing. On the north-west new housing was provided on the Bellevue estate and beyond it to the east. Victoria Road was extended eastward in 1964–6. From 1965 Wick Farm was developed and by 1970 the fields of Sunnyside Farm[33] had been covered.

In the town centre slum clearance took place chiefly in New Park Street,[34] Church Walk, Sheep Street, and the Nursery; 500 technically substandard houses were removed between 1957 and 1973[35] to be replaced in Sheep Street by two- and three-storey flats. In 1969 a large car park, with an approach road from the north covering the former Vale's Lane and Read's Court,[36] was built over the gardens behind the south side of the Brittox and the east side of High Street.[37]

CASTLE AND LORDSHIP TO c. 1550. At an unknown date a bishop of Salisbury, perhaps Osmund,[38] built a castle upon certain boundaries (*divise*), which gave the castle and adjacent town their name.[39] The fortified area, as a document of 1149 shows, was carved out of the manor of Bishop's Cannings.[40] Devizes castle is first mentioned in 1106, when Robert of Normandy was imprisoned in it.[41] He seems to have remained

29 W.R.O., Tithe Map, Devizes, St. John's par. For Gillett's Fm. see pp. 67, 111.
30 See p. 66.
31 O.S. Map 1/500, Wilts. XXXIV. 13. 20 (1886 edn.).
32 W.A.S. Libr., Devizes, Kite's Notes, iv. 188.
33 See pp. 66, 111.
34 In New Park St.: Powell's Ct., on E. side, in 1957 (ex inf. Devizes Motor Co.), hos. opposite, beside Wadworth's, in 1964 (*Wilts. Times*, 5 June 1964).
35 Ex inf. Public Health Inspector, Devizes.
36 For their position see O.S. Map 1/500, Wilts. XXXIV. 14. 6 (1886 edn.).
37 Wilts. Cuttings, xxiii. 225, 258.
38 H. M. Colvin, *King's Works*, i. 626.
39 Not the boundaries of hundreds (*P.N. Wilts.* (E.P.N.S.), 243), for hundreds did not then kiss at Devizes. More likely the boundaries of the manors of Potterne and Cannings.
40 *Sar. Chart. and Doc.* (Rolls Ser.), 15.
41 Mat. Paris, *Hist. Anglorum* (Rolls Ser.), i. 206; cf. ibid. 212 for his possible release and reimprisonment.

there, perhaps not quite continuously, until 1126.[42] In 1113 the castle was burnt, as were the Tower of London and the castles at Lincoln and Worcester.[43] In 1121 Bishop Roger (d. 1139) held an ordination in it,[44] so the ravages of fire must by then have been at least partly repaired. In or about 1138 Bishop Roger was undertaking extensive works at the castle.[45] It seems indeed to have been practically rebuilt at this time, and one chronicle even calls Roger its founder (*fundatorem*).[46] The strength, magnificence,[47] and lavish cost[48] of the fortress and the large area that it covered[49] impressed Roger's friends and enemies alike, and Henry of Huntingdon, doubtless hyperbolically, asserted that it was the most splendid in Europe.[50]

The years 1139–41 were probably the most stirring in the town's history. The castle building in which Roger and his nephews Niel, bishop of Ely, and Alexander, bishop of Lincoln, had been recently indulging led Stephen to suspect the intentions of the builders. Accordingly in June 1139 he seized the bishops of Salisbury and Lincoln, and Roger le Poor, the bishop of Salisbury's natural son. The bishop of Ely fled to Devizes and fortified it against the king. Stephen followed with his captives. He imprisoned the bishop of Salisbury in an ox stall in a byre (*bostario*) and the bishop of Lincoln in a mean hovel, and threatened to hang Roger le Poor before the castle gate unless the castle were handed over. The threat to her son's life moved Maud of Ramsbury (Roger le Poor's mother), who was within, and Bishop Roger himself, and together they prevailed upon the bishop of Ely to surrender. He did so three days from Stephen's arrival[51] and the castle fell into the king's hands. About

42 Ordericus Vitalis, *Hist. Eccl.* ed. A. Le Prevost, iv. 486 says he was there in 1128, but this is unlikely as the empress had removed him from Roger's custody in 1126. A.-S. *Chron.* ed. Dorothy Whitelock (1961), 192.
43 *Ann. Mon.* (Rolls Ser.), ii. 44.
44 John of Worcester in *Florentii Wigorn. Chron. ex Chronicis*, ed. B. Thorpe, ii. 76.
45 *Annals of Winchester* in *Ann. Mon.* (Rolls Ser.), ii. 51.
46 *Chron. ex Chronicis*, ii. 107.
47 'Mirando artificio sed et munimine inexpugnabili firmatum', 'ornanter et inexpugnabiliter muratum' (*Gesta Stephani*, ed. K. R. Potter, 52, 69).
48 'Multis et vix numerabilibus sumptibus … aedificatum' (Wm. of Malmesbury, *Hist. Novella*, ed. K. R. Potter, 27).
49 'Rogerius … plura apud Sciereburnam, et apud Divisas multum terrarum aedificiis amplexus, turritas moles erexerat' (ibid. 25).
50 Hen. of Huntingdon, *Hist. Angl.* (Rolls Ser.), 265.
51 The best original accounts of the story, which has been repeatedly retold, are in *Gesta Stephani*, ed. Potter, 52; Ordericus Vitalis, *Hist. Eccl.* ed. A. Le Prevost, v. 120; *Chron. ex Chronicis*, ed. Thorpe, ii. 107–8.

the end of October Stephen began to besiege the Bohun fortress at Trowbridge but soon abandoned the siege and returned to London. He left, however, in Devizes castle a party of armed soldiers (*succinctissimam ad martios congressus militiam*) to conduct future operations against Trowbridge.[52] About Easter 1140 Robert FitzHubert, a Flemish soldier of Earl Robert of Gloucester, stole away from his lord and seized the castle by night, scaling the walls by means of ladders stretched from the ramparts. Most of the sleeping garrison fell into his hands. A small party, indeed, escaped to an upper tower but were starved out in a few days. Gloucester's son was sent to recover Devizes from FitzHubert but was refused admittance. FitzHubert, however, was himself captured by John le Marshal, keeper of Marlborough castle, and imprisoned there. In August he was taken back to Devizes and hanged by Gloucester. After his execution his companions sold the castle to Hervey of Brittany, the king's son-in-law. Hervey defended the king's interest for some time, but eventually, being hard pressed by the surrounding inhabitants, surrendered it to the Empress.[53]

In September 1141 the Empress herself, fleeing from Winchester, was taken from Ludgershall to the castle, disguised and bound upon a bier.[54] She was in Devizes again during Lent and at Whitsun 1142 and the castle was in her hands at her death.[55] From her it passed to the future Henry II who was holding it in 1152.[56] In 1157 Archbishop Theobald ratified the existing state of affairs by confirming an exchange between the king and the bishop of Salisbury.[57] The king took the castle and its appurtenances in fee and gave the bishop in return the manor of Godalming (Surr.).[58] Thenceforth until the 17th century the castle belonged to the Crown.

A town grew up below the castle walls and by 1141 was called a 'borough'.[59] To this in course of time town lands were added. Presumably it was the combination of castle, town, and town lands that formed the lordship of Devizes, or 'manor' as it is actually called on eight occasions

52 *Gesta Stephani*, ed. Potter, 64.
53 Ibid. 69–72.
54 John of Worcester, *Continuatio* in *Florentii Wigorn. Chron. ex Chronicis*, ed. Thorpe, ii. 134.
55 Wm. of Malmesbury, *Hist. Novella*, ed. Potter, 71.
56 *Sar. Chart. and Doc.* (Rolls Ser.), 22.
57 Ibid. 29.
58 First stated in *Pipe R.* 1160–1 (P.R.S.), 42. Cf. *Bk. of Fees*, i. 67.
59 See p. 126.

between 1217[60] and 1248.[61] It is the lordship, rather than the castle alone, whose descent must now be traced.

That lordship formed the centre of a small liberty under the charge of the farmer or keeper of the castle, who often managed at the same time the manor of Rowde and the adjacent forests of Chippenham and Melksham.[62] Into this liberty, once or twice called a castellary[63] or honour,[64] the sheriff could not enter.[65] It was the constable who had return of writs,[66] and he alone was responsible for escheat[67] and wardship[68] and later for indicting offenders.[69] Also, no doubt, it was he who commanded the knights, by whom, as shown below, the castle was in early times defended.

The first known constable, Guy de Diva, occurs in 1192[70] and 1194–5,[71] but there is not evidence enough to show what the system of custody then was. In 1195–6 William of Ste. Mère Eglise was farming the estate,[72] though for the rest of the reign it was managed by the sheriff.[73] From 1199 Thomas de Sandford was farmer and so remained until July 1216.[74] Richard de Sandford, presumably his son, handed over the castle to a successor in March 1217.[75] From 1195–6 the customary farms for Devizes were £30 8s. and for Rowde £18 17s. 5d.[76] Out of them allowances for custody were made, £20 in 1195–6 and rather

---

60 *Rot. Litt. Claus.* (Rec. Com.), i. 330.
61 *Cal. Lib.* 1245–51, 163.
62 For the association of the constable with these forests see *V.C.H. Wilts.* iv. 409.
63 *Rot. Litt. Claus.* (Rec. Com.), ii. 5.
64 *Pat. R.* 1216–25, 299; 1225–32, 198.
65 *V.C.H. Wilts.* v. 5.
66 *Rot. Hund.* (Rec. Com.), ii (1), 252; *Plea R. of Exch. of Jews*, ed. H. Jenkinson (Jewish Hist. Soc.), iii. 42, 204 (1275–6).
67 Writ of *amoveas manum* of 1231: *Close R.* 1227–31, 506.
68 The wardship of Gillian daughter of Thos. of Rowde was granted to Wm. of Cardiff by Wm. Brewer *ante* 1226–8 (*Bk. of Fees*, i. 381). Roger son of Hen. le Oyseleur was a minor in the constable's custody in 1255 (*Rot. Hund.* (Rec. Com.), ii (1), 236).
69 *c.* 1346: J.I. 3/130 m. 33.
70 *Pipe R.* 1192 (P.R.S. N.S. ii), 186.
71 *Cur. Reg. R.* 1194–5 (P.R.S. xiv), 109.
72 *Chanc. R.* 1196 (P.R.S. N.S. vii), 197.
73 *Pipe R.* 1197 (P.R.S. N.S. viii), 214; 1198 (P.R.S. N.S. ix), 71; 1199 (P.R.S. N.S. x), 173.
74 *Pipe R.* At any rate he had joint charge of some boys in the castle in that month: *Rot. Litt. Pat.* (Rec. Com.), 191.
75 *Pat. R.* 1216–25, 51.
76 *Chanc. R.* 1196 (P.R.S. N.S. vii), 197.

more in Sandford's earlier years.[77] Later the joint farm was reduced, with retrospective effect, to 20 marks for 1199 to Easter 1206 and to £30 thereafter. Above those limits Sandford was to enjoy all profits.[78] Some time before John's death he seems also to have received a fee of 100 marks for the custody.[79]

From 1217 until 1234 the custody passed frequently from hand to hand. In this period the keepers were John Marshal, 'Strongbow's' nephew (1217–19),[80] Philip Daubeny (1219–21),[81] the legate Pandulf, elect of Norwich (1221),[82] Simon, abbot of Reading (1221), Alexander de Bassingbourne (1221),[83] William Brewer (1221–5),[84] Richard le Poor, bishop of Salisbury (1225–8),[85] Richard de Gray (June 1228–9),[86] Gilbert Basset (1229–33),[87] Ralph de Wilington (1233),[88] Peter de Rievaux (c. 1233),[89] Peter de Mauley (1234).[90] Apart from Marshal, Abbot Simon, Bassingbourne, Brewer, and Rievaux, about whom we are not informed, all these were granted the custody during pleasure. Brewer, Gray, and Basset received fees, Brewer's amounting to £30 or more,[91] Gray's[92] and Basset's to £20.[93] Gray[94] and Wilington[95] farmed the estate for £30 and Gray deducted his fee from his farm.

In May 1234 begins the long connexion of John du Plessis, later earl of Warwick, with the castle, which seems to have lasted

77 e.g. *Pipe R.* 1201 (P.R.S. N.S. xiv), 78.
78 *Rot. Litt. Claus.* (Rec. Com.), i. 69. The later fixed farm is once stated to be £30 and once £20.
79 *Pipe R.* 1218 (P.R.S. N.S. xxxix), 9 .
80 *Pat. R.* 1216–25, 51.
81 Ibid. 196.
82 Ibid. 293.
83 *Rot. Litt. Claus.* (Rec. Com.), ii. 7, which implies that he and Abbot Simon were the next keepers in succession to Pandulf.
84 Ibid. i. 549.
85 *Pat. R.* 1216–25, 419.
86 Ibid. 1225–32, 198.
87 Ibid. 317.
88 *Cal. Pat.* 1232–47, 20. Though the grant is dated 6 July 1233, he accounted for the period 6 Oct. 1232–9 Jan. 1234: S.C. 6/1117/13.
89 He had the custody 'antequam rex [eam] … committeret P. de Malo Lacu': *Close R.* 1231–4, 367.
90 Ibid. 361.
91 *Rot. Litt. Claus.* (Rec. Com.), ii. 109.
92 *Cal. Lib.* 1226–40, 158.
93 Ibid. 159.
94 E 372/73 m. 1.
95 S.C. 6/1117/13.

uninterruptedly until his death. At first the Crown let to him for 10 years (i) the castle and manor and Rowde manor for £25 and (ii) Chippenham forest for £2 10s.[96] In 1236 the arrangement was temporarily altered, the lands and forests being granted to Walter de Burgh, keeper of the king's manors, and the castle alone committed to du Plessis.[97] In 1238, however, the manors of Devizes and Rowde were restored to du Plessis during pleasure.[98] In 1240 they were again let to him for five years, though his fee was continued.[99] In 1255 this arrangement was changed again. The earl, as he then was, received the castle alone, during pleasure, at a reduced fee; the sheriff was to farm the rest.[1] In 1261 the sheriff lost the appurtenant lands, no doubt for political reasons,[2] and those lands were again restored to the earl.[3]

The troubled years during and after the civil war saw several changes in the custody: Robert de Neville (1263),[4] Philip Basset, the justiciar (1263–4),[5] Hugh le Despenser, also justiciar (1264),[6] Basset again (1264–71),[7] and Ellis Rabeyn (1271–2)[8] held it in rapid succession. At some time before April 1272 Henry III committed the castle to the lord Edward,[9] and Roger Mortimer (d. 1282), as trustee during the prince's absence in the Holy Land, accounted in 1272–3.[10] After this interlude John de Havering, constable of Marlborough (1272–5),[11] and Ralph de Sandwich (1275–?87) were successively keepers.[12] All these, apart from the lord Edward, about whose tenure nothing is known, received grants during pleasure. Basset was granted increasingly favourable terms owing to the need to munition the castle. He was promised his full expenses[13] which were eventually secured on lands in Dorset.[14]

96 *Cal. Pat.* 1232–47, 51.
97 *Cal. Lib.* 1226–40, 259.
98 *Cal. Pat.* 1232–47, 234.
99 *Cal. Lib.* 1240–5, 20.
1 *Cal. Pat.* 1247–58, 417.
2 *V.C.H. Wilts.* v. 11.
3 *Cal. Pat.* 1258–66, 171.
4 Ibid. 257.
5 Ibid. 264.
6 Ibid. 335
7 Ibid. 574.
8 *Ex. e Rot. Fin.* (Rec. Com.), ii. 551.
9 *Cal. Pat.* 1266–72, 646, 659.
10 E 159/49 m. 9.
11 *Cal. Pat.* 1266–72, 646.
12 Ibid. 1272–81, 127.
13 Ibid. 1258–66, 266.
14 Ibid. 307.

Repeatedly keepers were not in effective charge, for in 1195–6, 1204–5,[15] 1224,[16] 1238,[17] 1239,[18] and 1275–8[19] there were constables or under-constables in addition to the keepers. Apart from these, there is only one other castle officer, if he may be called that, who is mentioned in this period. This was a chaplain, who from 1237 to 1260 received an annual wage.[20]

The castle-guard of Devizes had originally been entrusted to knights holding fees or fractions of fees in Bratton, Calstone Wellington, Etchilhampton, Keevil, Market and West Lavington, Littleton Pannel, Stert, Bupton (in Clyffe Pypard), 'Cannings', Coate (in Bishop's Cannings), Horton, Hurst (in Worton), Mere, Orchardsleigh (Som.), and Potterne.[21] Possibly an entire or fractional fee had also lain in Broughton Gifford, but it is not mentioned before 1448.[22] At Devizes, as so often elsewhere, castle-guard services were not enumerated until they were already in decay. The first surviving list for Devizes was drawn up in 1255 and by that time the services in the last eight places named above, and part of the services in 'Lavington', had been withdrawn for thirty years back.

According to the declarations of 1255 each entire fee owed 40 days' service in wartime. Occasionally there are other definitions. Thus the tenant of the land in Calstone had to appear at the castle accompanied by an armed serjeant.[23] Late definitions of services arising in Market Lavington (1349)[24] and Stert (1355)[25] prescribed the defence of a tower in the castle. It is not known when corporal wartime service ceased, but

15 Walt. son of Ralph was constable in 1195–6: *Chanc. R.* 1196 (P.R.S. N.S. vii), 197. He was under arrest in 1204–5: *Pipe R.* 1205 (P.R.S. N.S. xix), 161.
16 W. de Radley: *Rot. Litt. Claus.* (Rec. Com.), i. 589.
17 *Cal. Pat.* 1232–47, 228.
18 Phil. de Munham: *Cal. Lib.* 1226–40, 380.
19 Walt. Lyllebon, John of Havering: *Plea R. of Exch. of Jews*, ed. H. Jenkinson (Jewish Hist. Soc.), iii. 43, 204; J.I. 3/71 m. 14.
20 *Cal. Lib.* 1226–40, 297; 1240–5, 41, 255, 301, 323; 1251–60, 355, 534. Presumably John, chaplain of the king's chapel in 1268, and rector of Devizes in 1268 (J.I. 1/998A m. 25 [24]) was the same officer.
21 Unless otherwise stated these three paragraphs are drawn from *Rot. Hund.* (Rec. Com.), ii (1), 232, 235–6. The service in Bratton is also mentioned in a feodary of 1242–3 (*Bk. of Fees*, ii. 736) and in *Valor Eccl.* (Rec. Com.), ii. 142. The fee or fractional fee out of which Calne hosp. paid a rent in 1535 has not been identified: *Valor Eccl.* (Rec. Com.), ii. 132. It was perhaps in Calstone Wellington.
22 *Cal. Close*, 1447–54, 11.
23 *Rot. Hund.* (Rec. Com.), ii (1), 236.
24 *Cal. Inq. p.m.* ix, p. 309.
25 Ibid. x, p. 219.

between 1224 and 1228 a tenant was excused his service on the ground that he was on duty elsewhere,[26] which suggests that the service was then sometimes still exacted.

In peacetime quit-rents, rated in 1255 at 10s. or £1, were payable on each fee or half-fee. The estimated optimum yield was then 25 marks, but when the withdrawn services have been deducted it can only have been £7 10s. This in fact is the sum which was later customarily collected and which was in fact being collected in 1541–2.[27] Such rents were still being paid to the Crown in 1609, though their then amount is unknown.[28] By 1647–8 and again in 1689–90 they were being enjoyed by the borough corporation,[29] but were lost by 1833.[30]

One serjeanty belonged to the castle, that of finding an armed serjeant for 40 days in wartime. This inhered in a small estate in Rowde and is traceable from 1249[31] to 1288–9.[32]

By the 13th century, no doubt, reliance was being placed at least as much on hired soldiers as on tenants by castle-guard or serjeants-in-fee and payments to members of a garrison are recorded in 1198–9,[33] 1221,[34] and 1233.[35] Quarrels were made in or sent to the castle in 1215,[36] 1225,[37] and 1226,[38] and corn was purchased in 1191–4[39] and 1216.[40] Evidently the castle was kept in a defensible state throughout the reigns of Richard I and John and the minority of Henry III.

Throughout the 13th century kings and notables constantly stayed in the castle. Between 1204 and 1216 King John visited it at least once in every year but two,[41] and there in June 1216 he received the countess

26 *Rot. Litt. Claus.* (Rec. Com.), ii. 5, 144; *Close R.* 1227–31, 77.
27 S.C. 6/Hen. VIII/6668.
28 S.P. 14/49 no. 82.
29 Cunnington, *Annals*, i (2nd pagin.), 116, cf. ibid. 109. In 1663 they seem to have been paid over to the king's auditors: ibid. 139. For 1689–90 see ibid. 189.
30 *Rep. Com. Mun. Corps.* H.C. 116, p. 1269 (1835), xxiv. Attempts to collect them were made up to 1735: Waylen, *Hist.* 98.
31 *W.R.S.* xvi, no. 408 and n. thereon at p. 272.
32 J.I. 1/1006 m. 59d.
33 *Pipe R.* 1199 (P.R.S. N.S. x), 168.
34 *Rot. Litt. Claus.* (Rec. Com.), i. 458, 467.
35 *Cal. Lib.* 1226–40, 231, 233.
36 *Rot. Litt. Claus.* (Rec. Com.), i. 198.
37 Ibid. 589.
38 *Cal. Lib.* 1226–40, 3.
39 *Pipe R.* 1192 (P.R.S. N.S. ii), 281; 1194 (P.R.S. N.S. v), 256.
40 *Rot. Litt. Claus.* (Rec. Com.), 273.
41 T. D. Hardy, *Description of Pat. Rs.* [and] *Itin. of King John*, index.

of Aumale and her children.[42] Henry III was there at his father's death[43] with many other boys,[44] and visited the castle as king in 1217, 1222, and 1224.[45] The cardinal-legate Otto stayed there in 1238,[46] Edward I paid six visits between 1278 and 1302,[47] and at Easter 1282 the King's Bench was there too.[48] In 1302 the royal children were in the castle for a while.[49]

The castle was also used as a prison, though never to a great extent. Robert of Normandy's captivity has already been referred to.[50] Queen Margaret and other hostages were held in custody there in 1174,[51] Isabel of Angoulême in 1209.[52] Approvers and others were received in it or removed from it to other places of custody in 1219,[53] 1221,[54] and 1242.[55] The most famous prisoner, however, was Hubert de Burgh who was committed after his arraignment in November 1232. He was guarded by four knights[56] to whom the keep was handed over as Hubert's prison on the understanding that the king had free access to the rest of the castle.[57] After a few months the king began to suspect that Gilbert Basset, a neighbouring landowner and former constable, would try to restore Hubert's cause and enlarged the guard in June and July.[58] These measures were evidently useless and on 28 September Hubert was entrusted to Ralph de Wilington, the constable, and more rigorously restrained. The following night, however, two of Hubert's guards carried him to St. John's church.[59] They were swiftly restored to the castle and orders were at once reissued for Hubert's rigorous confinement. Hubert's removal

42 *Rot. Litt. Pat.* (Rec. Com.), 187.
43 F. M. Powicke, *Hen. III and the Lord Edw.* i. 2.
44 *Rot. Litt. Pat.* (Rec. Com.), 191.
45 P.R.O., Round Room, Itin. of Hen. III. TS.
46 E 372/82 m. 1; *Close R. 1237–42*, 98.
47 P.R.O., Round Room, Itin. of Edw. I. TS.
48 *Sel. Cases in K.B.* ii (Selden Soc. lvii), p. lxxiv.
49 E 101/593/1.
50 See pp. 36–7.
51 *Pipe R. 1174* (P.R.S. xxi), 21; R. W. Eyton, *Court, Household and Itin. of . . . Hen. II*, 180.
52 Gervase of Canterbury, *Gesta Regum* (Rolls Ser.), ii. 107.
53 *Rot. Litt. Claus.* (Rec. Com.), i. 395.
54 Ibid. 450, 472.
55 *Cal. Lib. 1240–5*, 107, 122, 159; *Close R. 1237–42*, 415.
56 Unless otherwise stated this paragraph is drawn from Powicke, *Hen. III and the Lord Edw.* i. 127–8, 139–40.
57 *Cal. Pat. 1232–47*, 19.
58 Ibid. 19–20.
59 See p. 183.

from the church had, however, involved the violation of sanctuary and the bishop of Salisbury ordered his restoration. His guards refused and were excommunicated. Hubert was restored to sanctuary and never returned to the castle.

The great strength of the castle made it an obvious safe deposit. On several occasions between 1206 and 1242 both jewels and specie were placed within it.[60]

By the later 13th century the castle was becoming less and less a fortress and more and more the administrative centre of a territorial complex. This transition can perhaps be dated from 1287 when castle and manor were granted for life to Matthew son of John, knight, at a yearly rent.[61] Later in that year Rowde and other manors were added, and, by a separate grant, the forests of Melksham and Chippenham.[62] The wardenship of the forests had usually been linked with the constableship since the days of Thomas de Sandford and the connexion with that office or later with the stewardship was preserved into the 17th century.[63]

A few months after the initial grant the premises were regranted to Matthew in the name of the king and queen.[64] This suggests that Edward I had already begun to look upon Devizes as a potential means of support for his consort. In 1290 the king granted Queen Eleanor the rent reserved upon Devizes[65] and in 1299 when he married Margaret of France as his second wife he assigned Devizes to her as part of her jointure.[66] The grant of 1299 was presumably a mere expectancy contingent upon Matthew's death, but in 1301 Matthew actually surrendered the castle and its appurtenances and shortly afterwards was recompensed elsewhere.[67] After this, for a long time to come, the estate more often than not formed part of the jointure of queens consort or dowager.

Margaret held the estate until her death in 1318, except for a few months in 1308 when it was granted to Hugh le Despenser during

60 *Rot. Litt. Claus.* (Rec. Com.), i. 71, 138, 153, 602; ii. 73; *Pipe R.* 1207 (P.R.S. N.S. xxii), 202; 1214 (P.R.S. N.S. xxxv), 40; *Cal. Pat.* 1232–47, 118, 213; *Close R.* 1237–42, 392; *Cal. Lib.* 1240–5, 132.
61 *Cal. Pat.* 1281–92, 270.
62 Ibid. 279, 280.
63 *V.C.H. Wilts.* iv. 436–7.
64 *Cal. Pat.* 1281–92, 279; *W.R.S.* i, p. 68.
65 *Cal. Pat.* 1281–92, 368.
66 Ibid. 1292–1301, 452.
67 *Cal. Fine R.* 1272–1307, 529.

pleasure.[68] She was in residence in 1311.[69] At her death the estate was assigned to Queen Isabel[70] who held it until her forfeiture in 1324, when it was resumed.[71] By 1326 it appears to have been again granted away,[72] but, however that may be, the Crown held it again in 1327[73] and in 1330 assigned it,[74] as part of her jointure, to Queen Philippa, who kept it until her death in 1369.

Matthew son of John and his three successors appointed keepers or constables. One is known by name from Matthew's time,[75] one from Margaret's,[76] one from Despenser's,[77] and three from Isabel's.[78] In 1330, the year of the grant to Philippa, the practice began of leasing the whole estate, apparently for life, to farmers. Gilbert of Berwick was the first of these[79] and he remained farmer until at least 1338.[80] In 1340 he was succeeded by Roger, Lord Beauchamp (d. c. 1379), who farmed all the Devizes complex except Rowde.[81] After Philippa's death in 1369 he remained in possession, in which in 1344 he had been expressly confirmed by the king,[82] to whom he paid direct[83] the farm that he had formerly paid to the queen. In 1372 he granted away the custody of the parks and woodlands belonging to the castle,[84] and in 1376 his farm was reduced.[85]

68 *Cal. Pat.* 1307–13, 51, 96.
69 *Household Bk. of Queen Isabella*, ed. F. D. Blackley and G. Hermansen (Edmonton, Alberta), 206.
70 *Cal. Pat.* 1317–21, 115.
71 *D.N.B.* s.v. Isabella of France.
72 S.C. 6/1090/15 (Hil. 1326): a roll of receipts from lands late in the king's hands.
73 *Cal. Mem. R.* 1326–7, no. 137.
74 *Cal. Pat.* 1330–4, 55.
75 John Flavel: *Cal. Inq. Misc.* i, p. 412.
76 John Bluet, who was ordered to deliver the castle from the queen to Despenser (*Cal. Pat.* 1307–13, 51), was constable in 1309–10 (S.C. 6/1090/7).
77 John of Mountsorrel: B.M. Add. Ch. 7066.
78 John de Rameshalle (in office Sept. 1302): Hist. MSS. Com. 55, *Var. Coll.* iv, p. 106; Robt. Lewer (appointed Dec. 1321 by the king but without the queen's approval): *Cal. Pat.* 1321–4, 40; Robt. de Batelescombe (in office 1322 and 1326): S.C. 6/1090/12; S.C. 6/1090/15.
79 *Cal. Fine R.* 1327–37, 214.
80 *Cal. Pat.* 1338–40, 47.
81 Ibid. 1340–3, 115. At least Rowde is not expressly mentioned in the grant, though the farm that he was paying before 1376 (ibid. 1374–7, 352) is high enough to suggest that it may in fact have been included.
82 Ibid. 1343–5, 270. A Nic. of Rowde, constable c. 1346, was presumably Beauchamp's deputy: J.I. 3/130 m. 33.
83 Ibid. 1374–7, 352.
84 Inspeximus of 1378: *Cal. Pat.* 1377–81, 183.
85 Ibid. 1374–7, 352.

Early in 1380 Beauchamp was succeeded as farmer by Sir Nicholas de Sharnesfield, to whom Rowde was also assigned.[86] He lasted only until 1381, when the same farm was transferred to John, Lord Lovel.[87] Next year the king married Anne of Bohemia and the Devizes complex, apparently without Rowde, was granted to her.[88] Anne kept the estate until her death in 1394[89] and before April 1395 it was, with Rowde, granted or confirmed to Lovel, who had farmed it under her. In that April all rent was remitted.[90] In 1405 the same estate was settled upon Queen Joan of Navarre for life,[91] subject to Lovel's life interest. Lovel accounted in 1405–6,[92] and in 1408, the year of Lovel's death, the queen was confirmed in possession. It may be supposed that she retained it until she died in 1437. During the period 1408–15 Edward 'Plantagenet', duke of York, farmed it under the queen,[93] and in 1423 it was again being farmed to the queen's profit.[94]

It may be assumed that the castle was still munitioned in 1287, for Sandwich handed over crossbows, baldrics, and quarrels.[95] In 1307–8 orders were given to fortify and guard the castle with many others throughout the land.[96] After this there are but few references to munitioning. Beauchamp was indeed suspected of appropriating arms, furniture, artillery, and victuals,[97] but it is unlikely that the castle was strictly defensible in his time. At any rate the castle was not garrisoned and victualled against the French in 1360, as Old Salisbury and Marlborough were.[98] On the other hand it was well enough maintained to serve occasionally as a residence or a prison, and efforts to keep it in repair continued until well into the 15th century.[99] The evidence for such use is somewhat sporadic. In 1294 buildings in the castle were assigned to John Tregoze as a home for his wife while the king was in

86 *Cal. Close*, 1377–81, 359.
87 *Cal. Pat.* 1381–5, 62.
88 Ibid. 192.
89 *Cal. Inq. Misc.* vii, p. 169.
90 Inspeximus of 1397; *Cal. Pat.* 1396–9, 208.
91 *Cal. Close*, 1402–5, 455; *Cal. Pat.* 1405–8, 438.
92 E 364/41 m. 3.
93 S.C. 6/1093/1.
94 *Cal. Close*, 1422–9, 23.
95 *Cal. Inq. Misc.* i, p. 399.
96 *Cal. Close*, 1307–13, 30, 50.
97 *Cal. Pat.* 1377–81, 510.
98 *Cal. Close*, 1360–64, 9.
99 See p. 56.

Gascony—an arrangement paralleled in other castles.[1] Four Scots prisoners were received in 1296,[2] two of them remaining for over a year,[3] the king's children stayed there in 1302,[4] and between 1307 and 1312 Sir David Lindsey, another Scots prisoner, was honourably confined.[5] Eleanor la Zouche was imprisoned there c. 1330,[6] venison trespassers in 1283,[7] 1288,[8] 1294,[9] 1358,[10] and 1383,[11] and a suspect felon in 1274.[12] In 1373 the two sons of Charles de Blois were taken from confinement in the castle but returned thither in 1377.[13] The last reference to the castle as a prison occurs in 1405.[14] In 1411–12 the queen was in residence.[15]

Apart from the constables the only castle officer of any importance seems to have been the porter. The first known incumbent was in office in 1299[16] and others occur in the later 14th century[17] when the porter's only recorded function was rent-collecting.[18]

The fate of the castle immediately after the death of Joan of Navarre is uncertain. There was in any case no queen consort to whom it could be assigned. Before March 1443, however, it had reached the hands of Humphrey, duke of Gloucester, who had by that time appointed Sir Edmund Hungerford as constable during pleasure.[19] Humphrey spent Christmas 1446 at Devizes[20] but he died in 1447 and the castle and lordship, which he had held in tail male, were at once transferred to

1 *Cal. Close*, 1288–96, 391.
2 Ibid. 482.
3 *Rotuli Scotiae*, i. 46.
4 E 101/593/1.
5 *Cal. Close*, 1307–13, 17, 371, 463.
6 *Rot. Parl.* ii. 58.
7 *Cal. Fine R.* 1272–1307, 242.
8 Ibid. 249.
9 *Cal. Close*, 1288–96, 406.
10 *Cal. Pat.* 1358–61, 149.
11 K.B. 27/492 m. 14.
12 J.I. 3/35A m. 1d.
13 *Cal. Pat.* 1370–4, 325, 331; 1374–7, 417–18.
14 Ibid. 1401–5, 454.
15 S.C. 6/1062/25.
16 *Cal. Pat.* 1292–1301, 396.
17 Ibid. 1364–7, 39; 1370–4, 207; 1377–81, 183. Also perhaps Robt. Porter, collector of rents of assarts in 1368–9: E 364/4 m. D.
18 *Cal. Close*, 1377–81, 25, 30, 43; see also E 364/11 m. G (1377–8) and preceding n.
19 *Cal. Pat.* 1441–6, 168.
20 *Camden Misc.* xxiv (Camd. Soc. 4th ser. ix), 194.

Margaret of Anjou, whom Henry VI had married two years before. The term was at first unspecified but became a life tenure in 1452.[21] Hungerford remained undisturbed as constable at least until 1455.[22]

Margaret was presumably deprived on her attainder in 1459, and in 1461 Edward IV, enlarging a grant that he had made in the previous April,[23] bestowed the Devizes lordship upon Richard Beauchamp, bishop of Salisbury, for 20 years in fee farm.[24] The bishop's interest was protected from the operation of the Acts of Resumption of 1461 and 1464,[25] but he appears to have surrendered by March 1465 when the same bailiwick was bestowed upon Queen Elizabeth in part support of the expenses of her chamber.[26] In January 1466 the bailiwick was regranted to her by a new patent,[27] confirmed in Parliament in 1467.[28] It was she perhaps who appointed Sir Roger Tocotes steward. He was deprived in 1483 for complicity in the duke of Buckingham's rebellion,[29] but restored in 1485.[30] Meanwhile Thomas Stafford filled the office.[31] Elizabeth Woodville kept the estates until deprived of them in 1483–4.[32] She was reinstated in 1485[33] but in March 1486 the estates were granted in dower to Elizabeth of York.[34] The new queen appointed Richard Beauchamp, Lord St. Amand, to the stewardship in 1492.[35]

After Elizabeth's death (1503) the estates were kept in hand for some time, until in 1509 they were granted as part of her jointure to Catherine of Aragon, then Princess of Wales.[36] During the interval stewards were in charge. In 1504 the grant of the stewardship was renewed to St. Amand during pleasure.[37] In 1508 Anthony St. Amand and Edmund Dudley were appointed stewards for Anthony's life,[38] and in 1526 Sir Edward Baynton succeeded them.[39] By 1534 Catherine's jointure had

---

21 *Cal. Pat.* 1446–52, 559.
22 *Rot. Parl.* v. 318. The date of Hungerford's death has not been ascertained.
23 *Cal. Fine R.* 1461–7, 11.
24 *Cal. Pat.* 1461–5, 95.
25 *Rot. Parl.* v. 470, 519.
26 *Cal. Pat.* 1461–7, 430.
27 Ibid. 482.
28 *Rot. Parl.* v. 627.
29 Ibid. vi. 245.
30 Ibid. 273; *Cal. Pat.* 1485–94, 22.
31 Waylen, *Hist.* 584.
32 1 Ric. III, c. 15.
33 *Rot. Parl.* vi. 288.
34 Ibid. 386.
35 S.C. 6/Hen. VII/885.
36 *L. & P. Hen. VIII*, i (1), p. 49.
37 *Cal. Pat.* 1494–1509, 386.
38 Ibid. 589.
39 *L. & P. Hen. VIII*, iv (2), p. 1151.

been transferred to Anne Boleyn.[40] There is no evidence that the castle and lordship ever formed part of Jane Seymour's jointure. In 1540, however, the usual group of estates was bestowed on Anne of Cleves for life.[41] It was bestowed on Catherine Howard in 1541[42] and on Catherine Parr in 1544.[43] Catherine Parr made Sir William Herbert steward in 1544–5 and the king confirmed the appointment in 1546.[44] In August 1547 the same group of estates was granted to Lord Seymour of Sudeley, Catherine Parr's husband, to support the dignity of his creation.[45] He was attainted in 1549 and the Crown resumed possession.

By this time the portership had died away. In 1447–55 Hungerford held it while he was constable,[46] but presumably he merely took the profits and devolved the work. In 1451 a lesser man is named[47] and in 1484 the office was granted to a yeoman of the king's chamber.[48] In 1526[49] and 1544–5[50] the stewards of the lordship were appointed to the office, which presumably was then a sinecure. It is not heard of afterwards. In his later days the porter acquired the presidency of the court held at the castle gate, which sat once yearly from 1446–7 to c. 1543.[51] The court's function is not clear, but in 1576–7 the large sum of £5 was collected there as a relief.[52]

The first known steward had died by March 1463, two others occur in the later 15th century,[53] and in the next century appointments seem fairly regular. The emergence of a steward emphasizes the fact that the castle was by then of small account, even as a residence, and that what the Crown was granting away was a block of rural and urban property with some rents and perquisites. The cash revenues from 1446–

40 L. & P. Hen. VIII, vii, p. 146.
41 Ibid. viii, p. 52.
42 Ibid. xvi, p. 240.
43 Ibid. xix (1), p. 52.
44 Ibid. xxi (1), p. 359.
45 Cal. Pat. 1547–8, 32–3.
46 S.C. 6/1055/17–19; Rot. Parl. v. 318.
47 Edm. Butterfield, late porter: C 145/318 Pt. 1, no. 55.
48 Cal. Pat. 1476–85, 408.
49 L. & P. Hen. VIII, iv (2), p. 1151.
50 Confirmation of 1546: ibid. xxi (1), p. 359.
51 The statement rests on the relevant ministers' accts. in D.L. 29, S.C. 6, S.C. 6/Hen. VII, and S.C. 6/Hen. VIII, and on L.R. 2/191 f. 164v. The fact that the porter presided is only mentioned in S.C. 6/Hen. VII/1137.
52 S.C. 6/Hen. VIII/3760.
53 Cal. Pat. 1461–7, 274; 1485–94, 22.

7 to 1508–9 consisted of the rents of burgages, castle-guard rents, rents and farms of pasture and parks, tolls of the borough market, the profits of three courts, amercements of the borough's brewers and bakers, and the agistment and pannage of the forests.[54] After 1510 the market tolls, the amercements of bakers, and the profits of two of the courts were commuted into a fixed annual sum paid by the borough.[55] Out of these receipts the fees and wages of divers officers had to be met[56] and the expenses of maintaining the property.

The jurisdiction of the steward, whether appointed directly by the Crown or by a queen consort, represents the ancient authority of the constable, whose liberty, as has been shown, existed in the early 13th century.[57] After the charter of 1381 had been granted to the borough it was before him that the townsmen were mustered to arms.[58] He is found holding a view of frankpledge in 1366, at which a forger was indicted,[59] and from 1446–7 until 1508–9 he normally held one view and four courts each year.[60] From 1492–3 to 1507–8 he dealt with the amercement of brewers, who, in the period from 1477–8 to 1483–4 had been justiciable before the mayor.[61] But the story of this jurisdiction perhaps more properly belongs to that of the liberties of Wiltshire.

CASTLE BUILDINGS. The castle lay on the south-west side of the town, on a little hill with steeply sloping sides.[62] It was originally protected to the north-east and south by four concentric ditches. The outer two

---

54 The statement rests on the relevant ministers' accts. in D.L. 29, S.C. 6, S.C. 6/Hen. VII, and S.C. 6/Hen. VIII.
55 See p. 129.
56 In 1380 the keeper of the castle was expressly bound to pay the wages of porter, parker, and forester: *Cal. Fine. R.* 1377–83, 182. The wages of the yeoman ranger of Melksham and Pewsham forests were charged upon the castle, manor, and lordship of Devizes and Rowde in 1409: *Cal. Pat.* 1408–13, 55.
57 See p. 39.
58 See p. 128.
59 J.I. 3/156 m. 6d.
60 These courts were perhaps somewhat like the Dover court of castle gate: Katherine M. E. Murray, *Constit. Hist. of the Cinque Ports*, 103–5.
61 These statements rest on the relevant ministers' accts. in D.L. 29, S.C. 6, S.C. 6/Hen. VII, and S.C. 6/Hen. VIII.
62 Unless otherwise stated this paragraph is based upon W.A.S. Libr., Devizes, H 258 (drawing of ruins c. 1800), LL 58 (plan and drawing of 1858), map of 1654; Dore, Map, 1759; plans in E. H. Stone, *Devizes Castle* (1920); R. H. Cunnington, 'Devizes Castle', *W.A.M.* li. 496; W.R.O. 844, town deeds, box 9, Corp. Lease Bk., corp. lands, nos. 12, 115.

have been mentioned already, since, eventually at least, they formed town rather than castle fortifications.[63] Within these two lay the outer castle ditch. It started in Station Road near Craven House, ran beneath the Corn Exchange and the Bear yard, and cut through the roadway connecting the castle with St. John Street. It came close to the north side of St. John's churchyard and then joined the inner town ditch somewhere on the former railway track. Near the Corn Exchange it was double with steep sides 20 ft. deep. Its course behind the Pelican inn was marked in 1787 and 1832 by a town sewer. Within this ditch lay the inner castle ditch or moat, with almost vertical sides, which, on excavation, was found *c.* 1860 to be 45 ft. deeper than the exposed portion.[64] No doubt the outer ward or bailey of the castle lay originally between the inner town ditch and the outer castle ditch. As the town encroached, however, the outer bailey apparently contracted to the area between the outer and inner castle ditches. From the outside world this area was reached by the Brittox[65] and possibly a continuation of it. The roadway passed through an outer or 'foreign' gate of uncertain location and entered the inner precincts on the north by the inner gate. Inside that gate was a courtyard, called eventually the inner ward,[66] out of which a postern may have led a little to the south of west.[67] Somewhere on its course the roadway crossed two bridges, between which in 1380 was a barbican.[68] One of the bridges, probably that on the west, was a swing- or draw-bridge, mentioned in 1248.[69]

The earthen wall above the inner castle ditch was crowned by a stone curtain, of which some vestiges survive. It was probably this curtain which, having then recently fallen down, was repaired in 1240,[70] and, with its battlements, was repaired again on the south and east sides with Hazelbury stone in 1379–81.[71] Behind this stood the keep or 'great' tower, first mentioned when repaired in 1240.[72] It is perhaps the same as

63 See pp. 15–16.
64 W.A.M. xix. 175. It is, however, hard to be sure whether that dimension refers to this or the outer castle ditch.
65 See p. 17.
66 In 1461: C 145/318 Pt. 1, no. 55.
67 There is no documentary evidence of this gate, but Stone marks it on his plans.
68 *Cal. Inq. Misc.* iv, p. 65.
69 *Cal. Lib.* 1245–51, 192; cf. W.A.M. xliv. 83.
70 E 372/84 m. 3; *Cal. Lib.* 1226–40, 446.
71 E 101/593/46; E 101/593/48.
72 E 372/84 m. 3; *Cal. Lib.* 1226–40, 446.

the 'high' tower, joisted in 1309–10.[73] Work was done on the 'great' tower in the lower ward in 1411–14 including repairs to the foundations.[74] This was probably the same as the 'outer keep' which was fitted with a door in 1379–80.[75] Other towers or turrets abounded. New turrets were erected in 1240[76] and 1251[77] and others mended in the former year. The tower called 'Gent' was roofed with Corsham slates in 1309–10, and at the same time the 'Johan' tower was repaired.[78] The 'Everard' tower is first mentioned in 1385.[79] In 1610 five 'very high' towers partially survived.[80]

Adjoining the keep on the west stood an aisled hall of 6 bays, about 70 ft. x 25 ft., the foundations of which were laid bare in the 19th century.[81] It is first mentioned in 1236–7,[82] and from time to time until 1379–80, when it was equipped with new boarding.[83] In 1328 a pentice was attached to it.[84] Excavations in 1858 showed that various lesser buildings surrounded the hall, and that in the most northerly was a well. It is not now possible to determine their purpose. It is known, however, what some of the domestic buildings were within the castle precincts. The king's 'chamber', mentioned in 1236–7,[85] had become the 'chambers' by 1248.[86] A fireplace was put into the queen's chamber in 1256[87] and that building is mentioned again in 1309–10.[88] In the later year we hear of the chamber by the inner bridge, roofed with Corsham slates, the chamber attached to the tower, the tailor's chamber, and the kitchen.[89] In 1328 the king's chamber occurs, a 'great' chamber (with a cellar beneath) beside it, a wardrobe for the king's and queen's clothes, the

73 S.C. 6/1090/7.
74 S.C. 6/1062/25.
75 E 101/593/46.
76 E 372/84 m. 3; *Cal. Lib.* 1226–40, 446.
77 *Cal. Lib.* 1251–60, 8.
78 S.C. 6/1090/7.
79 E 101/593/76.
80 Hist. MSS. Com. 9, *Salisbury*, xxi. 224.
81 E. H. Stone, *Devizes Castle*, 29, 114, 142, plan facing p. 114 and pl. facing p. 142.
82 E 159/15 m. 14d.
83 E 101/593/46.
84 E 101/476/4.
85 E 159/15 m. 14d.
86 *Cal. Lib.* 1245–51, 192.
87 Ibid. 1251–60, 311.
88 S.C. 6/1090/7.
89 Ibid.

nursery, the queen's larder, the great saucery, and a 'cuphous'.[90] In 1377–81 the kitchen and tailor's chamber are mentioned again, and, for the first time, 'the esquires' chamber', a bakehouse with 2 ovens, a pantry, a separate queen's wardrobe, a stable for 40 horses, a garner, and an aviary.[91]

A chapel is first mentioned in 1237[92] and an 'outer' chapel in 1244,[93] which implies that by that time there was more than one. Two chapels certainly existed in 1385:[94] the 'old' one in the outer ward, which by 1287 possessed a bell,[95] and another in the inner ward, with glazed windows. It is not clear which of these was the 'great' chapel 'within the bailey' which lacked its glass in 1328.[96] Even as late as 1461 orders were celebrated within the chapel,[97] and in 1610 Norden noticed traces of both chapels.[98]

Two lesser buildings deserve mention. A treasury was repaired in 1242[99] and in 1287 there was a prison in the outer gate.[1]

The lack of ancient masonry and imprecision of the records make it very hard to describe the castle's development. It may be said, however, that for almost a century from 1195–6 expenditure on the buildings was very frequent.[2] Some of this was certainly for current maintenance, but large sums suggesting works of greater magnitude were at certain times laid out. Particular mention may be made of the years 1205–6 and 1215–16. In the first period £35 18s. 8d. was spent,[3] in the second £81 16s.[4] Much of the latter sum was devoted to a ditch, and ditchers and a miner were employed. But wages were also paid to 22 carpenters and in that year or the next to masons and hodmen as well. The next period of activity extended from December 1237 to September 1240, when John

90 E 101/476/4.
91 *Cal. Inq. Misc.* iv, p. 65; E 101/462/5.
92 *Cal. Lib.* 1226–40, 297.
93 Ibid. 1240–45, 255.
94 E 101/593/76.
95 *Cal. Inq. Misc.* i, p. 400.
96 E 101/476/4.
97 Sar. Dioc. Regy., Reg. Beauchamp, Ep. Sar., i, f. 183v.
98 Hist. MSS. Com. 9, *Salisbury*, xxi. 224.
99 *Cal. Lib.* 1240–5, 164.
1 *Cal. Inq. Misc.* i, p. 400.
2 This paragraph is largely based upon the *Pipe Rolls* (P.R.S.); *Rot. Litt. Pat.* (Rec. Com.); *Rot. Litt. Claus.* (Rec. Com.), i; *Cal. Lib.*; *Close R.*
3 *Pipe R.* 1206 (P.R.S. N.S. xx), p. 183; 1207 (P.R.S. N.S. xxii), p. 202; 1208 (P.R.S. N.S. xxiii), p. 201.
4 *Rot. Litt. Claus.* (Rec. Com.), i. 213, 353.

du Plessis spent over £383 on building.[5] The work, as has been said, affected the wall and towers. The years 1248–9 were at least as important, for £40 was spent on repairing the swing bridge of the 'donjon' and in reroofing,[6] and in 1249 expenditure up to £600 was authorized.[7] Less was spent for a while thereafter, but with the coming of Philip Basset payments rose again and continued to the end of the reign.[8] In 1280 orders were given for £300 to be divided between the works at Devizes and Odiham (Hants).[9] A report prepared after the close of Sandwich's constableship described the castle as 'well kept'[10] and the preceding expenditure would suggest that it was accurate.

After this the castle became decreasingly defensive and probably was not so well maintained. Extensive works were done in 1309–10,[11] but repairs valued at £260 were again needed in 1328.[12] Writs of aid for repairs were issued in 1350,[13] 1364,[14] and 1371,[15] but their effect is uncertain. Many repairs were done from 1376 to 1381,[16] but the institution of an inquiry into their adequacy in 1382[17] suggests that they did not reach far enough. Repairs continued in 1384–5, when Hazelbury stone and Corsham slates were used.[18] Despite this an inquest taken in 1405 after Queen Anne's death found the building so decayed as to be valueless.[19] Further repairs were accordingly carried out in 1411–14 to equip the castle for use by Joan of Navarre who was in residence in 1411–12. For the purpose stone was again brought from Hazelbury and slates from Corsham. Stone came also from Box and Corsham, tiles from Ludgershall.[20] This, however, was to be almost the last overhaul. A

---

5 E 372/84 m. 3d.
6 *Cal. Lib.* 1245–51, 192.
7 Ibid. 269.
8 Ibid. 1251–60, 49, 314, 529; 1260–7, 201; 1267–72, nos. 960, 1322.
9 *Cal. Fine R.* 1272–1307, 123.
10 *Cal. Inq. Misc.* i, p. 399.
11 S.C. 6/1090/7.
12 E 101/476/4.
13 *Cal. Pat.* 1348–50, 571.
14 Ibid. 1364–7, 8.
15 Ibid. 1370–4, 97.
16 E 364/9 m. H(d.); E 364/11 m. G; E 364/12 m. C(d.); E 364/14 mm. C and E; E 364/15 m. G.
17 *Cal. Pat.* 1381–5, 134.
18 E 364/20 m. E(d.); E 101/593/76.
19 *Cal. Inq. Misc.* vii, p. 169.
20 S.C. 6/1062/25.

writ of aid was indeed issued in 1420,[21] but an inquiry in 1461 showed that parts of the walls of the 'outer' and 'inner' wards were broken, that the kitchen was roofless, and the bridge outside the castle almost completely gone.[22] It was, however, still habitable, for Bishop Beauchamp, to whom it had then just been granted, dated a letter from it in September of the same year.[23] Minor repairs took place in 1501–2.[24]

Leland described the building as 'in ruin'. Part of the towers of the gate of the keep and the chapel in it had been taken away to help to build Bromham House.[25] If that house was indeed the destination of the materials, then the plundering presumably took place after 1526 when Sir Edward Baynton, its builder, was steward of the castle.[26] In the castle gate Leland noticed places for six or seven portcullises—an indication of how formidable the defences had been.[27]

In 1578 the county justices thought they might use the building as a house of correction,[28] but either the Crown refused consent or the building proved to be too decayed. In 1596 the castle was said to be 'utterly ruinated and decayed', its walls having 'fallen down for the most part'.[29] Quarter Sessions met in it, however, from 1598 until 1612.[30] It can hardly have been comfortable, and was presumably abandoned as a court room when the market-house was built in the town in 1615–16.[31] But, as has been shown, substantial fragments of towers and chapels still stood in 1610, together with the 'large ruined hall' 'within the keep',[32] and even in 1619 some part of the buildings was fit to house a bishop.[33]

During the first four years of the Rebellion Devizes was almost continuously in Royalist hands[34] and the castle may have been used as a barracks, a magazine, a strong point, or all three. The defences are known

21 *Cal. Pat.* 1416–22, 274.
22 C 145/318 Pt. 1, no. 55.
23 E 179/53/235.
24 S.C. 6/Hen.VII/878.
25 Leland, *Itin.* ed. Toulmin Smith, v. 82; cf. *V.C.H. Wilts.* vii. 179.
26 See p. 49.
27 Leland, *Itin.* ed. Toulmin Smith, v. 82.
28 *W.R.S.* iv. 45.
29 E 310/26/155.
30 Waylen, *Chrons.* 149 (2nd pagin.); Cunnington, *Annals*, i (2nd pagin.), 39, 40, 42, 48.
31 See p. 150.
32 Hist. MSS. Com. 9, *Salisbury*, xxi, 224.
33 Waylen, *Chrons.* 151 (2nd pagin.).
34 See pp. 9–10.

to have been altered during this period.[35] The castle, however, is not expressly referred to until Cromwell besieged it in September 1645, planting ten cannon in the Market Place on 21 September and on the two following days bombarding it. On the second day a 'grenado' fell into the keep, which was being used as a powder magazine. This did not ignite the powder but the incident convinced the governor of the vanity of further resistance. He accordingly surrendered on 24 September.[36] The castle was ordered to be slighted in 1646[37] but the work was not finished until 1648.[38]

The stone of the castle was promptly used for building. Already by 1654 the castle house, constructed from the spoil,[39] stood at the south-west end of what is now Castle Lane.[40] Stukeley complained in 1724 that the castle was then 'ignobly mangled, and every day destroyed by people that care not to have a wall standing, though for a fence to their garden'.[41] George Flower (d. 1729),[42] who bought a part of the site in 1728,[43] is said to have been a notable despoiler.[44] John Strachey (d. 1743),[45] in an undated letter, said that no stone of the castle remained, although a sketch of his, assigned *c.* 1700, showed the inner gatehouse.[46] Two windmills[47] then stood on the top of the mound which was ascended by an ill-kept spiral walk. The castle yard had become an orchard. The castle house, though still erect,[48] was already in decay.[49]

PARKS. A park at Devizes is first mentioned in 1149,[50] and in 1157 two parks are said to have belonged to the castle.[51] This imparked area remained

35 Waylen, *Chrons.* 123–4.
36 Waylen, *Hist.* 244–6.
37 *W.A.M.* xxvi. 374.
38 Cunnington, *Annals*, i (2nd pagin.), 116, 118.
39 *W.A.M.* xliv. 83.
40 W.A.S. Libr., Devizes, Map, 1654.
41 *Itinerarium Curiosum* (1776 edn.), Cent. i. 145.
42 Phillipps, *Wilts. M.I.* 72.
43 C.P. 25(2)/1232/1 Geo. II Hil.
44 C 12/725/7.
45 *D.N.B.*
46 W.A.S. Libr., Devizes, Cunnington MSS. iii, f. 35.
47 See p. 95.
48 W.A.S. Libr., Devizes, Cunnington MSS. iii, f. 35.
49 *W.A.M.* xliv. 83.
50 *Sar. Chart. and Doc.* (Rolls Ser.), 15.
51 Ibid. 29.

a castle appurtenance until at least 1570 (see below), and from the end of the 13th century it and the castle were often expressly passed together in royal grants.[52] There were probably two parks from very early times,[53] though draftsmen did not always use the plural.

The parks were the 'old'[54] or 'great'[55] park, lying to the south-west of the castle and within St. John's parish, and the 'new'[56] or 'little' park,[57] lying north of the town and mainly in Bishop's Cannings parish. The first had been disparked by 1595;[58] the second was subsequently incorporated into Roundway park, and, from having been the smaller, became the larger by accretion.[59]

In 1157 both parks were surrounded by a high bank and deep ditch, considerable traces of which still flanked the old one in 1972.[60] Until at least 1229 the 'park', presumably the old one, was bounded by a stone wall which was then in part removed.[61] Later there was a paling which was repeatedly repaired up to 1534–5[62] and in 1477–8 was heightened on the north side of the castle and spiked to hinder clambering boys.[63] By 1595 the paling or some part of it had disappeared.[64]

The old park, if not both parks, naturally sheltered deer. Bucks are referred to in 1256.[65] In 1460 the herd of deer numbered 20 bucks and 140 rascals.[66] Deer are last mentioned in 1576.[67] To tend these and other parkland beasts a keeper lived on the site. His house stood in the middle of the old park and is first referred to under the name of the 'driving lodge' in 1477–8.[68] About 1543 it comprised 4 chambers, a

52 e.g. in 1330: *Cal. Pat.* 1330–4, 55.
53 *W.A.M.* vi. 126.
54 First so called in 1646–7; Cunnington, *Annals,* i (2nd pagin.), 115.
55 First so called early in Chas. I's reign: S.C. 12/4/5.
56 First so called in 1327–8: C 143/194/10.
57 First so called in 1255: *Rot. Hund.* (Rec. Com.), ii (1), 236.
58 Waylen, *Hist.* 585.
59 The later history of this park is traced in *V.C.H. Wilts.* vii. 191–2.
60 *Sar. Chart. and Doc.* (Rolls Ser.), 29.
61 *Close R.* 1227–31, 164.
62 E 364/11 m. G; E 364/14 m. C; E 364/15 m. G; E 364/20 m. E d.; E 101/462/5; E 101/593/48; S.C. 6/1055/19; S.C. 6/Hen.VII/878; S.C. 6/Hen.VII/1135; S.C. 6/Hen.VII/1136; S.C. 6/Hen.VII/1137; S.C. 6/Hen.VIII/3776; D.L. 29/724/11802.
63 D.L. 29/724/11801.
64 Waylen, *Hist.* 586.
65 *Cal. Lib.* 1251–60, 311.
66 C 145/318 Pt. 1, no. 55.
67 *W.R.S.* iv. 22.
68 D.L. 29/724/11801.

parlour, a buttery, and a kitchen, and a stable and dairy house stood beside it.[69] In 1654 'grounds' surrounded it,[70] perhaps sown with the oaks which still abounded in 1859.[71] It seems to have been pulled down not long before 1839.[72] The building or its site was surrounded by a moat, named in 1835,[73] and represented in 1839 as an oblong area called Moat Mead. It was then fed by a stream passing south-westwards through the park. The moat was not a perfect quadrangle, for there was solid ground, suggesting a causeway, at the north-east corner.[74] In 1859 it could be described as 'broad and deep'.[75] When viewed in 1952 it was c. 90 ft. square and partially wet.[76] In 1480–1 a hedge and ditch were built around the park meadow to protect the beasts' winter feed.[77] About 1543 the hedge was in decay.[78] Possibly the present moat originated in the 15th-century ditch. In 1460 the 'park' contained a fishpond, then largely unstocked.[79]

Out of the ancient park area assarts had begun to be carved by 1275–6.[80] Some of these, in the old park, clung to the castle mound in 1382, when parcels, already alienated, are referred to as *supra* or *subtus montem*.[81] Assarts in the new park, in Bishop's Cannings, were being called Parklands by 1380,[82] and the name continues until 1651.[83]

Between 1304 and 1570 eleven parkers or park-keepers, though hardly forming an unbroken sequence, are known.[84] When the castle

69 L.R. 2/191 f. 164v.
70 W.A.M. xli. 191. Its site is marked on the contemporary map: W.A.S. Libr., Devizes, Map, 1654.
71 Waylen, *Hist.* 404.
72 It is not marked on W.R.O., Tithe Map, Devizes, St. John's par., but it was said in 1923 that it had stood within living memory: *W.A.M.* xlii. 392.
73 *Lond. Gaz.* 8 Dec. 1835, p. 2429.
74 W.R.O., Tithe Map, Devizes, St. John's par.   75 Waylen, *Hist.* 404.
76 Personal observation.
77 S.C. 6/1094/3.
78 L.R. 2/191 f. 164v.
79 C 145/318 Pt. 1, no. 55.
80 L.R. 2/191 f. 164v.
81 W.R.O. 189/34, deed, Gilbert to chwdns. 1382.
82 Hist. MSS. Com. 55, *Var. Coll.* iv. 104.
83 E 317/Wilts./20.
84 Hen. Hart (1304): *Cal. Pat.* 1301–7, 258; 1313–17, 627; 1330–4, 332. Roger de Sheffield (1371): ibid. 1370–4, 97, 209; 1377–81, 183. Robt. Tyndale (1408): ibid. 1408–13, 81. John Dyer (in office 1448–9): S.C. 6/1093/14. Hugh the parker (in office 1460): C 145/318 no. 51. Ralph Banaster (1461): *Cal. Pat.* 1461–7, 64. John Webbe (1484): ibid. 1476–85, 408. John Burleigh (1487): S.C. 6/Hen.VII/885.

was in a queen's hands it was she who filled the office, though usually the king confirmed her grant. Otherwise the Crown appointed direct. The first eight keepers were not men of social standing; the last three, however, were the stewards of the lordship—Baynton (1526),[85] William Herbert (cr. earl of Pembroke 1551, d. 1570) (1544/5–70), and Henry (d. 1601),[86] his successor in the earldom.[87] The terms of the appointments, when specified, were for the life of either the grantee or the grantor.

In 1583, long before Pembroke's death, Sir John Danvers was also said to hold the parkership for life.[88] The duplication is unexplained. Danvers, however, certainly claimed some local interest, for in 1584 he was at issue with the borough over the profits of the fairs and markets.[89] The earl of Essex (d. 1601) tried unsuccessfully to purchase the estate at the end of the century.[90] Howbeit by 1595 both parks appear to have belonged outright to Henry, earl of Pembroke.[91] They descended to his grandson Philip, earl of Pembroke (cr. earl of Montgomery 1605, d. 1650). They were mortgaged by him in 1609 to Peter Vanlore, who soon after foreclosed the mortgage and acquired the castle, and with the castle they descended for several generations.[92]

CASTLE ESTATE SINCE c. 1550. William, earl of Pembroke, constable and steward,[93] died in 1570 and his son Henry (d. 1601) succeeded him.[94] He was probably the last to hold those offices, for the integrity of the old jointure of the queens consort was already in decay. Rowde was let off on long leases and then sold in 1591;[95] the borough was let to farm to the burgesses.[96] The castle, by now of little value, was leased in 1596 to Richard Brackenbury.[97] In 1611 James I, in pursuance of his policy of alienating small and unprofitable parcels of Crown land,[98]

85 See p. 49.
86 See below.
87 See below.
88 S.P. 12/162 no. 34, I and II.
89 E 123/10 f. 85.
90 Soc. Antiq., Jackson MSS. v, f. 165.
91 Waylen, *Hist.* 585–6.
92 W.R.O. 212A/36/44, case concerning Old Park; E. H. Stone, *Devizes Castle*, 120.
93 See p. 50.
94 *Cal. Pat.* 1569–72, 78.
95 *V.C.H. Wilts.* vii. 218–19.
96 See p. 129.
97 E 310/26/155.
98 R. B. Pugh, *Crown Estate*, 12.

granted it in fee to Philip Herbert (d. 1650), 1st earl of Montgomery, afterwards also 4th earl of Pembroke.[99] The estate so conveyed (*c.* 20 a.) comprised the castle ruins and the meadow and pasture between the ruins and the town. In 1614 the earl in conjunction with other feoffees sold it to Peter Vanlore (knighted 1621), a native of Utrecht,[1] who also acquired the parks.[2] He died seised in 1627,[3] having first settled the castle and the two parks on his daughter Mary, who had married Sir Edward Powell, Bt., with remainder to his right heirs.[4] In September 1651 Powell induced her, it was alleged under duress, to levy a fine to the use of them both for life with remainder to Thomas Levingston and Anne, Thomas's wife, who was Lady Powell's niece. Lady Powell died childless in October 1651 before the fine could be recorded, but Powell falsely procured its entry. Attempts by Vanlore's granddaughters, the daughters of his son Peter, who predeceased him, to undo the fine proved vain, and in 1656 Chaloner Chute bought the premises from the Levingstons.[5] In 1660 one of Vanlore's granddaughters, Mary countess of Stirling, was dead, but her son with the two surviving granddaughters again petitioned for the restitution of the property. It was decided that the fine was false but could only be set aside by Act of Parliament[6] which was passed in 1662.[7] Chaloner Chute, son of the purchaser of 1656, petitioned against the Bill,[8] but seems to have received no compensation. The three heirs of Sir Peter the elder thus secured the estate in coparceny, which in 1664 they partitioned. Henry Alexander, earl of Stirling (d. 1690), son of the granddaughter, Mary, and his wife Judith took the castle itself, the new park, two tenements in Bishop's Cannings parish, some pasture and meadow, which was part of the old park, and a section of the castle ditch. Sir Robert Croke, of Chequers (Bucks.), and his wife Susan, a granddaughter, took arable, pasture, and meadow belonging to the old park, including the Bear grounds, and another part of the ditch. Henry Zinzan, or Alexander, of Tilehurst (Berks.), and his wife Jacoba, the second surviving granddaughter, took

99 C 66/1882 no. 5.
1 C.P. 25(2)/3701/11 Jas. I Hil.; Pevsner, *Berks.* 242.
2 See above.
3 C 142/441/13.
4 Hist. MSS. Com. 6, *7th Rep.* 110.
5 Ibid. 145.
6 Ibid. 110–11.
7 13 & 14 Chas. II c. 27 (Priv. Act).
8 Hist. MSS. Com. 6, *7th Rep.* 149.

other such lands in the old park.[9] Lord Stirling still held lands there in 1682.[10] It seems likely, however, that his family, which failed in the male line in 1739, parted with most of the property to the owners of Roundway in the earlier 18th century, for with Roundway the new park was eventually fused and house and park came to be known as New Park.[11] Part of the castle site was bought by George Flower in 1728[12] but in the end seems to have been acquired by the Wyndham family.

In 1666 the Croke portion was sold to Sir Wadham Wyndham, a justice of the King's Bench,[13] and descended to his son Wadham (d. 1736), his grandson Henry (d. 1788), and his great-grandson Henry Penruddocke (d. 1819).[14] This portion seems to have amounted to 295 a. in 1724.[15] It was stated in 1819 that the Zinzan portion, then 230 a., also passed into the hands of Sir Wadham Wyndham and descended upon a William Wyndham,[16] probably H. P. Wyndham's second cousin, who was a Wyndham of Dinton. The Croke portion is said to have been sold in 1793, at least in part, to William Salmon, the Devizes attorney,[17] who seems to have been already an occupier in 1773.[18] It is not at present clear how James Everard Arundell (d. 1803), father of Lord Arundell of Wardour (d. 1817), was in a position to lease the portion to Charles Penruddocke (d. 1788) in 1773 and 1783 in trust for Anne, the lessor's wife.[19] Anne was the granddaughter of John Wyndham, of Norrington (Alvediston), Sir Wadham Wyndham's eldest son.

Salmon bought that part of the property which surrounded the mound and this with the adjacent land he converted into pleasure grounds.[20] He cut the present road connecting St. John's Street with the mound and he or someone else built a new house, which stood isolated

9 Waylen, *Hist.* 304, 588–90; W.R.O. 84/47, Zinzan's title.
10 W.R.O. 212A/36/44, case concerning Old Park.
11 *V.C.H. Wilts.* vii. 191–2.
12 See p. 57.
13 Waylen, *Hist.* 304.
14 Waylen, *Annals*, 148 (2nd pagin.). There is an outline Wyndham pedigree in H. A. Wyndham, *Family Hist. 1688–1837*.
15 The 'north' part of the disputed park: W.R.O. 727, Wyndham accts.
16 W.R.O. 212A/36/44, case concerning Old Park.
17 Waylen, *Annals*, 148 (2nd pagin.). For Salmon see p. 143.
18 *W.R.S.* viii, pl. 11.
19 W.R.O. 332/187, deed, Arundell to Penruddocke.
20 Except where otherwise stated the rest of this paragraph and the next is based on E. H. Stone, *Devizes Castle*, 133–4, 136–8, 140–1.

in the castle grounds.[21] In 1809 he transferred the estate to his son William Wroughton Salmon (d. 1855), from whom it passed in 1813 to the younger Salmon's brother-in-law, Thomas Tylee, the banker and brewer.

In 1838 the castle estate, in its shrunken condition, had become the purlieus of the bank in St. John's Street and was in the hands of J. N. Tylee[22] who sold it to Valentine Leach (d. 1842), a Devizes tradesman. Leach built himself an imposing castellated residence on the site of the southern windmill tower.[23] On his death his son Robert Valentine (d. 1888) tried to sell the house,[24] which by then was styled Devizes Castle. The attempt failed, some parts of the estate were sold off, and Leach left the town. The castle was let and the grounds were opened as a pleasaunce to a limited public. About 1860 Leach returned and, for the next 20 years, occupied himself in enlarging the castle and introducing 'Norman constructions' into the grounds. Extensive excavations were carried out in 1858–9[25] and it was at that time that the footings of the former hall piers were examined. When Leach died the property was bought at what was then thought to be a bargain price by Sir Charles Rich, Bt. (d. 1913). He altered the house but seems not to have shared Leach's antiquarianism, for in 1903 the earthworks were much overgrown.[26] On the death of Lady Rich in 1918 the property was purchased by E. C. Reed, whose trustees sold it after his death to R. J. Clappen. In 1951 Mr. H. Brown, a Birmingham builder, bought it from Clappen[27] and divided it into two lots. One, the 'North Tower', he sold to W. B. Medlam who sold it in 1955 to Mr. E. B. M. Kemp. The other, the 'South Tower', he sold to Mr. T. G. Waugh, from whom it was purchased by R. N. Newsome and Miss Delia G. M. Tudor-Hart in 1956. From them Mrs. I. M. Durand bought it in 1961.[28]

The irregularly-shaped stone mansion owes much to the two Leaches. Valentine replaced the southern windmill tower by a massive circular one, the principal part of his new residence. The building was

21 W.R.O., Tithe Map, Devizes, St. John's par.
22 W.A.S. Libr., Devizes, sale cat. viii, no. 30, which states unexpectedly and possibly incorrectly that W. M. Nurse, of London, bought it.
23 See p. 57.
24 W.A.S. Libr., Devizes, sale cat. viii, no. 30.
25 Gillman, *Dir.* (1859).
26 *W.A.M.* xxx. 100; Soc. Antiq., Jackson MSS. v, ff. 6. 180.
27 *Wilts. Times*, 27 Oct. 1951.
28 Ex inf. Mrs. E. B. M. Kemp, Devizes Castle.

The castle from the south in 1972

designed to suggest an embattled Norman castle by H. E. Goodridge of Bath.[29] On the east front was a large round-arched entrance with machicolations and a portcullis, and above the tower parapet rose a lookout turret containing a spiral staircase.[30] The northern windmill tower was preserved and crowned with battlements. R. V. Leach's northward extensions, built piecemeal between about 1860 and 1880, trebled the size of the house. They incorporated the windmill tower of which the original brickwork is still visible. Leach inspired the design but J. A. Randell co-operated with him as architect.[31] They carried on the 'Norman' theme, but their work, both inside and out, is far more ornate and fanciful than that of Goodridge. At the north end of the house they built an octagonal conservatory, connected to his drawing room by a curved and arcaded 'fernery'.[32] Various ornamental features in the grounds, notably the so-called St. John's or Bishop's gate, are partly con-

29 Pevsner, *Wilts.* 188.
30 For views see Stone, *Devizes Castle*, pl. facing p. 136.
31 W.A.S. Libr., Devizes, R. H. Cunnington, 'R.V.L.' (TS. acct. of R.V. Leach, 1958–9); *Devizes Gaz.* 15 Sept. 1898.
32 For photographs see W.A.S. Libr., Devizes, sale cat. viii, no. 53. See also illustration on this p.

structed of genuine 12th-century fragments from St. John's church, the west end of which was being rebuilt in 1862–3.[33] Leach's last work was the entrance lodge, in the form of a Norman gatehouse, on the approach road from St. John's Street. Alterations made to the house by Sir Charles Rich at the end of the century included the replacement of many 'Norman' windows by larger ones of Tudor design.[34] He also built a billiard room and new stables. In 1971 the mansion was occupied as three dwellings and the gatehouse lodge was being converted into a substantial house.

That part of the Vanlore property which came into the hands of William Wyndham was sold by him to at least two purchasers. John Eldridge (d. 1807), of Abingdon (Berks.), bought the largest share and soon after the purchase built within it a house called Old Park.[35] A modest dwelling, north-west of Hartmoor, approached by a drive, already existed by 1773,[36] and may have been incorporated by Eldridge. It had not been there in 1736–7,[37] although by the mid 17th century a few small dwellings, some of them farm-houses, had begun to dot the area enclosed by ditch and bank.[38] The house descended to William Eldridge, John's son.[39]

In 1823 Old Park was owned by A. H. Hardman.[40] In 1825 it was bought by Alfred Smith (d. 1877) and passed to his son, the Revd. A. C. Smith (d. 1898), antiquary and rector of Yatesbury, who wintered there.[41] By 1885 Old Park Farm, with farm-land, adjoined.[42] In 1909, after the death of Smith's relict,[43] the property with 142 a. of land passed to Sir Reginald Butler, Bt. (d. 1933),[44] whose family were trying to sell it in 1924.[45] From 1923 to c. 1937 Sir Beauvoir de Lisle occupied and eventually bought it and from him it passed to Joshua Bower (d. 1951).[46]

33 See p. 186.
34 For a west view in 1919 see Stone, *Devizes Castle*, pl. facing p. 142.
35 Waylen, *Hist.* 403–4; *Gent. Mag.* 1807, pt. 1. 385; W.R.O. 212A/36/44, case concerning Old Park.
36 W.R.S. viii, pl. 11.
37 W.A.S. Libr., Devizes, Map, 1736–7.   38 Ibid.
39 *W.A.M.* xxx. 199.
40 Ibid. xlii. 393; Gillman, *Annals*, 27.
41 *W.A.M.* xxx. 199.
42 O.S. Map 1/2,500, Wilts. XXXIV. 13 (1886 edn.).
43 She died in 1908: *W.A.M.* xlii. 393.
44 W.A.S. Libr., Devizes, sale cat. xix, no. 50, with pictures.
45 Ibid. no. 45.
46 *Kelly's Dirs. Wilts.*; ex inf. Lt.-Col. S. M. C. Theyre, Allington Ho., Devizes.

On Bower's death the estate was split up. Some of the land fronting Hartmoor was then built upon.[47] The house itself was sold to the county council to become by 1953 a branch of Roundway Hospital.[48] It is a large irregularly-shaped two-storeyed building faced with stone ashlar. The western end may date in part from c. 1773 but the house was obviously much extended in the early 19th century. Facing east is an imposing entrance front, its central portion concave on plan; the curved Tuscan portico is flanked by niches and surmounted by a cast-iron balustrade.

The rest of William Wyndham's portion of the park, or some of it, was sold by him to B. W. Anstie.[49] It comprised three farms. On the west side of the area lies Lower (or Lower Park) farm, first located in 1808[50] and first named in 1839, when it was occupied by Jacob Clark.[51] In 1897 it was still owned by the Ansties and was occupied by C. E. Everett.[52] By 1901, when it measured 105 a., it had been acquired by Thomas Lavington, an estate agent.[53] In 1920, when it was occupied by R. H. Jefferies, it was sold to the county council as a small holding.[54] Sunnyside farm, on the north side of the area close to the Bath road, is first mentioned in 1839, when it was occupied by Joseph New.[55] In 1876, when it measured 45 a., it belonged to the trustees of Mrs. G. W. Anstie, deceased, whose husband had owned it in 1859.[56] Presumably it was the agricultural appendage of Anstie's house, Park Dale, erected shortly before 1834[57] and in his occupation in 1839.[58] In 1896 the farm was occupied by Joshua Hampton, dairyman. He bought it, later if not then, for in 1920 it was sold by his executors to J. M. Giles of Melksham.[59] The purchaser was dead by 1924 and the land was again put on sale.[60] Between 1965

47 See p. 36.
48 Gillman, *Dir.* (1953).
49 W.R.O. 212A/36/44, case concerning Old Park.
50 1" O.S. drawings, 1808.
51 W.R.O., Tithe Map, Devizes, St. John's par.
52 W.A.S. Libr., Devizes, sale cat. viii, no. 63, with plan.
53 Ibid. xvii, no. 40.
54 Ibid.; Co. Council Mins., Original, Finance Cttee. x. 19–20.
55 W.R.O., Tithe Award, Devizes, St. John's par.
56 W.A.S. Libr., Devizes, sale cat. viii, no. 66; Waylen, *Hist.* 404.
57 Cunnington, *Annals*, ii. 195.
58 W.R.O., Tithe Award, Devizes, St. John's par.
59 W.A.S. Libr., Devizes, sale cat. viii, no. 66; xiii, no. 7, with plans; W.R.O., Tithe Award, Devizes, St. John's par. altered apportionment.
60 W.A.S. Libr., Devizes, sale cat. xix, no. 8.

and 1970 the house and some of the land had been covered by the houses in the western part of Avon Road.[61] Gillett's farm, standing to the south-west of the castle, in open ground, is first identifiable in 1869[62] and first mentioned in 1885.[63] In 1895, when it measured only 15 a., it was sold by H. C. Lewis at a loss.[64]

LESSER ESTATES. In an urban area so strait and commercial no territorial estate of any size, apart from the castle, could be expected to emerge. Burgages were naturally numerous, as conveyances ranging from 1196[65] to 1636[66] attest, and are to be found in both the Old Port and the New.

Much work has already been done on the descent of particular urban properties.[67] It is perhaps sufficient to single out four of these. Brownston House, New Park Street, stands on the site of a house said to have been occupied by a Bayley in 1570, by Christopher Henton in 1613, and by a Filkes later. Thomas Browne substantially rebuilt it in 1720 in brick with stone dressings. It is of seven bays with four storeys and a basement with a three-bay projection. The gate piers are original. Here lived John Garth (d. 1764) and for a time his son Charles (d. 1784), both borough M.P.s and recorders. It came into the hands of the Locke family and Wadham Locke (d. 1835), borough M.P., was born there. Charles Trinder, physician, the Misses Bidwell, who kept a school in it, and the Misses Milman from 1901 until at least 1920 were successive occupiers.[68]

Hazelands, New Park Street, has been considered to be the town house of the Nicholas family of Roundway from the late 16th to the late 18th century.[69] In 1780 it was sold by Robert Nicholas (d. 1826) to John Anstie, clothier, and passed on his death in 1830 to the Hazeland family. They sold it in 1887 to John Llewellin (d. 1913) from whom it passed to S. H. Ward (d. 1952).[70] Greystone House, Long Street, stands

61 Development approved 1965: ex inf. Town Clerk. See also p. 36.
62 Weaver, Map, 1869.
63 O.S. Map 1/2,500, Wilts. XXXIV. 13 (1886 edn.).
64 W.A.S. Libr., Devizes, sale cat. viii, no. 12.
65 *Pedes Finium* (Rec. Com.), ii, no. 12.
66 C 66/2684 no. 1.
67 Mainly by Edw. Kite. For a list of his works see *W.A.M.* xlv. 95–9.
68 Ibid. xli. 204; Pevsner, *Wilts.* 192.
69 *W.A.M.* xli. 315.
70 Ibid. xxxviii. 502, 525; xli. 314–15.

Brownston House in the 1960s

on the site of a house occupied in 1603 by Richard Flower. It passed through marriage to the Lockes, who sold it in 1714 to James Sutton (I), who rebuilt it in 1731.[71] In 1784 it was occupied by Stephen Hillman, tenant of James Sutton (d. 1801), who sold it to Richard Carpenter.[72] It is ashlar-faced and of three storeys. The Tuscan doorway is surmounted by a window with Ionic columns and a pediment. Within, the staircase, panelling, and plasterwork are notable. Parnella House, no. 23 Market Place, c. 1740–50, ashlar-faced with a rusticated ground floor, is adorned with a statue of Aesculapius and was once the home of William Clare (d. 1829), surgeon.[73] The statue was renewed in 1960.[74]

Outside the central area, nos. 2 and 3 Church Walk, Southbroom, have been plausibly identified with 'Bluet's Court',[75] whose story presumably begins in 1315 when a house and other lands in Wick,

71 W.A.M. xxxviii. 451; Pevsner, Wilts. 191.
72 W.R.O. 402/86, deed, 12 Jan. 1784.
73 W.N. & Q. iii. 288.
74 Wilts. Gaz. 21 July 1960.
75 W.A.M. xliv. 386–7.

Nursteed, Bedborough, and Roundway were conveyed to Ralph Bluet.[76] By 1447–8 the property, then expressly called 'Bluet's Court', belonged to the Gilbert family.[77] In 1545, when it was described as three cottages, it was owned by William Page and in 1570 by his son Matthew.[78] It apparently passed to the Drews and thence descended like Southbroom House to the Watson-Taylors. About 1929 Mrs. Oliphant owned it. Originally the house seems to have fronted the Green. It is timber-framed, and had a central range and two gabled wings. The east wing has been demolished, that on the west has a fireplace and a ceiling with moulded beams of the 17th century.

About 1766 James Maynard (d. 1786) built a villa or 'summer house' to the designs of Thomas Collins Overton[79] on the north side of the Bath road, very near or upon the site on which Braeside stood in 1971. It passed to his sister Jane (d. 1826)[80] and by 1831 was being called Brow Cottage.[81] Thence it descended to Jane's kinsman, the Rev. Joseph Mayo (d. 1859).[82] In 1829 the Revd. Henry Bayntun of Bromham sold a house in the Bath road, called the Brow or Browfort.[83] In 1835, then a small squat house of two storeys and three bays, this house was again offered for sale.[84] It probably passed into Mayo's hands, for on his death the Brow, then woodland, was devised, together with his original home, to his son Joseph.[85] Mayo is said to have enlarged Brow Cottage, where he lived until 1839. It may be, however, that he actually enlarged not the house alone but the whole estate by an amalgamation. Which house he occupied must be uncertain. Mayo's house, tenanted in his absence by John Hayward, surveyor, was sold c. 1861 by the second Joseph Mayo to William Brown of the firm of Brown and May. Brown, whose initials appear upon the house, rebuilt it at the top of Dunkirk further to the west than the Brow Cottage of 1831. It was acquired c. 1907 by the Revd. P. L. Bayly who still owned it in 1927.[86] Since 1947 it has been

76 W.R.S. i, p. 88.
77 W.N. & Q. iii. 49 n.
78 Ibid. ii. 370.
79 Edw. Kite in *Wilts. Gaz.* 10 Mar. 1927.
80 Ibid.
81 *Rep. Bdy. Coms.* H.C. 236 (1837), xxvi, Map.
82 *Wilts. Gaz.* 10 Mar. 1927.
83 Gillman, *Annals*, 29; W.A.S. Libr., Devizes, sale cat. xviii, no. 15; Pigot, *Nat. Com. Dir.* (1830).
84 Wilts. Cuttings, ii. 142.
85 *Wilts. Gaz.* 10 Mar. 1927.
86 Ibid.

the offices of the Devizes R.D.C.[87] The adjacent Prospect House was the home of a Mr. Banister in 1828 and a Mr. Crowe in 1959.[88]

Apart from the Castle and Old Park the only substantial property within the ancient borough bounds was Hillworth House. Hillworth, as a field name, is traceable from 1668.[89] In 1779 it came into the hands of William Ludlow,[90] the snuff-maker, who built a house upon it, larger than the present one, and laid out a park of 22 a.[91] By 1803 it seems to have been called the Folly.[92] When the estate was sold in 1813 on Ludlow's bankruptcy there was a brick building, then of recent erection, which has been thought to have been a factory.[93] In 1822 the house was used as a preparatory school. About 1832 Thomas Hall bought and rebuilt it.[94] When he left the town in 1841, the property was sold to Alexander Meek who altered and extended it.[95] The estate remained in his descendants' hands until 1923,[96] when it was bought by a Mrs. Seaton, of Taunton.[97] In 1945 it was bought by the corporation. The house was then converted into flats and the grounds into a public park.[98]

The present house, as altered by Meek, has a long stucco front flanked by two Italianate gables. A continuous verandah on the garden side is carried round a central bay window. To the east, facing the road, is a pair of stucco-fronted terrace houses and, still further east, another pair. Both have recessed arcading to the ground floor and were either built or assumed their present form in the earlier 19th century. A summerhouse in the garden survives from Ludlow's time.

Beyond the original boundaries but long since within the borough was Southbroom House. This estate had come into the possession of John Trew or Drew, a clothier, reputedly of Devonian origin, by 1501–2.[99] By c. 1586 it consisted of a house, dovehouse, orchards, and gardens,

87 Ex inf. Mr. Cox, Devizes R.D.C.
88 Waylen, *Hist.* 530.
89 W.R.O. 402/74, deed, Wythers and May to Hope, 1668.
90 Ibid. 402/74, deed, Stone and others to Ludlow. The property is there called 'Willworth'.
91 Wilts. Cuttings, ii. 227.
92 Cunnington, *Annals*, ii. 277.
93 Wilts. Cuttings, ii. 227.
94 Ibid.; Gillman, *Annals*, 31.
95 Gillman, *Annals*, 35; Wilts. Cuttings, ii. 227.
96 Mrs. Grant Meek died there in 1923: *Wilts. Gaz.* 1 Mar. 1923.
97 W.A.S. Libr., Devizes, sale cat. xviii, no. 21.
98 *Official Guide* (1946), 43.
99 *W.A.M.* iii. 177; pedigree in *Wilts. Pedigrees* (Harl. Soc. cv, cvi), 50.

and had passed to John, the first John's grandson, who died seised in 1614 and was succeeded by his son Robert (d. 1645). The house is said to have been burned by Sir Charles Lloyd early in 1645,[1] but it was still depicted on a map of 1647.[2]

Before his death Robert settled Southbroom upon his wife Elizabeth, who remarried and conveyed the dovehouse to John Drew, her son. John died soon after, leaving the dovehouse to Elizabeth, his relict, who *c.* 1664 married Sir Henry Andrews, of Lathbury, Bt.[3] The bulk of the property seems to have remained in the main Drew line until it was bought *c.* 1680 by Sir John Eyles, a London merchant and eventually Lord Mayor, who belonged to a Devizes tradesman's family.[4] The house then stood further to the north-east than does the present one and was of six bays with a gatehouse front and rear. Southwards stood the dovehouse, and formal gardens lay to the south and west. In the early 18th century a second building lay westward of the western garden. An avenue led southward across the park to end in Southbroom Lane. In the later 17th and earlier 18th centuries what seems to have been a public track led south-westwards across the park to Half Moon Lane.[5]

A new house was built by Edward Eyles in 1773 with imported Bath labour.[6] Eyles is said to have pulled down the old one. This cannot have been wholly true, for it was included in the sale of 1812,[7] but it had gone by 1826.[8] A fire occurred in the new building in 1779.[9] The property descended to Edward's daughter who married George Heathcote of London. George's son, Josiah Eyles Heathcote, died in 1811 possessed of the estate which was sold to William Salmon in 1812. The park (22 a.) was by this time encircled by a full-grown plantation, and was adorned by romantic walks. The whole estate, part of which lay outside the present boundary, amounted to about 269 a. William Salmon (d. 1826) seems to

1 Waylen, *Hist.* 232–3.
2 W.A.S. Libr., Devizes, Map, 1647.
3 B.M. Add. Ch. 37592.
4 *W.A.M.* vi. 133.
5 W.A.S. Libr., Devizes, Maps, 1647, *c.* 1680 x 1703, and 1737–8.
6 Waylen, *Chrons.* 272.
7 Cunnington, *Annals,* ii. 255–6; Wilts. Tracts, clxiv. 7.
8 Map of Southbroom (undated). Its date cannot be before 1826 when W.W. Salmon, whose name appears on it as owner, succeeded. In 1973 the map was in W.A.S. Libr., Devizes.
9 Waylen, *Chrons.* 272.

have added a maze to the grounds.[10] He was succeeded in the estate by his son W. W. Salmon, who left the town in 1828. Then or later the property was sold to George Watson-Taylor. One account states that his son, Simon, owned it in 1860,[11] another that it was owned by Robert Parry Nisbet (d. 1882), who was certainly the occupier by 1841[12] and whose crest and that of his wife appeared upon the two lodges,[13] one of which was demolished in 1968. In 1913 and 1914 R. H. Caird owned the property. He then left the town and sold the house, with its private golf course and rare trees, to Sir Horace McMahon. The residue of the estate was put up for sale shortly afterwards[14] and much of it has now been built upon.[15] The county council bought the house and grounds in 1926 and established in them what had become Devizes School by 1971.

The house was altered and extended in the 19th century and in the 20th century for use as part of the school. The original building, dating mainly from 1773, is of Bath stone ashlar and consists of a two-storeyed central block flanked by much lower service wings, also of two storeys. The wings have been considerably altered but retain a few original round-headed openings on the ground floor with some oval windows above. The entrance front of the main block is of seven bays, having a pediment over the three central bays with the arms of Nisbet inserted in the tympanum. The classical portico may also have been added by R. P. Nisbet c. 1861.[16] On the garden front there is a central bay window rising through both storeys. Internally a few late 18th-century features survive.

The town contained very little monastic property. Bradenstoke priory held two crofts in 1207, one of them in the 'Reawe'.[17] The property was valued at 2s. in 1291.[18] By 1275 Stanley abbey held a burgage,[19] said to belong to its tannery.[20] In both cases the property was lost before the

10 Map of Southbroom, *c.* 1826 (see n. 8).
11 *W.A.M.* vi. 133; Wilts. Tracts, clxiv. 7; Waylen, *Hist.* 526–7.
12 W.R.O., Tithe Map, Southbroom.
13 *W.A.M.* vi. 133; Burke, *General Armoury* (1842).
14 W.A.S. Libr., Devizes, sale cat. x, n. 9; Wilts. Cuttings, ii. 83.
15 See pp. 34–5.
16 Gillman, *Annals*, 43.
17 *V.C.H. Wilts.* iii. 282.
18 *Tax. Eccl.* (Rec. Com.), 185.
19 *Rot. Hund.* (Rec. Com.), ii (1), 252.
20 *W.A.M.* xv. 257.

Dissolution. In 1540–2 the preceptory of the knights hospitallers at Ansty held four houses,[21] which were granted to John Zouche in 1546.[22] One of these is perhaps the tenement of the hospital of St. John of Jerusalem in the New Port, referred to in 1437.[23] The grant to Zouche was revoked in 1557–8 but confirmed in 1584. The houses seem to have been conveyed in 1795 to the currier, Bristow.[24] There is no clear evidence that the hospital of St. John the Baptist, Devizes, held any land in the town besides its own site, though it certainly owned some within that part of Bishop's Cannings which has been later brought within the borough.[25] A tenement of the house of St. John, mentioned in 1433,[26] may belong to the hospital or to the hospitallers. In 1447 John St. Lo had leave to alienate in mortmain a small amount of land to the chantry of St. Mary Magdalen in Calne church.[27] Salisbury chapter, who owned the manor of Cannings Canonicorum (in Bishop's Cannings) had a house at Southbroom in 1289.[28]

THE TOWN AS A COUNTY CENTRE. Although Wilton, the ancient county town, was inevitably the original meeting-place of the county court,[29] it was already being debated in 1280 whether the court should not rather sit at Devizes or Marlborough. No change was then made,[30] but centuries later, during the Interregnum, the advocates of Devizes secured a temporary success. In 1655, partly owing to the then favourable temper of the townsmen, Wilton was abandoned for five years in favour of Devizes. Though the sheriffs were responsible for the move, Devizes corporation supported them, and after a return to Wilton in 1660 Devizes tried to restore the *status quo*.[31] This attempt failed, but the court was again at Devizes on adjournment in 1676–7[32] and in 1695 a fruitless

21 S.C. 6/Hen. VIII/7262 m. 6d.
22 *L. & P. Hen. VIII*, xxi (1), p. 687.
23 W.R.O. 212B/23/8, deed, Hall and Hall to Marler.
24 *W.A.M.* xli. 206–7; and see p. 93 n. 7.
25 E 301/58/73.
26 W.R.O. 212B/23/6, deed, Rous to Grenyng.
27 *Cal. Pat.* 1441–6, 459; 1446–52, 61.
28 J.I. 1/1011 m. 42.
29 *V.C.H. Wilts.* v. 9; vi. 15.
30 Ibid. vi. 16.
31 *W.A.M.* xxvii. 113–20; Cunnington, *Annals*, i (2nd pagin.), 124, where '1665–6' should read '1655–6'.
32 Cunnington, *Annals*, i (2nd pagin.), 163.

effort was made to transfer the election of knights of the shire to Devizes.[33] By 1759,[34] however, if not by 1752[35] the court seems to have met regularly at Devizes,[36] though presumably not for polling. In 1847 the town became the centre of a County Court District.[37]

From 1383 Devizes was a county quarter sessions town.[38] It so remained until 1972, when it became a third-tier centre under the Courts Act, 1971.[39] In 1867 men tried to fix quarter sessions at Devizes and abandon the other three Wiltshire meeting-places. They failed, but later attempts, though no more successful, were aimed at making Devizes the quarter sessions town for north Wiltshire.[40] Both efforts show the 'metropolitan' standing that Devizes was assuming in county affairs. Nevertheless when the county council was established in 1889 it was Trowbridge and not any quarter sessions town that was chosen as its base and the attempt to transfer the county offices to Devizes, after rebuilding had been resolved upon in 1929, was set at nought.[41]

In 1578 the Wiltshire justices set a county rate to provide a house of correction. They chose Devizes as its seat, because they hoped to site it in a part of the castle. They failed in this, but by 1579 had built a bridewell there. This remained the only county bridewell until c. 1631.[42] It almost certainly stood from the outset in Bridewell Street where the Grange is now.[43] It was damaged by fire in 1619[44] and more seriously burnt in 1630.[45] In 1771 it was refronted in brick.[46] In 1774, at Howard's first visit, there were two night- and two day-rooms, a yard, a workshop and an infirmary somewhat recently constructed.[47] The prison was structurally improved in 1784–5[48] and it was no doubt the improved

33 C.J. xi. 464.
34 Dore, Map, 1759.
35 Cunnington, *Annals*, ii. 162.
36 Waylen, *Hist.* 536.
37 *Lond. Gaz.* 10 Mar. 1847, p. 990.
38 *V.C.H. Wilts.* v. 35.
39 1971, c. 23.
40 *V.C.H. Wilts.* v. 232.
41 Ibid. vii. 147.
42 Ibid. v. 96.
43 It was there in 1737–8: W.A.S. Libr., Devizes, Map 1737–8.
44 Hist. MSS. Com. 55, *Var. Coll.* i. 92.
45 *Wilts. Q. Sess. Rec.*, ed. Cunnington, 97.
46 Cunnington, *Annals*, ii. 254. The date appears in studs on the front-door of the Grange.
47 J. Howard, *State of the Prisons* (1780 edn.), 338–9.
48 *V.C.H. Wilts.* v. 186.

structure in which between 1801 and 1806 Nield found six yards, the infirmary as before, a 'small and neat' chapel, and 12 cells.[49]

After the 'New Bridewell' had been opened (see below) the 'old' bridewell was used mainly for detaining pre-trial suspects.[50] It was closed in 1836.[51] By 1882 it was being called the Grange and was used successively thereafter as a day-nursery and a home for old women, with whom for a while the town nurse had her residence.[52] Much of the old building survives. Bridewell Square beside it may have been an exercise yard.

The 'New Bridewell', so named at first and renamed the 'New Prison' in 1836,[53] was begun in 1810[54] and opened in 1817.[55] It stood on the north side of the old park and was designed by Richard Ingleman as a two-storeyed polygon, of brick and stone, surrounding a central governor's house.[56] It thus reflected the panopticon principle.[57] In the attics of the house were two infirmaries. There was a chapel. Sixteen wards, each with a yard and radially arranged, were planned.[58] Not all, however, were built; there were ten of each in 1819[59] and eleven, one for women, in 1836[60] and afterwards.[61] The women were reckoned to be poorly housed in 1836[62] and in 1841–2 new cells were erected for their better accommodation. These probably formed a third storey above five bays of the polygon on the side facing the gate. At demolition there was certainly an extra storey at that point. The women were also given a separate laundry and day-room and a new infirmary at the same

49 J. Neild, *State of the Prisons*, 158–9.
50 *V.C.H. Wilts.* v. 188.
51 For its later use see p. 169.
52 See p. 244.
53 *V.C.H. Wilts.* v. 239.
54 Date-stone on the gatehouse: photo. in Town Hall, Devizes. The architects' accts. with the gaol cttee. (in W.A.S. Libr., Devizes) cover 1810–15.
55 The governor said in May 1819 that the prison was finished two years before and that the first committals were in 1817: *Rep. Sel. Cttee. on Gaols*, H.C. 579, pp. 354, 359 (1819), vii.
56 Waylen, *Chrons.* 318.
57 *Rep. Sel. Cttee. on Gaols* (1819), vii. 359.
58 W.R.O., Q. Sess., prison plans 1808; the ground floor plan is reproduced in *V.C.H. Wilts.* v, pl. facing p. 187.
59 *Rep. Sel. Cttee. on Gaols* (1819), 354.
60 *Second Rep. of Prisons Inspectors, Southern and Western District* [89], p. 9 (1837), xxxii.
61 W.R.O., Q. Sess., prison plans, 1867.
62 *Second Rep. of Prisons Inspectors, Southern and Western District*, 9.

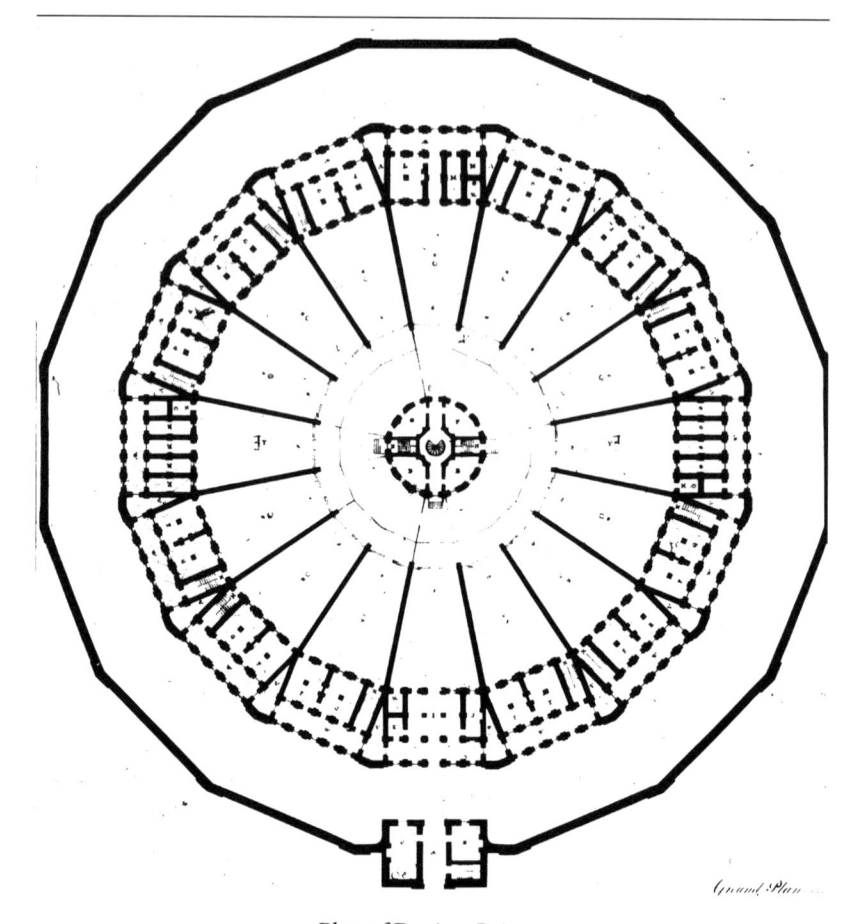

Plan of Devizes Prison

time.[63] A tread-mill was authorized in 1823.[64] It worked a corn-mill which lay outside the walls.[65] A schoolroom existed by 1842.[66] Further alterations, including the addition of ten cells and the enlargement of

63 W.R.O., Q. Sess. Min. Bk. 1841–3, Mich. 1841; prison plans, 1841; *Seventh Rep. of Prisons Inspectors, Southern and Western District*, [421], p. 136, H.C. (1842), xxi. For the appearance of the prison just before demolition see aerial photograph in Devizes Mus.
64 *V.C.H. Wilts.* v. 188.
65 *Twenty-third Rep. of Prisons Inspectors, Southern Districts*, [2411], p. 134, H.C. (1857–8), xxix.
66 *Seventh Rep. of Prisons Inspectors, Southern and Western District* (1842), p. 136.

the chapel, were authorized in 1868.[67] When Fisherton Anger gaol was closed, Devizes became the only county prison, and, as such, was transferred to the state in 1877.[68] Between 1912 and 1914 it was used only for prisoners on remand. It was a military detention barracks from 1914 until 1920, when it fell completely out of use,[69] and then or in 1921 it was closed.[70] In 1922 it was bought as a building site,[71] and in 1927 was being demolished.[72]

Devizes Prison in 1889

Although Salisbury was always the principal Wiltshire assize town, assizes were sometimes held at Devizes. This was so *c.* 1618[73] and in 1642[74] and possibly *c.* 1610.[75] In 1765 trials were held at Devizes as well

67 W.R.O., Q. Sess. Min. Bk. 1864–78, f. 260; plans, specifications, and estimates, 1867.
68 *V.C.H. Wilts.* v. 242.
69 *W.A.M.* xlii. 105.
70 Wilts. Co. Council Mins. Orig. x. 154.
71 *W.A.M.* xlii. 105.
72 Ibid. xliv. 85.
73 Waylen, *Chrons.* 151 (2nd pagin.).
74 G.A. Harrison, 'Royalist Organization in Wilts.' (Lond. Univ. Ph.D. thesis, 1963), 448.
75 The Chief Baron then lodged in the town: Waylen, *Chrons.* 150 (2nd pagin.).

as Salisbury.[76] The Assizes Act, 1833,[77] which enabled the Crown to appoint new assize towns, provoked a petition to the Privy Council from Devizes and the subscription in 1834 both from the townsmen and the neighbouring gentry for a law courts building.[78] Accordingly a classical building with an Ionic portico, designed by T. H. Wyatt, was built in Northgate Street in 1835, and site and building sold to the county by the subscribers in the same year.[79] Thenceforth the summer assize for Wiltshire was held at Devizes until in 1857 the spring assize was substituted.[80] The last assize was held in October 1971.

The Assize Court c. 1840

Money was also raised in 1834 to provide judges' lodgings.[81] It is not known how it was spent but c. 1832 the judges stayed at no. 11 Long Street[82] and at some other time at Handel House, Sidmouth Street.[83] In

76 Waylen, *Hist.* 538.
77 3 & 4 Wm. IV, c. 71.
78 Waylen, *Hist.* 538.
79 *W.A.M.* xlvi. 537; Waylen, *Chrons.* 322–3; Pevsner, *Wilts.* 187–8.
80 *V.C.H. Wilts.* vi. 96.
81 H.O. 52/25, Lord Lieut. to Home Sec., 26 May 1834.
82 Wilts. Cuttings, v. 151.
83 *W.A.M.* xxxvi. 200.

1868 the corporation bought Northgate House[84] and there from 1869[85] the judge resided. It was abandoned by the judge in 1956 and became the borough offices.[86] Thereafter the judge had no official residence.[87]

The county militia stores, after resting for a while in the 'old' hall,[88] were in 1856 accommodated in a purpose-built structure in the Bath road, designed by T. H. Wyatt.[89] In 1879 a part of this was converted into the headquarters of the county police[90] and so continued until 1962, when a new building was opened on the west side of the London road.[91]

Other forms of evidence prove that from the 18th century Devizes regarded herself or was regarded by others as the proper centre of the county. In 1710 the Commissioners of Stamps thought that, being 'in the heart' of Wiltshire, Devizes was a better seat for their chief collector than Salisbury.[92] In 1832 a Calne resident argued that the county hospital should be established in Devizes rather than remain exclusively in Salisbury.[93] In 1853, after long debate, the newly-formed Wiltshire Archaeological and Natural History Society chose Devizes as the home for its museum and activities not only because William Cunnington (III), its chief promoter lived there, but because it was 'the geographical centre of the county'.[94] Whether the headquarters of the Wiltshire Friendly Society, founded in 1828, was placed in Devizes because T. H. S. Sotheron Estcourt set it up[95] or for geographical reasons may be left an open question. It has there remained in a 'gothic' building facing down Long Street.

County-wide meetings were convened in the town in 1780 to support Burke's 'economical' reform,[96] in 1794 to support the French war,[97] in 1813 to consider Catholic emancipation,[98] in 1718 to

84 Gillman, *Annals*, 50.
85 Ibid. 52.
86 Wilts. Cuttings, xxi. 12.
87 Ex inf. Mr. S. O'Brien, Deputy Town Clerk, 1970.
88 Waylen, *Hist.* 476.
89 Gillman, *Annals*, 40.
90 Wilts. Co. Council, *Guide to the Rec. Office*, pt. i, p. 21.
91 *Wilts. News*, 14 Sept. 1962.
92 *Cal. Treasury Bks.* xxiv (2), 14.
93 Wilts. Cuttings, iii. 90.
94 *W.A.S. Centenary Hist.* (1953), 6–7.
95 Gillman, *Annals*, 28; *Sarum Almanack*, 1937, 255.
96 Cunnington, *Annals*, ii. 259.
97 Gillman, *Annals*, 21.
98 Waylen, *Chrons.* 276.

congratulate the Regent on escaping assassination,[99] in 1831 to support Parliamentary reform,[1] and in 1850 to challenge 'papal aggression'.[2] Such meetings have reinforced the view, however wrongly held, that the management of the affairs of Wiltshire from what was called in 1660 'the skirt of the shire'[3] was misconceived.

TRADE AND INDUSTRY. There is little means of establishing the prosperity or size of Devizes before the 14th century. There is faint evidence of a 12th-century mint at which both Stephen and his Angevin opponents may have struck coins.[4] The inhabitants were described as burgesses in 1141,[5] and it is reasonable to conclude that the town was, or contained, a 'borough' from that time. To taxes and tallages between 1172 and 1214 the town was invariably rated below Marlborough. Usually it was below Wilton and above Salisbury and Melksham.[6] In 1212, with Marlborough, Salisbury, and Wilton, it was one of four Wiltshire towns to furnish the king with a company of ten for service overseas.[7] Its trading position was strengthened by the grant of a merchant guild in 1218[8] and by its possession of a market, first mentioned in 1228.[9]

Its Jewish community, some index of the town's commercial maturity, was settled late. While there were Jews in Marlborough in 1241 and in Wilton in 1254,[10] it is not until 1268 that a Devizes jewry begins to emerge.[11] A Jew then appears to have been living in the town and four years later the Devizes Jews are referred to as an established community.[12] In 1275 that community was enlarged by the removal of the jewry at Marlborough to Devizes.[13] At the time of the deportation

99 Waylen, *Hist.* 509.
1 *V.C.H. Wilts.* v. 299–300.
2 Ibid. 38.
3 *W.A.M.* xxvii. 115.
4 *Arch. Jnl.* civ. 116, 122; G. C. Brooke, *Eng. Coins*, 95–6.
5 See p. 126.
6 *Pipe R.* 1172–1214 (P.R.S.); 1189 (Rec. Com.).
7 *Rot. Litt. Claus.* (Rec. Com.), i. 131.
8 See p. 126.
9 See p. 112.
10 H. G. Richardson, *Eng. Jewry under Angevin Kings*, 16.
11 *Plea R. of Exch. of Jews*, ed. J. M. Rigg (Jewish Hist. Soc.), i. 179, 199. Levi of Devizes occurs in 1191: *Pipe R.* 1191 and 1192 (P.R.S. N.S. ii), 139, but there is no reason to conclude that he formed the nucleus of a jewry.
12 *Select Pleas from Exch. of Jews* (Selden Soc. xv), 69.
13 Ibid. 85.

the Devizes jewry possessed an *archa*[14] and a synagogue.[15] Two Devizes Jews, one possessed of several books, suffered in the prosecutions of 1278–9.[16] After this Jews do not recur and at the suppression in 1290 only two houses were in Jewish occupation and only one in Jewish ownership. There were two *arche*, but the synagogue was gone.[17]

When in 1334 it becomes possible to judge the relative wealth of Wiltshire settlements from tax assessments Devizes is found in a somewhat low position. It is not among the eighteen most highly rated communities, several rural areas ranking well above it, and only four boroughs, of which Old Salisbury is one, below it.[18] In population, however, judged by the number of poll-tax payers, it stood thirteenth by 1377[19] and though the correlation between prosperity and population must not be pressed it is perhaps fair to conclude that it rose in economic importance as the 14th century wore on. Such a view is confirmed by its constitutional development.[20] It is reasonable to suppose that the prosperity of early Devizes, such as it was, rested on its market which supplied the needs of the castle garrison, but that pure commerce decayed with the waning military importance of the castle and that the town's fortunes were restored by the gradual establishment of industry.

While there was a skinner as early as 1196[21] and a dyer in 1281[22] it is only from the early 14th century that there is any recognizable group of craftsmen. At first they were all practitioners of the leather trades: a glover in 1302, a cordwainer in ?1306, a tanner possibly as early.[23] A tanner recurs in 1362[24] and another is mentioned several times between 1370 and 1385.[25] A skinner and a net-maker are mentioned in 1417[26] and Thomas Skinner, a glover, in 1425.[27] The metal trades are also represented early: in 1379 there was a brazier, before 1416 John Brasyere

14 *Cal. Pat.* 1272–81, 127.
15 *Plea R. of Exch. of Jews*, ed. H. Jenkinson (Jewish Hist. Soc.), iii. 61.
16 *Jewish Hist. Soc. Miscellanies*, ii. 61, 68.
17 Richardson, *Eng. Jewry*, 19.
18 *V.C.H. Wilts.* iv. 296, 303.
19 Ibid. 312.
20 See pp. 127–9.
21 *Feet of Fines*, 1196–7 (Pipe R. Soc. xx), p. 10.
22 *V.C.H. Wilts.* iv. 120, 137; J.I. 1/1005 m. 144 (146).
23 *W.A.M.* ii. 302.
24 *Cal. Pat.* 1361–4, 256.
25 Ibid. 1367–70, 383; J.I. 3/156 m. 16 and d.; B.M. Add. Ch. 59676, 59677.
26 *Cal. Pat.* 1416–22, 93–4.
27 *V.C.H. Wilts.* iv. 237.

had been a resident,[28] and in 1476 John Brownsmith was party to a deed.[29] Metal-working may have been stimulated by the presence of iron ore, found in small quantities near by and once smelted in the old park.[30]

The origins of the Devizes textile industry stretch back to a dyer of 1281[31] and a Southbroom weaver of 1347.[32] When Devizes 'blankets' are first expressly mentioned in 1429,[33] west Wiltshire had become well known for its white woollen broadcloth. Devizes, if on the edge, was a part of that area. It now had begun to rival Salisbury and ranked next to that city in an aulnage account of the 1420s.[34] A Devizes man farmed the Wiltshire aulnage from 1421 to 1425[35] and over ten more townsmen within the century are named as weavers or clothiers. One of these is known to have manufactured white cloth,[36] another russet,[37] and two were rich enough to own lands within the borough.[38] William Smith, who largely rebuilt St. Mary's church, is thought to have been a clothier,[39] and another clothier, William Salmon (fl. 1404), the possessor of two looms, was also a benefactor to the town.[40]

In the 16th century the town remained an important source of white broadcloth and now exported the product direct to London[41] instead of through the port of Bristol as heretofore.[42] The manufacturers prospered and became locally influential although they no doubt experienced the slack trade that sometimes prevailed in Henry VIII's reign. In 1528 something like a riot occurred in the town probably from this cause.[43] But prosperity was general. Of those expressly called 'clothier' or 'clothman', ten were wealthy enough to have their wills proved in the

28 W.R.O. 189/34, nos. 5, 7, deeds, 1379 and 1416.
29 Ibid. 189/41, deed, 1476.
30 V.C.H. Wilts. iv. 250; Waylen, *Chrons.* 329.
31 V.C.H. Wilts. iv. 120.
32 *Devizes and Wilts. Gaz.* 16 July 1903.
33 *Rot. Parl.* iv. 361.
34 V.C.H. Wilts. iv. 128.
35 E 101/345/5.
36 E 101/345/6.
37 Ibid.
38 C 1/544/11; B.M. Add. Ch. 37529.
39 *W.N. & Q.* vii. 196; see below, p. 190.
40 Waylen, *Chrons.* 283–6.
41 Ibid. 139–40.
42 Ibid. 137.
43 *L. & P. Hen. VIII*, iv (2), p. 1851.

Prerogative Court. Among the ten, Henry Morris (probate 1572)[44] owned a workshop containing at least two broad looms and engaged in a number of long-term transactions.[45] He, Walter Bayly (probate 1560),[46] Richard Batt (probate 1569),[47] and John Batt (d. 1600)[48] owned land within the borough and without.[49] Moreover Richard Batt was taxed on the level of most country gentry.[50] The Batts, Morris, and Thomas Hull (probate 1576)[51] were more than once mayors[52] and Hull a borough M.P. At least ten other clothiers can be detected, even if not always so labelled. Among these Walter Trymnell (probate 1511) died possessed of a 'warping bar' and two looms,[53] John Baker (fl. 1551) was mayor,[54] and Henry Blackborrow (fl. c. 1595) was lessee of no little land.[55] Of five persons labelled 'draper' or 'woollen-draper' John Willos (or Willis), the elder, was taxed at £2 in 1545[56] and Thomas Tymmer owned houses in the town.[57] Both were mayors.[58]

The 'weavers' were presumably of less account, but Edward Haynes (fl. 1555, 1576) became mayor[59] and the clothier Richard Batt had been a weaver first.[60] About mid century a 'weaver' called Catherine Brede made white and coloured cloths on contract, marked with her own mark, for sale in Gloucestershire through a Gloucestershire agent.[61] A cardmaker first appears at the beginning of the century[62] and another occurs in 1582[63] and was perhaps still living in 1618.[64] No fullers are

44 Prob. 11/55 (P.C.C. 2 Peter).
45 Ramsay, *Wilts. Woollen Industry*, 18, 27.
46 Prob. 11/43 (P.C.C. 13 Mellershe).
47 Prob. 11/51 (P.C.C. 4 Sheffelde).
48 Prob. 11/95 (P.C.C. 21 Wallopp).
49 Their wills: *W.N. & Q.* iii. 124 (Ric. Batt); Cunnington, *Annals*, ii. 140–1 (Morris).
50 Ramsay, *Wilts. Woollen Industry*, 48.
51 Prob. 11/58 (P.C.C. 11 Carew).
52 Cunnington, *Annals*, i, pp. xviii–xix.
53 Prob. 11/17 (P.C.C. 1 Fetiplace).
54 W.R.S. x. 14; W.R.O. 212A/36/2, deed, mayor to Truslow, 1551–2.
55 Sta. Cha. 5/87/4.
56 W.R.S. x. 14 (here called Willons).
57 Prob. 11/22 (P.C.C. 22 Porche).
58 W.R.O. 212A/36/2, deed, mayor to Cowrtes, 1563–4; Page to Spray, 1523–4.
59 Ibid. 844, Skippet deed, no. 29; W.R.S. iv. 23; Cunnington, *Annals*, i. p. xviii.
60 Ramsay, *Wilts. Woollen Industry*, 16.
61 C 1/1214/5–8.
62 *L. & P. Hen. VIII*, i (1), p. 272.
63 W.R.O. 212B/Dv. 3a, deed, Burd to Stephens.
64 W.A.M. ii. 308.

then known. Although little cloth was dyed in Wiltshire,[65] a dye-house existed in the town by 1549.[66]

All this suggests that Leland was not wrong in declaring that the town was in his time 'most occupied by clothiers'.[67] Nevertheless the leather trades continued. A glover and gauntlet-maker died in 1582[68] and there is record of four tanners. Of these James Webb died *c.* 1559 possessed of a tan-house, tanner's tools, and a dwelling in the Brittox,[69] and Jeremy Webb inherited a tan-house in Bishop's Cannings from George Reynolds in 1577.[70] By 1559 there was a craft guild or 'company' jointly comprised of cardmakers, smiths, wiredrawers, saddlers, and cutlers,[71] an unexpected combination but one which shows the persistence of the metal trades which provided locally the wire for cards. While no founder is expressly named, the bells of St. Peter and St. Paul, Marlborough, were recast in Devizes in 1579.[72]

There had already been a tailor before 1443.[73] Other tradesmen directly serving the sophisticated consumer now appear: a capper in 1555;[74] three haberdashers between 1560 and 1569;[75] a joiner in 1564;[76] a barber in 1576;[77] a painter in 1582;[78] and a jerkin-maker in 1583.[79]

The 'company' referred to above is the first evidence of the way in which the craft guilds, perhaps existing somewhat earlier,[80] were organized. At the herald's visitation of 1565 such a company is mentioned again. It was officially called 'the fellowship and corporation of the burgesses and merchant adventurers', was presided over by the mayor, its 'head and governor', and divided into three sections, each under two wardens. Those sections were the clothiers and weavers, the drapers and

65 *V.C.H. Wilts.* iv. 150.
66 *Cal. Pat.* 1549–51, 139.
67 Leland, *Itin.* ed. Toulmin Smith, v. 82.
68 *W.A.M.* xlii. 113.
69 Sar. Dioc. R.O., Detecta Bk. 1550–3, f. 227.
70 Prob. 11/59 (P.C.C. 45 Daughtry).
71 Cunnington, *Annals*, i (1st pagin.), 29, 46–7.
72 *W.N. & Q.* v. 576.
73 *Cal. Pat.* 1441–6, 163.
74 W.R.O. 212A/36/2, deed, mayor and commonalty to Swayne, 1555–6.
75 Ibid.; B.M. Add. Ch. 37542
76 W.R.O. 212A/36/2, deed, mayor to Cowrtes, 1563–4.
77 *W.R.S.* iv. 23.
78 Ibid. 79.
79 Ibid. 90.
80 See pp. 129–30.

The Devizes Guilds. *Barry wavy of six azure and argent a pegasus salient or and in chief palewise* (i) *argent a roundel azure charged with a paschal lamb argent holding a staff or,* (ii) *gules a demi-virgin couped below the shoulders issuing from clouds, all proper crowed with an Eastern crown or,* (iii) *argent a fountain on a bend gules a lion passant guardant or*

tailors, and the mercers, 'etc.'.[81] A grant of arms was registered.[82] The relationship of the three sections of 1565 to the 'company' of 1559, which consisted only of practitioners of the leather and metal trades, is obscure, unless, which is unlikely, it is to be identified with the mercers' guild. But it has been concluded that its creation about this time arose from the wish to restrict competition in an age of declining prosperity for the Wiltshire cloth towns, which set in about the middle of the century.[83]

In 1523 as many as eight townsmen were assessed at £40 in anticipation of the subsidy.[84] In the assessments of both 1545 and 1576 Salisbury stood out far above all other towns, followed in that order by Marlborough and Devizes. Trowbridge and Warminster were not far

81 *W.A.M.* iv. 160–1.
82 The arms are tricked out but without any indication of tinctures: B.M. Harl. MS. 1565 (publ. in *Gen.* N.S. xii. 24);W.A.S. Libr., Devizes, MS.Visitation. In *Gen.* N.S. xii the trick has been converted slightly inaccurately into a blazon.The arms are fully blazoned (i) on a wooden panel, dated 1606 (in Town Hall, Devizes, 1973), (ii) in the 'Constitutions' (in W.A.S. Libr., Devizes) but with variations upon theVisitation version. First on (i) the field is azure four bars argent and in (ii) azure three bars wavy argent. Secondly in (ii) the sinister roundel is not a fountain but a roundel azure charged with three bars wavy argent. In (i) the drawing is too crude for certainty but is either a fountain or azure five bars wavy argent.The tinctures given above are taken from the wooden panel and the 'Constitutions'.
83 *V.C.H.Wilts.* iv. 148.
84 *L. & P. Hen.VIII*, iii (2), p. 1478.

behind.[85] The demographical evidence, such as it is, seems to point towards the same ranking.[86]

By the earlier 17th century wages in the cloth trade had fallen and there was distress among the weavers, some of whom were sent to the house of correction.[87] Shortly before 1630 the Devizes poor-rate rose.[88] This was but a local reflection of the prevailing widespread destitution in the trade.[89] Between 1611 and 1618 no fewer than eleven Devizes men were prosecuted in the Exchequer for engrossing.[90] Moreover since country clothiers competed with town clothiers some attempt was made by the latter to enforce apprenticeship. A reorganization of the merchants' 'fellowship' which took place in 1614,[91] with a constitution which insisted on apprenticeship, perhaps had such an aim. By the middle of the century Devizes weavers were finding it hard to retain their apprentices,[92] and a list of a dozen apprentices and their masters, drawn up apparently ten years before, contains the name of only one master-weaver.[93] None the less the old 'clothier' or woollen-draper families such as the Batts,[94] the Morrises,[95] and the Flowers[96] continued to govern the town and fill the mayoralty. New ones who now arose did the same: Pierces,[97]

85 W.R.S. x, where the assessments are printed.
86 See p. 4.
87 Ramsay, Wilts. Woollen Industry, 80; Cunnington, Annals, i (2nd pagin.), 71.
88 S.P. 16/216 no. 66.
89 V.C.H. Wilts. iv. 151.
90 W.R.S. xv. pp. 63–4, 73, 84, 88, 94, 98. One of these was Wm. Erwood, four times mayor: W.N. & Q. viii. 551; Cunnington, Annals, i (1st pagin.), p. xix.
91 V.C.H. Wilts. iv. 149.
92 Wilts. Q. Sess. Rec. ed. Cunnington, 190.
93 S.P. 16/377 no. 183.
94 Ric. (d. 1612) son of John, referred to already: W.N. & Q. iii. 37. John, probably his brother, a warden of the drapers' company: W.A.M. iv. 162.
95 John: W.R.S. xv, pp. 49–51 (1620); member of the drapers' company (1614): W.N. & Q. viii. 551.
96 One of the large Devizes capitalist clothing families in the preceding century: Ramsay, Wilts. Woollen Industry, 41. Devizes members of the family in the early 17th century were Roger (fl. c. 1600): Wilts. Q. Sess. Rec. ed. Cunnington, 2; Ric. and Robt. (fl. c. 1600–20): W.N. & Q. viii. 551; Thos. (fl. c. 1630): Gen. N.S. xxvii. 176; Robt. (1625), a master weaver (W.R.O. 189/23) ? the same as the above Robt.; Edw. (married 1642) was a mercer: Gen. N.S. xxxi. 187.
97 Members of the family were Thos. (fl. 1603): Gen. N.S. xxxviii. 82; John (mayor 1603): Cunnington, Annals, i, p. xix; John (married 1633): Gen. N.S. xxvii. 174; Edw. (married 1642): Gen. N.S. xxxi. 188; and Ric. (married 1664): Gen. N.S. xxxii. 207. Thos., later dean of Salisbury (see p. 11), was presumably the son of the second of these.

Erwoods,[98] Webbs,[99] and Paradises.[1] William Erwood and Richard and Robert Flower were all mayors and so were Edward Northey and John Stephens, also clothiers.[2] That some at least of these manufacturers possessed gentle status and were prosperous is in various ways attested. Northey[3] and John Pierce (d. c. 1642)[4] sent their sons to Oxford, and Richard Batt bequeathed £130 in cash.[5]

The effect of the changes in the guild structure of 1614 seems to have been to turn the three sections of 1565 into three separate companies. The new constitution was agreed upon in the common council of the borough, and the mayor remained the 'chief head and governor'.[6] The parent company or merchant guild was now implicitly abolished. The three companies were the drapers, the mercers, and the leather-sellers, each under a master and two wardens, called in the case of the drapers master-wardens. The first included clothiers, weavers, woollen-drapers, tailors, hosiers, fullers, shearmen, and spinners, i.e. the textile manufacturers and leading textile retailers, and it extended also to coopers, carpenters, masons, tilers, joiners, cutlers, smiths, and ironmen, in fact the constructional workers and most metal-workers. The second company included mercers, grocers, linen-drapers, haberdashers of both small wares and headgear, vintners, innholders, brewers, bakers, apothecaries, barbers, surgeons, chandlers, painters, braziers, and glasiers, i.e. the catering trades and leading retail tradesmen. It has been concluded that the leather-sellers comprised dealers in hides, patten-, boot-, bellows, and harness-makers, saddlers, and girdlers.[7] The regulations promulgated required the registration of those free of the companies, the admission and regulation of apprentices and journeymen, the correction of trade abuses,

---

98 Members of the family were Wm. (fl. c. 1596–1615) and John (fl. c. 1614): *W.N. & Q.* viii. 551.
99 Members of the family were Alexander (1620): *W.R.S.* xv, p. 49; Thos.: *Gen.* N.S. xxiv. 169 (1615); *Cal. S.P. Dom.* 1640, 272, 528 (1640); and Ric. (fl. c. 1620): *Gen.* N.S. xxv. 235.
1 Thos. (1637): *Gen.* N.S. xxxiii. 54. The family, however, was more notable in the later century: Ramsay, *Wilts. Woollen Industry*, 128.
2 Cunnington, *Annals*, i, p. xix. For Northey see W.R.O. 130/58A, deed, Northey to Bartlett, and for Stephens *W.N. & Q.* viii. 551.
3 Foster, *Alumni Oxon. 1500–1714*, 1078.
4 *D.N.B.*; and see p. 11.
5 *W.N. & Q.* iii. 37.
6 Unless otherwise stated, this paragraph is based on *W.A.M.* iv. 161–72, where the constitutions, recorded in 1628, are printed.
7 Waylen, *Chrons.* 288, quoting petitions to Parl.

and the restriction on outsiders seeking to trade in the borough. Small changes in the mercers' constitution were made in 1620 and 1623, and in 1651 the whole of the drapers' constitution was ratified, which suggests that the company was still of some account. In general it may be doubted whether the companies were ever of much economic, as distinct from social, importance. Nevertheless the charter of 1685 sought to restrict trade within the borough to those free of one of the companies, unless they were locally apprenticed.[8]

While white broadcloth no doubt continued to be the staple product, felt and serge now began to be manufactured. There were felt-makers in 1633 and 1637,[9] a serge-weaver in 1637,[10] and a serge-comber in 1631.[11] There was a hosier in 1615[12] and, somewhat unexpectedly, a silk-weaver two years later.[13] Hosiers had market standings by 1630.[14] Besides combers practitioners of processes subsidiary to weaving began to show themselves. Thomas Blackborrow, doubtless a kinsman of the 16th-century clothier already mentioned, is labelled both 'fuller'[15] and 'shearman',[16] and two other fullers existed in 1620.[17] William Watton (1620)[18] and Robert Showring (1631, 1652) were cardmakers.[19]

The leather trades continued conspicuous, as the creation of the leather-sellers' company implies. Between 1605 and 1640 Edmund and Edward Potter,[20] Philip Godfather,[21] James Fidsell,[22] Richard Godbye, and Richard Palmer[23] are named as glovers, Richard Attwood[24] and John Miles[25] as curriers, John Thorer as a saddler,[26] a Paradise[27] and Thomas

8 S.P. 44/335 ff. 403–6 (wt. for charter).
9 W.N. & Q. viii. 552; Gen. N.S. xxx. 186.
10 Gen. N.S. xxx. 126.
11 Ibid. N.S. xxviii. 56.
12 W.R.O. 212B/Dv. 5, deed, Lewen to Drew.
13 Ibid. 189/23, indentures of apprenticeship.
14 See p. 119.
15 Gen. N.S. xxx. 185.
16 Ibid. N.S. xxix. 120; N.S. xxx. 246.
17 W.R.S. xv, p. 49. One of them, however, Philip Godfather, is also called 'glover': ibid.
18 Ibid. p. 50.
19 W.R.O. 189/23.
20 Ibid. 130/58A, deed, Button to Potter; W.R.S. xv, p. 50.
21 W.R.S. xv, p. 49. Also a fuller: ibid.
22 Sta. Cha. 8/181/27.
23 S.P. 16/377 no. 183.
24 W.R.O. 212A/36/2, deed, Nicholas to Attwoode, 1605; W.R.S. xv, p. 49.
25 S.P. 16/377 no. 183.
26 W.R.S. xv, p. 50.   27 Cunnington, Annals, i (2nd pagin.), 82.

Merryweather[28] as tanners. Cordwainers or shoemakers are numerous enough to suggest the presence of an industry catering for far more than a local market.

By the turn of the century Devizes had not significantly changed its relationship to other Wiltshire towns. With Salisbury and Marlborough it was the only Wiltshire town to whom the Crown appealed in 1614 for money and plate.[29] In 1622 it was the only town, apart from Marlborough, which was asked for a benevolence.[30] In 1635 and 1638 it contributed somewhat less to ship-money than Marlborough, but more than Chippenham and much more than Wilton.[31] In the middle of the century, however, it outstripped Marlborough and in 1662 Fuller called it 'the best and biggest town for trading (Salisbury being a city) in the county'.[32]

There is no evidence that Devizes engaged in the making of medley cloths which elsewhere in the county was undertaken with success around the middle of the 17th century. Consequently the town lost ground and the centre of Wiltshire textiles shifted westward.[33] If petitions of 1696,[34] 1719,[35] and 1731[36] are to be trusted, the Devizes manufacturers suffered considerable losses. Yet cloth-making did not leave the town; it changed its form. In the later 17th century the town became a chief centre of serge manufacture,[37] producing a strong variety of 'German' serge much used by country people.[38] Edward Bowman was a serge-weaver in 1657[39] and between that year and 1753 23 other people are described as serge-clothiers, serge-makers, or serge-weavers.[40] The last of these was George Pead, serge-weaver of St. James's chapelry,[41] but serge was still being made in 1779.[42]

28 Ibid. 79; W.R.O. 212B/Dv. 6b, deed, Stevens to Merryweather.
29 *Acts of P.C.* 1613–14, 495.
30 Ibid. 1621–2, 176–7.
31 Waylen, *Hist. of Marlborough*, 127; Hist. MSS. Com. 47, *15th Rep.* X, Radnor, p. 166.
32 *Worthies of Eng.* (1840 edn.), iii. 333; cf. above, pp. 80–1.
33 *V.C.H. Wilts.* iv. 154–5, 160.
34 *C.J.* xi. 583–4.
35 Ibid. xix. 179.
36 Ibid. xxi. 645.
37 Ramsay, *Wilts. Woollen Industry*, 110.
38 *V.C.H. Wilts.* iv. 159.
39 W.R.O. 632/122, indentures of apprenticeship.
40 *Cal. S.P. Dom.* 1683–4, 83 (cf. *Gen.* N.S. xxxvii. 211, 213); *W.R.S.* xvii, pp. 26, 148; *W.N. & Q.* viii. 552; W.R.O. 632/122.
41 W.R.O. 632/122.   42 Julia de L. Mann, *Cloth Ind. in West of Eng.* 40 n.

A slightly later Devizes product, noted by Defoe as a speciality of the town, was drugget, popular for its lightness.[43] Four members of the Phillips family engaged in its manufacture between 1716 and 1734,[44] and ten other drugget-makers or drugget-clothiers can be found.[45] They include Morgan Price who was so described in 1734[46] and who was a serge-clothier in 1748.[47] Devizes druggets were being exported to Russia up to 1753.[48] Felt-making continued. A felt-maker is mentioned c. 1669[49] and there are four new ones in the 18th century, the last in 1750.[50]

Another industrial event of the 18th century was the inception of 'cassimere'-making. 'Cassimeres', closely-woven fancy fabrics sometimes shot with silk, cotton, or mohair, were the speciality of John Anstie,[51] who was trading from at least 1779[52] and who c. 1785 built a factory in New Park Street at the corner of Snuff Street on a site acquired about ten years earlier.[53] Anstie was said in 1788 to have kept 300 looms at work.[54] His cloths were exported to the Continent and he himself was a leader among West of England clothiers. He went bankrupt, however, in 1793, partly perhaps through over-diversification,[55] and partly because the French War made the discharge of debts impossible.[56]

Between the Restoration and the Reform Bill fresh families of Devizes clothiers and drapers arose, notably the Suttons, who succeeded by marriage to New Park,[57] the drugget-making Phillipses[58] and others

43 V.C.H. Wilts. iv. 159.
44 Geo. (1716): W.R.S. xvii, p. 113; Edw. (1721): p. 5; Sam. (1729, 1734): p. 110, W.R.O. 234/6; Ric. (1734): W.R.O. 234/6, deed relating to meeting-ho. in St. John's par.
45 Nic. Phip (1715): W.R.O. 943; Wm. Pyle (1715): W.R.S. xvii, p. 50; Ric. Brooks (1716, 1719): p. 23; W.N. & Q. viii. 551; John Clark (1721, 1722, 1725): W.R.S. xvii, pp. 51, 60; W.N. & Q. viii. 551; Wm. Richman (1720), Joseph Peck (1722), Tim. Lott (1728), Hen. Beal (1728): W.N. & Q. viii. 551; Ric. Anstie (1728): W.R.O. 844, Corp. Lease Bk., St. John's lands, no. 1; Thos. Beal (1729): W.N. & Q. viii. 551.
46 W.R.O. 234/6. He was still living in 1767 when he was described simply as a clothier: W.R.O. 402/74, deed, Williams and others to Rowden.
47 Ibid. 212A/29/2, deed, mayor and burgesses to Price.
48 Mann, Cloth Ind. West of Eng. 40 n.   49 Gen. N.S. xxxiii. 206.
50 W.N. & Q. viii. 552; W.R.S. xvii, p. 70.
51 Mann, Cloth Ind. West of Eng. 61–2.
52 W.R.O. 402/74, deed, Stone, Anstie, and Mayo.
53 W.A.M. lv. 139–43, where the buildings are described. The argument that they were meant only for silk-weaving does not seem sustainable.
54 Cunnington, Annals, ii. 266.
55 V.C.H. Wilts. iv. 164, 168. He was b. c. 1745: Waylen, Chrons. 352.
56 Mann, Cloth Ind. West of Eng. 86.
57 For their lineage see Waylen, Hist. 553–4.   58 See above.

of that name, i.e. Edward (1733–67)[59] and Edward White Phillips (d. by 1767),[60] and John Waylen (1687–1727) who married a Paradise[61] and founded a dynasty. Of these the elder James Sutton was a white clothier in 1715,[62] his son, also James, was admitted to the drapers' 'fellowship' in 1719,[63] and a John Sutton, not in the direct line, was a clothier in 1767.[64] Stephen Hillman, trading in 1791,[65] was worth £800 yearly in 1797.[66] Such were some of the new-comers. Some of the older families, however, continued, such as the Paradises[67] and the Webbs.[68]

There were still six clothiers in 1783–4[69] and three in 1791.[70] By c. 1828 all had departed.[71] The last of any account was Robert Waylen (d. 1841), who in his hey-day employed a thousand[72] and used the best steam engine in the district.[73] His factory, afterwards a brewery,[74] stands behind the houses on the west side of Northgate Street.[75] It ceased to make broad cloth in 1824 but was still making fancy waist-coatings in 1826, which continued to be made for a few more years by one Holloway, Waylen's foreman.[76] Though the firm of J. J. Fox & Co. was still listed in 1839 as making linsey-woolsey[77] and as woollen cloth manufacturers and wool-staplers in 1865,[78] they seem to have been primarily retail drapers.[79]

59 Phillipps, *Wilts. M.I.* 79.
60 W.R.O. 402/74, deed, Williams and others to Rowden.
61 *Gen.* N.S. xxxvii. 152; *W.N. & Q.* viii. 551.
62 *W.R.S.* xvii, p. 111.
63 *W.N. & Q.* viii. 551.
64 W.R.O. 402/74.
65 *Univ. Brit. Dir.* ii.
66 P.R.O. 30/8/279 Pt. 1 f. 79.
67 John, junior (1712): *W.N. & Q.* viii. 551; Hen. junior (1705, 1726): W.R.O. 335/23, deed, to Hen. Paradice, 1705; *Gen.* N.S. xxxvii. 81; will, archdeaconry of Wilts.; Wm. (c. 1760): *W.N. & Q.* viii, pedigree at p. 49. The last Devizes Paradise seems to have d. 1817: Gillman, *Annals*, 25.
68 Thos. (b. 1676): W.R.O. 189/17 (1701); Waylen, *Hist.* 337 (1711).
69 Bailey, *Dirs.* (1783–4).
70 *Univ. Brit. Dir.* (1791), ii.
71 Waylen, *Chrons.* 326.
72 Gillman, *Annals*, 35.
73 Wilts. Cuttings, v. 151.
74 See p. 99.
75 Wilts. Cuttings, ii. 171; W.R.O., Tithe Award, Devizes, St. John's par. A survey of the building (c.1818) is in W.A.S. Libr., Devizes.
76 Wilts. Cuttings, v. 151. Patterns of fancy waistcoats survive in Devizes Mus.
77 Robson, *Com. Dir.* (1839), ii.
78 Harrod, *Dir.* (1865).
79 Cf. *W.A.M.* xlii. 239.

The industries ancillary to cloth manufacture were more sparsely represented after the Rebellion than they had been in early times. Between 1654 and 1679 five card-makers[80] and four worsted-combers[81] are named. Wool-combers are not conspicuous in the next century. They seem, however, to have been grouped into an informal company, for in 1739 they collectively attended a public ceremony.[82] A comber was still living in 1776.[83] In 1756 there was a dyer,[84] and in 1743 Richard Brooks, clothier, patented a machine for drying yarn.[85] There was a fuller in 1734 and shearmen in 1723 and 1759.[86]

Among the ancillaries silk-throwing must be included. As has been shown, silk might be needed in weaving 'cassimeres' and Robert Waylen spun his own.[87] A distinct trade is said to have arisen about 1815 and by 1855 was employing some 100 men.[88] Belvedere, once Snakesmead mill, in Roundway parish, can be traced from 1823, when Peter Walker owned it. In that year Walker joined Robert Waylen to work another factory.[89] This was in Anstie's former building.[90] What came of this enterprise is not known but Belvedere mill, then owned by Frederick Walker, lasted until 1859.[91]

Wool brought wealth to Devizes not only through those who wove from it but also through those who dealt in (or jobbed) it. By c. 1637 there was already a market spinner.[92] William Ludlow and his ancestors seem to have been wool-broggers throughout the later 16th and earlier 17th centuries[93] and there are four known wool-staplers within the period 1672–86.[94] During the first sixty years of the 18th century

80 John Tyley (fl. 1658) and Thos. Andrewes (fl. 1659): W.R.O. 632/122; Walt. Bennett (fl. c. 1667): *Gen.* N.S. xxxiii. 115; Wm. Tylye (mar. 1674): N.S. xxxv. 240; Thos. Harrie (mar. 1679): N.S. xxxvii. 104.
81 John Rogers (1654), Peter Coole (1658), Thos. White (1678): *W.N. & Q.* viii. 552; Edw. Pannell (fl. c. 1672): *Gen.* N.S. xxxiv. 239.
82 Cunnington, *Annals*, i (2nd pagin.), 209.
83 W.R.O. 212B/4/241, deed, Grubbe to James.
84 *W.R.S.* xvii, p. 17.
85 *W.N. & Q.* i. 4, 363.
86 W.R.O. 632/122, indentures of apprenticeship.
87 *V.C.H. Wilts.* iv. 176–7.
88 *Kelly's Dir. Wilts.* (1855).
89 *W.A.M.* lv. 143–4.
90 See p. 90.
91 *Kelly's Dir. Wilts.* (1859); *W.A.M.* lv. 144.
92 S.P. 16/377 no. 183. For market-spinners see *V.C.H. Wilts.* iv. 154.
93 Aubrey, *Nat. Hist. Wilts.* ed. Britton. 110.
94 *W.N. & Q.* viii. 551.

the staplers continue numerous. Thirty-three of them, including one cloth factor, are then known by name.[95] Moreover they lasted on for another century. Four are known between 1783 and 1839,[96] the last being William Cunnington (d. 1846), the nephew of Colt Hoare's collaborator. Cunnington established his wool business at Southgate House in 1827 and in 1836 began additionally to deal in wine and spirits. His sons William (d. 1906), Henry (d. 1887), and Edward carried on after their father's death, though it is not clear for how long they acted as wool-staplers, certainly not after 1887.[97]

After the Rebellion there were no more tanners. Glovers, however, continued. Four are known in the middle years of the 18th century[98] and one Baster, fell-monger, glove-, breeches-, and gaiter-maker, enjoyed a reputation well beyond the borough bounds.[99] A few such men were still similarly employed in 1861[1] and the firm of V. C. Boulton of Westbury maintained a workshop in 1956.[2] In the earlier 18th century three curriers,[3] four saddlers,[4] and eight cordwainers[5] are known. The last are perhaps still too numerous for an exclusively local trade. Curriers were in business in 1783–6[6] and 1791[7] in Bridewell Street, hence the Curriers Arms.[8] Reference to curriers and 'leather-cutters' continue far on into the 19th century. The Reynolds family practised their craft in Maryport

---

95 *W.N. & Q.* viii. 551; ii. 531; iii. 80; *W.R.S.* xvii, *passim*; W.R.O. 234/6, deed, 3 Jan. 1734; 402/84–5, deeds, 10 Oct. 1759, 20 June 1740; 130/58B, deed, mayor and burgesses to Phillips; *Gen.* N.S. xxxvii. 153; *W.A.M.* xlii. 304; Phillipps, *Wilts. M.I.* 74.
96 Bailey, *Dirs.* (1783–4); *Univ. Brit. Dir.* (1791), ii. 779; Pigot, *New Com. Dir.* (1822–3); Robson, *Com. Dir.* (1839), ii.
97 *W.A.M.* xxx. 160–1; xxxiv. 324. The wine and spirit business was conducted for a while after 1887 by B. H. Cunnington.
98 Robt. Lewis (1743), Sam. Beaven (1753), Robt. Haggard (1755), Wm. Neale (1758): *W.R.S.* xvii, pp. 157, 175, 48, 91.
99 Baster, whose name appears upon a token: *W.A.M.* xliv. 5. See also Soc. Antiq., Jackson MSS. v, f. 174.
1 *V.C.H. Wilts.* iv. 237. 2 Ibid. 238.
3 *W.R.S.* xvii, pp. 61, 121, 137, 165.
4 John Eyles (1757), John Forman (1716), John Herne (1720, 1723), Edw. Moxham (1715, 1716, 1722, 1729–30): ibid. pp. 38, 145, 130, 139, 102, 149, 172.
5 Thos. Bailey (1713, 1721, 1725), Stephen Bell (1710, 1716, 1722), Gabriel Butcher (1730, 1751), Wm. Fennell (1742), John Harwood (1711), Sam. Slade (1750), John Tonnell (1719), Thos. Twinney (1758): ibid. pp. 48, 159, 162; 3, 161, 172; 79, 168; 101, 154; 172; 123; 46; 112.
6 Thos. Garlick or Goulick: Bailey, *Dirs.* (1783–4); Cunnington, *Annals*, ii. 265.
7 William Bristow: *Univ. Brit. Dir.* (1791), ii. 779.
8 *W.A.M.* xli. 206; and see below, p. 108.

and Monday Market Streets until at least 1885[9] and in that year there was a tannery in the latter.[10] Throughout the 19th century there were never fewer than two firms in the town.[11]

The braziers of earlier times remain in evidence. Among them James Bartlett[12] and James Burrough were also bell-founders. The latter, who is thought to have kept his foundry at the Ark,[13] was active locally between 1738 and 1755 but with two exceptions never plied his trade outside the county.[14] William Box, an iron-founder, cast one Wiltshire bell.[15] Braziers continue into the 19th century. Two are named in 1822–3 and also an iron- and brass-founder.[16] Around 1825 much good ironwork seems to have been executed by Devizes men, especially H. and J. Burt, and a Mr. Hope who succeeded Burrough in his business.[17] There were four braziers and tinmen in 1830[18] and five in 1851,[19] but they and their successors were probably in general only retailers.

A spoon-maker (Henry Showring) appears in 1631[20] and in the mid 18th century there are two whitesmiths.[21] There was still a wiredrawer in 1694[22] and perhaps also in 1740.[23] There was a cutler in 1620[24] and two in the 18th century.[25] The names of just over 30 clock-makers have been recorded, active, judging by their dated products, between 1660 and 1819.[26] They were probably of little more than local consequence,[27] although a list compiled in 1911 shows that there were far more clock-makers in Devizes than in any other Wiltshire town.

9 Robt. Reynolds (d. 1849): *W.A.M.* xliii. 236; Pigot, *New Com. Dir.* (1822–3). The firm became S. Reynolds & Co.: *Kelly's Dirs. Wilts.*; cf. *Letters of Stephen Reynolds*, ed. H. Wright, p. xi.
10 O.S. Map 1/2,500, Wilts. XXXIV. 14 (1886 edn.).
11 Pigot, *New Com. Dir.* (1822–3) and later *Dirs.* (national and local).
12 W.R.O. 402/1, bond, 16 Apr. 1666.
13 Ibid. 130/58B, deed, Beavan to Burrough; W.R.S. xvii, p. 4; Wilts. Cuttings, v. 151.
14 Walters, *Wilts. Bells*, 315.
15 Ibid. 316.
16 Pigot, *New Com. Dir.* (1822–3).
17 Wilts. Cuttings, v . 151.
18 Pigot, *Nat. Com. Dir.* (1830).
19 Slater, *Dir.* (1851).
20 W.R.O. 189/23, indentures of apprenticeship.
21 W.R.S. xvii, pp. 22, 38.   22 W.R.O. 130/58A, deed, West to Watton.
23 Wm. Leach, tobacco- and snuff-maker, was a 'wire-maker' before entering that business: *W.N. & Q.* ii. 538.
24 W.R.S. xv, pp. 50–1.   25 Ibid. xvii, pp. 98, 159.
26 *W.A.M.* xlviii. 313–17; *W.N. & Q.* vi. 312–14.
27 Only 2 have been traced in F. J. Britten, *Old Clocks and Watches* (7th edn. 1956).

Eighteenth-century trade labels

Tobacco and snuff were cured and ground in Devizes from the early 18th century.[28] The firm, later known as E. & W. Anstie Ltd., traces its origin to Richard Anstie, a grocer, who in 1698 occupied a shop at the junction of Snuff Street with the Market Place. John Anstie, Richard's son, was for a short time in partnership with William Leach (d. 1780), a former wire-maker,[29] who ground his snuff in the two windmills on the castle motte. These mills existed in 1716, when a half share of them was conveyed to William Maple,[30] and originally expressed rape oil.[31] They were used by William Ludlow, who was still in trade in 1784.[32] The Anstie–Leach partnership was dissolved before 1740 but in 1769 Leach was still trading alone.[33]

28 Except where otherwise stated this and the following paragraphs are based on *V.C.H. Wilts.* iv. 240–1.
29 *W.N. & Q.* ii. 538. For the date of death see Cunnington, *Annals*, ii. 259.
30 C.P. 25(2)/1077/2 Geo. I Hil. no. 6; another moiety was conveyed to Geo. Flower, who owned the castle site, in 1721: C.P. 25(2)/1078/8 Geo. I Hil. no. 14; and see p. 57.
31 Waylen, *Chrons.* 326.
32 Bailey, *Dir.* (1784).
33 *W.N. & Q.* ii. 482.

Anstie's snuff factory, formerly a cloth factory

Ansties tenanted land on both sides of Snuff Street from 1731[34] and presumably at some time later in the century used it for their tobacco trade. The firm was mechanized in the 1830s and the works completely rebuilt in 1831.[35] In 1894 offices, designed by J. A. Randell,[36] were put up on the site of the shop of 1698.[37] By 1917 the former factory of John Anstie the clothier, at the junction of Snuff and New Park Streets, had been taken over.[38] In 1925 the tobacco-making business of I. Rutter & Co., of Mitcham (Surr.), was absorbed. In 1944 the firm was sold to the Imperial Tobacco Co. and thus the six-generation link with the Anstie family was severed. Snuff ceased to be made in 1957[39] and tobacco to be cured in 1961.[40] In the second year the factory and office buildings were sold to C. H. Woodward, Ltd., printers.[41]

34   Lease of 1731 to John Anstie, grocer; of 1817 to B. W. Anstie, snuff manufacturer: W.R.O. 844, Corp. Lease Bk., St. John's lands, nos. 9 and 10.
35   W.A.M. lv. 142 n.   36   *Devizes Gaz.* 15 Sept. 1898.
37   Date stone.
38   W.A.M. lv. 145; and see above, p. 90.
39   *Wilts. News*, 11 Oct. 1857.
40   *Wilts. Times*, 3 Mar. 1961.
41   Ibid. 17 Nov. 1961.

From the mid 16th century brewing and malting have been carried on[42] and in the 1670s malt was reckoned one of the town's more important articles of merchandise.[43] Between 1620 and the mid 18th century ten maltsters[44] and three brewers are known.[45] A malt-house in St. John's parish, once Thomas Lewen's, is mentioned from 1618[46] to 1626[47] and a 'millhouse' was conveyed to John Hollis, maltster, in 1707.[48] In 1645 a malt-mill 'opposite' the castle was destroyed,[49] before 1752 a brewhouse and millhouse seems to have stood on the site of the Ark,[50] and from 1726 until at least 1842 a malt-house and subsequently a brewery stood next to the Bridewell.[51] By 1819 the Bridewell Street brewery had come into the hands of James and Joseph Dredge, represented in 1844 by Joseph Dredge & Co.[52] In 1797 Samuel Adlam, a clothier in 1783–4,[53] was a prosperous maltster.[54] Charles Rose and John Tylee, his nephew, were inn-holders in 1766 and in partnership as brewers by 1768.[55] By 1783, Rose being dead, the firm had been transformed into Tylee and Gent,[56] which under the subsequent names of Gent and Tylee, J. & T. Tylee, and Tylee & Co. is traceable to 1844.[57] By 1822–3 the brewery was at the maltings, Northgate Street,[58] on a site now forming a branch of Wadworth's. By 1841 it had become a foundry.[59] The firm of

42 The first brewer to be noted was John Mathews, a member of the corporation, fl. 1551: W.R.O. 212A/36/2, deed, mayor to Truslow, 1551–2.
43 Richard Blome, *Britannia*, 242.
44 *W.R.S.* xv, p. 39; S.P. 16/377 no. 183; *Wilts. Q. Sess. Rec.* ed. Cunnington, 186; Cunnington, *Annals*, i (1st pagin.), 92, (2nd pagin.), 200; W.R.O. 402/74; *W.N. & Q.* vi. 6; *W.R.S.* xvii, p. 166; W.R.O. 130/58B, deed, Beaven to Burrough.
45 *W.N. & Q.* vii. 142; *W.R.S.* xv, p. 49.
46 W.R.O. 632/107, accts. 1619–20; cf. acct. 1618–19.
47 Cunnington, *Annals*, i (2nd pagin.), 80.
48 W.R.O. 844, town deeds, box 9, 16 Apr. 1707.
49 *Wilts. Q. Sess. Rec.* ed. Cunnington, 186.
50 W.R.O. 130/58B, deed, Beaven to Burrough. The premises were at a place called 'Steps Head', which is near the SW. corner of St. John's chyd. The deed is endorsed in a later hand 'now the Ark'.
51 W.R.O. 844, town deeds, box 9, 24 Mar. 1728; Pigot, *Nat. Com. Dir.* (1842).
52 Ibid.   53 Bailey, *Dirs.* (1783–4).
54 P.R.O. 30/8/279 Pt. i f. 79.
55 *Wilts. Gaz.* 5 Feb. 1925.
56 Ibid.
57 Pigot, *New Com. Dir.* (1822–3); Pigot, *Nat. Com. Dir.* (1830, 1844); Robson, *Com. Dir.* (1839), ii.
58 Pigot, *New Com. Dir.* (1822–3).
59 W.R.O., Tithe Map, Southbroom; *Wilts. Gaz.* 5 Feb. 1925.

Figgins and Gent coexisted from 1783 to 1791.[60] James Gent, whose income in 1797 might be reckoned a large one,[61] remained a partner until his death in 1829.[62]

Wadworth's brewery c. 1968

60 Bailey, *Dir.* (1783); *Univ. Brit. Dir.* (1791), ii. 779.
61 P.R.O. 30/8/279 Pt. i f. 79.
62 *Wilts. Gaz.* 5 Feb. 1925.

The two connected trades continued to flourish throughout the 19th century, often as adjuncts to liquor retailing. Seven firms are found in 1839, three of them 'large',[63] and six in 1898–9.[64] In test years they average four.[65] Few survived for long. One of the brewers of 1839 was James Oram of Northgate Street,[66] successor to the younger Robert Waylen and J. O. Anstie.[67] In 1864 Oram sold out to Sainsbury Brothers,[68] who established the Northgate Brewery[69] in the elder Robert Waylen's cloth factory,[70] which by 1970 had become Messrs. May's premises. They then sold in 1875 to H. A. Wadworth, a farmer, who founded the present firm of Wadworth & Co. Ltd. The brewery and maltings at the corner of Northgate and New Park Streets were designed by J. A. Randell[71] and built by direct labour in 1885.[72] Four years later Wadworths became a limited company and absorbed J. F. Humby's business, otherwise the Southbroom Brewery in the present Southbroom Road traceable from 1854.[73] Later they acquired other enterprises: in Devizes the Estcourt Brewery, traceable from 1889,[74] and Chandler & Co.'s maltings, once Tylee's, in Northgate Street, in 1904. The last two of Wadworth's Devizes competitors are recorded until 1911 and 1933 respectively. They were the Hare and Hounds Brewery,[75] which had been in existence, if intermittently, since 1839,[76] and the Three Crowns brewery.[77] Between 1904 and 1968 Wadworths bought various public houses and liquor stores. In 1964 they ceased to malt and converted the Northgate Street maltings into a warehouse called Kennet House.

The development of brewing in the 18th century led to the building-up of a cooperage industry. Three Paradises were then coopers[78] and four others are known.[79]

63 Robson, *Com. Dir.* (1839), ii.
64 *Kelly's Dir. Wilts.* (1898–9). 65 *Dirs. passim.*
66 Robson, *Com. Dir.* (1839), ii. 67 Wilts. Cuttings, ii. 171.
68 Unless otherwise stated the rest of this paragraph depends upon *Wadworths* (priv. print. ?1968).
69 O.S. Map 1/2,500, Wilts. XXXIV. 13 (1886 edn.).
70 See p. 91. 71 *Devizes Gaz.* 15 Sept. 1898.
72 O.S. Map 1/2,500, Wilts. XXXIV. 13 (1886 edn.).
73 *Kelly's Dirs. Wilts.* The brewery stood between Sidmouth St. and Hare and Hounds St.
74 *Kelly's Dirs. Wilts.* 75 Ibid.
76 W.R.O., Tithe Map, Devizes, St. John's par.; *Kelly's Dirs. Wilts.*
77 W.A.S. Libr., Devizes, sale cat. xx, no. 26; and see below, p. 109.
78 Hen. junior (1714, 1722); Wm., of the Brittox (1741, 1744); Edw. (1751, 1753, 1757): W.R.S. xvii, pp. 76, 112; 40, 82, 99; 4, 85, 104.
79 Ibid. pp. 31, 43, 103, 119.

A HISTORY OF DEVIZES

In the 17th century Devizes was well known for the manufacture of metheglin, in which Thomas Pierce, of the Swan, did a large trade.[80] One or two Devizes tobacco-pipe-makers of the late 17th or early 18th century have been identified.[81]

Until the 17th century[82] there is no mention of wind- or water-mills. The castle occupied the only suitable site for the former and the flow of water in the parkland streams was too feeble to sustain the latter. A horse-mill, however, occurs in 1363 and 1451.[83]

In the course of the 19th century some completely new industries arose. Two firms of agricultural engineers played a large part in the town's prosperity. The first of these was Brown and May, established in 1854 and liquidated in 1913.[84] Its works, the North Wilts. Foundry, which in 1885 lay north of Estcourt Street close to the then workhouse,[85] were badly burnt in 1873.[86] The firm made agricultural steam engines and ultimately oil engines, which seem to have led to their undoing. A limited company from 1895,[87] the firm employed 350 workmen in 1901. The other firm was T. H. White, Ltd., originating in an ironmongers' firm (1830) of that name in the Brittox and another (Thomas Carter) in Sidmouth Street. It was founded about 1855 by George White, whose grandson (d. 1899) bore the same initials as the ironmonger of 70 years before. It became a limited company in 1914 and absorbed other Wiltshire firms, including those of Richard and William Box, active in and around Devizes in the 1840s.[88] The firm built the Phoenix factory (burnt 1864)[89] in the angle formed by Sidmouth Street and Gains Lane. In 1973 the works were moved to Nursteed Road.[90]

The firm of W. E. Chivers & Sons Ltd., building contractors, dates from 1884, when the first Chivers set up a small business close to the Rising Sun in Southbroom Road. It moved in the late 1890s to a joinery

---

80 Aubrey, *Nat. Hist. Wilts.* ed. Britton, 68, 70.
81 *W.A.M.* lxvi. 159.
82 For 17th- and 18th-cent. mills see pp. 95, 97.
83 W.R.O. 844, Skippet deeds, nos. 12, 27.
84 *V.C.H. Wilts.* iv. 196–7.
85 O.S. Map 1/2,500, Wilts. XXXIV. 14 (1886 edn.).
86 Gillman, *Annals*, 53.
87 Ibid. 66.
88 For Wm. see *V.C.H. Wilts.* iv. 195. Ric. occupied what had once been Tylee's brewery in Northgate St. in 1841: W.R.O., Tithe Map, Southbroom; and see above.
89 Gillman, *Annals*, 46.
90 Ex inf. Messrs. T. H. White, Ltd.

at the corner of Hare and Hounds and Sidmouth Streets and in 1912 took over Brown and May's foundry, which it still occupies. It came to prosperity in the First World War when it was employed by the government partly in building construction and partly in furnishing steam lorries to transport troops and munitions. The transport business was given up in the early 1930s but the construction side has continued on a large scale. Since the Second World War Chiverses have built the Atomic Energy establishments at Harwell (Berks.) from 1946, and at Aldermaston (Berks.) from 1955. In 1970 about 1,500 were employed of whom 300–400 were based on Devizes. Branches have been opened in several parts of southern Britain. The main offices in Estcourt Street were rebuilt c. 1965.[91]

The North Wilts. Dairy Co., formed in 1889 by (Sir) Reginald Butler, had its depot in Estcourt Street[92] and later a factory in Pans Lane.[93] By fusion with a similar company in Melksham this became the Wilts. United Dairies, Ltd., in 1897 and took over other dairying concerns.[94] Headquarters remained in Devizes until 1913. The Pans Lane factory then became the chief centre for the firm's soft cheeses until its closure in 1941. In 1915 the company was merged in United Dairies, Ltd.[95]

The Central Wiltshire Bacon Company, Bath Road, was formed in 1899. Shut down during the Second World War, it revived its prosperity shortly after,[96] but was closed finally in 1960,[97] when its buildings were taken over by Cross Manufacturing Co. (1938), Ltd., light engineers. Two small electrical manufacturing firms operate: Savage Transformers, Ltd., with a factory in Nursteed Road, started in 1926, and the Hinchley Engineering Co., started in 1949 in the former cheese factory in Pans Lane.[98]

Several neighbouring brick and tile factories provided outlets for the local labour force, especially the works on Caen Hill, established by

---

91 Ex inf. Mr. Bruce Chivers, Managing Director, 1970; illustrated booklet (priv. print. 1919).
92 W.A.M. xlvi. 529.
93 V.C.H. Wilts. iv. 225.
94 Gillman, Annals, 67.
95 V.C.H. Wilts. iv. 225–7.
96 Ibid. 223.
97 Wilts. News, 7 Oct. 1960.
98 V.C.H. Wilts. iv. 203, and see above.

1855.[99] Apart, however, from the works which existed 1831–9 at the foot of Dunkirk and in the latter years belonged to G. T. Sainsbury,[1] none of these has ever been within the borough bounds.

By the early 19th century Devizes had been transformed from a mainly manufacturing into a mainly commercial town. In the preceding century economic life had been growing more sophisticated and so the way for this evolution had been smoothed. In 1740 attempts were still being made to restrict retail trading to the members of the three companies.[2] Thirty years later the companies were dissolved.[3] Luxury trades were set up. Thus there was a bookseller before 1719,[4] a goldsmith by 1712.[5] Mantua-makers abounded.[6] Henry Axford (fl. 1720),[7] John Locke,[8] his son Wadham Locke (fl. 1744, 1755),[9] Solomon Hughes (fl. 1751),[10] and William, his son,[11] were attorneys. By 1783 there were six firms of attorneys in practice,[12] by 1797 seven.[13] A physician existed in 1711[14] and two surgeons by the middle of the century.[15] By 1791 there were two physicians and four surgeons.[16]

In 1775 the first bank was opened. It was owned by James Sutton, William Leach, John Beaven, and Richard Read.[17] Sutton was probably the former clothier of that name,[18] Leach perhaps the tobacco-manufacturer.[19] By 1783 the house was known as Sutton, Read & Tylee.[20]

99 *Kelly's Dir. Wilts.* (1855).
1 Wilts. Cuttings, v. 151; Robson, *Com. Dir.* (1839), ii; *Rep. Bdy. Coms.* H.C. 141, map facing p. 103 (1831–2), xl. The map shows it to have lain SW. of the Devizes–Chippenham rd.
2 Cunnington, *Annals,* i (2nd pagin.), 210–11.
3 In 1769–70 the companies then released their right to the Weavers' Hall and surrendered their plate: ibid. 227; *W.A.M.* iv. 173.
4 W.R.O. 130/58B, deed, Stephens to Williams.   5 *W.R.S.* xvii, p. 99.
6 Ibid. *passim.*   7 Ibid. p. 150.
8 Waylen, *Hist.* 562.
9 Ibid.; *W.R.S.* xvii, pp. 18, 61, 93, 174.
10 *W.R.S.* xvii, p. 137; Waylen, *Hist.* 125–6.
11 Waylen, *Hist.* 125.
12 Bailey, *Dir.* (1783).
13 P.R.O. 30/8/279 Pt. i f. 23.
14 John Standfield: *W.R.S.* xvii, p. 148.
15 Joseph Needham (1741): ibid. p. 31; Geo. Gibbs (1753): W.R.O. 130/58B, deed, Saunders and others to Gibbs.
16 *Univ. Brit. Dir.* (1791), ii. 778.
17 Gillman, *Annals,* 19.
18 Bailey, *Dir.* (1783); and see above, p. 91.
19 See p. 95.
20 Bailey, *Dir.* (1783).

Tylee was John Tylee, the brewer,[21] by 1797 the richest man in town.[22] Under a variety of names this bank existed for two generations. It had disappeared by 1851.[23] Its offices were in the Market Place in the 1820s,[24] and in Northgate Street in 1839.[25] The firm of Locke, Hughes & Co., presumably composed of members of the local lawyers' firms, may be traced from 1822–3 under a succession of different names.[26] It was then in the Brittox[27] and moved to purpose-built offices at no. 41 St. John's Street, on the site of the old gabled home of the Mayos, in 1826,[28] where it remained until 1851.[29] The bank was fused with the Capital and Counties in 1883.[30]

INNS. Nine Devizes innkeepers were licensed in 1600.[31] In 1620 15 innholders or innkeepers, 13 alehouse keepers, and a taverner, all of Devizes or Southbroom, bound themselves in Lenten recognizances.[32] If the earlier figure is complete, even for the hosts of the larger establishments, there must have been an enormous increase in taverns over a short period. A reduction in the number by 12 in 1623 causes no surprise.[33] In 1686 the inns of the town contained 97 beds, many fewer than Salisbury, Chippenham, or Marlborough could provide; even Warminster and Bradford could do better.[34] On the other hand stabling was ampler in 1686 than that of any other Wiltshire town apart from Salisbury.[35] In 1766 licensed premises in the borough and on the Green numbered 41,[36] in 1818–19 30 within the borough,[37] in 1844 28 within the extended borough,[38] in 1903 30,[39] and in 1970 26. Several of the early inns belonged to the corporation either absolutely or in trust.

21 See p. 97.
22 P.R.O. 30/8/279 Pt. i f. 79.
23 Slater, *Dir.* (1851).
24 Pigot, *New Com. Dir.* (1822–3).
25 Robson, *Com. Dir.* (1839), ii.
26 Pigot, *New Com. Dir.* (1822–3).
27 Ibid.
28 *Wilts. Gaz.* 10 Mar. 1927.
29 Slater, *Dir.* (1851).
30 Gillman, *Annals*, 59.
31 *W.A.M.* xx. 329.
32 *W.R.S.* xv, pp. 38, 49–50.
33 Cunnington, *Annals*, i (2nd pagin.), 71.
34 *W.R.S.* xv, p. xv.
35 Ibid.
36 *W.A.M.* xxxi. 108.
37 Cunnington, *Annals*, ii. 210–11.
38 Pigot, *Nat. Com. Dir.* (1844).
39 *Kelly's Dir. Wilts.* (1903).

The first named inn, mentioned in 1514, was called 'Dokemannys'.[40] It stood on the Green and does not recur. Next comes the Crown, which occurs in 1538–44.[41] It seems to have continuously occupied the same site in St. John's Street[42] until its closure in 1966.[43] Its use in the 17th century by lodgers of good social standing suggests that it was then one of the best inns in the town.[44]

There is record of six other 16th-century inns, four of which may be specially mentioned. The Hart, represented by no. 12 St. John's Street, is first mentioned in 1546,[45] and under the successive names of the Boot,[46] and the Wheatsheaf, and possibly the Rose[47] can be traced to 1836.[48]

A Swan is first mentioned in 1563[49] and in 1580[50] stood in the New Port. In 1668 there was a Black Swan, approachable from Short Street, near the butchers' shambles. It was still an inn in 1673[51] but closed soon after. It is probably the Swan of 1580. In 1693 no. 22 High Street, previously a private house, had become the Black Swan and so remained until 1732[52] or later. Its yard may have lain across the street, for in 1900 no. 6, on the east side, was still called 'Old Swan Yard'. By 1750 the building had become a private house, but by 1766 there was once again a Black Swan.[53] This may have been the present one, which is dated 1737,[54] was partly burnt in 1798,[55] and has stood in the Market Place since at least 1778.[56] A White Swan, now represented by no. 39

---

40 Longleat MS. 8055.
41 C 1/1062/50–4.
42 *Devizes and Wilts. Gaz.* 26 Apr. 1900.
43 Wilts. Cuttings, xxii. 362.
44 The Chief Baron, 1610: *Devizes and Wilts. Gaz.* 26 Apr. 1900; the warden of New College, Oxf., 1670: *W.R.S.* xiii. 31.
45 *W.A.M.* ii. 235.
46 *W.N. & Q.* i. 390; *Endowed Char. Wilts.* (1908), lxxx, p. 387; W.R.O. 844, Corp. Lease Bk., St. John's lands, no. 4.
47 *Devizes and Wilts. Gaz.* 12 and 19 Sept. 1895.
48 Pigot, *New Com. Dir.* (1822–3); *W.A.M.* xli. 315.
49 *Devizes and Wilts. Gaz.* 26 Apr. 1900.
50 Prob. 11/62 (P.C.C. 34 Arundell).
51 W.R.O. 212B/Dv. 13A, deed, Eyles to Rose. For the site of the shambles see pp. 115–16.
52 Deeds *penes* Mrs. Pamela Mullings, 22 High St., Devizes.
53 *Devizes and Wilts. Gaz.* 26 Apr. 1900.   54 Pevsner, *Wilts.* 189.
55 Cunnington, *Annals*, i (1st pagin.), 163.
56 W.R.O. 844, Corp. Lease Bk., St. John's lands, no. 1.

Market Place,[57] existed in 1676–7,[58] and perhaps changed prefixes with the Black Swan when that inn set up in High Street. In 1758 it was made a dining-place for militia officers.[59] It was still an inn in 1775, was a private house in 1791,[60] and an inn again from 1808[61] to 1864,[62] when it became the Wilts and Dorset Bank.[63] Thomas Pierce, the metheglin-maker,[64] once occupied the Swan and was presumably the descendant of John Pierce, its licensee in 1600,[65] and Richard Pierce, the Royalist mayor, its owner in 1649.[66] The inn was probably the Black Swan in 1668. An Angel, in the New Port, existed in 1596.[67] It is often referred to afterwards, for out of it a rent was payable to the poor.[68] It has been claimed that it stood in the Market Place on a site later occupied by Ansties' offices, and at an uncertain date to have been renamed the White Lion.[69]

The Bear, now and for long the chief inn, is first mentioned in 1600.[70] In 1678 it was called the Black Bear[71] and in 1738 alternatively the Bear and Castle.[72] It seems to have possessed ornamental grounds by 1664[73] and a bowling alley ten years before.[74] As a staging point on the Bath road it became well known to the fashionable world and under its licensee George Whatley (d. 1767) was evidently well conducted. A near successor to Whatley was Thomas Lawrence, the painter's father, who became licensee in 1772 and remained until at least 1779,[75] when he

57 *Kelly's Dir. Wilts.* (1859).
58 W.R.O. 212A/31/5, deeds to property called White Swan.
59 Waylen, *Hist.* 412.
60 W.R.O. 212A/31/5.
61 W.R.O. 844, Corp. Lease Bk., corp. lands, no. 45.
62 W.A.S. Libr., Devizes, Licensing Justices' Min. Bk. 1842–66.
63 Gillman, *Dir.* (1866).
64 See p. 100.
65 *W.A.M.* xx. 329.
66 Waylen, *Hist.* 265; and see p. 9.
67 Cunnington, *Annals*, i (2nd pagin.), 32.
68 *Endowed Char. Wilts.* (1908), lxxx, p. 390.
69 *Devizes and Wilts. Gaz.* 10 May 1900.
70 *W.A.M.* xx. 329.
71 W.R.O. 844, town deeds, box 9, 26 Sept. 1678.
72 Ibid. Corp. Lease Bk., corp. lands, no. 1.
73 Waylen, *Hist.* 589.
74 *W.A.M.* xli. 192. The bowling alley belonged to E. Effington whose house was associated with the Bear grounds in 1664: Waylen, *Hist.* 589.
75 D. E. Williams, *Life and Correspondence of Sir Thomas Lawrence*, i. 66 gives this date. Waylen, *Hist.* 447, 454 gives 1781. It has been plausibly conjectured (D. Goldring, *Regency Portrait Painter*, 43) that the father went at the earlier date, the mother and son at the later. The son was certainly there in 1780.

was replaced by William Halcombe (d. 1801), licensee of the King's Arms.[76] During Lawrence's time Fanny Burney and David Garrick were lodgers[77] and the young Thomas (1769–1830) entertained such visitors by reciting poetry and showing his precocious drawings.[78] Halcombe maintained the standards, so that the inn could still be described in 1788 as 'remarkable' for its goodness.[79] In his time 30 coaches a day halted in the yard.[80] He may have been responsible for building new assembly rooms to the north of the inn where the Corn Exchange now stands. The likeness of a black bear, holding a bunch of grapes, reared upon two columns in the Market Place, was moved to the north entrance porch c. 1801,[81] after when the prefix 'black' was dropped.[82] The Archduke of Austria in 1786, George III and Queen Charlotte in 1789, and Queen Charlotte alone in 1817 all stopped at the inn.[83] The Duchess of Kent and Princess Victoria did the same in 1830,[84] and Edward VII, when Prince of Wales, visited it in 1893.[85] The construction of the Corn Exchange and Station Road c. 1857 much reduced the size of the yard.[86]

In the 18th and 19th centuries, especially before the Town Hall was remodelled and the Corn Exchange erected, the inn was an administrative and social centre; the first board of Improvement Commissioners were required by statute to assemble there,[87] and it was an appointed dining-place for militia officers.[88] In 1828 a subscription reading-room was established in it.[89]

The northern half of the inn was originally timber-framed and has an L-shaped plan, consisting of a front range and a long rear wing.

76 *Devizes and Wilts. Gaz.* 3 May 1900.
77 Waylen, *Hist.* 448, 450–1.
78 Williams, *Life . . . of . . . Lawrence*, i. 37–41, 50–5, 60, 65–7; *Diary and Letters of Madame D'Arblay*, ed. Muriel Masefield, 44–5.
79 *N. & Q.* cxcii. 185.
80 *Devizes and Wilts. Gaz.* 3 May 1900.
81 Waylen, *Hist.* 408, 476 gives 1801, but the column is still shown in a water-colour in W.A.S. Libr., Devizes, dated 1804 (not necessarily correctly).
82 Still called the Black Bear in 1789; licensed under the name Bear in 1818: Cunnington, *Annals*, ii. 174, 210.
83 E. Kite, *Bear Hotel, Devizes* (priv. print. 1924).
84 Waylen, *Hist.* 453.
85 Kite, *Bear Hotel.*
86 *Devizes and Wilts. Gaz.* 3 May 1900.
87 21 Geo. III, c. 36, s. 3.
88 Waylen, *Hist.* 412.
89 Kite, *Bear Hotel.*

The front range may once have had an open passage running through it. Its oldest visible features are two Tudor-arched stone fireplaces of a type which persisted from the late 16th to the mid 17th century. The gabled rear wing is likely to be of the latter period. The front range was remodelled and raised in height in the 18th century; its three-storeyed front is now stucco-faced and has sash windows and a columned porch. Other 18th-century alterations, perhaps Whatley's work, included a curved staircase with a Venetian window above it housed in a bowed projection facing the yard. Three stone Tuscan columns, each with a detached entablature, rise through two storeys of the rear wing and support the ceiling of what may originally have been an open first-floor gallery. The monumental character of the columns, incongruous in this position, suggests that they may have come from elsewhere; they appear to match those which formerly supported the Bear sign in the Market Place. Early in the 18th century the inn frontage was extended by the erection of a new south block. It originally had a flat two-storeyed front of five bays with a central pediment.[90] Between c. 1804 and 1816 the front was faced with stone ashlar and given two-storeyed bay windows, fluted pilasters, and other embellishments;[91] the wrought-iron verandah above the central doorway and double flight of steps may be of later date. The former assembly room, displaced by the Corn Exchange, appears to have been reconstructed in much its original form at the far end of the rear wing. The street front had a low ground floor with, above it, three tall sash windows set in arched recesses.[92] The present assembly room has similar windows and an enriched plaster ceiling in the 'Adam' style.

The Elm Tree may possibly be the corner tenement, 'forynst an elme', mentioned in 1512.[93] As the Salutation Inn it occurs from 1665–6[94] to 1681.[95] It had acquired its present name by 1818.[96] A tree which stood in front of it was removed in 1826.[97]

The Black Horse occurs from 1657[98] to 1848. It then changed its name to the Wiltshire House and disappeared in the next year.[99] It stood

90 W.A.S. Libr., Devizes, water-colour dated 1804.
91 Ibid. photograph of drawing by G. N. Burton, 1816.
92 Ibid. grangerized version of Waylen, *Chrons.*, photograph of c. 1850.
93 W.R.O. 212B/23/1/18, deed, 20 May 1512.
94 Cunnington, *Annals*, i (2nd pagin.), 144.
95 *Endowed Char. Wilts.* (1908), lxxx, p. 392.
96 Cunnington, *Annals*, ii. 210.
97 Ibid. 185.   98 Ibid. i. (1st pagin.), 90.
99 W.A.S. Libr., Devizes, Licensing Justices' Min. Bk. 1842–66.

on the site of the Wiltshire Savings Bank, Long Street,[1] and in the late 18th century was occasionally the meeting-place of the licensing justices.[2]

There was a Bull in 1663.[3] It may be identifiable with the Bull's Head in the Little Brittox, recorded from 1740[4] to 1821[5] or later,[6] whose sign is said to have been painted by Sir Thomas Lawrence in childhood.[7] The Castle, New Park Street, still open, was built soon after 1768 and was inviting custom in its 'genteely furnished' state in 1770.[8] In the later 18th century it was the meeting-place of the Improvement Commissioners and of local insurance societies[9] and in 1836 it was a posting house,[10] fair proof of its size and importance. The Curriers' Arms formed part of the Bridewell Street brewery.[11] It was the Chartists' headquarters in 1839.[12] Between 1841 and 1845 it became the Duke of Wellington and so survived until 1865.[13] The Hare and Hounds in the street of that name, has existed since 1766.[14] The King's Arms (Northgate House in 1973), first mentioned in 1766,[15] the approximate date of all but the western block, which is a little later, became soon after a coaching house with 40 beds, garden, and bowling green, the scene of aristocratic balls. Halcombe was the landlord in the early 1770s until he left it for the Bear.[16] The inn had closed by 1823.[17] The Leg of Mutton, Sidmouth Street, is named from 1739[18] to 1830.[19] It seems likely that it became the Odd Fellows or Odd Fellows Arms in or before 1844.[20] That inn changed

1 *Devizes and Wilts. Gaz.* 10 May 1900.
2 Cunnington, *Annals*, ii. 209.
3 W.R.O. 6/3, deed, Drew to Andrewes.
4 Ibid. 844, town deeds, box 9, 23 Aug. 1740.
5 Ibid. 844, Corp. Lease Bk., corp. lands, no. 82.
6 *Endowed Char. Wilts.* (1908), lxxx, p. 412.
7 *W.N. & Q.* vi. 273.
8 *Wilts. Gaz.* 5 Feb. 1925.
9 Cunnington, *Annals*, ii. 167, 172, 174, 235, 237.
10 *Wilts. Gaz.* 5 Feb. 1925.
11 W.R.O. 137/66, draft assignment with plan, 2 Jan. 1840.
12 *Chartist Studies*, ed. Asa Briggs, 178, 183.
13 W.R.O. 137/66; W.A.S. Libr., Devizes, Licensing Justices Min. Bk. 1842–66; *Devizes and Wilts. Gaz.* 10 May 1900.
14 *Devizes and Wilts. Gaz.* 3 May 1900.
15 W.R.O. 844, Corp. Lease Bk., St. John's lands, no. 12.
16 *Devizes and Wilts. Gaz.* 3, 10 May 1900; *W.A.M.* xlviii. 264.
17 W.R.O. 844, Corp. Lease Bk., St. John's lands, no. 12.
18 Cunnington, *Annals*, ii. 161.
19 Pigot, *Nat. Com. Dir.* (1830).
20 *W.A.M.* li. 179.

its name to the Unicorn in 1866,[21] was still open in 1966,[22] but had closed by 1970. Another Unicorn existed in 1687.[23] A Pelican (not the present one) was the headquarters of the royal troops during Monmouth's rebellion.[24] This still existed in 1737–8.[25] The Queen's Head has stood at the foot of Dunkirk Hill since 1769.[26] The building of chequered brickwork with stone dressings and a pedimented Tuscan porch may be of that period; a two-storeyed bay window was added later. The Three Crowns, Maryport Street, probably a 17th-century building, has existed since 1849.[27] When it was put up for sale in 1933 by J. F. Phipp, whose family had owned it since 1862, it was said to be the only free house in town.[28] The White Bear, Monday Market Street, a building of similar if not earlier date, has existed since 1673.[29] The timber-framed building on a corner site, which it still occupies, probably dates from the earlier 17th century.

AGRICULTURE. Until the boundary extensions began in 1831 the only significant amount of agricultural land in the borough was the comparatively well-watered tract of the old park. In 1227 the king had a meadow in it[30] and in 1225 its herbage and pannage were let at a fixed rent. The herbage and pannage of the other park was also let in 1255 and the whole of that park, by which may have been meant the pasturage, was let as well.[31] In 1281–2 the constable of the castle converted the meadow in the old park into pasture.[32]

In 1408 a parker, then newly appointed, was authorized to take a fee for every beast agisted.[33] Such fees continued to be collected until at least 1447–8.[34] From 1465–6[35] until the later 16th century the agistment

21 W.A.S. Libr., Devizes, Licensing Justices' Min. Bk., 1842–66.
22 Fletcher, *Dir.* (1966).
23 Cunnington, *Annals*, ii. 155, where it is spelt 'Wincorne'.
24 Waylen, *Chrons.* 351.
25 Cunnington, *Annals*, i (2nd pagin.), 239.
26 *Devizes and Wilts. Gaz.* 31 May 1900.
27 W.A.S. Libr., Devizes, Licensing Justices' Min. Bk., 1842–66.
28 Ibid. sale cat. xx, no. 26, with illustration.
29 *W.A.M.* xliv. 388. The identification with the Talbot there made is doubtful.
30 *Rot. Litt. Claus.* (Rec. Com.), ii. 204; *Close R.* 1227–31, 179.
31 *Rot. Hund.* (Rec. Com.), ii (1), 236.
32 *Cal. Inq. Misc.* ii, p. 49.
33 *Cal. Pat.* 1408–13, 81.
34 S.C. 6/1055/17.
35 S.C. 6/1094/1.

and also the pannage were customarily let, often to the stewards.[36] The herbage or hay crop was let from 1468 to 1478–9 to the parker with or without a partner[37] and was let with the agistment and pannage to Henry Herbert, earl of Pembroke (d. 1601), the steward within the period 1574–82.[38] It seems probable that these leases affected the old park alone. In 1570 Pembroke had also secured for a term the agistment and pannage,[39] which in 1581 were granted for life to his son William (d. 1630), later earl of Pembroke, and in 1592 to feoffees, one of whom was steward to the earl of Essex.[40]

Between 1446–7[41] and *c.* 1543[42] the summer and winter pasture of the new park were leased to parkers.[43] In 1570 Pembroke acquired the pannage for a term[44] and in 1581 the lease was extended.[45] In 1592 it was, like the pannage of the 'old' park, settled upon feoffees.[46]

Encroachments on the new park, for the needs of husbandry, had begun in 1275–6,[47] when a rent, unchanged until at least 1505–6,[48] was collected for the farm of the lands therein. In 1327–8 this encroachment, later known as Parklands,[49] amounted to 135 a., mostly arable, and was divided between eight people.[50] By 1412 an area within it was both arable and pasture[51] but by 1446–7 was referred to only as pasture.[52]

Land 'under' the castle ditch, and therefore in the old park, was let sporadically from 1443 to 1481 but was waste in the years immediately

36 S.C. 6/Hen.VIII/3776; S.C. 6/Hen.VIII/6668; and see p. 60.
37 D.L. 29/724/11800; D.L. 29/724/11802; L.R. 2/191 f. 164v. The surveys in the third source seem to be assignable to 1543 and 1551. See also below.
38 L.R. 2/86 ff. 136–7.   39 *Cal. Pat.* 1569–72, 49.
40 E 308/4/35 no. 63; cf. E 310/26/154 nos. 5 and 44. Leases in reversion were also granted to two feoffees in 1589. Presumably they never took effect.
41 S.C. 6/1055/16. It is not, however, until 1477–8 that the pasture is expressly said to lie in the New Park: D.L. 29/724/11801.
42 S.C. 6/Hen.VIII/6668.
43 Ralph Banaster (1478–9): D.L. 29/724/11802; cf. *Cal. Pat.* 1461–7, 64; John Burleigh (1516–17): S.C. 6/Hen.VIII/3760; Sir Edw. Baynton (1534–5, 1541–2, *c.* 1543): S.C. 6/Hen.VIII/3776; S.C. 6/Hen.VIII/6668; L.R. 2/191 f. 164.
44 *Cal. Pat.* 1569–72, 49.
45 E 308/4/35 no. 63; cf. E 310/26/154 nos. 5 and 44 and see n. 40.
46 Ibid.
47 E 372/120 m. 23.
48 S.C. 6/Hen.VII/882. It was 69*s.* in 1565–6; L.R. 2/269 f. 132.
49 See p. 59.
50 *Wilts. Inq. p.m.* 1327–77 (Index. Libr.), 19.
51 W.R.O. 189/34, deed, chwdns. to Swyft, 1412.
52 S.C. 6/1055/16.

following.[53] A survey of c. 1565–6 shows 'gardens' near the castle[54] and in 1611 there were meadow and pasture, 'gardens', and orchards around the same area.[55] The pattern was the same in 1651[56] and 1654.[57] In particular there was a cherry orchard on the south side of the castle mound. In 1654 the whole of the old park was split up into small 'grounds'. The partition of 1664[58] implies the existence of arable, meadow, and pasture in all parts of the park.[59] The land-use in the next century is uncertain, but between 1710 and 1740 Wadham Wyndham's portion[60] was split into 25–35 parcels. In 1720 these parcels included a withy bed, which between 1729 and 1738 was converted into a grove.[61] About 1551 rabbits abounded in what was called the ditch about the castle without the park.[62] References in 1715 to the Little Conyger[63] and in 1828 to the Upper Conyger, the latter lying south of the Congregational church,[64] attest the presence of a rabbit warren.

In the 19th century the old park was split up between Old Park and Lower Park, Gillett's, and Sunnyside farms.[65] The last of these, occupied in 1896 and later by a dairyman,[66] was watered by the clarified effluent of the sewage works.[67] In 1920 it was said to consist of 'exceptionally rich pasture land'[68] and in 1924 its pasturage potential was even more enthusiastically praised.[69]

Cartographical evidence shows the whole town to have been a mass of gardens and orchards in 1759. In particular the map of that year marks a belt of 'nurseries and gardens' running outside the then borough boundary from the site of the Assize Courts to Gains Lane.[70] The area

53 S.C. 6/1055/16–19; S.C. 6/1094/1–3; S.C. 6/Hen.VII/1135, quoting earlier acct.; D.L. 29/724/11800.
54 L.R. 2/269.   55 C 66/1882 no. 5.
56 E 317/Wilts./21.
57 W.A.M. xli. 191–3; W.A.S. Libr., Devizes, Map of 1654.
58 See p. 61.
59 Waylen, *Hist.* 589.
60 See p. 62.
61 W.R.O. 727, Wyndham accts.
62 L.R. 2/191 f. 164.
63 W.R.O. 943.
64 Ibid. 844, Corp. Lease Bks. corp. lands, no. 94.
65 See pp. 66–7.
66 Ibid.
67 W.A.S. Libr., Devizes, sale cat. viii, no. 63.
68 Ibid. xiii, no. 7.
69 Ibid. xix, no. 8, with pics. of the farm buildings of recent date.
70 Dore, Map, 1759.

seems large but may be no more than is to be expected on the outskirts of a rather sophisticated town of this sort and with a soil as fertile as that of the Upper Greensand. Perhaps in one of these nurseries worked the gardener Adam Taylor, author of a treatise on pineapples published in Devizes in 1769.[71] Three later nurseries may need special mention. An estate called Rotherstone was bought by George Sloper in 1775 and converted into a nursery garden in 1794.[72] It probably ceased by 1839 when the terrace of that name was built.[73] In 1841 there was a nursery, occupied by James Durnford, at the corner of Pans Lane and Southbroom Road[74] and in 1885 Northgate Nursery ran from the malthouses in Northgate Street southwards to the station.[75] The second was still a nursery in 1971.[76]

An allotment garden, said to be the first of its kind in England, was laid out by William Ewart, of Broadleas, Potterne, in 1855, south of Hillworth Park and west of Potterne Road. In 1956 it began to be built over.[77]

By the time of statutory inclosure (1819) there was already a number of old inclosures in the tithings of Southbroom and Wick,[78] but little has been gathered about their exploitation. An analysis published in 1834 of the land-use of Southbroom chapelry[79] is not illuminating because there is no ready means of knowing how the classification applies to the parts that lie within the present borough bounds.

MARKETS AND FAIRS. As might be expected in a town on royal demesne, Devizes market, first mentioned in 1228,[80] sprang up without express grant. In 1275 the burgesses claimed that Edward I's predecessors had forbidden the establishment of any rival market within seven miles (*leucas*)[81] but cited no precise authority. They claimed that the recent establishment of a market at Market Lavington[82] had infringed their

---

71 *A treatise on the Ananas or Pine Apples, ... Melons, etc.*
72 Cunnington, *Annals*, ii. 256, 270.
73 See pp. 30–1.
74 W.R.O., Tithe Award, Southbroom.
75 O.S. Map 1/2,500, Wilts. XXXIV. 13 (1886 edn.).
76 Mr. L. G. Painter's.
77 Wilts. Cuttings, xx. 73; and see above, pp. 35–6.
78 W.R.O., Inclosure Award, Bishop's Cannings, Southbroom, etc. 1819.
79 *First Ann. Rep. Poor Law Com.* H.C. 44, p. 568 (1834), xxx.
80 *Close R.* 1227–31, 76.
81 *Rot. Hund.* (Rec. Com.), ii (1), 252.   82 *V.C.H. Wilts.* x. 99.

monopoly and reduced their tolls.[83] Their market, however, was not permanently injured and has continued to the present day. It is held on Thursdays as it has been since 1609 at least.[84] In 1567 the Crown expressly granted a second market to be held in St. Mary's parish on Mondays.[85] It was still held in 1803[86] but had apparently ceased in 1814.[87]

Leland described the Thursday market as 'very celebrate'[88] and so it has remained almost until now. Corn, wool, and yarn seem to have formed the chief merchandise in the 16th and earlier 17th centuries.[89] In 1605 both townsmen and strangers might sell corn, foodstuffs, cattle, wool, and woollen yarn, but cloth, unless of the strangers' own making, and other commodities were restricted to townsmen.[90] Later in the 17th century cheese, bacon, and butter became important.[91] Aubrey thought Devizes the best fish market in the county.[92] A writer in 1673 described it as a mart for horses, cattle, and corn.[93] Stukeley said in 1724 that the townsmen viewed it as 'one of the best weekly markets in England'.[94] In 1759 it was called one of the best markets in the west for corn, wool, cheese, black cattle, and sheep.[95] The cattle market seems to have lapsed about this time but was revived in 1776.[96] By the early 19th century there was a twice-weekly market for butcher's meat.[97] Britton (1814) singled out horses, cattle, corn, wool, and cheese.[98] In 1830[99] and 1842 corn seems to have been the staple commodity and in the later year, when malt was also sold, it was possible to describe the corn market as one of the most important in England.[1] In that generation the wool

83 J.I. 1/998A m. 25; J.I. 1/1006 m. 60d.; *Rot. Hund.* (Rec. Com.), ii (1), 252.
84 C 66/1680 m. 13.
85 *Cal. Pat.* 1566–9, p. 65.
86 Cunnington, *Annals,* ii. 19.
87 J. Britton, *Beauties of Eng. and Wales* (1814), xv. 424.
88 *Itin.* ed. Toulmin Smith, v. 82.
89 Cunnington, *Annals,* i, *passim*; Ramsay, *Wilts. Woollen Industry,* 7.
90 See p. 132.
91 Cunnington, *Annals,* i, *passim.*
92 The fish came from Poole (Dors.): Aubrey, *Nat. Hist. Wilts.* ed. Britton, 115.
93 R. Blome, *Britannia,* 242.
94 W. Stukeley, *Itinerarium Curiosum* (1776 edn.), Cent. i. 145.
95 Dore, Map, 1759.
96 *Wilts. Advertiser,* 2 Sept. 1909.
97 *Rep. Com. Munic. Corps.* H.C. 116, p. 1268 (1835), xxiv; cf. T. B. Oldfield, *Rep. Hist. of Gt. Britain,* v. 153.
98 *Beauties of Eng. and Wales* (1814), xv. 424.
99 Pigot, *Nat. Com. Dir.* (1830).
1 Ibid. (1842).

market lapsed and the cattle market lapsed again, but both had been revived by 1837, though held but four times yearly.[2] In 1848 corn and cattle were looked upon as the chief commodities.[3] The cheese market, having lapsed at some uncertain time, was restored in 1862.[4] It had ceased by 1903.[5] It was the local view in 1888 that the market as a whole had recently lost ground to Chippenham, but that the cattle market had increased and the yield of the corn market doubled since 1858.[6] In 1903 the market was said to be for corn, poultry, butter, and vegetables,[7] in 1939 for corn, cattle, pigs, and poultry,[8] though cattle and corn were then of minor importance.[9] A Christmas stock market in December was being held in 1903 and 1939,[10] but had ceased well before 1961.

It is clear from the plaint of 1275 that the borough enjoyed at least a part of the profits of the market. In practice, however, it possessed no monopoly, for it was also complained that the constables of the castle had damaged the market by erecting stalls and letting them at a fixed rent,[11] and in 1275–6 the constable received over £18 in tolls.[12] As is elsewhere shown,[13] the borough seems to have lost some independence in the earlier 14th century and perhaps during that period the burgesses forfeited the tolls. At all events the profits were enjoyed by the lord of the fee between 1446 and 1509. They consisted of petty customs, which from 1501–2 included the 'yarn lane',[14] and the toll of the grain. The former was always the richer source and both sources declined fairly steadily in the half-century.[15]

In 1510 Catherine of Aragon leased the profits of the fairs and markets to the burgesses[16] who so enjoyed them until 1624 when they

2 *Wilts. Advertiser*, 2 Sept. 1909; W.R.O. 844, Corp. Mins. 1835–46, 30 May, 19 Aug. 1836.
3 *Kelly's Dir. Wilts.* (1848).
4 Ibid. (1862).
5 Ibid. (1903).
6 *Rep. Com. Mrkt. Rights* [C. 5550–ii], pp. 355–6, H.C. (1888), liv.
7 *Kelly's Dir. Wilts.* (1903).
8 Ibid. (1939).
9 Fry, *Land Utilisation Wilts.* 200.
10 *Kelly's Dirs. Wilts.*
11 *Rot. Hund.* (Rec. Com.), ii (1), 252.
12 E 372/120 m. 23.
13 See p. 127. 14 See p. 119.
15 These conclusions are based upon the relevant ministers' accts. in D.L. 29, S.C. 6/Hen. VII, and S.C. 6/Hen. VIII.
16 S.C. 6/Hen. VIII/3760.

secured them in fee farm.[17] From the late 16th century until the early 19th the profits were normally let to contractors, together with the halls in which the market activities were severally carried on.[18] The practice seems to have been abandoned with unhappy results between c. 1808 and c. 1822.[19] It was resumed in 1837[20] but discontinued, except for the corn tolls, ten years later.[21] The tolls of all the markets, except the general market, were still let by the corporation in 1888,[22] but taken in hand again in 1889.[23]

In earlier times the chief market-place lay in front of St. Mary's church,[24] where there is still an irregular open space. The corn market was held beside the White Bear, at the corner of Monday Market Street, and the cattle market further to the north-west, at the west end of St. Mary's church.[25] There was once a cross here. It was marked by a tree in 1759[26] which had apparently disappeared by 1814.[27] In 1366 there was a special market, of unknown location, where horses were sold.[28] Gradually the market spread from the Old Port to the New and invaded many quarters of the town. As the castle lost its military significance, its outer bail provided an admirable open space for marketing, and here and in the streets around the chief market was eventually concentrated. That concentration had begun by 1378. Probably the old market-place was never abandoned but continued as the locale of the Monday market.

For many generations the market was really not a single entity but a group of markets. There was a fish market by 1378[29] and a district *ubi carnes venduntur* by 1454.[30] Both these were in the New Port. By 1463 the latter district was being called the flesh shambles[31] and in 1489 the butchers' shambles.[32] Later evidence suggests that the place of sale

17 See p. 129.
18 Cunnington, *Annals*, i and ii, *passim*.
19 *Rep. Com. Munic. Corps.* (1835), xxiv, p. 1268.
20 W.R.O. 844, Corp. Mins. 1835–46, 11 Jan. 1837.
21 Ibid. 1846–62, 21 May 1847.
22 *Rep. Com. Mrkt. Rights* (1888), liv, pp. 352–3.
23 W.R.O. 844, Corp. Mins. 1889–95, 2 Aug. 1889, 27 June 1890.
24 Marked as 'The Old Market Place' on Dore, Map, 1759.
25 *W.A.M.* xliv. 385.   26 Dore, Map, 1759.
27 Cunnington, *Annals*, ii. 54.
28 J.I. 3/156 m. 6d.
29 W.R.O. 189/54, deed, proctors to Lufwyke.
30 Ibid. chwdns. to Clark.
31 Cunnington, *Annals*, i (1st pagin.), 12.
32 Prob. 11/8 (P.C.C. 23 Milles, Hen. Pole's will).

was at the corner of Wine Street and High Street. In 1617 a town weighing beam was erected over the site which by 1728 was covered by a dwelling house.[33]

In 1568 new shambles were built, in Short Street,[34] and rebuilt in 1600.[35] By 1737–8, however, they were in the present Market Place, north-east of the cross, and in 1759 were a set of uncovered stalls surrounded by trees.[36] Between 1769 and 1771 the corporation, using the benefaction of their M.P. George Willy, replaced these stalls by a permanent building, once again in Short Street,[37] and in 1791 Addington gave £500 to enable this building to be completed or rebuilt.[38] The accretions to the building are mentioned below.[39] In 1803 the building also became a mart for pig-meat.[40] The butchers, however, boycotted it soon after.[41]

A corn market is mentioned in 1502[42] and in 1534 was in the New Port.[43] It probably occupied the present Market Place. In 1610 it was also called the tanners' market-place.[44] A corn market in the Old Port is still mentioned in 1569.[45] A corn hall existed in 1560.[46] In 1615 a 'Measuring House' for corn was set up.[47] Later this stood a little to the north of the then recently erected shambles in the present Market Place.[48] Perhaps it was planted there at the outset and the corn market moved northwards. In 1625–6 the Measuring House was being leased[49] and in 1646–7 the beadle and ale-taster became perpetual lessees.[50] It was

33 W.R.O. 844, town deeds, box 4, 25 Mar. 1728; Cunnington, *Annals*, i (2nd pagin.), 64. For the beam see below, p. 121.
34 *W.A.M.* xliv. 386; *Chantry Report*, 3.
35 Cunnington, *Annals*, i (2nd pagin.), 63.
36 W.A.S. Libr., Devizes, Map, 1737–8; Dore, Map, 1759.
37 Cunnington, *Annals*, i (2nd pagin.), 224, 226, 228.
38 Ibid. ii. 2.
39 See pp. 120–1.
40 Cunnington, *Annals*, ii. 20.
41 See p. 145.
42 W.R.O. 844, Skippet deed, no. 4.
43 Ibid. 212A/36/2, deed, corp. to Webbe, 1534.
44 *Chantry Report*, 5. For the tanners' market-place see p. 119.
45 W.R.O. 212A/36/2, deed, corp. to Blanford, 1569.
46 Cunnington, *Annals*, i (1st pagin.), 35.
47 Ibid. (2nd pagin.), 64.
48 Dore, Map, 1759.
49 Cunnington, *Annals*, i (2nd pagin.), 80.
50 Ibid. 113.

The Bear Inn and the Corn Exchange

somewhat expensively repaired in 1674–5.[51] In 1678–9, when troops were stationed in the town, it was used as a guard house.[52] It appears to have been demolished between 1787 and 1791.[53] After that time, so far as is known, corn was both sold and measured in the open against the Market Cross railings, until it was resolved in 1856 to build a Corn Exchange on part of the Bear Hotel yard.[54] The building, designed by William Hill of Leeds, was opened in 1857. C. Darby Griffith, M.P., gave the clock and the statue of Ceres that crowns the entablature. The cost was largely met by public subscription.[55]

The market in early times centred upon the cross. A 'corn cross', very near St. Thomas's chapel,[56] is mentioned in 1527[57] and a cross, perhaps the same, was mended in 1645–6.[58] In 1673–4 it was furnished

51 Ibid. 160.
52 Ibid. 165–6.
53 Ibid. 242.
54 W.A.M. xlvii. 149.
55 Ibid.; Gillman, Annals, 41.
56 See p. 193.
57 Prob. 11/22 (P.C.C. 22 Porche, Thos. Tynmer's will).
58 Cunnington, Annals, i (2nd pagin.), 111.

with 'gernard', globe, and neckstone and the whole construction gilded.[59] Presumably it was this cross, standing west of the old shambles,[60] that remained in use until 1814. It was then replaced by a new one, the gift of Lord Sidmouth, somewhat further to the east.[61] On one side is recorded the story of Ruth Pierce, a market-woman of Potterne who fell dead in the Market Place in 1753 after lying to her neighbours.[62] This testimony to the consequences of perfidy, placed in the Measuring House in 1760,[63] was removed from the Market Place in 1788, and fixed to the sign of the Bear.[64] The original is now in the Devizes Museum.[65] The cross, designed by Benjamin Wyatt and L. J. Abington, was first 'laid open' when peace was proclaimed in 1814.[66] The adornment of the Market Place was completed in 1879 when T. H. S. Sotheron Estcourt presented a fountain, designed, it is said, by Henry Woodyer.[67]

Market Place

59 Cunnington, *Annals*, i (2nd pagin.), 160–1 corrected from MS.
60 Dore, Map, 1759; W.A.S. Libr., Devizes, water-colour of Market Place, 1804. See also illustration on p. 120.
61 Cunnington, *Annals*, ii. 57–8; Waylen, *Hist.* 496–502.
62 For Ruth Pierce see Cunnington, *Annals*, ii. 58–60, 281; Waylen, *Hist.* 388–9; *W.N. & Q.* vi. 241.
63 Cunnington, *Annals*, ii. 281; *W.N. & Q.* vi. 241–2.
64 Waylen, *Chrons.* 317.
65 *W.A.M.* xxvi. 172.
66 Cunnington, *Annals*, ii. 54.
67 Wilts. Cuttings, xxii. 84.

A yarn cross existed in 1559.[68] It was no doubt the mart for wool and textiles and perhaps stood in the (unlocated) 'yarn lane', already leased to the borough in 1516–17.[69] By 1575 the cross had been replaced by a yarn hall.[70] This was rebuilt in the early 17th century and its history is told elsewhere.[71] A butter cross is mentioned in 1599, when it was repaired,[72] and such repairs were periodically done until 1650–1.[73] In 1661–2 the cross yielded a small rent.[74] It is not heard of again and its site is not known. In the later 18th century butter appears to have been sold in the 'New' hall.[75] Since 1803 the mart has been the Market House.[76]

'Chescrosway' is mentioned in 1553.[77] The cross from which it took its name still existed in 1657,[78] but in 1687–8 the stones of which it was made were ordered to be removed and a wooden platform erected in their place.[79] Next year there is a reference to the cheese market,[80] in which no doubt the cross had stood, but like the cross itself its location is unknown. Cheese was later marketed successively in the 'Old' hall, the 'New' hall, the Town Hall (as the 'Old' hall had become),[81] and the new Market House.[82]

Among the places set apart for the sale of special commodities 'millers' places' or 'standings' and the 'tanners' standings' are mentioned in 1599–1601. The corporation could not then let them and perhaps in consequence they disappeared.[83] In 1741 the tanners' market, in earlier times probably in the present Market Place, lay or had recently lain at the north end of the present Town Hall.[84] By regulations of 1630 the hosiers were confirmed in their immemorial standing in High Street.

68 Cunnington, *Annals*, i (1st pagin.), 41.
69 e.g. S.C. 6/Hen. VII/878.
70 Cunnington, *Annals*, i (1st pagin.), 59.
71 See p. 150.
72 Cunnington, *Annals*, i (2nd pagin.), 35.
73 Ibid. 118.
74 Ibid. 135.
75 See p. 152.
76 See below.
77 C.P. 25(2)/46/321 no. 3.
78 *W.A.M.* xliv. 386.
79 Cunnington, *Annals*, i (2nd pagin.), 182.
80 Ibid. 183.
81 See pp. 150, 152.
82 See below.
83 Cunnington, *Annals*, i (2nd pagin.), 34, 36, 37.
84 *W.A.M.* xliv. 386; li. 179; *W.N. & Q.* i. 390–1 and see above, p. 116.

The Market Place in 1798. The Market House is on the left, the Market Cross and the 'Bear' monument in the centre, and the Bear Hotel on the right

Greengrocers were to stand from the White Swan southwards, smiths, fishmongers, and shoemakers in St. John's Street.[85] In 1642 the shoemakers were to move to their former standing at a vacant plot called 'the Gun', presumably the site of an inn of that name,[86] and the hosiers were anchored to their existing pitch 'near' the corn market.[87] On the map of 1737–8 the word 'poultery' is written in the middle of Wine Street.[88]

Addington's gift for the butchers' shambles in 1791 was matched in the same year by an equal sum from his fellow M.P. Joshua Smith. This the corporation used to improve the Market Place[89] by building a covered market for merchandise other than butchers' meat, corn, cheese, and live-stock to the west of the butchers' shambles. The new Market House seems to have been partly complete by 1793, for it then had a bell. In the same year hides and skins were ordered to be moved from the west end of the butchers' shambles,[90] probably so that further building might not be obstructed. By 1803 the building was finished and orders were given that it should become the only market-place for eggs, poultry, fruit, and vegetables.[91] In 1822 it was also the butter market.[92] The

85 Cunnington, *Annals*, i (2nd pagin.), 86.
86 Ibid. 103.
87 Ibid. 104–5.
88 W.A.S. Libr., Devizes, Map.
89 Cunnington, *Annals*, ii. 3.
91 Ibid. 19.
90 Ibid. 6.
92 Ibid. 78.

butchers' shambles was roofed in 1838 and the two buildings fused for all practical purposes.[93] One Pollard, of Frome (Som.), is said to have designed these changes.[94] In 1869 the Market House was described, perhaps inadequately, as a cheese market.[95] In 1921,[96] as in 1970, a wide variety of goods was exposed for sale upon its benches.

Weighing beams, which by Statute of 1429 all cities and boroughs were required to possess,[97] are first mentioned at Devizes in 1592 when a capital burgess surrendered his grant of them.[98] In 1617 new beams for weighing meat, butter, cheese, grease, and other victuals were erected on the site of the old butchers' shambles.[99] By 1614 there was a beam for wool and yarn[1] and one for bacon in 1698.[2] From the late 16th century to the late 17th the beams were usually let or put up for lease.[3] The public had to be repeatedly enjoined to weigh goods (or certain types of goods) elsewhere than at the common scales. Such orders can be traced from 1614 to 1737 and a provision to the same effect was included in the charter of 1685.[4] In 1793 there was a weighing house in Short Street[5] and this was most probably on the site of the pre-1617 shambles.[6] It seems likely that ultimately only food, and perhaps only butchers' meat, was weighed there. At all events the terms of a lease of 1726 suggest that wool, yarn, and cheese were all weighed in the Wool Hall, where they were marketed.[7]

A 'rudder' market lay in the New Port in 1666, probably in the present Market Place. There or near by cattle were sold in 1888[8] and

93 W.R.O. 844, Corp. Mins. 1835–46, 30 May, 19 Aug. 1836; inscr. on bldg.
94 Waylen, *Hist.* 576. The name Pollard cannot be traced in Robson, *Dir. Som.* for 1839 or in *A Gen. Dir. for Co. of Som.* (1840).
95 Weaver, Map, 1869.
96 *The Times*, 24 June 1921.
97 8 Hen.VI, c. 5.
98 Cunnington, *Annals*, i (2nd pagin.), 61.
99 Ibid. 55, 64; see above, p. 116.
1 *Constitutions*.
2 Cunnington, *Annals*, i (2nd pagin.), 199.
3 Ibid. 85, 135.
4 S.P. 44/335 ff. 403–6 (wt. for charter).
5 Cunnington, *Annals*, ii. 6.
6 See p. 116.
7 Cunnington, *Annals*, ii. 159.
8 *Rep. Com. Mrkt. Rights* (1888), liv, p. 352. In 1885 there were pens for cattle, sheep, and pigs in the Black Swan yard, grandiloquently called 'The Repository': O.S. Map 1/2,500, Wilts. XXXIV. 13 (1886 edn.).

have been since. A sheep market was being constructed in 1673–4,[9] and was promptly leased out.[10] It seems to have contained the sheep 'cubs'[11] or cribs.[12] In 1737–8 the cribs were in the Market Place adjacent to the butchers' shambles,[13] and, like the shambles, were often leased out. In 1791 there was a comprehensive lease to a single individual of the sheep, pig, and cattle markets and fairs and the stalls and standings in them altogether with the corn tolls.[14] No other reference has yet been found to cattle tolls, which by 1888 the corporation had given up exacting.[15] In 1819, apparently for the first time, horses were ordered to be tolled,[16] but by 1888 the horse market was not of much account.[17]

In 1208 a yearly fair on the eve and feast of St. Denis (8 and 9 Oct.) was granted to the lepers of Devizes.[18] In 1223 the bishop of Salisbury was at variance with the constable of the castle over the right to make attachments at it. How the bishop had displaced the lepers, who from now disappear from view, is not known, but the lepers' house, in Southbroom, was in the bishop's fee and outside the borough. Litigation ensued and in 1224, while the outcome was pending, the constable and bishop were charged to make attachments jointly (*communiter*).[19] After an inquiry the fair was granted in 1227 to the bishop to be held on the days already appointed and the two following.[20] The constable, however, continued his claim for a while, for in 1229 it was necessary to order him expressly to let the bishop have his fair.[21] The grant of 1227 was confirmed in 1393.[22]

In 1223 a fair was established on 23–25 June to endure until Henry III's majority in 1227.[23] If it continued after 1227, it is not heard of for many centuries. An early summer fair, perhaps this one, was,

9 Cunnington, *Annals*, i (2nd pagin.), 158–60.
10 Ibid. 60.
11 e.g. ibid. 158.
12 e.g. ibid. 165.
13 W.A.S. Libr., Devizes, Map, 1737–8.
14 Cunnington, *Annals*, ii. 3.
15 *Rep. Com. Mrkt. Rights* (1888), liv, p. 352.
16 Cunnington, *Annals*, ii. 73.
17 *Rep. Com. Mrkt. Rights* (1888), liv, p. 353.
18 *Rot. Litt. Claus.* (Rec. Com.), i. 105.
19 Ibid. 633.
20 *Cal. Chart. R.* 1226–57, 51.
21 *Close R.* 1227–31, 258.
22 *Cal. Chart. R.* 1341–1407, 343.
23 *Rot. Litt. Claus.* (Rec. Com.), i. 539.

however, being held on Ascension day 1557—27 May in that year.[24] In 1576 one was held on Corpus Christi day (Trinity Thursday)—27 June in that year.[25]

In 1567 the corporation was granted two fairs of its own, one on Candlemas eve and the two days following (1–3 Feb.) and another on the eve of the Decollation of St. John the Baptist and five days following (28 Aug.–1 Sept.).[26] Finally in 1685 the Crown granted it a new fair on 10 April and the two following days for wool and woollen cloth, cattle, and merchandise, to be held somewhere in St. John's parish.[27] This was called by contemporaries 'the wholesale fair'. Woollen goods brought for sale were to be exposed in and about the Wool Hall.[28] Aubrey said that in his time the October fair lasted about a week.[29]

In 1759 fairs were held on 13 February, Holy Thursday, Trinity Thursday, 5 July, 9 September, 2 October, and 20 October.[30] The first, fourth, fifth, and seventh respectively represent the Candlemas, Midsummer, Decollation of the Baptist, and St. Denis fairs of the past, thrust forward by the Calendar Act. The sixth, later called the nine days before Michaelmas or Lamb Fair and held on 1 October,[31] was new. In 1792 the fairs were the same as those of 1759 except that 20 April and 13 June have replaced Trinity Thursday and 9 September as fair days.[32] The April fair is perhaps the same as that granted by the 1685 charter,[33] which in that respect the corporation found to be not 'obnoxious' but benign. The June fair had lapsed by 1830.[34] The Holy Thursday fair is still referred to in 1836[35] but seems to have ceased by 1839, possibly because of a temporary revival of the Ascension day fair. The Candlemas fair was then held on 14 February.[36] By 1848 the fairs had been reduced to three, namely, 14 February, 20 and 21 April, and 20 and 21 October.[37]

24 Cunnington, *Annals*, i (1st pagin.), 19.
25 Ibid. 67.
26 *Cal. Pat.* 1566–9, p. 65.
27 S.P. 44/335 ff. 403–6.
28 Cunnington, *Annals*, i (2nd pagin.), 180.
29 Aubrey, *Nat. Hist. Wilts.* ed. Britton, 114.
30 Dore, Map, 1759.
31 *c.* 1770: *Devizes and Wilts. Gaz.* 16 July 1903.
32 *Univ. Brit. Dir.* (1792).
33 See p. 138.
34 *Rep. Com. Mrkt. Rights* [C. 5550–i], App. p. 214, H.C. (1888), liii.
35 W.R.O. 844, Corp. Mins. 1835–46, 19 Aug. 1836.
36 Robson, *Com. Dir.* (1839), ii.
37 *Kelly's Dir. Wilts.* (1848).

By 1907 the July fair had been revived, though it was then held on the second Tuesday in that month.[38] By 1939 the fairs on 21 April and 21 October had been discontinued.[39] The July fair ceased in 1939 and the February fair in 1942.[40]

St. Denis's fair was being held on the Green by 1560 and that is probably its original, as it is its present, site. The April fair was held in the same place from at least 1789.[41] The Candlemas fair was held in Monday Market Street in 1790 and there remained throughout its life.[42] In 1888 it swamped over into New Park Street.[43] In 1839 the July fair was held in the Market Place,[44] in 1907 in the Corn Exchange and the shambles.[45]

About 1224 St. Denis's fair was described as a wake (*vigilia*).[46] In 1790 the Candlemas fair was for horses; the 20 April fair, a very large one, the Holy Thursday fair, a 'considerable' one, and the 5 July fair, a 'very considerable' one, were all for cattle. The early October fair, which was small, was for cattle and pleasure, and the later one, for cattle, hops, and cloth.[47] The later October fair was also a pleasure fair, wild beasts assembling there from all over England.[48]

As elsewhere in England the fairs fell off in importance in the next half-century. The October fair of 1838 was described as 'the smallest ever recollected at this season'. About 20,000 sheep changed hands, but little trade was done in horned cattle or horses. The display at the pleasure fair was 'meagre'.[49] In 1839 the February, Ascension day, and early October fairs were said to be for sheep and cattle and the April and October fairs, described as 'large', for cheese, hops, and cattle.[50] In 1848 the April and October fairs were said to be for cattle, toys, and pedlary.[51] They were more authoritatively defined in 1888 as for cattle, sheep, and horses on

38 *Mate's Guide* (1907).
39 *Kelly's Dir. Wilts.* (1939).
40 Ex inf. Messrs. Ferris & Culverwell, Devizes.
41 Cunnington, *Annals*, ii. 267.
42 *Univ. Brit. Dir.* (1791), ii. 777; *Kelly's Dir. Wilts.*; Robson, *Com. Dir.* (1839), ii says, no doubt wrongly, that it was held in the Market Place.
43 *Rep. Com. Mrkt. Rights* (1888), liv, p. 353.
44 Robson, *Com. Dir.* (1839), ii.
45 *Mate's Guide* (1907).
46 S.C. 1/4/64.
47 *Univ. Brit. Dir.* (1791), ii. 777.
48 A schoolboy's impression of 1788: *N. & Q.* cxcii. 185.
49 *The Times*, 25 Oct. 1838.
50 Robson, *Com. Dir.* (1839), ii.
51 *Kelly's Dir. Wilts.* (1848).

The Green c. 1840

the first day and for pleasure on the second.[52] Definitions of 1903 and 1939 do not mention horses,[53] and the last horse was sold on the Green in April 1956.[54] From 1839 the July fair was for wool.[55] In 1873 it was described as the largest in the west of England. Fleeces then sold numbered 100,000.[56]

As has been said, the borough has enjoyed the profits of fairs continuously since 1624.[57] The grant was limited to the fairs within the borough. The Green, to which the fairs later mainly gravitated, lay outside until 1835 and was not borough property, and, even when it came within the bounds, the corporation, on grounds of private ownership, felt itself debarred from collecting tolls. Private rights were, however, extinguished

52 Rep. Com. Mrkt. Rights (1888), liv, p. 353.
53 Kelly's Dir. Wilts. (1903).
54 Ex inf. Messrs. Ferris & Culverwell, Devizes.
55 Robson, Com. Dir. (1839), ii; Rep. on Markets and Fairs in Eng. and Wales, (H.M.S.O. 1929), iv. 209.
56 Gillman, Annals, 54.
57 See pp. 114–15.

in 1899 when the corporation bought the Green.[58] The town clerk said in 1888 that tolls were not collected at the Candlemas fair, as the expense of doing so would have exceeded the receipts.[59]

BOROUGH GOVERNMENT. A charter, acquitting them of toll, passage, and lastage throughout the realm and its ports and promising them royal protection, was granted to the burgesses by Maud the empress in 1141. It was confirmed by Henry II[60] and again in 1200[61] and 1229.[62] In 1218 the privileges of Marlborough, granted to that borough in 1204,[63] were bestowed upon the burgesses. Those privileges consisted of a long string of exemptions, such as Winchester and Oxford enjoyed, from burdens both financial and judicial, from suit of shires and hundreds and, in the main, from attendance at forest courts; the right to hold their dwellings (*mansiones*) in chief; a guild merchant; the trial of pleas by the law of Winchester and not by combat; the cessation of customs unjustly raised (*levata*) in the recent war; the recovery of debts by bailiffs of their own; except for debtors and their pledges, immunity from distraint; exemption from external pleading in pleas of land, but the trial of those pleas by the law of Winchester.[64]

The burgesses through the town bailiffs appear to have been farming the borough in 1239 and 1240,[65] and by 1245,[66] if not by 1244,[67] Pewsham forest as well. They were separately represented at the eyres of 1194, 1249, 1268, 1281, and 1289,[68] at the fiscal eyre of 1255,[69] and at

58 Gillman, *Annals*, 68; see above, p. 4.
59 *Rep. Com. Mrkt. Rights* (1888), liv, p. 353.
60 The text of this and the preceding charter are known only from the 1371 confirmation: *Cal. Chart. R. 1341–1417*, 217. The date of the first was confirmed by Prof. H. A. Cronne, 16 Jan. 1956. The names of the witnesses to the second charter suggest 1158 or less probably 1155 as the date. In Feb.–Mar. 1158 Henry was in Salisbury, where the charter is dated, and the witnesses were with him for at least part of the time.
61 *Rot. Chart.* (Rec. Com.), 78.
62 *Cal. Chart. R. 1226–57*, 93.
63 *Rot. Chart.* (Rec. Com.), 135.
64 *Pat. R. 1216–25*, 142. This merely confers the privileges of Marlborough in general terms. For the details see *Cal. Chart. R. 1341–1417*, 218.
65 *Cal. Lib. 1226–40*, 371, 464.
66 Ibid. 1240–5, 307.
67 *Close R. 1242–7*, 216.
68 W.R.S. xvi, pp. 124–5.
69 *Rot. Hund.* (Rec. Com.), ii (1), 236, 241.

the investigations of 1275.[70] In 1249 the borough was called a free manor.[71] In 1255 it was headed by its bailiff, William the parker, who is the first town officer to be named.[72] It claimed return of writs, made declarations about castle-guard, and returned its own value at £39 2s. 4d. This value was made up of rents of assize, the herbage and pannage of the two parks with two 'gardens', the rent of the new park, market profits, and court perquisites.[73] The next declaration of its constitutional condition was made in 1275. The burgesses claimed that they could plead pleas of *vee de naam*, and, foolishly, that the castle and the borough were ancient demesne. They extended the rents of assize at £9 11s. and the perquisites of court at £5. Writs, however, were now said to be returned by the constable of the castle and the profits of the assize of bread and ale were said to belong to the Crown and therefore by implication were not accounted for by the burgesses. There is a reference to two beadles.[74]

So far as the scanty evidence permits a judgement, the borough was ascending in the scale of autonomy until the earlier years of Edward I. Then, at the time when the castle began to lose its military importance[75] and the burgesses the prosperity they had won through the proximity of a garrison, a decline set in; once even, in 1315, the town was taxed at a fifteenth.[76] The presumption of decline is supported by a Parliamentary petition of 1330 in which the townsmen pray to have the town by the 'old' extent. They were impoverished, they said, by farmers and strangers who made execution by unknown bailiffs; they claimed the right to elect their own bailiffs and to have the return of writs, which the farmers withheld. The Crown was willing to restore past usages, if investigation confirmed their genuineness,[77] but it was not until 1371 that there was any express renewal of privileges. In that year the charters of Maud, Henry II, John, and Henry III were confirmed, with the addition of the clause *licet*, and the privileges of Marlborough, conceded in general

---

70 Ibid. 252.
71 W.R.S. xvi, p. 230.
72 *Rot. Hund.* (Rec. Com.), ii (1), 241.
73 Ibid. 236.
74 Ibid. 252.
75 See p. 45.
76 *Hist. Essays in Honour of James Tait*, ed. J. G. Edwards, V. H. Galbraith, and E. F. Jacob, 435.
77 *Rot. Parl.* ii. 43.

terms in 1218, were defined.[78] By another charter[79] with the same clause, granted in 1381, the old charters were again confirmed and the burgesses were granted return of writs, exemption from the authority of the county keepers of the peace and coroners, and the right to elect a coroner of their own. This charter also stipulated that the principal men of the town should be arrayed before the keeper of the castle or his lieutenant and none other, and should be required to furnish themselves with arms. The charter was confirmed without alteration in 1404, 1414, 1423, 1462,[80] and 1559.[81]

Until 1555, when its own records begin, there is little to show what were the organs of borough government. It has been seen that in the 13th century the borough was managed by one or two bailiffs and that in 1275 it possessed beadles. It was to the bailiffs that the Crown addressed an order in 1355 to provide a guard of burgesses for Charles of Blois and his children,[82] but by the end of the 14th century the authority of the bailiffs, whatever it may have been, had begun to be encroached upon by the mayor. A mayor is named in 1306[83] and thereafter mayors are repeatedly encountered. While the charter of 1381 was addressed to the burgesses alone, that of 1391 was addressed to mayor and burgesses together. Nevertheless the bailiffs do not disappear. By twos they are known by name for various years between 1398[84] and 1481.[85] They appear to have been the officers jointly or severally responsible with the parker, the collector of castle-guard rents, and others for paying to the Crown the profits of the borough. They were acting in this way in 1461–4,[86] and were still town rent collectors in 1499–1500 and 1533–4.[87] In 1539 they witnessed a deed together[88] and in 1561

78 *Cal. Chart. R.* 1341–1417, 217–18.
79 Ibid. 273–4.
80 *Brit. Boro. Chart.* 1307–1660, ed. M. Weinbaum, 120.
81 *Penes* Devizes Corp.: *W.R.S.* x. 12. *Rep. Com. Munic. Corps.* H.C. 116, p. 1261 (1835), xxiv, says that there were confirmations by Hen. VIII and Edw. VI but these have not been found.
82 *Cal. Close,* 1354–60, 158.
83 *W.A.M.* ii. 303. The statement by Kite in Waylen, *Hist.* 578, that there was a named mayor in 1302 has not been confirmed.
84 W.R.O. 212B/4/9, deed, Coventr' to Olcombe.
85 S.C. 6/1094/1–3; D.L. 29/724/11800.
86 E 368/98 m. O (d). But in 1405–6 the constable accounts: E 364/41 m. 3.
87 W.R.O. 189/1, chwdns.' accts.
88 Ibid. 212B/1/25, deed, 20 Jan. 1539.

were present at a livery of seisin.[89] In the attestation clauses of deeds dated between 1398 and 1539[90] two constables appear, ranking before the bailiffs. Their then function is obscure as is that of a *prepositus*, who witnessed a charter of 1379.[91]

As shown above, the borough had power to determine civil pleas by 1371 and perhaps certain Crown pleas by 1381. A mayor's court is known to have sat from 1446–7. Between that year and 1504-5, when the details cease to be recorded, the number of sessions was variable: 19 in 1480–1, 6 in 1503–4 and 1504–5. The average was between ten and eleven.[92] Until 1510 the profits went to the Crown and fluctuated greatly. The respective functions of the mayor's court and the two courts held by the steward[93] are not known, but in the earlier 16th century a dispute between a townsman and the mayor was referred to the steward for settlement.[94]

Civic autonomy was significantly advanced in 1510 when Catherine of Aragon let the borough to the burgesses to farm, to hold during pleasure at £5 yearly. The grant included all courts, leets, and profits of fairs and markets within a 40s. limit.[95] This ran by prescription until renewed by the Crown c. 1540–1.[96] It was renewed again in 1563[97] and 1585[98] for 21-year terms and made perpetual in 1624.[99]

Shortly after the first lease, in an arbitration award upon a disputed mayoral election, the nature of the constitution becomes more evident. The award states that some held that the 'yeldens', which must mean either the men of the guild merchant or the craft guildsmen of whose

89 B.M. Add. Ch. 37542.
90 W.R.O. 212B/4/9 (1398); 844, Skippet deed, no. 3 (1452); 212B/1/20 (1527); 212B/1/25 (1538).
91 B.M. Add. Ch. 59676.
92 S.C. 6/1055/16; S.C. 6/1094/2–3; S.C. 6/Hen.VII/878–81; S.C. 6/Hen. VII/1135–7; D.L. 29/724/11800–3.
93 See pp. 50–1.
94 Req. 2/4/171. The petitioner claimed that the mayor had entered his house and taken his goods. The petition can be dated from internal evidence between 1526 and 1541.
95 E 315/38/157.
96 *Constitutions*.
97 E 309/Box 1/5 Eliz. I no. 3.
98 C 66/1257 m. 24. A lease of 1573 in reversion to Brian Fitzwilliam (C 66/1095 m. 33) never took effect.
99 C 66/2333 no. 5. The burgesses bought out a reversionary interest which Edw. Wardour had acquired in 1609: *Constitutions*; Cunnington, *Annals*, ii. 142.

prior existence there is no evidence, should choose the mayor and present the name of the chosen candidate to 'the twelve' who are 'chosen to the rule of the town'. Others, however, held that the 'yeldens' and 'the twelve' should join together in the election.[1] Though the members of the guild merchant may have been the burgesses, as in some other 16th-century towns,[2] this is the only evidence that the guild played a part in government. The arbitrators' decision is not extant but whatever it may have been the 'yeldens' were ultimately excluded. After this time the senior men of the borough or even the whole mass of 'burgesses' begin to play their part in local affairs. Conveyances of borough lands, once made by the mayor alone, are now often made in the name of the mayor and his brethren or of the mayor, the brethren, and the commons or burgesses.[3]

The mayor's 'brethren' were almost certainly in part ex-mayors. They are known as *majores sive prefecti* in 1580,[4] and are the same as the body called 'capital burgesses' in 1592[5] and 'burgesses being councillors' at the 'end' of Elizabeth I's reign.[6] Below them were 'the twelve', not meant to correspond mathematically with that number,[7] who are first mentioned in 1561.[8] They are called in 1592 'common councillors' and usually thereafter 'capital burgesses of the common council'. Below them stood the freemen or 'burgesses'. In 1574, 1580, 1592, and at the 'end' of the reign the number of these three classes, when tested, were respectively: 9, 17,[9] 10, and 9; 13, 14, 10, and 22; and 26, 21, 35, and 30. The figures for the first two years and the fourth are drawn from tables purporting to be complete, though subsequent amendments sometimes create uncertainty; those for the third are taken from a court attendance list.

It is clear that already the inhabitants and the burgesses did not coincide. The court admitted or created burgesses in 1556[10] and 1560[11] and in 1560–1 disburgessed them. Where cause is assigned, disburgessing

1 *L. & P. Hen. VIII*, i (2), p. 1024.
2 C. Gross, *Gild Merchant*, i. 123–4.
3 W.R.O. 212A/36/2. The formulae cited ran from 1523 to 1571.
4 Cunnington, *Annals*, i (1st pagin.), 72 compared with MS.
5 Ibid. (2nd pagin.), 20.
6 *Constitutions*.
7 *Rep. Com. Munic. Corps.* (1835), xxiv, p. 1261; cf. E. Gillett, *Hist. of Grimsby*, 136 n.
8 Cunnington, *Annals*, i (1st pagin.), 51.
9 For this year there are two lists of *majores*, the relationship of which is not clear.
10 W.R.O. 844, Ct. Bk. 1556–7.   11 Cunnington, *Annals*, i (1st pagin.), 45.

is for misbehaviour towards the mayor, the mayor and brethren, or another burgess.[12] Once a vote was taken on a man's fate,[13] and once it was said that thenceforth the disburgessed person 'standeth as a commoner and not otherwise'.[14]

In the 16th century the governing body seems to have gathered in only one assembly, the court, or 'court of assembly' as it is called in 1592.[15] The headings in a court book running from 1574 imply that the court was also one of pie powder and *vee de naam* but pie powder proceedings seem lacking.[16] The court sat frequently and its business was varied. There were 13 sessions between 21 April and 23 October 1556, 16 in 1574–5, and 12 in 1575–6. Here the mayor and other officers were elected, burgesses admitted and removed, tradesmen licensed, prices fixed, and vagrants, night-walkers, slanderers, minor thieves, and those who played unlawful games, evaded price-fixing, and trespassed against the assizes of bread and ale were punished.[17] The court also entertained private suits. Actions of debt are numerous and there are also actions of detinue (1557),[18] trespass on the case (1582),[19] and breach of promise of marriage (1560).[20] Leases were sometimes ratified or at least recorded in court.[21] Little is known of procedure but a suitor once (1556)[22] waged his law and inquest juries might be summoned to present customs or nuisances.[23] The court amerced delinquents and often committed them to 'ward', usually no doubt the town prison[24] but once in 1583 to the county bridewell.[25]

The governing body, who in 1567 had acquired a market and two fairs in indisputable ownership[26] and in 1586 a lien upon landed

---

12 Ibid. 44, 52–3.
13 Ibid. 53.
14 Ibid. 52.
15 Ibid. (2nd pagin.), 20.
16 W.R.O. 844, Ct. Bk. 1574–6.
17 Except where otherwise stated this paragraph is based on Cunnington, *Annals*, i (1st pagin.), 1–89 (*passim*); ii. 108–19; W.R.O. 844, Ct. Bks. 1556–7, 1574–6, 1582–4.
18 Cunnington, *Annals*, i (1st pagin.), 29.
19 W.R.O. 844, Ct. Bk. 1582–4.
20 Cunnington, *Annals*, i (1st pagin.), 39–40.
21 e.g. 1556: W.R.O. 844, Ct. Bk. 1556–7.
22 Cunnington, *Annals*, i (1st pagin.), 6.
23 e.g. 1556, c. 1582: ibid. 8–11, 75.
24 See p. 154.
25 Cunnington, *Annals*, ii. 129.
26 See pp. 113, 123.

property which was or was thought of as once chantry land,[27] obtained their first charter of incorporation in 1605.[28] By this instrument, which was addressed to the mayor and burgesses, the mayor, town clerk, and 36 capital burgesses were declared to be the common council and were empowered to choose the mayor each year from the twelve capital burgesses councillors and to appoint other officials. A mortmain licence was granted. Courts of record and of quarter sessions were established and certain steps were at the same time taken to protect retail trade in textiles.[29] The corporation was to control internal trade and to promulgate by-laws. In pursuance of the charter a commission of the peace was formed the same year, consisting of the mayor, town clerk, and the common council or its greater part.[30] When recorded in 1614 the new corporation was made up of the mayor, 15 *magistri* or *capitales burgenses et consiliarii* (who included the town clerk), 26 *capitales burgenses de communi consilio*, and 33 free burgesses.[31] The titles for all practical purposes were the same in 1630 but the numbers were then respectively 21 (including the mayor), 30, and 47.[32] On the first occasion the number of capital burgesses, however reckoned, exceeded the charter limits, on the second it was within them. In general the structure does not differ much from that of pre-charter times. After 1614 'and' drops out of the title used for the senior body,[33] the word *consilarius* being in apposition to *capitalis burgensis*. The alias *magister* is still found in 1730.[34] The phrases used for the three classes in 1834 were 'capital burgesses councillors', 'capital burgesses of the common council', and 'free burgesses'[35] and were common in the preceding two centuries apart from the period 1685–8.

The corporation received two other charters shortly after 1605. In 1610 the chantry lands which in 1586 had been secured to trustees to the corporation's use passed to them as an outright gift.[36] Secondly in 1609 the corporation purchased from the Crown, after the determination

27 See pp. 234–5.
28 C 66/1680 m. 13.
29 See pp. 87–8.
30 Cunnington, *Annals*, i (2nd pagin.), 63.
31 W.R.O. 844, Ct. Bk. 1583–1621.
32 Ibid. Entry Bk. 1572–1660.
33 Phillipps, *Wilts. M.I.* 79.
34 There is no *et* in 1636: W.R.O. 844, Entry Bk. 1572–1660.
35 *Rep. Com. Munic. Corps.* (1835), xxiv, p. 1262.
36 See pp. 234–5.

of a lease to an Exchequer official, the reversion of the bailiwick of the borough and the profits of markets, fairs, courts, and other customs under 40s. in value, which that official had himself secured in reversion after the termination of the corporation's own lease.[37] In 1624 they obtained this in absolute possession, subject to a fee farm rent of £5,[38] and they paid for the purchase by granting long leases of their own and their trust lands.[39] Such benefits as these were an outcome of the civic maturity which the charter of 1605 bespoke.

In 1636 the rents and profits reserved in 1624 and the rents reserved in 1610 were conveyed at the request of a Crown creditor (Sir John Heydon) to two nominees.[40] He and they in the same year sold them to ten persons, doubtless members of the governing body, in trust for the corporation. By this means the borough liquidated any abatement of the interest that they had acquired in 1624, subject only to the payment to the Crown of a chief rent of £10 and a fee farm rent of £5. It is not clear why this circuitous course was adopted. In 1658 the trust was renewed. The corporation bought the rent or rents in 1650[41] but surrendered them at the Restoration. It was they and not the trustees who paid them in 1660–1.[42] In 1701 the Crown sold the rents to Francis Bourman[43] and from him they descended to others.[44] The last parcel was redeemed by the corporation in 1971.[45]

In 1639 a new charter was secured under which the borough was governed, with but a brief intermission, until 1835. It did not, like its predecessor, require that the mayor should be chosen from among the capital burgesses councillors; it declared the corporation's right, partly exercised already, to hold pleas of account and mixed actions not

---

37 *Constitutions*; Cunnington, *Annals*, ii. 142.
38 *Constitutions*.
39 Cunnington, *Annals*, i (2nd pagin.), 77–8.
40 B.M. Add. MS. 34008, ff. 31–8. The nominees were speculators acting elsewhere: W. M. Palmer, *Cambridge Castle* (priv. print. 1928), 25. For the creation of the precedent legal estate see C 66/2684 no. 1. The originals of the letters patent of 1636, the conveyance of that year, and the conveyance of 1658 were in 1973 in the custody of the Devizes Town Clerk.
41 E 307/D/2/13.
42 Cunnington, *Annals*, i (2nd pagin.), 133, 145, 148; B.M. Add. MS. 34008, f. 51. An attempt made in 1683 to create a new trust seems to have been abortive: Cunnington, *Annals*, i (2nd pagin.), 169–70.
43 B.M. Add. MS. 34008, f. 72.
44 *W.N. & Q.* ii. 268; Waylen, *Hist.* 119.
45 Ex inf. Town Clerk.

extending to debt or damages above £40; it limited the mortmain licence to lands of the net yearly value of £100; it replaced the 'common clerk', as it called him, by a recorder who was to be a barrister; it limited the commission of the peace to the mayor, recorder, and a single common councillor chosen by the council.[46] These last two provisions tended to make the borough courts more professional. Otherwise the new instrument wrought little change.

In the earlier 17th century the corporation began to admit the county notables to its fellowship, a practice of course paralleled elsewhere.[47] Such persons sometimes also represented the borough in Parliament, as Sir Edward Baynton and Sir Henry Lee, capital burgesses councillors in 1623, did or had done.[48] The earl of Marlborough was a capital burgess councillor in 1630.[49] In 1654 when 46 'burgesses and inhabitants' participated in the election of a member of Parliament, nine were labelled 'gentlemen'.[50] Such persons, and indeed lesser men, were no doubt elected by the capital burgesses councillors including the mayor and town clerk or recorder.[51] The governing body continued also to eject the unworthy and unfit. Richard Maundrell, once mayor, was disburgessed in 1607 for contempts;[52] a man who had lived outside the borough for a year and a day in 1617;[53] burgesses who declined to pay forfeitures for straying beasts or fees to the bellman in 1623.[54] Sir Edward Baynton, the 'justice', who refused to sit, lost his office in 1656, probably for political reasons.[55]

By the time the 1639 charter was granted the appointed town officers had become numerous. A town clerk existed in 1556.[56] In 1565 he was stated, perhaps wrongly, to be also recorder.[57] He was receiving a

46 C 66/2877 no. 2.
47 e.g. E. Gillett, *Hist. of Grimsby*, 124.
48 G. W. Marshall, *Wilts. Visitation*, 1623, 88.
49 W.R.O. 844, Entry Bk. 1572–1660.
50 Cunnington, *Annals*, i (2nd pagin.), 121.
51 e.g. John Nicholas, chief burgess councillor, John Allen, common councillor, 1606: ibid. 41.
52 Ibid. 63–6.
53 Ibid. 54. He transgressed a by-law of 1614: *Constitutions*.
54 'Common' or other inhabitants suffered imprisonment: Cunnington, *Annals*, i (2nd pagin.), 73–5.
55 Ibid. 124.
56 Ibid. (1st pagin.), 13.
57 *Gen.* N.S. xii. 24.

salary in 1592 and 1596.[58] By the charter of 1605 he became a member of the governing body but at least until 1612 retained a salary.[59] John Kent (d. 1630), town clerk in 1628, compiled an illuminated register of the charters and constitutions, based upon a text of 1592,[60] whence comes much of our knowledge about the officers. Kent was also county clerk of the peace from *c.* 1601 until 1626[61] and had been a borough M.P. and mayor in 1602. It was perhaps his personal prestige that secured so eminent a position for the town clerkship in James's charter. The substitution of a recorder in the succeeding charter may betoken a local suspicion of over-mighty town clerks. No more such officers are heard of until 1662.[62] The first recorder was Robert Nicholas, who surrendered his office on becoming a justice of the Upper Bench in 1649.[63]

A steward and clerk of the courts, with the power of deputation, existed in 1614,[64] but the office probably dates from the establishment or reconstruction of those courts in 1605. Two chamberlains emerge in 1592[65] and are afterwards continuously traceable. They kept the borough property, collected the revenue, and accounted annually. In 1614 one was chosen from the capital burgesses councillors and the other from the 'twelve'.[66] They were salaried in 1630 and 1636.[67] The coroner, annually chosen up to 1605,[68] was dropped from the charter of that year.

The two constables, of 15th-century origin at least,[69] were the most senior of the 'inferior ministers', as Kent called them. With bailiffs and sub-bailiffs they are found taking offenders to court (1575)[70] or

58 Cunnington, *Annals*, i (2nd pagin.), 21, 32.
59 Ibid. 48, 64.
60 A normalized version of the Constitutions is in B.M. Add. MS. 15665, ff. 294 sqq. It states that the orders were agreed in 1592 but in its first article refers to the charter of 1605. The constitutions, as now known, were drawn or ratified in 1614: *Constitutions*. The 'constitution book' was being 'painted' *c.* 1615 (Waylen, *Chrons.* 151, 2nd pagin.), but its final form is signed 1628: *Constitutions*.
61 W.R.S. xi, pp. ix, x; *Wilts. Pedigrees* (Harl. Soc. cv, cvi), 105.
62 See pp. 137–8.
63 Cunnington, *Annals*, i (2nd pagin.), 116.
64 *Constitutions*.
65 Cunnington, *Annals*, i (2nd pagin.), 20.
66 *Constitutions*.
67 Cunnington, *Annals*, i (2nd pagin.), 86, 95.
68 e.g. 1556: W.R.O. 844, Ct. Bk. 1556–7; 1574: ibid. 1574–6.
69 See p. 129.
70 Cunnington, *Annals*, i (1st pagin.), 59.

summoning townsmen to join in suppressing a riot (1631).[71] The two bailiffs, if indeed they may claim any descent at all from their medieval predecessors, have lost some status, for they act like the constables or in their support by bringing captives into court (1557)[72] or distraining.[73] In 1614 they were also assigning stalls in fairs and markets.[74] Two serjeants or serjeants-at-mace, traceable from 1556,[75] and two sub-bailiffs, traceable from 1574,[76] were similarly minor policemen. By 1614[77] the sub-bailiffs were equated with the strangely-named 'aldermen' of 1556[78] and 'under-aldermen' of 1565.[79] In 1599 it was decreed that the sub-bailiffs should thenceforth be paid.[80]

The by-laws of 1614 refer also to surveyors of ways and streets, scavengers, carners of the market, searchers of leather, and an aletaster. There was already one 'wayman' in 1556[81] and two in 1561 and 1574.[82] In the last two years they seem to have been subordinate to two surveyors.[83] There was a scavenger, a carner, and a leather-searcher in 1556[84] and two of each by 1574,[85] 1574,[86] and 1625[87] respectively. The aletaster's office first appears in 1574, when it was linked with the beadle's.[88] An *apparitor* occurs from 1556[89] to 1614 at least.[90] In 1574 there was a crier (*preco*) and aletaster.[91] In 1614 when the two offices seem to have been separated the aletaster both examined the quality of liquor and presented the drunken; the beadle and crier collected tolls,

71 *Cal. S.P. Dom.* 1631–3, p. 198.
72 Cunnington, *Annals*, i (1st pagin.), 16.
73 Ibid. 18.
74 *Constitutions*.
75 Cunnington, *Annals*, i (2nd pagin.), 20; W.R.O. 844, Ct. Bk. 1556–7.
76 W.R.O. 844, Ct. Bk. 1574–6.
77 *Constitutions*.
78 W.R.O. 844, Ct. Bk. 1556–7.
79 *Gen.* N.S. xii. 24.
80 Cunnington, *Annals*, i (2nd pagin.), 62.
81 W.R.O. 844, Ct. Bk. 1556–7.
82 Cunnington, *Annals*, i (1st pagin.), 49; W.R.O. 844, Ct. Bk. 1574–6.
83 Ibid.
84 W.R.O. 844, Ct. Bk. 1556–7.
85 Ibid. 1574–6.
86 Ibid.
87 Cunnington, *Annals*, i (2nd pagin.), 79.
88 W.R.O. 844, Ct. Bks. 1574–6; 1583–1621.
89 Ibid. 1556–7.
90 Ibid. 1574–6; 1583–1621.
91 Ibid. 1574–6.

cleaned the corn market, impounded strays, and arrested vagabonds.[92] He has enjoyed subsequently a prominence out of keeping with his low estate.[93] In 1646–7 the offices were fused again.[94] A 'wayer' is found in 1556.[95] He was a rather senior officer and was presumably one of the weighers of wool and yarn or of the common beam whose duties were defined in 1614.[96]

Nearly all the 'inferior ministers', who seem almost ludicrously abundant for so small a place, were elected yearly in the borough court. But there were some others who figure neither in these annual lists nor in the by-laws. A town chandler was appointed for a short period in 1556 and between 1559 and 1586 such a person seems to have been regularly in office. A by-law, recorded by 1614, gave him monopoly of the purchase of tallow brought into the town by outside butchers, retailing at a controlled price candles so produced.[97] In 1585 a keeper of the toll booth took charge of strays.[98] In 1623 a bellman was appointed to patrol the streets in winter, and give warning of the danger of theft and fires.[99] The office seems to have lapsed but to have been revived in 1646–7.[1]

The court of record, established *eo nomine* in 1605, was in 1614 an all-purpose assembly meeting weekly.[2] In 1615 it was still possible to fill vacant offices at its meetings.[3] Presumably, however, it confined itself increasingly to litigation, and the court of common council, so styled in 1657,[4] with administrative decisions. An 'attorney in the borough court' is first named in 1621.[5]

When the corporation reassembled at the Restoration it consisted of the mayor, 14 capital burgesses councillors, 32 capital burgesses, and 53 free burgesses,[6] a larger total, 100, than is recorded before. In 1662 it

92 *Constitutions.*
93 A crier's death in 1770 is recorded in a diary: Cunnington, *Annals*, ii. 254; see below, p. 148.
94 Cunnington, *Annals*, i (2nd pagin.), 112.
95 W.R.O. 844, Ct. Bk. 1556–7.
96 *Constitutions.*
97 Cunnington, *Annals*, i (1st pagin.), 7, 29, 37, 46, 49, 80; (2nd pagin.), 10.
98 Ibid. (1st pagin.), 88.
99 Ibid. (2nd pagin.), 73–5.
1 Ibid. 113; cf. ii. 150 (1658–9).
2 *Constitutions.*
3 Cunnington, *Annals*, i (2nd pagin.), 79.
4 Ibid. 125.
5 Sta. Cha. 8/181/27.
6 Cunnington, *Annals*, i (2nd pagin.), 127.

was 'regulated' by the Corporation Act commissioners and six capital burgesses councillors, 10 common councillors, the town clerk, and seven free burgesses were removed,[7] whether on political or religious grounds cannot be said. Not all were replaced and the corporation was reconstituted to consist of the mayor, recorder, 11 capital burgesses councillors, 24 common councillors, and 31 'freemen, and burgesses',[8] a total of 69.

Despite a futile effort in 1671 to secure some changes,[9] the borough constitution was not disturbed until 1684 when under threat of *quo warranto* the corporation surrendered their governing charter.[10] The 'obnoxious' charter, granted in 1685,[11] provided for a corporation of 60: a mayor, recorder, deputy recorder, 11 aldermen, 15 capital burgesses, and 31 free burgesses. The deputy recorder was to be appointed by his principal; the limit of actions in the court of record was raised to £50; the Parliamentary franchise was restricted to the members of the corporation; and the free burgesses, not being aldermen or capital burgesses, were limited to 35. There were also three non-constitutional provisions. A new fair was granted;[12] the common beams were confirmed as the only places for weighing wool and yarn;[13] and trading by interlopers was restricted.[14] In personal terms the effect of the charter was that a new recorder, Sir John Talbot, was appointed by name to replace Charles Danvers, who, likewise named, was demoted deputy. Talbot was promptly elected M.P. The mayor was continued and eight members of the old common council were dropped and replaced by seven, but three of these later refused to serve. One free burgess also refused the oath.[15]

On three occasions in 1688 James II, taking advantage of the clause customary in 'obnoxious' charters, regulated the corporation by Orders in Council. In January the mayor, 5 aldermen, 8 capital burgesses, and 7 free burgesses were removed and replaced by new ones, one extra free burgess being added.[16] In February 5 aldermen, 7 capital burgesses,

---

7 Cunnington, *Annals*, i (2nd pagin.), 134.
8 B.M. Add. MS. 32324, f. 148.
9 *Cal. S.P. Dom.* 1671, 185.
10 Cunnington, *Annals*, i (2nd pagin.), 174–5.
11 Ibid. 177; S.P. 44/335 ff. 403–6.
12 See p. 123.
13 Ibid.
14 See p. 88.
15 Cunnington, *Annals*, i (2nd pagin.), 177; W.R.O. 844, Entry Bk. 'D'.
16 Cunnington, *Annals*, i (2nd pagin.), 181–2.

and 10 free burgesses were replaced.[17] In March there was a third regulation of which we have no details.[18] The effect was to erode the 1685 corporation by stages and replace it by new men. The new mayor was an Independent in religion[19] and at least two other dissenters were intruded. In suffering these changes Devizes was of course in no way singular.

The common council, constituted according to the 1685 charter, met finally on 12 October 1688, when the mayor, 9 other aldermen, and 16 capital burgesses attended.[20] By 18 October the proclamation in effect restoring all pre-1679 borough charters was issued and on 22 October a new mayor was elected.[21] He was the elder Francis Paradise who had been ejected in the preceding January.

Since there were no striking constitutional changes between 1688 and 1835 the state of local government institutions can be reviewed for the period as a whole. The corporation continued to consist of the mayor, recorder, capital burgesses, and free burgesses, the first three elements forming the common council. By 1705 it had been reduced to 27, probably for political reasons, but seems to have risen in the next year to 54 by new elections.[22] By 1690 capital burgesses councillors had come to be fixed at 12 in number.[23]

The mayor presided over the common council, quarter sessions, and court of record.[24] By order made in 1657,[25] rescinded in 1661,[26] but at an unknown date revived he remained a justice for the year following his mayoralty.[27] This arrangement naturally ended with the Justices of the Peace Act, 1968.[28] The mayor was chosen out of the capital burgesses councillors by a majority of the common council. Towards the end of the old corporation's life, in 1827, it was ruled that a simple majority of

17 W.R.O. 844, Entry Bk. 'D'.
18 Cunnington, *Annals*, i (2nd pagin.), 183.
19 Edw. Hope: see p. 207.
20 Cunnington, *Annals*, i (2nd pagin.), 85.
21 Ibid.
22 Soc. Antiq., Jackson MSS. v, f. 179.
23 *C.J.* x. 521.
24 Unless otherwise stated the following 12 paragraphs are based on *Rep. Com. Munic. Corps.* (1835), xxiv, pp. 1262–7 and Waylen, *Chrons.* 160–5 (2nd pagin.).
25 Cunnington, *Annals*, i (2nd pagin.), 125.
26 Ibid. 131.
27 It was so in C.W. Pugh's mayoralty, 1942–3.
28 1968, c. 69.

common councillors was enough to validate an election and that there need not be separate majorities of capital burgesses councillors and capital burgesses of the common council.

In 1615 it was decided that at each election two candidates should be proposed, by later custom by the mayor, and that the council should vote on these. In 1683 Pierce, a capital burgess councillor, proposed a third candidate which had the effect of eliminating the mayor's second candidate from the contest. Pierce's candidate won but for an unknown reason did not take up office.[29] The story of how in 1706 there were rival claimants to the mayoralty is so plainly a part of parliamentary history that it must be sought elsewhere.[30]

From at least 1614 the mayor was elected on Friday in Whitsun week and took up office, in accordance with the 1605 charter, on the following Michaelmas day. Persons refusing office were, by the same charter, liable to fines and this was also true of admission to other borough offices and to membership of the common council and to the free burgess-ship.[31] In 1673 a capital burgess renounced election to a capital burgess councillorship. He paid a voluntary fine and so retained his membership of the common council.[32] In 1741 the mayor's fine was fixed at £30 and in 1809 five capital burgesses of the common council paid the same fine in order not to proceed to the higher rank.

The mayor was receiving a salary before 1595, when it was raised substantially,[33] and there are constant references to such payments later on. In 1612 the allowance was as high as £30 because of the difficulty of getting mayors,[34] and in 1614 was higher still.[35] Thereafter there are repeated prohibitions[36] and restorations[37] of the allowance, which was reduced to £80 just before the Municipal Corporation commissioners arrived.[38] From at least 1653, the money, when paid, was often spent on feasting[39] but by the early 19th century was so insufficient for the purpose

29 Cunnington, *Annals*, i (2nd pagin.), 171.
30 See p. 171.
31 *Constitutions*.
32 Cunnington, *Annals*, i (2nd pagin.), 155–6.
33 Ibid. 29.
34 Ibid. 47, 64.
35 Ibid. 50.
36 Prohibitions in 1655, 1687, 1689, 1693, 1798: ibid. 122–3, 183, 186, 190–1; ii. 92.
37 It stood at £40 for a 'long period' before 1798, when it was stopped as a wartime economy: ibid. 92.
38 Ibid. 228.
39 Ibid. i (2nd pagin.), 131.

that capital burgesses, as explained above, preferred to be fined rather than qualify for the mayoralty and so assume its burdens. In 1971 the mayoral allowance was £300.[40]

The recorder was elected for life or during pleasure by the common council and was normally made a free burgess and councillor on the eve of his appointment. He did not in practice attend council meetings unless by-laws needed drafting.[41] He officiated at quarter sessions and was a judge in the court of record. In 1660 he received a salary[42] but by 1835 its payment had long ceased. By 1688 he was appointing a deputy[43] who commonly thereafter sat in council. None was appointed after 1826. The recorder was not required to reside and he often held his office concurrently with that of one of the borough M.P.s, the first office being a kind of stepping-stone to the second. Nearly all the known recorders up to 1844 at some time sat for Devizes.[44]

The capital burgesses councillors were elected by the common council out of the burgesses of the common council. The difficulty of finding candidates in the early years of the 19th century has been mentioned. It lessened after 1810. In the century after the Restoration importance was attached to both residence and good attendance, the second presumably being partially ensured by the first.[45] A laxer view was taken in 1784[46] and after.

The by-laws of 1614 enjoined attendance on the days on which the mayor was pre-elected and sworn and also on the two days of assembly, namely the Fridays after St. Andrew and Easter.[47] In 1631, however, the 'customary' election days were Michaelmas and the Fridays before and after.[48] In 1790 the 'Charter' days were these three, together with the mayor's election day, which was the Friday in Whitsun week.[49] Normally, of course, the council did not limit its meetings to these high days. It has been concluded that in 1688–1749 meetings were separated by a few days only and that the average frequency was monthly.[50] But the spirit of

40 *Municipal Yr. Bk.* 1971.
41 Regina *v.* Sutton: 10 Mod. 74.
42 Cunnington, *Annals,* i (2nd pagin.), 130.
43 Ibid. 185.
44 Cf. the lists in Waylen, *Hist.* 545–7, 581.
45 Cunnington, *Annals,* i (2nd pagin.), 155, 207–8, 211.
46 Ibid. 230.
47 *Constitutions.*
48 Cunnington, *Annals,* i (2nd pagin.), 87–8.
49 Ibid. ii. 1.
50 Ibid. i (2nd pagin.), 217 n.

the old by-laws, which aimed at compelling attendance, lived on despite the multiplication of meetings,[51] and could sometimes be effective.[52] After 1790, however, despite fines,[53] there were some poor attendances.[54]

The capital burgesses of the common council were elected by the common council from among the free burgesses. From 1731[55] efforts were made to keep all the vacancies filled, but latterly residence was laxly enforced. The number of free burgesses, by charter unlimited, steadily declined. In 1682, when Henry Baynton was admitted,[56] the practice still prevailed of introducing the local gentry. In 1688 the number was 34. In 1697 it was decided to limit the free burgesses to twenty[57] and thus to admit new ones only when vacancies on the common council had to be filled or compliments bestowed. In the end men were commonly admitted to the burgess-ship and the common council simultaneously. Addington was treated thus in 1784 and Thomas Tylee in 1805.[58] The honorary burgesses were either 'inferior' borough officers or M.P.s. Sir Paul Methuen, for example, M.P. 1708–10, was a free burgess by 1733.[59] The number stood at ten in 1728 and in 1738–1828 averaged a little over two. In 1835 there were four, none resident. At that time nomination had long rested with the mayor who was thus able to pack not only the corporation but until 1832 the constituency.

A few further remarks are needed about the 'lesser' borough officers. Of the three justices of the peace, one, called preeminently 'the justice', was chosen for life by the common council. He was unpaid and never in practice became mayor. He might, however, be also M.P., as T. G. B. Estcourt was in 1820–6, and this, especially when the recorder was also absent, was inconvenient. In 1835 there was a fortnightly petty sessional court, which, no doubt, the 'justice' effectively ran. He was not as such a judge of the court of record but probably he presided there as well. The steward and clerk of the courts was also town clerk and clerk of the peace and attended in practice the meetings of common council,

51 Cunnington, *Annals*, i (2nd pagin.), 146, 184.
52 Thus as many as 34 councillors attended in 1749 after an order of 1736 had imposed fines on unexcused absentees: ibid. 217.
53 Ibid. ii. 35.
54 Ibid. 1–2, 75, 81.
55 Ibid. i (2nd pagin.), 207–8.
56 Ibid. 166, which gives the date as 1683.
57 Ibid. 195–6.
58 Ibid. 231; ii. 26.
59 Ibid. i (2nd pagin.), 218.

of which he was at times a member. In 1707 he had power to depute.[60] He received a salary and court fees and was the corporation's solicitor. Over three generations from the mid 18th century the office was held by the Salmon family. The founder's son William amassed great wealth as an attorney and banker, and as manager of the corporation earned the name 'King Salmon'.[61] He it was who controlled the borough in 1816.[62]

The appointment of surveyors is not systematically recorded after Elizabeth I's reign but the office evidently continued[63] until abolished in 1780.[64] The chamberlains continued. They lost their salaries, like other officers in 1687,[65] but regained them later although they did not always collect them. In 1833 only one was effective at a time and they had then recently begun to serve two years or more. For some time before 1833 they habitually accounted only at the end of their terms but in 1832 an annual audit was established. The constables were already literate in 1662 when they were corresponding direct about enforcing tax payments by armed force.[66] In 1835 they were taken from the 'respectable' inhabitants and were regarded as the head of the police. The serjeants-at-mace, bailiffs, and sub-bailiffs continued up to 1833. The first two executed court judgements and were then paid, though the bailiffs' wages were cut off in 1682[67] and the sub-bailiffs' in 1687.[68] In 1833 the serjeants-at-mace had custody of those arrested or taken in execution by process in the court of record. One sub-bailiff was also beadle and the other hall-keeper. Searchers of leather and searchers or surveyors of fish and flesh also continued, though without duties in 1833. In 1688 the beadle was also aletaster.[69] The bellman still existed in 1674–5.[70] In 1736 a paid inspector of weights and measures was appointed.[71]

After the Restoration the common council was beginning to manage its affairs through committees. Two were set up in 1662[72] and

60 Ibid. 156–7.
61 Waylen, *Hist.* 465.
62 Oldfield, *Rep. Hist. of Gt. Britain*, v. 157–8.
63 Cunnington, *Annals*, ii. 151 (1658–9); and see above, p. 136.
64 21 Geo. III, c. 36, s. 48.
65 Cunnington, *Annals*, i (2nd pagin.), 183.
66 *Cal. S.P. Dom.* 1661–2, p. 275.
67 Cunnington, *Annals*, i (2nd pagin.), 167.
68 Ibid. 183.
69 W.R.O. 844, Entry Bk. 'D'.
70 Ibid. Entry Bk. 1660–81.
71 Cunnington, *Annals*, i (2nd pagin.), 209.
72 Ibid. 137.

again in 1685.[73] In 1666 something in the nature of a standing general purposes committee was created to meet at least quarterly. Not unexpectedly such committees are less frequent in the next century, though two were convened in 1732.[74] In 1809, during a period of stringency, there was a committee on market and fair tolls.[75] It seems to have stood until 1821,[76] although in 1812 a similar committee concerned with all aspects of the borough revenue was intercalated.[77]

The court of record, composed of the recorder (or his deputy) and three other common councillors, was required to sit weekly. Pleading was the same as in superior courts except in ejectment proceedings. The surviving records begin in 1653.[78] Owing to the low scale of fees and low level at which costs were taxed the court began to lose business by c. 1776 and there was hardly any after 1813. In 1810, however, it still possessed enough life to formulate practice rules and revise its table of fees.[79] In 1754–66 the assize of bread, which with the assize of ale and beer the mayor had been required to keep since 1614 at least,[80] was promulgated in the court.[81]

The court of quarter sessions, with a quorum of two justices, could try misdemeanours and minor felonies. Its records begin in 1657.[82] Then and until c. 1815 presentment juries, each of twelve, were summoned from the Old and New Ports.[83] After that time only trial juries were summoned. By 1833 there were few trials. In practice the county justices were excluded but they possessed in theory a concurrent jurisdiction.

It has been shown that the corporation had long owned much landed property and held much charity land in trust. It had also effectively enjoyed the profits of markets, fairs, and justice since 1510, and it raised money by penal fines from its members. As is to be expected, it had no rate income. When analysed in 1833 revenue arising from land made up

73 Cunnington, *Annals*, i (2nd pagin.), 177–8, 180.
74 Ibid. ii. 160.
75 Ibid. 34.
76 Ibid. 78.
77 W.R.O. 844, Min. Bk. ct. of common co. 1790–1826.
78 *W.R.S.* x. 14.
79 Cunnington, *Annals*, ii. 224. The rules were not known in 1833.
80 *Constitutions*.
81 Cunnington, *Annals*, ii. 223.
82 Ibid. i (1st pagin.), 90.
83 e.g. ibid. 90–5.

about 70 per cent of the total, the rest coming from tolls which since *c.* 1826 had been farmed as they often were in the past.[84] Of the land revenue about two-thirds was yielded by renewals of leases and the rest from chief and quit rents. The rents whether upon freeholds or leaseholds were numerous and low, and the property was widely scattered. By long-standing custom most leases were for 99 years though a by-law of 1722 made provision for a shorter term, in practice 60 years, or for lives. Leases were commonly renewed when half their terms had run. It had been the recent practice to sell the reversion where corporation property was mixed with another owner's.

The chief sub-heads of expenditure were salaries (*c.* 36 per cent), mainly to the mayor, and the service of debt (*c.* 25 per cent). In the mid 18th century much of the latter arose from borrowings from charity funds especially from the alms-houses. In the late 18th and early 19th centuries the borough M.P.s presented the corporation with substantial sums for the liquidation of the debt,[85] some of which gifts were spent on public buildings.[86]

As one of its first tasks the reformed corporation inquired into its financial legacy. The chamberlains, whose report was presented in 1836,[87] examined their predecessors' accounts from 1785. They discovered a debt of over £4,500, only partly secured, and excessive expenditure on mayors' feasts, loyal addresses, law expenses, and the decoration of the Town Hall. There was also no proper record of debts and contracts. On the revenue side insufficient income had been drawn from market tolls, owing in part to the cessation of the butchers' market to which the commissioners of 1833 had drawn attention.[88] While there is no doubt that by the standards of 1835 there had been much irregularity, it may be noted that one of the chamberlains was a Baptist,[89] to whom some of the expenditure could have seemed morally objectionable. The chamberlains also seem to have ignored the fact that before they reported the old corporation had resumed the farming of the tolls which they told the commissioners of 1833 was a better method of raising the revenue

---

84 See p. 115.
85 e.g. in 1812: Cunnington, *Annals*, ii. 23, 51.
86 See pp. 116-18, 120, 152.
87 Cunnington, *Annals*, ii. 227–34; Gillman, *Annals*, 33.
88 *Rep. Com. Munic. Corps.* (1835), xxiv, p. 1268.
89 Paul Anstie, a member of the late New Baptist chapel congregation: personal inf.

than the use of direct labour.[90] The corporation solved their problems by selling reversions and increasing rents. They also resolved to eliminate renewal fines.[91]

In 1781 a body of improvement commissioners to clean, light, and watch the town and repair the streets was appointed under an Act of 1780.[92] The Act provided for a board, made up of the corporation and 97 substantial townsmen, with a quorum of five. Seventeen persons attended the first meeting. The then mayor presided and William Salmon, to whom no doubt the innovations were due, became clerk and treasurer.[93] During the period for which minutes survive (1781–95) there is little to suggest that the board were very effective. From 1782 adjournments were frequent[94] and in 1790 it was necessary to find 22 new trustees to replace those who had died since 1780.[95] The board set rates, as statute allowed, both to defray capital expenses such as lamp standards and toll-houses and also to carry out its day-to-day routine. They were also empowered to levy a double Sunday rate on those passing through the turnpikes on that day and this power they exercised.[96] Most notable, perhaps, is the success with which they extracted gifts from James Sutton for the furtherance of their work and loans from him on the credit of the tolls.[97]

The first Act, having been officially pronounced insufficient, a new one was passed in 1825 in which paving was given first place and cleansing last. It appointed the corporation and 111 substantial inhabitants commissioners and repealed all the provisions of its predecessor except the power to impose Sunday tolls, which was retained for fourteen years. The quorum was nine. The Act was stronger and more professional than its predecessor. It required the audit of accounts, the separation of the offices of clerk and treasurer, and the maintenance of proper records. It prohibited fees and enjoined salaries. More important, however, were the clauses which vested the streets in the board and gave them power over the ensuing five years to acquire by what amounted to compulsory

90 *Rep. Com. Munic. Corps.* (1835), xxiv, p. 1268.
91 Waylen, *Chrons.* 216–20.
92 21 Geo. III, c. 36.
93 Cunnington, *Annals*, ii. 166.
94 Ibid. 170.
95 Ibid. 175.
96 Ibid. 166.
97 Ibid. 167–9, 173–5.

purchase specified properties and to compel builders to make up the service roads. None of the rating powers bestowed by the last Act was surrendered.[98]

William Salmon (II) was concerned with the successful promotion of the Act as were the borough M.P.s.[99] The latter also contributed to the improvements and in 1826 the public was incited to do the same.[1] The board certainly did not ignore its paving responsibilities, even making a proper road through the Market Place[2] which was vested in the corporation.[3] As Parliament had allowed, they also started a gas works in 1825, revised the watching arrangements in 1826, overhauled fire precautions in 1825 and 1827, condemned thatched roofs in 1826–7, and made minor improvements in the urban plan. All these achievements are elsewhere rehearsed.[4] The board also investigated and corrected nuisances in 1831.[5] In 1833 they sought to enlarge their powers by a new Act,[6] but the appointment of the Municipal Corporation Commissioners in that year no doubt discouraged them. Their minute books ceased in 1843,[7] and in 1867 their powers, which perhaps had been for some time dormant, were transferred to the corporation acting as the local board of health.[8]

By the Municipal Corporations Act, 1835,[9] the borough was reincorporated under the title, traditional since 1605,[10] of the 'Mayor and Burgesses of the Borough of Devizes', with 6 aldermen and 18 councillors. North and South wards were created, whose boundaries as delimited in 1835[11] were slightly varied shortly after.[12] An East ward was added in 1960 without altering the number of councillors.[13]

98   6 Geo. IV, c. 162 (Local and Personal).
99   Cunnington, *Annals*, ii. 180.   1   Ibid. 184.
 2   Ibid. 86.
 3   *Rep. Com. Munic. Corps.* (1835), xxiv, p. 1269; cf. 6 Geo. IV, c. 162, s. 25 (Local and Personal).
 4   See pp. 29, 166–7, 169.
 5   Cunnington, *Annals*, ii. 193–5; cf. 6 Geo. IV, c. 162, s. 39 (Local and Personal).
 6   Cunnington, *Annals*, ii. 194.   7   Ibid. 199.
 8   Gillman, *Annals*, 49–50.
 9   5 & 6 Wm. IV, c. 76.
10   This was the name in 1833: *Rep. Com. Munic. Corps.* (1835), xxiv, p. 1262. The charter of 1605 confirmed all liberties to the mayor and burgesses of the borough of Devizes or to the burgesses of the town of Devizes by whatever names of incorporation.
11   *Lond. Gaz.* 8 Dec. 1835, pp. 2428–9.   12   Waylen, *Chrons.* 195.
13   Stat. Instrum. 1960, no. 446.

A court of quarter sessions, of seven persons with the mayor, was set up on petition in 1836[14] and survived the Justices of the Peace Act, 1949. Devizes was the smallest town in 1949 to possess such a court.[15] A court of record was preserved in 1835[16] but had not met by 1840[17] and perhaps never did. It can have been little use after the creation of county courts.[18] Besides the statutory watch committee the council set up a finance committee, and appointed a treasurer, a town clerk (who was also registrar of the court of record), and a clerk of the peace. They retained the two chamberlains, who remained as unpaid custodians of borough property, the (chief) constables, and the liveried beadle, who was also hall-keeper and a policeman, and they abolished the serjeants-at-mace, and the steward and clerk of the courts.[19] The recordership was also preserved and the coronership restored.[20] No coroner, however, has been appointed since 1939 when the last one retired and all county coroners' districts were abolished.[21] Mock antiquarianism had by 1864 reunited the office of beadle with that of aletaster,[22] and by 1915 had fused aletaster and town crier.[23]

Fines for not attending council meetings and for declining office were preserved. New by-laws were presented.[24] Somewhat unexpectedly select newspaper reporters were from 1836 admitted to council meetings.[25]

Pursuant to the advice given in 1835 the borough treasurer had by 1837–8 sold off a number of reversions and rents, thus converting the properties into freeholds, and had leased many of the tolls. He had liquidated his debt to various charities. He had, however, inevitably ordered a borough rate since, despite savings, the borough had to bear new burdens formerly shouldered by the county or the parishes.[26]

14 Waylen, *Chrons.* 187.
15 Wilts. Cuttings, xxiii. 188.
16 Waylen, *Chrons.* 190.
17 *Return of Cts. of Request*, H.C. 619, pp. 164–5 (1840), xli.
18 See p. 74.
19 Waylen, *Chrons.* 182–5; H.O. 52/40, abstr. of accts.
20 Waylen, *Chrons.* 186.
21 *Wilts. Times*, 4 Feb. 1939, quoting Order under Coroners (Amendment) Act, 1926.
22 Gillman, *Annals*, 46.
23 *W.A.M.* xxxix. 133.
24 W.R.O. 844, Corp. Min. Bk. 1835–46, 23 Feb., 15 Mar. 1836.
25 Ibid. 5 June 1837.
26 H.O. 52/40, abstr. of accts.

Immediately after the Municipal Corporations Act the corporation fell into the hands of Whigs This situation lasted only until 1841.[27] Though there was a mayoral contest in 1845,[28] the corporation's conservative complexion remained unchanged until at least 1889.[29] Two Liberals, however, were elected in 1857 and Liberal mayors assumed office after 1889.[30] The first Labour councillor, R. P. Sheppard, was returned in 1929.[31]

In 1867 a local board of health was set up, coincident in membership with the borough council and in practice meeting on the same day.[32] At the same time much of the Improvement Act of 1825 was repealed and the commissioners abolished.[33] A paid clerk (who was the town clerk), surveyor, inspector of nuisances and collector, clerk of the gas works, and an unpaid treasurer were appointed.[34] In the natural course of events the local board became an urban sanitary authority in 1872 and was fused with the borough in 1889. The borough, however, for reasons which are not apparent, continued additionally to style itself an urban district up to 1933.[35]

During the later 19th century the borough officers remained substantially the same with the important exception that a medical officer of health was appointed in 1873.[36] In 1892 the clerk of the peace lost his fees and began to receive a salary.[37] The part-time offices of borough treasurer and town clerk were converted into full-time ones in 1948 and 1965 respectively.[38]

MUNICIPAL BUILDINGS. An 'old' town hall (*pretorium vetus*) stood in the New Port in 1451.[39] Beneath its successor, first mentioned in 1541,[40] a shop, called the Tolsey House, stood in 1563,[41] and six stalls in

27 Soc. Antiq., Jackson MSS. v, f. 176.
28 Gillman, *Annals*, 36.
29 Soc. Antiq., Jackson MSS. v, f. 176.
30 *Devizes Advertiser*, 20 May 1897.
31 Ex inf. Miss B. Sheppard.
32 W.R.O. 844, Min. Bk. Local Bd. 14 Dec. 1866, 1 Feb. 1867.
33 30 and 31 Vic. c. 67, confirming a provisional order. Twenty-six sections of the Act of 1825 were saved.
34 W.R.O. 844, Min. Bk. Local Bd. 5 and 25 July 1867.
35 e.g. Min. Bk. 9 Nov. 1933.
36 W.R.O. 844, Corp. Mins. 1862–75, 19 Sept. 1873.
37 Ibid. 1889–95, 6 May 1892.
38 Ex inf. Town Clerk.
39 W.R.O. 844, Skippet deed, no. 12.
40 *W.A.M.* l. 487 which gives the date wrongly. See W.R.O. 212A/36/2, deed, mayor to John Jonys.
41 *W.A.M.* l. 488.

1586.[42] In the later 16th century the council house, with a shop below it, adjoined the guildhall.[43] In 1648–50 a turret was added to the building, into which the market-bell and a new clock were then inserted; at the same time the building was gilded and ceiled.[44] In 1669–71 turret, 'town hall', and council house were repaired together.[45] From the earlier 16th to the later 17th century the guildhall was used for administrative assemblies and sessions of the borough courts;[46] the town armour was housed in the hall in 1625–6[47] and documents in the council house in 1635.[48]

In 1615–16 the yarn hall of earlier date[49] was rebuilt as the market-house for wool and yarn to the designs of one Andrews and other masons.[50] It was intended additionally as a meeting-place for county quarter sessions.[51] The corporation began to let it in 1625–6[52] and after 1641 did so commonly. The hall was repaired in 1627–8[53] and extensively in 1631–4.[54] In 1663–4 it needed 'propping up'.[55] From the late 17th century until its reconstruction in the early 19th century, it is nearly always called the Wool Hall, or else, to distinguish it from the hall built c. 1752, the Old Hall.[56] The cheese markets and fairs were moved into it in 1689[57] and by 1726 were located in what was called the 'lower Wool Hall'.[58]

In 1733 it was decided to build 'a new guild hall' 'behind' the Wool Hall[59] and next year to spend £300, offered by Sir Joseph Eyles, on 'rebuilding and repairing' the hall.[60] The designs of a Mr. Lawrence

42 E 178/2429.
43 W.R.O. 543/3, list of St. Mary's tenements (undated but later-16th-cent.).
44 Cunnington, *Annals*, i (2nd pagin.), 117–18.
45 Ibid. 154.
46 Ibid. i and ii *passim*.
47 Ibid. i (2nd pagin.), 80.
48 Ibid. 92.
49 See p. 119.
50 Cunnington, *Annals*, i (2nd pagin.), 64; W.R.O. 844, Entry Bk. 1583–1621, f. 270.
51 Cunnington, *Annals*, i (2nd pagin.), 64.
52 Ibid. 80.
53 Ibid. 82.
54 Ibid. 90–1.
55 Ibid. 141.
56 See below.
57 Cunnington, *Annals*, ii. 155.   58 Ibid. 159.
59 Ibid. 160. The undated min. so directing stands between mins. of the 14 Dec. 1733 and 27 Apr. 1734 meetings.
60 Ibid. 208.

were approved soon after.[61] It seems that the construction of a completely new hall was discarded in favour of altering the existing Wool Hall by adding to it a council chamber in which the common council sat from 1735.[62]

The 'old' hall, as depicted in 1759,[63] was a two-storeyed brick building with a hipped slate roof. The lower storey formed an open courtyard, presumably for the display of merchandise. The principal front was of five bays, having a Tuscan colonnade below, supplied in 1629,[64] and sash windows above. The central entrance was flanked by Corinthian columns which rose through both storeys and supported a pediment; above was the clock turret surmounted by a bell cupola. By 1792 the lower storey seems to have been enclosed by walls in which windows were inserted.[65]

St. John's Street in the earlier 18th century, showing the Wool or 'Old' Hall, rebuilt between 1806 and 1808

In 1750 it was decided to pull the guildhall down and in its place to erect a 'public hall' to be set upon piazzas.[66] The site chosen was on

61 W.R.O. 844, Entry Bk. 'D', 17 May 1734.
62 Cunnington, *Annals*, ii. 160.
63 Dore, Map, 1759.
64 Waylen, *Chrons.* 152 (2nd pagin.).
65 A. Robertson, *Topog. Survey of the ... Road from London to Bath*, ii, pl. facing p. 84. The building here appears to be of 3 bays.
66 Cunnington, *Annals*, i (2nd pagin.), 220.

the south side of Wine Street. A decision reached in 1751 to build the new hall around a courtyard, which might be used as a poultry market,[67] cannot have been effective, for the building of 1973 is a solid block. The hall seems to have been nearly finished by 1752[68] and completely so by 1759.[69] Unexpectedly the corporation used it mainly as a market-house, banishing the markets from the Wool Hall, and using the latter for its current business. Of this there are two signs. When in 1791 the corporation gave a lease of the Wool Hall, they reserved to themselves not only the 'upper' hall but their right to use the whole building on certain 'public occasions'.[70] Secondly, when the hall was condemned to reconstruction (see below), directions were given to fit up the 'new' one for public business.[71] If the 'new' hall had become the corporation meeting-place, such directions would have been meaningless. In 1785–7 the hall was being used as a militia arsenal.[72] On completion of the covered Market House in 1803 many marketing activities were transferred to it.[73]

In 1803 James Wyatt condemned the 'old' hall as beyond repair[74] and with further benefactions, each of £1,000, from Smith and T. G. B. Estcourt, M.P., (Addington's successor) it was substantially rebuilt between 1806[75] and 1808[76] to the designs of Thomas Baldwin of Bath.[77] The front was pulled down and replaced by a new sessions court on the ground floor and a spacious assembly room with fine plasterwork above. The walls forming the rear of the old building were retained[78] but the interior was altered to provide a council chamber, with attached muniment room, on the first floor. Below it was an enclosed open space into which the cheese market was moved from the 'New' hall in 1810.[79] This area was still called the cheese hall in 1972. The sessions court had

67 Cunnington, *Annals*, i (2nd pagin.), 221.
68 Ibid. ii. 162.
69 Dore, Map, 1759. This depicts the hall, but shows it with a turret that it no longer possesses, if it ever did.
70 Cunnington, *Annals*, ii. 3.
71 Ibid. 19, 29.
72 Ibid. i (2nd pagin.), 241.
73 See p. 120.
74 Cunnington, *Annals*, ii. 17.
75 Ibid. 27.
76 Ibid. 279.
77 Ibid. 26.
78 Ibid. 34.
79 See p. 119.

Town Hall, as rebuilt 1806–8, depicted *c.* 1840

been converted into offices by 1961. Between 1825 and 1830 iron palisades were placed at the north end of the building.[80]

In 1809 it was resolved to lease out the 'New' hall. With an unexpected regard for amenities the corporation resolved to preserve its external appearance.[81] In 1825 the hall was sold[82] and has since been put to literary and commercial uses.[83] William Cunnington (II) bought it in 1836 to house his wine and spirit business[84] and in 1871 his son William (III) erected a clock on the façade.[85]

A weavers' hall is first mentioned in 1586, when it was described as very ruinous.[86] The corporation, then its *de facto* owners, mended it in 1595–7.[87] Fruitless attempts to let it were made in 1599–1601.[88] In

80 Cunnington, *Annals*, ii. 233.
81 Ibid. 38.
82 *Guide* (1946), 32.
83 Waylen, *Hist.* 576.
84 *W.A.M.* xxx. 160.
85 Gillman, *Annals*, 53.
86 E 178/2429. Presumably it had been the hall of the guild or company of weavers and clothiers, existing in 1565 (see p. 84). Kite (*W.A.M.* iv. 163) spells it Weaver's Hall.
87 Cunnington, *Annals*, i (2nd pagin.), 27; W.R.O. 844, Ct. Bk. 1583–1621, ff. 167, 171v.
88 Cunnington, *Annals*, i (2nd pagin.), 34, 36, 37 and see below, p. 235 n. 56.

1607 it was a seat for county quarter sessions.[89] In 1614 it was assigned to the three craft guilds and remained to their use until upon their dissolution in 1770 they surrendered it.[90] In 1707 a common council was held in it.[91] It possessed a chapel (1586)[92] with a little room in it (1595),[93] stairs (1595),[94] and a buttery (c. 1617).[95] It seems to have stood on the north side of Wine Street.[96] The map of 1737–8, however, shows the guildhall in this position[97] and marks a 'Drapers' Hall' on the other side of the street exactly where the 'New' hall now stands. That hall appears to have covered the guildhall site after that building had been demolished. 'Drapers' Hall' could be another name for the weavers' hall assigned to the craft guilds, which included drapers. The map, however, must not be trusted too far since it assigns at least one improbable street name.[98]

A town prison is first mentioned in 1556[99] and is doubtless 'the ward' to which from 1559 delinquents were committed by the borough court.[1] By 1581 both bailiffs' and serjeants' wards existed.[2] The first of these can be traced from 1560,[3] and in 1643[4] was distinguishable from the 'blind house', mentioned from 1584[5] until 1737–8.[6] About 1655 a new prison was built 'at the end' of the market-house or Wool Hall,[7] but, somewhat unexpectedly, this was 'pulled down' in 1660–1 and the 'old prison' repaired.[8] In 1737–8[9] what is called the 'Mayor's new prison',

---

89 Cunnington, *Annals*, i (2nd pagin.), 42.
90 *W.A.M.* iv. 163, 167, 174.
91 W.R.O. 844, papers concerning disputed mayoral election, extract order 21 Apr. 1707.
92 E 178/2429.
93 W.R.O. 844, Ct. Bk. 1583–1621, f. 157v.
94 Cunnington, *Annals*, i (2nd pagin.), 27.
95 Ibid. 55.
96 *W.A.M.* iv. 174 and n.
97 W.A.S. Libr., Devizes, Map, 1737–8.
98 See p. 22.
99 Cunnington, *Annals*, i (1st pagin.), 5.
1 e.g. ibid. 29.
2 Ibid. 75.
3 Ibid. 39.
4 Waylen, *Hist.* 144.
5 Cunnington, *Annals*, ii. 130.
6 Ibid. i (2nd pagin.), 239.
7 Ibid. 122.
8 Ibid. 132.
9 W.A.S. Libr., Devizes, Map, 1737–8. The words sprawl so that the exact location is speculative.

probably replacing the 'blind house', seems to have stood near the south end of the Wool Hall. It may have been out of use in 1774, for Howard found town prisoners in the bridewell.[10] When the Town Hall was rebuilt in 1806–8 a cell, which still survived in 1973, was fitted into its southern end.

A gallows was mended in 1596 and 1623[11] and new made in 1642.[12] Its name was long preserved in Gallows Ditch,[13] which in 1787–8 was a suicides' graveyard.[14]

Apart from such shelter as the Town Hall could provide the corporation had no central offices until 1959 when they moved to Northgate House.[15] The town clerk, being until then a part-time officer, worked from his own premises.[16]

SEALS, INSIGNIA, RECORDS, AND CHIEF OFFICERS. The first common seal, of which the latten matrix broken in four and soldered together survives, is round, 2.375 in., and depicts the borough arms.[17] Legend, black letter: SIGILLUM COMMUNE BURGENSIUM DOMINI REGIS DIVISAR'. Impressions of the seal have not been traced. The matrix has been conjecturally assigned to the 14th or 15th century.[18]

The second common seal, of which the bronze matrix survives, is round, 2½ in., and also depicts the borough arms.[19] In base '1608', the year of execution.[20] Legend, humanistic: SIGILLUM COMUNE MAIORIS ET BURGENSIUM BURGI DOMINI REGIS DE DEVIZES IN COMITATU WILT'. Impressions survive appended to documents of 1748[21] and 1792.[22]

The mayor's seal, of which the silver matrix survived until about 1951 but has not since been traced, was round, 1.31 in., and also depicts

10 See p. 74.
11 Cunnington, *Annals*, i (2nd pagin.), 32, 76.
12 Waylen, *Chrons.* 153 (2nd pagin.).
13 See p. 22.
14 Cunnington, *Annals*, ii. 265–6.
15 Ex inf. Mr. S. O'Brien, Deputy Town Clerk, 1970.
16 See p. 149.
17 B.M. *Cat. of Seals*, ii, no. 4866. For illustrations see Cunnington, *Annals*, i, pl. facing p. xiii and *W.A.M.* iii, pl. facing p. 236.
18 Ll. Jewitt and W. H. St. John Hope (*Corporation Plate and Insignia*, ii. 412) suggests the earlier, Kite (*W.A.M.* x. 236) the later date.
19 B.M. *Cat. of Seals*, ii, no. 4865. For illustration see n. 17 above.
20 Cunnington, *Annals*, i. 45.
21 W.R.O. 212A/29/2, deed, mayor and burgesses to Price.
22 Ibid. 130/58B, deed, mayor and burgesses to Whitlock.

the borough arms.[23] Legend, humanistic: SIGILLUM OFFICII MAIOR*IS* BURGI DOMINE [sic] REGI [sic] DIVISAR'. Round the edges were the words 'Mr. Mathew Allar maior anno do' 1681'.[24] Impressions have not been traced. The dating is a puzzle. Kite thought the matrix was struck early in Elizabeth I's reign,[25] which the use of 'domine' would support. If he is right, then 1681 must be the year of recasting. A mayor's seal was, however, struck in 1665–6 by James Hughes.[26] This was either lost or abandoned in the more distant past or the matrix described above is much later than has been supposed.

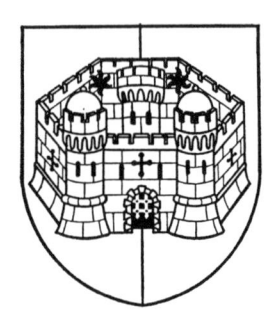

Borough of Devizes. *Parted palewise gules and azure, a gold six-sided castle in perspective, the port flanked by two domed towers, each dome surmounted by a star sable, and another tower rising above the gate* [Recorded 1565]

A silver seal was in the list of property to be surrendered by the old to the new mayor in 1660.[27] If this was the common seal, the 1608 seal, which is of bronze, must be its replica in base metal.

In 1893 an impress stamp die was substituted for the seals.[28] It was still used in 1971.

A mayor's mace existed in 1560[29] and by 1608 there were two, weighing 10 oz. each.[30] They were then replaced by two new ones, each

23 B.M. *Cat. of Seals*, ii, no. 4867. For illustration see *W.A.M.* iii, pl. facing p. 236.
24 Jewitt and Hope, *Corporation Plate*, ii. 412. A Matthew Allen was mayor 1681–2: Cunnington, *Annals*, i, p. xix.
25 *W.A.M.* iii. 236.
26 Cunnington, *Annals*, i (2nd pagin.), 144.
27 Ibid. 129.
28 Ibid. p. xiii.
29 Ibid. i (1st pagin.), 41.
30 Ibid. (2nd pagin.), 45.

weighing nearly 30 oz.[31] All or some of the maces were altered in 1625[32] and 1650,[33] to adapt them to new regimes. In 1660–1 the present two mayor's maces were made.[34] They are silver-gilt, 2 ft. 10½ in. long, chased with roses, thistles, and other floral devices, and divided into lengths by ornate bosses.[35]

In 1609 maces were provided for the serjeants.[36] These were no doubt the precursors of the two brass-headed constables' staves, which had existed shortly before 1895 and borne a portrait of Queen Anne and the royal arms, the date 1709, and an inscription testifying that they had been presented by John Smith, citizen of London and brazier to William III.[37]

A mayoress's mace, originally belonging to the rector, was discovered in St. John's church between 1838 and 1853 and was used by the mayoress, wife of Henry Butcher, its owner, when the foundations of the Corn Exchange were laid in 1857. In 1900 his relict presented it to the corporation.[38] It is not hall-marked.

The mayor's gold badge and chain, made by Messrs. T. and J. Bragg, were presented in 1879 by Sir Thomas Bateson, Bt., M.P., and the recorder, rector, town clerk, clerk of the peace, and coroner.[39] A replica for the mayoress, on a smaller scale, was acquired in 1952.[40]

A silver-gilt loving-cup, 15¼ in. high, hall-marked 1606–7, with 'AB' as the maker's name, was presented in 1620 by the mayor and twelve 'brethren'.[41] Known in 1940 and long before as a 'hanap cup', it is customarily carried before the mayor when he goes to church in state.[42] A silver punch bowl, hall-marked ?1734–5, and silver ladle, hall-marked 1740–1, both belonging to an obscure body called 'The Brittox Club', are also among the insignia.[43]

31 Ibid.
32 Ibid. 79.
33 Ibid. 118.
34 Ibid. 131.
35 Jewitt and Hope, *Corporation Plate*, ii. 411, with illustration.
36 Cunnington, *Annals*, i (2nd pagin.), 45.
37 Jewitt and Hope, *Corporation Plate*, ii. 411.
38 Gillman, *Dir.* (1940), art. by B. H. Cunnington; ex inf. Town Clerk.
39 Jewitt and Hope, op. cit. 411.
40 Ex inf. Town Clerk.
41 Jewitt and Hope, op. cit. 411, with illustration; ex inf. Town Clerk.
42 Gillman, *Dir.* (1940).
43 *W.A.M.* xxviii. 41–2.

Apart from the charters, nearly all the records up to 1900 were transferred to the county record office, Trowbridge, in 1966.[44] A list of those dated before 1836 has been published.[45] A list of mayors, 1302–1858, was published in 1859,[46] and for 1302–1906 in 1908.[47] A list from 1302 also hangs in the Town Hall, together with photographs of many ex-mayors since 1850. A list for 1554–1791 was issued in revised form in 1925.[48] Numerous additions, especially for the 14th and 15th centuries, can now be made. The names of a few recorders were published in 1859.[49]

PARISH GOVERNMENT. In a town in which borough government was fairly active the function of the parish officers was *pro tanto* lessened. Moreover the records, although for St. Mary's parish they are numerous and begin unusually early, are marred by chasms and do not tell a continuous story.[50] The two churches always possessed separate sets of parish officers and separate vestries. The churchwardens of St. John's have, so far as is known, always numbered two. By 1762 the practice of accepting the rector's nominee for one of the two offices was prevailing, a custom breached in 1805 but then resumed. It seems that from c. 1814 until 1830 the 'senior' churchwarden was reappointed from year to year.

There were three overseers for St. John's in 1762, one of whom was perhaps paid. In 1814 an 'extra' paid overseer was appointed, whose creation was held soon afterwards to have brought savings to the parish and comfort to the poor. In 1833 there were both a deputy and assistant overseers, the first of whom was paid. The vestry met with fair regularity from 1762. In April of that year the parish officers and eight others attended. In 1830 it was resolved to meet monthly to investigate minutely appeals for aid. This was at a time when the expenses of the poor were high.[51]

44 Ex inf. Mr. M. G. Rathbone, County Archivist.
45 *W.R.S.* v. 10–20.
46 Waylen, *Hist.* 578–81.
47 Gillman, *Annals*, 73–6.
48 Cunnington, *Annals*, i, pp. xviii–xx.
49 Waylen, *Hist.* 581.
50 Unless otherwise stated this paragraph and the next are based on W.R.O. 632/8–9, chwdns.' accts. 1758–1806 and vestry mins. and chwdns.' accts. 1805–54.
51 Higher in fact in 1829 and 1830 than in any other year between 1825 and 1832: *Poor Rate Returns*, 1830–1, 1835: H.C. 83, p. 221 (1830–1), xi; H.C. 444, p. 214 (1835), xlvii.

Between 1798 and 1812 rates were set by twelfths, one or two of such fractions being granted for the year. In 1812 it was said that the then poor-rate, which had stood at 19s. 6d. in the £ in 1803,[52] was 'unequal and defective' and a new one was ordered to be devised. After that time fractional calculations cease, and until 1832 rates, when set, are at 6d., 9d., and 1s. in the £, sums which occur with almost equal frequency. In 1822 agricultural land was derated by 12½ per cent and in 1831 by a further 15 per cent, except for the Old Park estate (Alfred Smith), which secured an abatement of 20 per cent.

Two churchwardens or proctors of St. Mary's may be traced from 1340–1.[53] In 1398 they are called keepers of church goods.[54] Since the church possessed landed property from the 14th century[55] the keepers needed a seal[56] of which there are a few 16th-century impressions. Between 1573 and 1576 they were chosen by the mayor 'and his brethren'.[57] From the mid-17th century it was the practice for each churchwarden to serve two years[58] and in 1655 it was settled in vestry that every rector should be empowered to choose one of the old churchwardens as his own warden.[59] This practice may not have lasted long. From 1772 the church property was managed by a body of feoffees.[60] In 1615 and 1618 there were four overseers, from 1619 only two.[61]

A vestry existed from 1655[62] and perhaps from 1637.[63] Long before this, however, the parishioners participated in parochial decisions, for in 1378 and in 1421 conveyances were made by the proctors, with the consent of the parish.[64] In 1655 the vestry ruled that the churchwardens might not spend more than £2 annually, except on the poor, without the consent of the parish.[65]

---

52 *Poor Law Abstract*, 1803, H.C. 175, p. 570 (1803–4), xiii.
53 W.R.O. 189/54, file of deeds, 1341–1589.
54 *W.A.M.* ii. 304.
55 In W.R.O. 189/34, files of deeds; cf. p. 177.
56 Two mutilated specimens (1584, 1588) will be found in W.R.O. 189/52. For a drawing, possibly somewhat imaginative, see *W.N. & Q.* vii. 193.
57 W.R.O. 189/1, chwdns.' accts. 1499–1633.
58 Ibid 189/2, chwdns.' accts. 1633–1734.
59 Ibid.
60 Ibid. 402/1, min. bk. of feoffees.
61 Ibid. 189/20, overseers' accts. 1614–72.
62 See above.
63 *W.N. & Q.* iii. 540.
64 W.R.O. 189/54–5, deeds 1341–1589, 1421–70.
65 Ibid. 189/2, chwdns.' accts.

The story of the Devizes poorhouses, with which the parish officers were naturally concerned, is obscure and patchy. In 1726 St. John's parish was trying to lease a site for a workhouse outside its own boundaries, at Gallows Ditch.[66] It is not known whether the attempt succeeded. In 1783 the 'Ark' was being used for this purpose.[67] Before 1776 there had also been a workhouse in New Park Street presumably belonging to St. Mary's parish.[68] In 1796 the two parishes were united for poor-law purposes under Gilbert's Act[69] and decided to buy a workhouse jointly.[70] By 1799 Anstie's former factory in New Park Street had been acquired as a 'house of industry'[71] but then,[72] as in 1802, St. Mary's parish was trying to withdraw from the agreement.[73] By 1809 the building had been abandoned[74] and in 1817 was sold.[75] The two parishes seem then to have parted company. St. John's moved its paupers to Short Street apparently to the alms-house which Sir John Eyles had given to the poor of the parish by 1668.[76] By 1826 that was thought to be unsafe.[77] Accordingly in 1828 a plot at the junction of Hare and Hounds Street and Southbroom Road was acquired by exchange and a combined alms- and poorhouse erected in 1829, known in 1885 as St. John's Buildings.[78] About 1834 there were 24 rooms of which 18 were occupied by paupers.[79] The building was not abandoned upon the building of the Union workhouse,[80] but was still used in 1901 when it comprised 16 rooms occupied by members of the Old and Eyles almshouse charities, who received no allowance but were relieved.[81]

66 Cunnington, *Annals*, i (2nd pagin.), 207.
67 Sar. Dioc. R.O., Glebe Terrier, 1783.
68 W.R.O. 212B/4/242, deed, Lacy to Beaven.
69 Wilts. Co. Council, *Guide to Rec. Office*, pt. ii, 86.
70 W.R.O. 632/107, overseers' accts. and memoranda, 3 Aug. 1796.
71 Ibid. 632/8, chwdns.' accts. 2 July 1799; see above, p. 90.
72 W.R.O. 632/8, chwdns.' accts. 2 July 1799.
73 Ibid. 11 May 1802.
74 Ibid. 632/9, chwdns.' accts. 14 June 1809.
75 Ibid. 23 Apr. 1817.
76 See p. 241.
77 W.R.O. 632/9 charity accts. 10 Nov. 1826.
78 *Endowed Char. Wilts.* (1908), lxxx, p. 392; W.R.O. 632/9, 18 Sept. 1828, 7 Apr. 1829; O.S. Map 1/500, Wilts. XXXIV. 14 (1886). For site plan see W.R.O. 632/27.
79 *Endowed Char. Wilts.* (1908), lxxx, p. 392.
80 See below.
81 *Endowed Char. Wilts.* (1908), lxxx, p. 445.

In 1810 the parish officers of St. Mary's sold some timber standing on their lands and therewith bought the site for a poorhouse, which they built.[82] It is not known for certain where this stood, but possibly near their Eyles houses in Short Street. In 1828 a combined alms- and poorhouse of 32 rooms was built at New Town in Commercial Road on the south of St. Mary's church, the Eyles's almspeople of St. Mary's being moved there too.[83] The parish paupers occupied 24 of the rooms but Eyles's benefaction was commemorated by a tablet on the new building which *c.* 1834 was said to be occupied as a 'parish poorhouse'.[84] After the Union workhouse was built the story of the New Town premises is part of that of the Eyles and St. Mary's alms-houses and is traced elsewhere.[85]

A Devizes Poor Law Union was formed in 1835[86] and a workhouse built in 1836[87] in Sedgefield Gardens. In 1947 it was renamed St. James's Home (Hospital from 1949) and became an old people's home.[88]

Churchwardens' accounts for St. John's exist for 1758–1806 after which year until 1853 they are combined with vestry minutes, which continue, perhaps only *quoad sacra*, until 1945.[89] There are overseers' accounts from 1613 until 1848 with some gaps.[90] Churchwardens' accounts for St. Mary's (1499–1734),[91] overseers' accounts (1614–1736),[92] and vestry minutes (1808, 1833–1928)[93] survive. The most significant *Nachlass*, however, is the parish deeds which are fairly abundant from the 13th century.[94]

PUBLIC SERVICES. The streams that flow through the old park can have been of little use as a town water supply. A spring once gushed from the slope which descends from Northgate Street to Station Road. It was called the King's Well from 1595,[95] and may originally have helped

---

82 Ibid. p. 403.
83 *Endowed Char. Wilts.* (1908), lxxx, p. 455.
84 Ibid. pp. 401, 455, 457.
85 See pp. 241–2.
86 *V.C.H. Wilts.* v. 253, 294
87 Gillman, *Annals*, 33.
88 Gillman, *Dirs.* (1947, 1949).
89 W.R.O. 632/7–13.
90 Ibid. 632/107–18.
91 Ibid. 189/1, 2.
92 Ibid. 189/20, 21.
93 Ibid. 189/4, 5.
94 Some of the documents have been published in *W.A.M.* ii. 302 sqq.
95 Waylen, *Hist.* 586.

to feed the castle, though there was a well within the castle walls.[96] As late as the 1830s it flowed from a grotto into a walled pond from which water was supplied to Waylen's factory in Northgate Street. When the railway and access road were built, the spring was sealed and now lies below the bed of both.[97] It is uncertain whether the watercourse at the north gate, mentioned in 1451,[98] is that same spring.

The town has had many wells, often sunk to a depth of more than 90 ft. to penetrate below the Greensand.[99] In 1905 a few were still in use, notably one under Wadworth's which survived in 1971.[1] In 1702 the well water was held to be bad and attempts were made to pipe a better supply from a spring under Roundway, presumably Mother Anthony's Well.[2] Nothing was then done and 27 years later Stukeley commented on the continuing shortage,[3] which may thenceforward if not earlier have limited the town's growth.

In 1792 James Sutton offered to build a reservoir near the shambles. The offer was accepted[4] and by 1837 such a tank lay below that building.[5] Between 1807[6] and 1838[7] vain efforts were made to induce the Canal Company to provide lock water for fire extinguishment and street-watering. By 1839, however, a tank for the latter purpose had been built and another was then under construction.[8] One of these was in Couch Lane.[9] In 1843, however, supplies were still considered inadequate for fire extinguishment.[10] Efforts to improve the supply were made between 1866 and 1868 but were fruitless, the view prevailing that wells were enough.[11] By 1877, however, it had become clear that this was wrong and a water-works was begun at Shepherd's Shore in Bishop's Cannings parish. Its history belongs elsewhere.[12]

96 E. H. Stone, *Devizes Castle*, plan facing p. 114.
97 *Devizes Gaz.* 21 Mar. 1895.
98 W.R.O. 844, Skippet deeds, no. 12.
99 Waylen, *Chrons.* 328.
1 *Water Supply Wilts.* (H.M.S.O. 1925), 57–8. In 1971 Wadworth's well was used only for cooling: ex inf. Mr. Bertwhistle, Wadworth & Co.
2 *V.C.H. Wilts.* vii. 187.
3 *Itinerarium Curiosum* (1776 edn.), Cent. i. 145.
4 Cunnington, *Annals*, ii. 10.
5 Ibid. 197.
6 Ibid. 31.
7 Ibid. 198.
8 Waylen, *Chrons.* 171.
9 W.R.O., Tithe Map, Southbroom.
10 Cunnington, *Annals*, ii. 198.
11 Gillman, *Annals*, 48, 51.
12 Ibid. 56; *V.C.H. Wilts.* vii. 188.

In early days street maintenance, when not provided charitably,[13] was a corporation responsibility. 'Waymen' and surveyors existed by the later 16th century.[14] In 1614 the waymen were levying a highway rate, managing lands allotted to the highways, and presenting defaulters.[15] Digging pits in the streets had been prohibited by 1614[16] and in 1632 frontagers were directed to repair the streets in which they lived;[17] the order was repeated with variations in 1641–2.[18] Surveyors were still being appointed in 1770.[19] It was stated in 1724 that the surface of two main roads through the town was so bad that carriages were often broken when they had crossed the borough boundary.[20] The Improvement Commissioners appointed in 1781 included paving among their functions. They were somewhat inactive on this front, but did promise in 1783 that those who paved their frontages should receive allowances.[21] In 1784 and 1787 they sought contractors to pave the turnpike roads from Rowde Ford to Shepherd's Shore and from the east end of the town to Redhorn Hill (in Urchfont) in their passage through Devizes.[22] The succeeding Improvement Act of 1825 vested the streets in the board and empowered them to pave.[23] Their most conspicuous work, however, was in effecting minor alterations in the plan.[24]

By 1614 frontagers had become obliged to clean the areas before their doors once a week and after fairs and remove the muck, and the town scavengers[25] were to see that this was done and to ensure the cleansing of gutters and ditches. Swine were not to wander.[26] The corporation expressed itself in favour of clean streets in 1732,[27] but systematic scavenging can be said to date only from 1781, when the Improvement Commissioners, charged to supervise this service, appointed the first paid scavenger.[28] For many years the work was carried out by

13 See p. 245.
14 See p. 136.
15 *Constitutions*.
16 Ibid.
17 Cunnington, *Annals*, i (2nd pagin.), 89.
18 Ibid. 98–100, 102.
19 Ibid. ii. 254.
20 Waylen, *Chrons*. 271.
21 Ibid. 171.
22 Ibid. 171, 173. This is road 1 mentioned in *V.C.H. Wilts*. iv. 266.
23 6 Geo. IV, c.162, ss. 22, 24 (Local and Personal).
24 See p. 29.
25 See p. 136.
26 *Constitutions*.
27 Cunnington, *Annals*, ii. 160.
28 Ibid. 167.

contractors, changing periodically.[29] In 1825 the second board seems to have appointed a permanent cleansing inspector.[30] In 1791 the town was divided into three scavenging districts[31] and in 1794 separate scavengers for the two parishes were chosen.[32] In 1785 the public were charged to cleanse the footways beside their houses,[33] a requirement that became statutory in 1825.[34]

By 1833 the corporation had long maintained a main sewer,[35] and the Improvement Commissioners of 1825 were empowered to explore for contaminated water.[36] The lack of water, however, already mentioned, impeded the development of good sewerage, since water closets could not be built in any number.[37] Although attention was drawn to the situation in 1848,[38] it was not until 1869 that a drainage system for the whole town was decreed.[39] Deep drainage below the Market Place had been sanctioned four years earlier.[40] At first the crude sewage seems to have been discharged into the two streams that traverse the old park. While the northern stream carried it away well enough, the southern one became clogged where it passed under Marsh Lane and aroused protests from the Rural Sanitary authority.[41] This led to the construction of a proper sewage works, modelled on that at Oswestry (Salop.), on the north side of the former parkland. It was completed by 1886[42] and extended in 1892[43] and 1895.[44] The septic system of disposal was in full operation by 1905.[45]

A cemetery at Belvedere was opened in 1879[46] and extended eastwards in 1958.[47] A bathing place in pound no. 24 on the canal, behind

29 Cunnington, *Annals*, ii. 171, 175–6.
30 Ibid. 183.
31 Ibid. 175.
32 Ibid. 176.
33 Ibid. 172.
34 6 Geo. IV, c.162, ss. 37–8 (Local and Personal).
35 *Rep. Com. Munic. Corps.* (1835), H.C. 116, p. 1267 (1835), xxiv.
36 6 Geo. IV, c. 162, s. 65 (Local and Personal).
37 W.A.S. Libr., Devizes, Devizes MSS. no. 28.
38 Ibid.
39 Gillman, *Annals*, 52.
40 Ibid. 47.
41 W.R.O. 844, Corp. Mins. 1882–9, 17 Dec. 1884.
42 Ibid. 1 May 1885; 17 Dec. 1886.
43 Ibid. 1889–95, 16 Dec. 1892.
44 Decision to enlarge: ibid. 9 Nov. 1894; works in progress: ibid. 1 Feb. 1895.
45 R. D. Gillman, *Popular Guide to Devizes*, p. iii.
46 Gillman, *Annals*, 57.
47 Wilts. Cuttings, xxi. 3.

the secondary school, was constructed in 1878[48] and opened to women in 1890.[49] In 1936 it was replaced by a public swimming bath in Colston Road.[50]

Devizes was visited by the plague in 1604, 1607, and 1644[51] and by the last year contained a pest house.[52] There were small-pox visitations in 1767, 1769, 1785, 1794, 1806, and 1810. Inoculation was being practised by the first year and there were general inoculations in 1785, 1806, and 1820.[53] A pesthouse stood, c. 1831, on the east side of Pans Lane,[54] and is perhaps the same as that mentioned in 1644 and between 1787 and 1791.[55] A cholera hospital was provided in 1832 by the local Board of Health which had been set up in the preceding year to contend with the threat from that disease. The board was dissolved in 1833.[56] Attempts in 1866 to provide such a hospital anew were defeated,[57] but in 1873 an infectious-diseases hospital was built beside the canal just north of the present course of Victoria Road.[58] It was transferred from the cottage hospital managers in 1875[59] and enlarged in 1883[60] and 1893.[61] Between 1903 and 1911 it moved to a new site in Pans Lane close to what is now Roundway Hospital,[62] but by 1956 the building which housed it had become a maternity hospital.[63]

In 1832 a dispensary was established in Snuff Street with one resident and a rota of visiting physicians.[64] Between 1859 and 1871,

48 W.R.O. 844, Corp. Mins. 1875–82, 15 Mar. 1878.
49 Ibid. 1889–95, 20 June 1890.
50 Date stone.
51 *V.C.H. Wilts.* v. 319–20.
52 Waylen, *Chrons.* 321.
53 Cunnington, *Annals*, ii. 48, 253, 264, 270; W.R.O. 632/9, chwdns.' accts.
54 *Rep. Bdy. Coms.* iii (i), H.C. 141, map facing p. 103 (1831–2), xl.
55 Cunnington, *Annals*, ii. 230.
56 Ibid. 193; Waylen, *Chrons.* 321. Although the St. John's vestry mins. state that the board was formed in Aug. 1832 there seems little doubt from the second source that it existed in 1831. The pest-house is marked on *Rep. Bdy. Coms.* (1831–2), map facing p. 103.
57 Gillman, *Annals*, 48.
58 W.R.O. 844, Min. Bk. Local Bd. 3 May 1872; O.S. Map 1/2,500, Wilts. XXXIV. 14 (1886 edn.).
59 W.R.O. 844, Corp. Mins. 1862–75, 23 Apr. 1875.
60 Gillman, *Annals*, 59. Site visible on plan of 1897: W.A.S. Libr., Devizes, sale cat. viii, no. 63.
61 Gillman, *Annals*, 64.   62 *Kelly's Dirs. Wilts.* (1903, 1911).
63 O.S. Map 6", SU 06 SW. (1961 edn.).
64 Gillman, *Annals*, 30; Wilts. Cuttings, v. 151.

when it was called the North Wilts. Dispensary, it had moved to Northgate Street[65] and by the next year to Monday Market Street.[66] It seems to have maintained a kind of independence in 1879,[67] although by 1873 it was in some form combined with the hospital, and served as an out-patients' department.[68] It was closed in 1888.[69] A cottage hospital in New Park Road was opened in 1872,[70] earlier efforts made in 1824 and 1832 to establish a local hospital having failed.[71] It was enlarged in 1887,[72] c. 1897,[73] as jubilee memorials, in 1911, with a benefaction from Alexander Grant Meek,[74] in 1921 as a memorial to Edward VII,[75] and in 1936, when private wards were provided.[76]

In 1815 Richard Trueman was licensed to receive into the Knoll, his home on Dunkirk Hill, a maximum of ten lunatics.[77] His daughter married Thomas Phillips, who took over the business and moved his patients before 1839 to a building behind the Old Crown, New Park Street.[78] By 1841 the establishment had moved again to Bellevue[79] and there it remained until at least 1862, although its licence for pauper patients was withdrawn in 1854, two years after the county lunatic asylum (now Roundway Hospital) had been opened.[80] It held 100 patients in 1841 and 156 in 1844, most of whom were paupers.[81]

Lighting was one of the responsibilities of the first board of Improvement Commissioners and in the year of their appointment lamp posts were erected throughout the town.[82] By 1824 the corporation discussed a plan to light the town by gas, and, favouring it, concluded

65 Gillman, *Dirs.* 1859, 1873.
66 Ibid. 1872.
67 Annual report: Wilts. Tracts, xcii.
68 Gillman, *Dir.* 1873.
69 Char. Com. recs.
70 Gillman, *Annals*, 53; *V.C.H. Wilts.* v. 343.
71 Waylen, *Chrons.* 322.
72 *Kelly's Dir. Wilts.* (1931).
73 Gillman, *Annals*, 67.
74 *W.A.M.* xxxvii. 492; xl. 80.
75 *Kelly's Dir. Wilts.* (1931).
76 Ibid. (1939).
77 Cunnington, *Annals*, ii. 209.
78 Wilts. Cuttings, v. 151; Pigot, *Nat. Com. Dir.* (1830); Robson, *Com. Dir.* (1839), ii.
79 Pigot, *Nat. Com. Dir.* (1842).
80 *V.C.H. Wilts.* v. 330–1, where there is a brief history; W. L. Parry-Jones, *Trade in Lunacy*, 255.
81 Parry-Jones, op. cit. 42.
82 21 Geo. III, c. 36, ss. 20, 25; Cunnington, *Annals*, ii. 167–8.

that a new Improvement Act would be required, with enlarged powers.[83] The Act was passed in the next year and the new Commissioners promptly set about promoting a gas supply not only for street-lighting but for private consumption. A site for a gas works beside the canal convenient for unloading fuel, was secured from the wharf company.[84] The works was opened in 1827 and by 1858 had been enlarged several times.[85] The gas company was taken over on nationalization and about 1955 the gas works was closed.[86] Since then gas has been piped into the town from Bath. The gas-works chimney was felled in 1961.[87]

The firm of Brown and May began to supply electric light in 1897.[88] By an Act of 1904, confirming Board of Trade orders, the corporation were constituted undertakers and mains were laid.[89]

Punishments for creating fire hazards were laid down in 1614.[90] The borough ordered its first known fire engine in 1641.[91] In 1731 it purchased one of Richard Newsham's.[92] In 1825 the second body of Improvement Commissioners tried to secure a proper supply of water for fire-fighting; they drew up regulations for stowing and mending the engine and provided fire-fighting appliances to be kept in the shambles. Master bricklayers and carpenters were to attend fires with axes and act as special constables.[93] There were still complaints about a lack of water in 1843[94] when a new fire engine was supplied.[95] A fire brigade was established in 1868[96] and reorganized in 1886.[97] From 1885[98] until c. 1962 the engine house stood at the west end of Short Street, but by 1927 the engine had been moved to Estcourt Street.[99] In 1967 a new

83 Cunnington, *Annals*, ii. 80.
84 Ibid. 82–3.
85 Gillman, *Dir.* (1858).
86 *Wilts. Gaz.* 24 Dec. 1958.
87 Wilts. Cuttings, xxii. 19.
88 *Devizes Advertiser*, 20 May 1897.
89 4 Edw. VII, c. clxxviii (Local Act).
90 *Constitutions*.
91 Cunnington, *Annals*, i (2nd pagin.), 98.
92 Ibid. 208. For Newsham see *D.N.B.*
93 Cunnington, *Annals*, ii. 181–2, 187; 6 Geo. IV, c. 162, s. 54 (Local and Personal).
94 Cunnington, *Annals*, ii. 198.
95 Ibid. 199.
96 W.R.O. 844, Min. Bk. Local Bd. 7 Feb. 1868.
97 Ibid. Corp. Mins. 1882–9, 19 Mar. 1886.
98 O.S. Map 1/500, Wilts. XXXIV. 14 (1886 edn.).
99 Ex inf. Mr. R. E. Sandell.

station was built by the county council, in opposition to local opinion, on the south side of Heathcote House.[1]

From the 16th century there was a formidable array of peace officers. Headed by the constables, they included bailiffs, serjeants-at-mace, and 'aldermen', all of whom were in some way involved under the by-laws of 1614. Arresting and imprisoning vagabonds and others, presenting offenders, especially the drunken and unlawful gamesters, and attendance upon the courts were among their functions. In addition all inhabitants were to store in their shops and other places such arms as might be needed to keep the peace and in theory they were, under the constables' superintendence, to keep watch.[2] A regulation of 1642 demanded that for a limited period all who paid the poor rate should act as or find wardsmen and watchmen, four of the former to be on duty by day and eight by night.[3] The duty of watch and ward was abolished in 1781.[4] The first Improvement Commissioners were among other matters to superintend the watching of the borough and were given power to correct a long list of nuisances.[5] They at once appointed four paid night watchmen to that end.[6] The men were ill-disciplined.[7] A superintendent was appointed in 1787 no doubt to check their behaviour,[8] but misconduct was still reported in 1795.[9] The ineffectiveness of the watchmen led to the formation of the Association for preventing Felony and other Offences. This was in existence by 1787 and remained so until at least 1793. It was succeeded in 1797 by the Devizes Prosecution Society which held meetings until 1867. It maintained a membership for some (probably a social) purpose until 1887 and a nominal existence until 1920. A competing body, the Devizes Mutual Protection Society, was formed in 1836. All three societies extended their membership to surrounding villages.[10]

1 Wilts. Cuttings, xxiii. 35.
2 *Constitutions.*
3 Cunnington, *Annals*, i (2nd pagin.), 102.
4 21 Geo. III, c. 36, s. 13.
5 Ibid. s. 48.
6 Cunnington, *Annals*, ii. 166.
7 Ibid. 170, 172.
8 Ibid. 173.
9 Ibid. 174, 176.
10 W.A.S. Libr., Devizes, Wilts. MSS. ii, nos. 9 and 10: Mins. of Assoc. for preventing Felony; mins., accts., etc. 1811–22, 1822–87, of Devizes Prosecution Soc.; *W.A.M.* xlviii. 444.

The second body of Improvement Commissioners, 1825, were required to watch the town as their predecessors had been.[11] They were at once impressed by the insufficiency of the police. This is not surprising since the regular appointment of watchmen had evidently lapsed. Four men were appointed in 1826 to work under the constable, and dissolute wanderers were placed under stricter control.[12] As before, however, there were cases of indiscipline,[13] and a new regulation of 1829 required the night constable, as he was now called, to patrol the town four times each night and report daily to the high constables.[14]

As soon as the Municipal Corporations Act, 1835, had transferred policing to the reformed corporation, the new watch committee informed the Home Office on the state of the police. Under the high (here called chief) constables there were four policemen, a night constable, and four constables acting as watchmen. By 1839 these last four seem not to have existed, but there were 30 special constables.[15] In 1835 the only station house was the night constable's house in the Brittox. The policemen were normally only on duty on market and fair days and on Sunday afternoons, but the night watchmen patrolled regularly. Shortly afterwards a single policeman was put in uniform and expected to be on duty six days a week.[16] The watchmen continued until the whole Devizes force was amalgamated with the county constabulary in 1847.[17]

The police station was in the old bridewell from c. 1836[18] until it was moved between 1855 and 1859 to the Town Hall.[19] It was in the Assize Courts from 1937[20] and in Barford House, St. John's Street, the former post office, from 1969.[21]

A postal service in Devizes is first recorded in 1674 and a postmaster in 1675.[22] In 1847 the post office stood at no. 44 Market

11 6 Geo. IV, c. 162, s. 66 (Local and Personal).
12 Cunnington, *Annals*, ii. 186–7.
13 Ibid. 189.
14 Ibid.
15 Waylen, *Chrons.* 185.
16 Cunnington, *Annals*, ii. 213–15.
17 Gillman, *Annals*, 37; cf. *V.C.H. Wilts.* v. 245.
18 It was closed as a prison in 1836: *V.C.H. Wilts.* v. 239. A writer in the *Devizes Advertiser* (20 May 1897) said that it became a police station 'after 1835'. In 1836 the grand jury room in the Town Hall had been surrendered as a police office: W.R.O. 844, Corp. Mins. 1835–46, 13 Apr. 1836.
19 *Kelly's Dirs. Wilts.*
20 Ibid. (1939).
21 *Wilts. Times*, 5 Dec. 1969.
22 Ex inf. P.O. H.Q.

Place where it remained until 1880. It was then successively at no. 39 (1881–7) and no. 24 (1888–1921).[23] In 1921 it was moved to Barford House,[24] St. John's Street, and thence in 1968[25] to the junction of Sheep and Maryport Streets, where it forms part of a block of offices consisting additionally of the local branches of the Departments of Health and Social Security and Employment and the County Court offices.

THE CONSTITUENCY. The borough of Devizes was first summoned to Parliament in 1295.[26] Out of the next 37 Parliaments to which boroughs were summoned and for which returns survive it was summoned to twelve. From 1331–2 until 1362, a period of decline,[27] it was not summoned at all. Of the 57 Parliaments, similarly defined, between 1363 and 1449 it was summoned to all but five. It was not summoned in 1459 or 1460. Afterwards, except in 1553, it was never omitted. In the first Protectorate Parliament of 1654 it was summoned with Salisbury and Marlborough alone,[28] a reflection of the true significance of Wiltshire towns at this time. Except in the first Parliament of 1384[29] and in 1654,[30] it was represented by two members until 1867. It then returned one until in 1885 it was merged with the Devizes division of Wiltshire.[31]

The return was made by the constable of the castle in 1322.[32] It has been said that in 1510–11 representatives were chosen in the county court.[33] In 1593,[34] and so far as is known at all other times, returns were made by the mayor and burgesses.

The uncertain element in the constitution was the body of burgesses, who were by charter unlimited in number. What looks like an attempt by the 'popular' element to contest the mayor's return in 1660 does not seem to have been pursued.[35] That element, however, apparently

23 *Devizes Advertiser*, 20 May 1897; Gillman, *Dirs*.
24 Ex inf. P.O. H.Q.
25 *Wilts. Gaz. and Herald*, 28 Nov. 1968.
26 The sources used for this computation are those given in *V.C.H. Wilts.* v. 72, n. 2.
27 See p. 127.
28 *V.C.H. Wilts.* v. 150.
29 *Return of M.P.s* i. 221.
30 *V.C.H. Wilts.* v. 150.
31 Ibid. 310, 312–13.
32 Ibid. 74.
33 T. B. Oldfield, *Rep. Hist. of Gt. Britain* (1816), v. 153.
34 Cunnington, *Annals*, i (2nd pagin.), 23.
35 Waylen, *Chrons.* 256–7.

swayed the election of 1679.[36] On petition the governing body's influence was re-established at the election to the Convention in 1688–9[37] and in 1697 the number of free burgesses was cut down.[38]

Over the years 1705–14 further election disputes troubled the peace of the town. On the death of a Whig member in 1706 the Tory recorder tried to secure the return of a Tory by alleging that the election precept had been addressed to a false mayor and by inciting to riot. The rioters were prosecuted, with Government support, and a Whig returned. In 1708 Tories again alleged that returns had been made by a false mayor. The House of Commons compromised by declaring both a Whig and a Tory elected. At the elections of 1710 and 1714 Tories secured both seats but on the second occasion attempts were made to unseat them. The disputes were characterized by each party trying to elect its own supporters as capital burgesses, forcing or persuading opponents to absent themselves from the council, and obstructing efforts to fill its vacancies.[39]

As shown elsewhere,[40] the corporation and therefore the electorate steadily declined in numbers from the end of the 17th century so that for the period 1715–54 the electorate could not unjustly be called 'a narrow self-co-opting oligarchy'.[41] As Oldfield cynically remarked in 1816, 'care is taken not to let the number of burgesses exceed that of the corporation who creates them'.[42] The estimates, however, of the size of the constituency, both at that time (32) and in the ensuing 35 years (c. 30), seem too low.[43] The statement made in 1816 that the voters numbered about 50[44] is, on the other hand, probably too high.

Although men who were not townsmen were beginning to sit in the 15th century,[45] the constituency was never in 'carpet-baggers'' hands.

36 V.C.H. Wilts. v. 156.
37 Ibid.; Waylen, Chrons. 259–61; Oldfield, Rep. Hist. v. 157.
38 See p. 142.
39 The incidents merit further exploration. The sources are Waylen, Chrons. 266–70 and Hist. 546; Cunnington, Annals, i (2nd pagin.), 203–5; Hist. MSS. Com. 29, Portland, viii, p. 352; Hist. MSS. Com. 7, 8th Rep. I, Marlborough, 45; the papers digested in W.A.M. xlvi. 533–4, now in the W.R.O.; W.R.S. x, p. 17; Cal. Treas. Bks. 1708, ii. 423, 442; Soc. Antiq., Jackson MSS. v, f. 179.
40 See p. 139.
41 Hist. Parl., Commons, 1715–54, i. 345.
42 Oldfield, Rep. Hist. v. 157.
43 Hist. Parl., Commons, 1715–54, i. 345; 1754–90, i. 411. The corporation consisted of 38 together with free burgesses who on the eve of the Reform Act were between two and four.
44 Oldfield, Rep. Hist. v. 157.
45 V.C.H. Wilts. v. 77.

No doubt the gentry were increasingly returned, but at least one member in each Parliament, through residence just outside or near the borough, maintained the local connexion.[46] In the 18th century large-scale clothiers dominated the constituency, but the local connexion continued to be preserved by the same means.[47] Only John Pearse (M.P. 1818–32), for long a director of the Bank of England and prosperous in the insurance world, was an interloper. Though the owner of an estate at Chilton Foliat,[48] he was a stranger to the town and twice had to fight election contests. T. H. S. Sotheron Estcourt, of New Park, who sat 1835–44, perpetuated the older tradition that at least one seat should be filled by a local gentleman.

During the 18th century the members were supporters of government.[49] In 1831 the representatives in Parliament, like the corporation, were opposed to Parliamentary reform and both members voted against this Bill.[50] After 1832 both parties were represented for a while,[51] but by 1841 the constituency had gone Tory and so remained for the rest of its existence.[52]

CHURCHES. The history of the churches of St. John the Baptist and St. Mary the Virgin is so closely interwoven that for part of its course it must be told as a single narrative. In 1194–5 the churches are called *ecclesie*.[53] In 1226–8,[54] however, they are *capelle* and that word was still being applied to them in 1275.[55] But from 1233,[56] they are again called 'churches', and even before that, in 1227, the 'parish' of St. John, with its 'parson', is referred to.[57] 'Church' is the word that has tended to prevail for both, but in the 17th[58] and 18th[59] centuries St. Mary's is sometimes

46 *V.C.H. Wilts.* v. 113, 121.
47 Ibid. 227, 229.
48 *Gent. Mag.* cv (2), 331.
49 *Hist. Parl., Commons,* 1715–54, i. 345; 1754–90, i. 411.
50 *V.C.H. Wilts.* v. 298–301.
51 Waylen, *Hist.* 547.
52 Ibid.; *V.C.H. Wilts.* v. 310.
53 *Cur. Reg. R.* 1194–5 (Pipe R. Soc. xiv), 109.
54 *Bk. of Fees,* i. 380.
55 *Rot. Hund.* (Rec. Com.), ii (1), 252. They were also called *capelle* in 1236 and 1247: *Close R.* 1234–7, 244; 1242–7, 525.
56 *Close R.* 1231–4, 327.
57 *Rot. Litt. Claus.* (Rec. Com.), ii. 204.
58 In 1648: *W.A.M.* ii. 329. In 1681 and 1690: P.R.O., Inst. Bks.
59 Ecton, *Thesaurus* (1763), 396.

called a 'chapel' once again. In 13th-century inquisitions St. Mary's is usually named before St. John's[60] but from the 14th century the order is reversed. An expression, first used in 1400,[61] namely, 'the church of St. John with St. Mary annexed', very fairly represents the subsequent relationship and seems by 1839 to have become the official designation of the cure.[62] But whether called 'churches' or 'chapels' the two have always formed a single cure under a single rector,[63] *rector ecclesiarum loci*, as he was called in 1322.[64] By a similar usage St. Mary's and St. Giles's in Reading have always counted as one church.[65] This unity, however, has not prevented St. John's and St. Mary's from enjoying distinct revenues and being served by distinct sets of parish officers.

It is a fair presumption that St. John's was originally the castle chapel, and in very early times the garrison may well have been large enough to fill it. As the town encroached upon the castle and the inner bailey in which the church or chapel originally stood contracted, the church became less convenient for castle use; the inmates of the castle were fewer and some of them were royal. Accordingly it became necessary to provide the castle with domestic chapels.[66] Nevertheless the connexion between the castle and St. John's remained for a while; in 1268 John, chaplain of the king's chapel, held both churches.[67]

Some time before 1194–5 Count John presented to the living.[68] This was presumably by usurpation and need not qualify the assertion that since 1226–8,[69] the Crown has been the patron, except during the currency of limited grants of the castle and castle estate. Thus the queens consort exercised it in 1310–92, 1412–14, and 1468–1547, and Humphrey, duke of Gloucester, in 1420–33. It has for long been exercised by the Lord Chancellor. The situation in the middle years of the 17th century

60 *Bk. of Fees*, i. 380 (1226–8); ii, p. 1422 (1249); *Rot. Hund.* (Rec. Com.), ii (1), 236 (1255); J.I. 1/998 m. 25 (1267); *Rot. Hund.* (Rec. Com.), ii (1), 252 (1275); J.I. 1/1005 m. 144 [146] (1281); J.I. 1/1006 m. 60d. (1289).
61 Phillipps, *Wilts. Inst.* i. 87.
62 The rectory of St. John the Baptist with the chapel of the Virgin Mary annexed: Waylen, *Chrons.* 224.
63 Phillipps, *Wilts. Inst. passim.*
64 Sar. Dioc. Regy., Reg. Martival, Ep. Sar. ii, f. 315v.
65 L. Harman, *Par. of St. Giles in Reading*, 7 and facsimile therein of bull of 1191.
66 See p. 54.
67 J.I. 1/998A m. 25 [24].
68 *Cur. Reg. R.* 1194–5 (Pipe R. Soc. xiv), 109.
69 *Bk. of Fees*, i. 380. Unless otherwise stated this paragraph is based on Phillipps, *Wilts. Inst.*

is not clear. In 1624 the corporation became perpetual lords of the borough in fee farm, and to them were assigned, in 1628, the 'advowson and possession' of the churches.[70] It is not known how far the corporation exercised its rights in practice. Between 1628 and 1681, when the Crown resumed presentation, four clerks held the cure: John Prestwich, Robert Byng, John Shephard, and Henry Johnson. The first was presented by an unstated patron in 1644,[71] Byng before 1646, when Shephard, instituted by order of the House of Lords in 1648, replaced him.[72] Johnson was presented in 1652,[73] it has been assumed by the corporation.[74] For unknown reasons the bishop presented in 1690.[75] It was said in 1839 that rectors had 'been usually appointed in accordance with the wishes and choice of the inhabitants',[76] a practice, if truly stated, which must have been due to the way in which the stipend was amassed.

The parishes formed part of an episcopal peculiar.[77] This was so in 1312,[78] and apparently remained so until the abolition of peculiars.[79]

The united rectory was valued at 3½ marks in 1194–5,[80] and between 1249 and 1281 at sums varying from 8 marks to £10.[81] In 1428 St. John's was valued at £9 and St. Mary's at £5.[82] The rectory, however, is not mentioned in the Taxation of Pope Nicholas, the Inquest of the Ninths, or the *Valor*. It has been suggested[83] that these silences imply that, at least for part of the time during which the castle was a royal residence, the rector was in effect a domestic chaplain and was paid out of the issues of the lordship. Devizes was, of course, a small area, and highly urbanized. There was, therefore, little land within it, apart from the parks, that could yield predial or mixed tithes.[84] Accordingly it would

70 Waylen, 'Nonconformity in Devizes', no. xxiv (a series of articles in *Devizes Advertiser*, 1877, mounted as bk. in W.A.S. Libr., Devizes).
71 Phillipps, *Wilts. Inst.*
72 *Walker Revised*, ed. A. G. Matthews, 370; *L.J.* x. 358.
73 *Walker Revised*, ed. Matthews, 370.
74 Waylen, *Hist.* 573.
75 P.R.O., Inst. Bks. The presentation is not in Phillipps, *Wilts. Inst.*
76 Waylen, *Chrons.* 224.
77 A. J. Camp, *Wills and their Whereabouts*, 81.
78 *Reg. Ghent* (Cant. & York Soc.), ii. 794.
79 Wilts. Co. Council, *Guide to the Rec. Offices*, pt. iv, pp. xiii, 49.
80 *Cur. Reg. R.* 1194–5 (Pipe R. Soc. xiv), 109.
81 W.R.S. xvi, p. 231 (1249); *Rot. Hund.* (Rec. Com.), ii (1), 236 (1255, 1279); J.I. 1/998 m. 25 (1267); J.I. 1/1005 m. 144 [146](1281).
82 *Feud. Aids*, v. 285.
83 Waylen, *Hist.* 570–1.
84 Cf. W.R.O. 212A/36/44, case concerning Old Park.

not be surprising if the owner or occupier of the lordship should make some direct contribution towards the support of the cure. This is the more probable since, at times, the tithability of the parks was in dispute.

In 1227 the constable was ordered to assign the tithe of the meadow to the rector[85] and in 1229 the tithes of hay.[86] In 1315 the rector claimed that this tithe arose in the park or parks, and that, owing to recent conversion of the meadow into pasture, he had been deprived of it, though he and his predecessors had once enjoyed it.[87] A jury found that no such tithe had been paid since Ralph de Sandwich's constableship (1275–?87). Nevertheless orders were issued that the queen, as tenant of the park, should pay tithe to the value of £1 2s.[88] Tithe arising in the park was certainly collected in 1483–4.[89] These instances seem enough to prove that the parks were tithable in the Middle Ages. What other sources of revenue the rector enjoyed in these earlier times is not exactly ascertainable, but 'church lands'[90] had already begun to accumulate. In 1502 and 1533 the churches were well enough supported for pensions to retiring rectors to be charged upon their revenues[91] and in 1573–4 the rector was receiving £8 out of St. Mary's parish stock.[92]

In return for the assignment of 1628 the corporation pledged itself to pay the rector's stipend, then £40, out of the town revenues. It did not keep its bond, but, acting like the impropriate feoffees,[93] paid the incumbent only a part of the stipend and reserved the rest for lecturers.[94] The foundation in 1642 of Pierce's charity[95] seems to suggest that the benefice was impoverished. In 1646 a yearly augmentation of £50 for each church was granted probably out of the proceeds of chapter lands sold, but of this only £70 was ever paid, and even that sum was eventually reduced. By 1655 this subvention had dried up and the living was said to be worth £9 10s.; the rest, it was added at the time, 'dependeth on good will of inhabitants'.[96] In 1661 the bishop was supplementing the stipend out of his own pocket.[97]

85 *Rot. Litt. Claus.* (Rec. Com.), ii. 204.
86 *Close R.* 1227–9, 179.
87 *Rot. Parl.* i. 319.   88 *Cal. Inq. Misc.* ii, p. 49.
89 D.L. 29/724/11803.   90 See below.
91 *W.A.M.* ii. 328–9.   92 W.R.O. 189/1, Chwdns.' Accts.
93 For them see J. E. C. Hill, *Econ. Problems of the Ch.* 261–2.
94 Waylen, 'Nonconformity in Devizes', no. xxiv (see n. 70 above).
95 See below.
96 *W.A.M.* ii. 330 n.; W. A. Shaw, *Ch. under Commonwealth*, ii. 547.
97 S.P. 29/43, no. 68.

In 1662 the rector tried to secure for the benefice the tithes arising in the old park.[98] He failed, but in 1682 was receiving a yearly composition in lieu out of the Wyndham share of the park.[99] The corporation thereupon stepped in and by 1666 was making a supplementary yearly gift of £10,[1] made permanent for the rector's life in 1670.[2] In addition to augmenting the benefice the corporation in the 17th century sometimes contributed to repairing St. John's.[3]

In time the living acquired other assets. By 1704 rent arose from the site of the parsonage, which no longer existed.[4] By then St. John's was also entitled to tithes on land (2 a.) in Eastcroft hill and St. Mary's to two gardens, which, with the parsonage site, formed the glebe. The rector collected in each church 4d. from every woman churched.[5] In 1743 (Sir) George Lee, M.P. for the borough, gave the corporation £200, which was handed over to the churches in equal shares for the provision of ornaments.[6] In 1764 the benefice was augmented by £200 out of Queen Anne's Bounty.[7] In the next year Thurman's charity[8] was founded. The benefice was further augmented by £200 in 1802,[9] and was valued at £132 in 1809.[10] Some time after 1833 the rector succeeded in securing the park tithes.[11] It was probably this achievement which made it possible to commute the tithes for £213 10s.[12] The benefice was valued at £518 in 1837,[13] and at £242 about 1901.[14] The glebe measured 3½ a. in 1887, at which figure it had apparently stood in 1783.[15]

---

98 W.A.M. ii. 330. For later (1801) transcript of the suit in the K. B. (Trin. 1662), see W.R.O. 212B/4/32.
99 W.R.O. 212A/36/44, case concerning Old Park.
1 Cunnington, *Annals*, i (2nd pagin.), 145.
2 Ibid. 152.
3 Ibid. 42 (1606), 163 (1676–7).
4 Sar. Dioc. R.O., Glebe Terrier, 1704; see p. 178.
5 Sar. Dioc. R.O., Glebe Terrier, 1704.
6 Cunnington, *Annals*, i (2nd pagin.), 213.
7 C. Hodgson, *Queen Anne's Bounty* (2nd edn.), p. clxv.
8 See pp. 177–8.
9 Hodgson, op. cit. p. clxv.
10 Waylen, *Chrons.* 226.
11 Waylen, *Hist.* 334 states that the tithes were recovered by E. J. Phipps, rector 1833–53.
12 Before 1847: *Rtn. of Tithes Commuted*, H.C. 298, p. 203 (1847–8), xlix.
13 *Rtn. Annual Value Benefices*, H.C. 439, p. 36 (1837), xli.
14 *Endowed Char. Wilts.* (1908), lxxx, p. 450.
15 *Rtn. of Glebe Land*, H.C. 307, p. 163 (1887), lxiv.

About the application of rates to church expenses little has been collected, but, as the next paragraph will show, St. Mary's at least had little need of them over a long period. In 1559 the mayor ordered a house-to-house collection for communion bread and wine[16] and in 1833 a like collection was ordered in St. John's parish so as to relieve the rates of the organist's salary.[17]

From the Middle Ages St. Mary's parish owned many plots of land[18] which eased financial difficulties. It is not certain whether St. John's did so too. By the early 17th century, however, both parishes possessed territorial estates, the income from which was used in each case partly for the church's direct benefit. So far as could then be known, it was shown c. 1834 that St. Mary's had always been supported out of charity lands and that no church rate had ever been levied. The fund, then called St. Mary's Church and Poor Lands, had also been used at times to support singers and ringers.[19] Its later history is told elsewhere as is that of the corresponding charity for St. John's.[20] The two parishes continue to benefit from the funds.

John Pierce, by will proved 1642, left £50 for the repair of St. John's. In 1834 the corporation, as trustees, held the capital and paid £3 a year into a poor fund. It was then recommended that the charity be applied to its proper use.[21] In 1900 it yielded £1 11s. and was distributed with the income of St. John's Church and Poor Lands.[22] Pierce also left £50 to augment the rector's stipend.[23] The later history of these two Pierce charities is told elsewhere.[24] By 1670 there was vested in the corporation in trust an eleemosinary charity, created under Robert Walter's will, out of which 6s. 8d. was deducted for the rector.[25] The deduction was apparently still being made c. 1900.[26] In 1765 Thomas Thurman gave a rent-charge of £8 to be paid to the rector to perform

---

16 Cunnington, *Annals*, i (1st pagin.), 32.
17 W.R.O. 632/9, Chwdns.' Accts.
18 e.g. stalls belonged to the chwdns. of St. Mary's in 1378 and 1411: W.R.O. 189/34, files of deeds, 13th-cent.–1467.
19 *Endowed Char. Wilts.* (1908), lxxx, p. 403.
20 See pp. 235–6.
21 *Endowed Char. Wilts.* (1908), lxxx, p. 389. For the date of probate see ibid. p. 441.
22 Ibid. p. 431.
23 Ibid. p. 442.
24 See p. 248.
25 *Endowed Char. Wilts.* (1908), lxxx, p. 404.
26 Ibid. p. 457.

services in one of the churches twice weekly or in default to be applied to his clothing charity. It seems to have been normally applied to its primary purpose at St. John's, except in 1854–60, and was again so applied c. 1900.[27] In 1942 it was redeemed for £320 stock,[28] which yielded about £7 in 1971.[29]

There were also several sermon charities founded by the donors of larger ones expressly or presumptively to encourage further almsgiving. The donors were Anne, relict of Sir Henry Sharington of Lacock (1594),[30] Elizabeth Strangwidge (1634),[31] Mary Collier (1670),[32] and Eleanor Powell (1743).[33] The second, third,[34] and fourth were still being paid c. 1900.[35] The first, attached to a loan charity, is not mentioned after its foundation. By will dated 1774 Thomas Bancroft, of Bristol, among larger benefactions,[36] left money, invested as £333 stock, for sermons on his birth- (2 May) and death-days (23 Nov.) and for rewarding the ringers ringing on those days. In 1779 the charity was so regulated as to provide at each church for the distribution of £2 for each sermon and £2 severally to the ringers on the same occasions.[37] The payments were still made in 1971.[38]

A rectory-house existed by 1525.[39] It was damaged in the Civil War and its repair ordered in 1646.[40] The house had gone by 1704 and the site been converted into gardens,[41] now covered by the parish room.[42] The present house was bought by Queen Anne's Bounty in 1776. It was then said to include two parlours, one with a Venetian sashed window.[43] It has been subsequently altered.

27 *Endowed Char. Wilts.* (1908), lxxx, p. 446.
28 Char. Com. file 201833/B1.
29 Ex inf. Mr. E. E. Lake, chwdn.
30 See p. 245.
31 See pp. 247–8.
32 See pp. 248–9.
33 See p. 221.
34 *Endowed Char. Wilts.* (1908), lxxx, p. 432.
35 Ibid. p. 457.
36 See pp. 221, 251.
37 *Endowed Char. Wilts.* (1908), lxxx, pp. 394–5.
38 Ex inf. Mr. E. E. Lake, chwdn.
39 *W.A.M.* ii. 310.
40 *C.J.* iv. 556.
41 Sar. Dioc. R.O., Glebe Terrier, 1704.
42 W.A.S. Libr., Devizes, Map, 1736–7.
43 Sar. Dioc. R.O., Glebe Terrier, 1776.

In the Middle Ages both churches were furnished with chantries. In 1392 Richard Cardmaker then mayor, was authorized to settle lands in the borough to support a priest celebrating at St. Leonard's altar in St. John's. The foundation was for the benefit of the king and queen, other royalties including Henry 'some time King of England and Maud his queen', and the mayor and commons who were the trustees, and their kindred. By the Dissolution it had come to be imagined that Cardmaker was the sole beneficiary. The lands, all of which lay in the New Port, included a part of what was doubtless the town ditch, some 36 houses and plots, and three stalls.[44]

By 1489 St. John's had four altars. One was presumably St. Leonard's. Another was dedicated to St. Catherine,[45] and is mentioned again in 1502, in which year the high altar was said to be dedicated to Our Lady.[46] Other altars, mentioned later, were dedicated to the Trinity (1529)[47] and to Our Lady and St. George (1541).[48]

A chapel of St. Catherine in St. John's is mentioned in 1508[49] and at sundry other times until 1529.[50] In the latter year it contained an 'image' of the Trinity.[51] This is perhaps the building, now called the Beauchamp but until the 1830s the Hungerford[52] chapel, whose erection has been attributed to Sir Roger Tocotes (d. 1492).[53] The Trinity altar, mentioned above, stood within it. Presumably the St. Catherine altar was also there.

St. Mary's contained at least three chantries. The first, founded by John Coventry the elder, was endowed with 14 tenements in the New

---

44 *Cal. Pat.* 1391–6, 115; *W.A.M.* ii. 235–6, where the chantry certs. are set out. The commemoration of Hen. and Maud raises a problem. The indexer of the Pat. R. Cal. was probably wrong in supposing that Maud is Hen. I's queen. She is more likely Maud the Empress, who gave the town its first chart. In that case for 'queen' read 'mother'. Hen. is probably Hen. II who confirmed that chart. and the exchange of Godalming with Devizes (see above p. 38). The cert. of 1548 calls the founder John Cardmaker and this mistake is repeated in 1590: C 66/1340 m. 10.
45 Prob. 11/8 (P.C.C. 23 Milles, Hen. Pole's will). For the location of the lands see W.R.O. 212A/36/2, deeds, 1551 and 1559.
46 Prob. 11/13 (P.C.C. 16 Blamyr, Hen. Smyth's will).
47 Ibid.
48 Prob. 11/23 (P.C.C. 7 Jankyn, Thos. Rede's will).
49 Prob. 11/28 (P.C.C. 32 Alenger, Wm. Larkstocke's will).
50 Prob. 11/15 (P.C.C. 34 Adeane, John Grendell's will).
51 Prob. 11/23 (P.C.C. 7 Jankyn, Thos. Rede's will).
52 Waylen, *Chrons.* 304.
53 *W.A.M.* xlix. 284–7.

Port and 2½ a. in Wick field.[54] The second, founded by John Coventry the younger (d. *ante* 1475),[55] was a comparatively wealthy one, for it was endowed with 33 tenements in Devizes and Bishop's Cannings, and 37 a. of arable, 5 of them in Seend.[56] One or other of these endowments appears to have supported an altar on the south side of the church.[57] The third chantry, founded by William Coventry, was endowed with 24 tenements, nearly if not quite all of them in the town.[58] The gross income was charged, under the founder's will, with an annuity of £1 13s. 4d. to four poor women in the alms-house.[59] John Ocle or Okelegh, by will proved 1398, left a house in the town out of which 4d. was to be paid for his own and his wife's anniversary and 6d. to St. Catherine's light in the church.[60] The foundation is not heard of again, but in or before 1466 John Field gave to the wardens of the light land in the Old Port for masses at that altar for himself, his parents, and Edward and Joan Daniel.[61] The proctors of the light are mentioned again in 1469[62] but neither they nor it thereafter.

Probably about the end of the 14th century[63] and certainly before 1461 Richard Gobett of Devizes endowed with land in the town an obit to be celebrated yearly on the Friday after Epiphany for the souls of himself, his wife, William Estmonde, a John Coventry and his wife, and their kin. A dole to priests and poor was to be distributed at the obit. William Smith (d. 1436) and Thomas, his son, the former presumably the rebuilder of the church, gave land for maintaining three sepulchre tapers and a font taper and for an obit for Thomas and his parents.[64] Smith's tapers still burnt in 1557,[65] and some of the lands that Gobett gave have been retained by the church.[66] Thomas Cardmaker's light and

54 E 301/58/37. For later details about the lands see *Cal. Pat.* 1555–7, 151.
55 For the date of death see *W.A.M.* ii. 251.
56 E 301/58/40. For later details about the lands see *Cal. Pat.* 1555–7, 151.
57 *W.A.M.* ii. 251. The cert. shows the chantry to have been in St. Mary's. In 1555 it was said to be in St. John's: *Cal. Pat.* 1555–7, 151.
58 E 301/58/38. For later details about the lands see *Cal. Pat.* 1555–7, 151.
59 E 301/58/38; E 301/59/24; and see p. 236.
60 W.R.O. 189/34, will dated 1397.
61 Ibid. 189/34, deed, Vyld to wdns. of St. Cath's. altar, which corrects *W.A.M.* ii. 252, 306.
62 Ibid. 189/55, deeds, for tenements in New Port.
63 Gobett was living in 1378 and 1390: W.R.O., Skippet deeds, nos. 18, 23.
64 *W.A.M.* ii. 252.
65 Ibid. 315.
66 Ibid. 252; *Endowed Char. Wilts.* (1908), lxxx, p. 399. For Gobett see also p. 246.

a light in Our Lady porch are mentioned in 1499–1500[67] and a lamp before the high altar in 1525.[68] The fate of these chantry lands is considered elsewhere.[69]

The ecclesiastical policy of the two parishes after the Reformation can only be glimpsed sporadically. Through an exceptional run of early churchwardens' accounts[70] the progress of the Reformation and Counter-Reformation at St. Mary's may be traced. In 1550–1 the altars were pulled down and next year copies of the Prayer Book were bought.[71] 'The scriptures' and the Commandments were inscribed upon the walls at about the same time, and the organs and rood-loft removed. In 1553–6 the high altar, a side altar, and the organs were re-erected, the rood-loft replaced and adorned with statues of the Virgin and St. John the Evangelist, and the mural inscriptions defaced.[72] Two more altars were built in 1557–8.[73] The restorations were themselves swept away under Elizabeth I. In 1561–2 the rood-loft went and next year the organ and the candlesticks,[74] and in 1575–6 the Commandments were reinscribed.[75] In 1573–4 bread and wine were bought for fourteen communicants, in 1575–6 for only five.[76]

The progress of the Reformation in St. Mary's suggests that the parish conformed to official tendencies. When the next century is entered such an impression is confirmed, for in 1637–8 the Communion table was railed in.[77] The use of lecturers and preachers[78] might indeed suggest a degree of Puritanism on the part of the corporation, patrons at this time,[79] and certainly one preacher became a noted Parliamentarian.[80]

---

67 *W.A.M.* ii. 308–9; cf. W.R.O. 189/1, Chwdns.' Accts.
68 *W.A.M.* ii. 311.
69 See pp. 234–5.
70 Now in W.R.O.
71 *W.A.M.* ii. 312.
72 Ibid. 312–14.
73 Ibid. 314.
74 Ibid. 316.
75 Ibid. 318. Date corrected from original acct. in W.R.O. 189/1, Chwdns.' Accts.
76 W.R.O. 189/1.
77 *W.A.M.* ii. 322.
78 Cunnington, *Annals*, ii. 145 (1628); i (2nd pagin.), 88 (1630–1); 105 (1641–2 and neighbouring years); ii. 151, 153 (1659–60); *Calamy Revised*, ed. A. G. Matthews, 286 (1638).
79 See p. 174.
80 Phil. Hunton (d. 1682), later vicar of Westbury: *Calamy Revised*, ed. Matthews, 286; *D.N.B.*; *V.C.H. Wilts.* viii. 177.

On the other hand, they may sometimes simply have stopped gaps during vacancies. Byng, at all events, rector c. 1646, was not a Puritan, for he joined the king's forces and his lands were sequestered.[81] The situation becomes clearer in 1661–2. A lecturer was then engaged, although a rector (Henry Johnson) was in office.[82] In 1662 certain members of the corporation were ordered to dine on each weekly lecture day with the lecturer.[83] Johnson left a reputation as a preacher[84] and was esteemed by Bishop Henchman a 'learned, prudent, and orthodox man', but the temper of the people was not altogether 'good'[85] and dissent was prevalent.[86]

In 1783 a morning and an evening service were held on alternate Sundays at the two churches, the same congregation going to both. There were also daily services at one church or the other. Communion was celebrated on six Sundays in the year and at St. John's on the great feasts. The average number communicating was 80–90 at St. John's and 60 at St. Mary's.[87] It was decided in 1800 that Sunday services should be held at both churches.[88] In 1810 there were two such services at each church,[89] the rector no doubt responding to Bishop Douglas's stipulation that every church in the county should be so provided for.[90] In 1833, when gas was installed, the second took place in the evening.[91] E. J. Phipps, rector 1833–53, introduced the practice of singing the doxology after each psalm.[92] In 1845 he aroused public protest by his ritualistic observances. A county meeting, summoned in December 1850 to protest against papal 'aggression', refused him audience. A memorial, criticizing his views, was lodged with the bishop next month. It split the congregation, part of which withdrew a year later. A sermon on the Real Presence preached in November 1852 by his assistant curate resulted in actions in the church courts and in the following August St. Mary's doors were locked against the rector, who left soon after for another cure.[93]

81 Waylen, *Hist.* 274–5.
82 Cunnington, *Annals*, i (2nd pagin.), 136.
83 Ibid. 134.
84 T. Dingley, *Hist. from Marble* (Camden Soc. 1st ser. xcvii), ii, no. cccccii.
85 S.P. 29/43 no. 68.   86 See p. 200.
87 W.R.S. xxvii, pp. 85–6.
88 J. J. Slade, 'Hist. St. John's Ch.' (see n. 2 below).
89 Cunnington, *Annals*, ii. 43.
90 Gillman, *Annals*, 22.
91 Ibid. 31.
92 C. Lucas, *Observations on the Modern Clergy* (n.d.), 29.
93 Gillman, *Annals*, 36, 38–9.

In 1864 there were two Sunday services at each church, morning prayer daily at St. John's, and evensong once a week at each church. Communion services were held monthly at each church on the great feasts, and at St. John's weekly in Lent and Advent. Average attendances were 70 at St. John's and 40 at St. Mary's. In general both churches were then well attended and St. John's was 'frequently crowded'.[94] In 1878 there was a monthly Sunday afternoon service for children at St. Mary's.[95] Evening services at that church do not seem to have started until 1883.[96] Dr. J. H. Burges, rector 1874–99, was remembered for his energy as a parish priest, also as a promoter of Anglican education and church repair.[97]

St. John's church is remembered outside Devizes as the place to which Hubert de Burgh fled for refuge in September 1233. As already related,[98] he was dragged back to the castle soon after his escape, but restored to sanctuary again. On his restoration a stockade was ordered to be fixed upon the bank round the churchyard to keep him safe.[99] He was, however, rescued from the church. The churches also acquired a more than local prominence during the Civil War. The tower of St. John's was used as a powder magazine and lead for bullets was taken from the roofs of both churches.[1]

The church of *ST. JOHN THE BAPTIST* is built of ashlar and has a chancel with north and south chapels, a crossing tower, transepts, an aisled nave, and north and south porches.[2]

---

94 Sar. Dioc. R.O., Vis. Queries, 1864.
95 *The Church Rambler* (1878) [anon.], ii. 462.
96 Gillman, *Annals*, 59.
97 *The Church Rambler* (1878) [anon.], ii. 432–3; see also pp. 187, 191, 224.
98 See pp. 44–5.   99 Close R. 1231–4, 329.
 1 G. A. Harrison, 'Royalist Organization in Wilts.' (Lond. Univ. Ph.D. thesis, 1963), 124, 200.
 2 The best acct. of the two chs. is probably still Edw. Kite's in *W.A.M.* ii (1855), 213–56, 302–32. See also J. H. Burges (rector) in *W.A.M.* xix (1881), 119 sqq.; C. E. Ponting in *Devizes Gaz.* 30 July 1903 (preserved in Wilts. Cuttings, ii. 18, 20), and J. J. Slade, 'Hist. St. John's Ch.' (cuttings from *Wilts. Gaz.* Feb., Mar. 1934, mounted as bk. in W.A.S. Libr., Devizes). Notes by Sir Stephen Glynne (d. 1874) are in *W.A.M.* xlii. 194. The first known pictures are on Dore, Map, 1759. Other illustrations of St. John's are (i) J. Britton, *Archit. Antiquits. Gt. Britain* (1807), pls. facing pp. 9, 11, 12 in vol. ii (1835 edn.), and *Beauties of Wilts.* iii (1824), after p. lxiv; (ii) water-cols. by J. Buckler in W.A.S. Libr., Devizes, vol. v. 27–9 and sketches therefor in B.M. Add. MS. 36391, ff. 91–3; (iii) drawing by W. Millington (1834 x 1844), lith. by J. Holloway in W.A.S. Libr., Devizes, T. f. 61.

The church of St. John the Baptist in the early 19th century

The later-12th-century cruciform church was of considerable size and quality.[3] The chancel was covered by a quadripartite vault of two bays and the walls were decorated internally by intersecting arcading. The oblong tower, more than 65 ft. high, was richly ornamented both inside and out and had a circular stair turret of still greater height at its north-west corner. Visible above the crossing arches on the inside there was a blind arcade with triple intersecting arches, perhaps the only example of this in England.[4] The transepts, like the chancel, had an eaves course decorated with carved corbels, and in each gable three windows arranged one over two.

Contrary to expectation in a church of this period,[5] the nave seems to have been unaisled; it terminated in a decorated west front. The evidence for changes in the next two centuries is slight but implies that the church was considerably enlarged. Parts of weathering courses

3 In 1881 Loftus Brock conjectured 1152–60 as the date of erection: *W.A.M.* xix. 123. Mr. R. A. Stalley, using different arguments, reached a similar conclusion in 1971: *Brit. Arch. Jnl.* xxxiv. 81–3.
4 A. W. Clapham, *Eng. Romanesque Archit. after Conquest*, 105.
5 Ibid. 108.

on the east walls of both transepts imply that there were chapels or apses before those of the 15th century, and it is unlikely that they were original apses in a church of later-12th-century design. The doorway and flanking buttresses of the north porch are 14th-century and their position implies both a porch and an aisle at that time. Both the nave, except for the west front, and the aisle were removed when the western part of the church was rebuilt in the 15th century. The nave then had matching north and south aisles with arcades of five bays and at least a north porch of two storeys. At the same time the lower part of the tower staircase was rebuilt and a doorway was made above the respond of the north arcade to give access to a rood-loft. During the same century, and possibly a little earlier, there were also alterations in the eastern end. Battlements and pinnacles were added to the tower and tracery was placed in the lower tower windows. Single large windows were inserted into both transept gables and the chancel east wall, and new chapels were built in the angles between the chancel and transepts.

The chapel on the north is of only one bay, since there was at one time another building, probably a sacristy, between its east wall and the first bay of the chancel, from which it was approached by a doorway. On a moulding of the east window a chantry inscription to Richard Lamb, otherwise unknown, was formerly painted.[6] The south, or Beauchamp, chapel[7] is of two bays and richly ornamented especially in the panelling of the roof and on the battlements and pinnacles. In the centre of the east wall is a canopied niche, which may once, like the similar one at St. Mary's, have contained a statue of the Virgin.[8] Both within and without are carved figures of angels, those without holding shields. Within the moulding at the apex of the arch between the transept and the chantry are two carved rudders. The numerous secondary altars already mentioned[9] account for the construction of a profusion of squints from the chapels and transepts towards the high altar. At some date, probably either at the rebuilding of the nave in the 15th century or as a result of damage during the Rebellion,[10] the west wall of the tower was rebuilt

6 The inscription was faint in 1903 (Ponting, see n. 2 above) and invisible in 1971.
7 See p. 179.
8 Ponting (see n. 2 above). 9 See p. 179.
10 Unspecified repairs were carried out in 1646: *C.J.* iv. 556. In the 1890s the E. wall was said to be scarred with bullet-marks and other signs of the 1643 siege: Wilts. Cuttings, v. 151. Ponting (see n. 2 above), however, conjectures that the rebuilding took place in the 15th cent.

following closely the original exterior design but omitting the internal decoration, perhaps implying that by this time the crossing was ceiled.

By 1759, if not by 1737–8, the south porch existed in its present form, perhaps following not very closely a late medieval predecessor, and at the earlier date there may also have been a porch to the west doorway.[11] During the 18th century the east window was blocked with brickwork to facilitate the fitting of a panelled reredos, the aisles ceiled, and the nave ceiled with a plaster barrel-vault and fitted with box-pews, a lofty pulpit, and a west gallery.[12] About 1800 a large Venetian window was placed in the west wall but only the side lights appear to have been open.[13]

The first major restoration was in 1844 when the reredos was removed, the east and south walls of the chancel covered with intersecting arcading in imitation of the 12th-century work, a window of Romanesque form put into the east wall, and the chancel and side chapels were cleaned.[14] Probably at the same time the nave ceiling was removed, three nave windows, blocked about ten years earlier, were reopened, and a stone spirelet, visible in 1759[15] and 1807,[16] above the tower stair-turret was taken down. By the late fifties the nave arcades and aisle walls had acquired a serious outward list. This demanded attention and extra seating was needed. Accordingly a large-scale restoration, directed by a W. Slater of London with the advice of (Sir) Gilbert Scott, was carried out in 1862–3.[17] The nave was extended by one bay, this securing 154 free sittings,[18] and the west wall, which still bore many traces of 12th-century work, rebuilt in 15th-century style. The piers of the nave were rebuilt in blocks of Box and Chilmark stone, set alternately. The nave roof was given a higher pitch, the aisle roofs reconstructed, and the aisle windows repaired. The interior walls of the aisles, transepts, and chapels were scraped. Those of the aisles seem to have retained up to that time their 15th-century plaster. The tracery in the chapel windows was renewed, and the door of the south chapel rebuilt and its floor repaved. The west gallery was demolished.[19]

---

11 W.A.S. Libr., Devizes, Map, 1737–8; Dore, Map, 1759.
12 W.A.M. ii. 223, 229 n.; Wilts. Cuttings, v. 151.
13 See illustration on p. 184.
14 Ibid. 15 Dore, Map, 1759.
16 Britton, *Archit. Antiquits. Gt. Britain* (1835 edn.), pl. facing p. 9.
17 Gillman, *Annals*, 44–5. 18 Sar. Dioc. R.O., Vis. Queries, 1864.
19 J.J. Slade, 'Hist. St. John's Ch.' (see n. 2 above).

In 1894 the gabled roof of the north chapel was replaced by a flat one, the floors of that chapel and of the transepts were removed, the aisles and south transepts unceiled, and the north transept opened to the roof. In 1897 colouring, which probably dated from the restoration of 1844, was removed from the east end.[20] Between 1900 and 1909 the tower was strengthened. In 1902 the south chapel was restored and fitted for service. Its eastern portion had been used as a vestry. The north chapel then became the vestry and the organ was moved into the north transept.[21] The tower was further repaired in 1922 and the south aisle in 1924.[22]

The pulpit incorporates 15th-century panels. The oak screen dividing the chancel from the chapels was presented in 1844 by T. H. S. Sotheron Estcourt. An organ was apparently being erected in 1743.[23] The upper part of the present organ case is of 17th-century date. The royal arms were repainted in 1606.[24] In 1855 James II's arms hung above the arch at the east end of the nave.[25] Two scratch-dials are cut upon the south wall.[26]

The corporation enjoyed the benefit of a special pew 'in church', probably in both churches, by 1730.[27] Corporation pews were still maintained in both churches in 1971. In 1806 after the town hall had been reconstructed the church acquired the clock that had hung in the turret of the old building since at least 1759.[28] This was replaced in 1901–2 by a new clock erected as a memorial to Queen Victoria.[29]

There is a brass to John Kent (d. 1630), town clerk. Sculptured monuments commemorate John Eyles (d. 1752) and his family (by Prince Hoare of Bath), George Willy (d. 1770), and Prince Sutton (d. 1779) (both by Richard Westmacott (d. 1808)), James Sutton (d. 1788), and Maria Heathcote (d. 1792) (both by T. King of Bath), James Sutton (d. 1801) (by Sir Richard Westmacott), and William Salmon (d. 1826) (by E. H. Baily). Other members of the Eyles, Heathcote, and Sutton families

20 Ibid.
21 *Devizes Gaz.* 27 Mar. 1902.
22 Slade, op. cit.
23 Cunnington, *Annals*, i (2nd pagin.), 213.
24 Ibid. 42.
25 *W.A.M.* ii. 231.
26 Ibid. xlv. 294, 533.
27 Cunnington, *Annals*, i (2nd pagin.), 207.
28 W.R.O. 632/9, Chwdns.' Accts.
29 *Devizes Gaz.* 27 Mar. 1902.

are also commemorated, as are members of the Bruges, Drew, Giddings, Jackson, Long, Merewether, Needham, Nott, Simpson, Tayler, Thurman, Trollope, and Wild families. In the churchyard is the tomb of five young people drowned in Drew's Pond on a Sunday in 1751. Its restored inscription extols sabbatarianism.[30]

Edward VI's commissioners left the church with a chalice weighing 14 oz. and took 5½ oz. of other plate. The chalice, however, seems to have been sold soon after. In 1783 there were 2 chalices, 2 patens, and a flagon. The last, of Britannia metal, was given by Sir Edward Ernle, Bt., in 1704. The rest seem to have been recast in 1839. There are three brass alms-dishes of 1846,[31] 1847, and 1967.[32] A Bible 'of the best and largest volume' was bequeathed in 1542.[33]

A bequest was made to the bells in 1515.[34] In 1553 there were 4 bells and a sanctus bell, but, like the chalice, all seem to have been sold soon after. There are now 8 bells: (iv) and (v) of 1610, (iii), (vii), and (viii) of 1677, by William Coney, (vi) of 1697, by William Cor of Aldbourne, (i) and (ii) of 1747, by James Burrough of Devizes.[35] A sanctus bell of 1807 by James Wells of Aldbourne was presented to Appleshaw church (Hants) in 1965 and stolen before hanging.[36] The tower is associated with some bell-ringing customs. It was decided in 1646–7 that the 'church' bell should be rung daily at 4 a.m. in the winter months.[37] This evidently applied to both churches. By 1875, when the practice ceased, the tolling occurred at 6 a.m.[38] A curfew was being rung at 8 p.m. in 1655, when the hour was changed to 9 p.m.[39] In 1934 it was decided that there should be no ringing in the three summer months.[40] Ringing continued until at least 1951.[41]

30 The attributions to the sculptors follow R. Gunnis, *Dict. Brit. Sculptors*, except in the cases of J. Sutton (d. 1788) and Maria Heathcote, where they seem to be wrong. For the Heathcote mon. see *W.N. & Q.* v. 374. For copies of the inscriptions in ch. and chyd. see Phillipps, *Wilts. M.I.* 69, and vol. vi of M.I.s in W.A.S. Libr., Devizes.
31 Nightingale, *Wilts. Plate*, 103–4.
32 Ibid. 104; ex inf. the Revd. W. D. C. Williams, Rector.
33 Prob. 11/29 (P.C.C. 4 Spert, Wm. Page's will).
34 Prob. 11/18 (P.C.C. 12 Holder, Thos. Spraye's will).
35 Walters, *Wilts. Bells*, 72–3.
36 Ibid. 72; ex inf. the Revd. W. D. C. Williams, Rector.
37 Cunnington, *Annals*, i (2nd pagin.), 113.
38 Gillman, *Annals*, 55.
39 Cunnington, *Annals*, i (2nd pagin.), 123.
40 Wilts. Cuttings, xviii. 134.
41 *Wilts. News*, 7 Aug. 1959.

The registers date from 1559 and are complete except for the period 1648–53.[42]

The church of St. Mary in the early 19th century

The church of *ST. MARY THE VIRGIN* is built of ashlar and has a chancel, aisled and clerestoried nave, south porch, and west tower.[43]

There is a tradition that it is not the first church on the site, for a churchwarden told Dr. Burges (rector 1874–99) that foundations had been discovered leading north-east across the chancel through the churchyard.[44] There is, however, no further evidence of such a building. The present chancel, like that of St. John's, is of the later 12th century

---

42 The registers are in W.R.O. Marriages 1559–1837 have been printed in *Wilts. Par. Reg.* ed. W. P.W. Phillimore and J. Sadler, xi. 43–140.
43 For preceding accounts see p. 183 n. 2. Water-cols. by J. Buckler are in W.A.S. Libr., Devizes, vol. v. 30–1 with sketches in B.M. Add. MS. 36391, ff. 88–90.
44 *W.A.M.* xix. 124.

and is of two bays with quadripartite vaulting and intersecting arcading decorating the internal walls. There is no certain evidence for the plan of the western part of the original church. The position of the 13th-century south wall of the south porch suggests that by that time the nave had achieved its present length and had at least a south aisle, although probably not as wide as that which exists. The porch doorway has an inner order of the 13th century with four orders of reset 12th-century ornament in the arch, perhaps taken from the earlier south doorway. The footings of the east wall of the north aisle are thicker than those of the other aisle walls and may be 13th-century or earlier.

No datable features of the later 13th and 14th centuries remain but both aisles were probably extended to their present dimensions during that period and much of the surviving walling, which incorporates many ashlar blocks of 12th-century character, may be of 14th-century construction. The appearance of the church, however, was radically altered in the 15th century. The first changes may have been in the south aisle where the walls were heightened and embattled and there was a new west window. Simultaneously the south porch was heightened to a full two storeys and provided with a stair-turret on the west. Perhaps even before that work was finished the nave arcades of five bays were rebuilt and a clerestorey, elaborately decorated on the outside, was added. The date of this work is recorded in a memorial inscription on the roof to the donor William Smith (d. 1436), a Devizes man of whom little is known. The next phase of the alterations was the refurbishing of the aisles with new windows, buttresses and roofs, the insertion of new windows into the chancel, and the enlargement of the chancel arch. Finally, but still before the end of the century, the west tower was built against the nave. The nave wall was then removed to reveal a tower arch of unusual height.

Changes made during the Reformation are described above;[45] the greatest structural loss was probably the removal, in 1561, of the rood-screen which had presumably been put up *c.* 1436. The porch was repaired in 1612[46] and again in 1638–9.[47] The lower part of the west window was bricked up in 1637–8[48] perhaps because it coincided with a gallery floor. Two doorways were cut in the tower, presumably those at

45 See p. 181.
46 *W.A.M.* ii. 242.
47 Ibid. 322.
48 Ibid.

gallery level and on the outside at the base of the stair in 1697–8,[49] and a new gallery was put in in 1706.[50] The spirited statue of the Virgin and Child in the earlier 15th-century niche on the east gable of the nave was probably put in during the 17th century.[51]

In 1852 the present Romanesque east window was inserted together with the arcading below it, modelled upon similar arcading in the chancel.[52] The church was repewed, a vestry built, and the restored church reopened in 1855.[53] Perhaps at this time the blocked windows of which there were at least five in the aisles and nine in the clerestorey, together with the east window, were reopened.[54] Extensive wall-paintings, then revealed, were almost invisible in 1878.[55] The church was again restored in 1876, when colouring was discovered on the canopied niches on each side of the chancel arch. A lath-and-plaster roof to the nave was then removed and the tie-beams and wall-plates consequently exposed. A little colour was then applied to them. The rood-loft door was opened up and the gallery blocking the west window removed.[56] In 1875 the chancel was paved with tiles at the cost of Thomas Badger. These works were crowned in 1897–8 by repairs to the tower which had begun to crack.[57] The tower was then underpinned and some of its battlements, pinnacles, and gargoyles were taken away, and the chancel reroofed.[58] Further repairs, particularly to the nave and tower roof, took place in 1923–4.[59]

Two 16th-century brasses to members of the Horton family existed in 1855 but have since disappeared, as have all but one of the matrices then surviving. There are also monuments to John Garth (d. 1764), M.P. and recorder, and to members of the Filkes and Hull families. A mural tablet commemorating Henry Johnson (d. 1681), rector,[60] is no longer

49   Ibid. 324.
50   Ibid. 325.
51   Ponting (see p. 183, n. 2 above) observes that it does not fit the niche. It is inscribed 'Ra. Moor' and the date 13 Mar. 1624.
52   W.A.M. xix. 124.
53   Ibid. vi. 120 (faculty for repewing, 1854).
54   B.M. Add. MS. 36391, ff. 89, 90.
55   The Church Rambler (1878) [anon.], ii. 465.
56   W.A.M. xix. 125.
57   Devizes Gaz. 24 Feb. 1898.
58   Ibid.
59   Wilts Gaz. 11 Oct. 1923; inscription on tower wall.
60   W.A.M. ii. 247–8. For Johnson see above, p. 174. For copies of inscriptions in ch. and chyd. see Phillipps, Wilts. M.I. 77–80 and vol. vi of M.I.s in W.A.S. Libr., Devizes.

visible, although noted in 1878.[61] Nor are the wall monuments to George Johnson (d. 1683) and Timothy Sacheverell (d. 1680), which were visible *temp.* Charles II.[62] There is a brass tablet to John Llewellin (d. 1913).

The church possessed a clock as early as 1498–9[63] and organs by 1500–1.[64] The fate of the organs during the Reformation is traced above.[65] The royal arms, dating from 1797,[66] were re-erected above the chancel arch in 1963.[67] A weather 'cock', perhaps of late-17th-century date, stands inside the tower.

In 1436 the church owned 3 dishes, 2 flagons, and a gilt ring.[68] A 16th-century letter to the bishop enumerates the goods that some of the then recent churchwardens had alienated over the preceding decade.[69] They were a large cross with St. Mary and St. John, a pair of candlesticks, 5 chalices, 2 censers, a large pyx, 2 cruets, an oil vat, a 'shep' with spoon, and 2 paxes. The letter has been assigned to Mary's reign and could be of 1554. If so, the pre-Reformation church must have been rich in plate, for even after these depradations the commissioners of 1553 found 13½ oz. They took only 3 oz. for the king. A silver plate for the communion table was bought in 1599–1600.[70] In 1607[71] and 1634–5[72] this plate survived together with a silver communion cup. This seems to have been lost soon after, for a new one was bought in 1654. In 1677–8 there was a silver cup and plate and a pewter flagon. The cup survived until 1783 by which time there was also a salver and flagon inscribed 1716–18. The church now possesses 2 chalices, 2 patens, and a flagon, all hall-marked 1789. There is also a brass alms-dish of *c.* 1848.[73]

At least 4 bells hung in the tower in 1498–1500.[74] The clapper of one of these, the 'great' bell, was repaired by John Smith of Bristol in the

61 *The Church Rambler* (1878) [anon.], ii. 464.
62 T. Dingley, *Hist. from Marble* (Camden Soc. 1st ser. xcvii), ii. 151.
63 W.R.O. 189/1, Chwdns.' Accts.
64 *W.A.M.* ii. 309.   65 See p. 181.
66 *W.A.M.* xlviii. 107.   67 Wilts. Cuttings, xxii. 202.
68 *W.N. & Q.* vii. 194.
69 Unless otherwise stated, the rest of this paragraph is from Nightingale, *Wilts. Plate*, 104–6, where the letter to bp. of Salisbury is printed. The writer was John Hall, mayor and M.P., 1554. It is dated Mon. 15 Jan., a possible date for 1554, but also for 1543, 1560, and 1565.
70 *W.A.M.* ii. 318.
71 W.R.O. 189/6, inventories of ch. goods.
72 *W.A.M.* ii. 320.
73 Ex inf. the Revd. W. D. C. Williams, Rector.
74 W.R.O. 189/1 Chwdns.' Accts.

latter year.[75] The letter to the bishop above referred to[76] mentions the loss of 2 great bells, but in 1553 there were 4 bells and a sanctus bell.[77] Some of the then existing bells were recast by J. Wallis of Salisbury in 1606, and a bell was recast in 1616.[78] In 1641 there were 5 bells.[79] There are now six: (i), (ii), (v), and (vi) of 1663, all apparently by the Purdues, (iv) of 1640, recast 1696 by Robert and William Cor of Aldbourne, (iii) of 1701, recast 1879.[80] The bells were rehung in 1878,[81] 1897–8,[82] and 1915.[83]

The registers date from 1569 and are complete.[84] A chest with 15 locks, holding title deeds, stood in the chancel in 1629.[85]

A church-house was 'taken down' in 1529, but such a building still existed in 1701.[86] The graveyard was enlarged *c.* 1768.[87] In it, south of the chancel, stands a dole-table, perhaps of 15th-century date.

A chapel of St. Thomas is mentioned in 1502, when money was left for its repair.[88] In 1527 it is said to have lain next door but one to the corn cross,[89] wherever that may then have been. It then disappears.

The church of St. James, Southbroom, first mentioned in 1461,[90] stands on the Green and from its location was sometimes called the church 'of the green'[91] or the Green Church.[92] It bore its dedication by 1505[93] and perhaps occupies the site of the chapel of St. James and St.

---

75 Ibid.
76 See preceding paragraph.
77 Walters, *Wilts. Bells*, 73–4.   78 Ibid.
79 W.R.O. 189/8, misc. docs., bond with Robt. Dismer to repair clapper of largest bell.
80 Walters, op. cit. Three cwt. of metal were added in 1664–5 to what were then called the 3rd and 4th bells: W.R.O. 189/2, Chwdns.' Accts.
81 Gillman, *Annals*, 57. If this date is correct, the date on no. 3 bell would seem wrong.
82 *Devizes Gaz.* 24 Feb. 1898.
83 *W.A.M.* xxxix. 296.
84 See *W.A.M.* liii. 449 for printed list of all par. recs. existing *c.* 1950. Some of the regs. have been transcribed: *W.A.M.* xlvii. 442.
85 *W.A.M.* ii. 244; B.M. Add. Ch. 37567.
86 *W.A.M.* ii. 311, 324.
87 W.R.O. 402/1, resolution of vestry, 13 Feb. 1769.
88 Prob. 11/13 (P.C.C. 8 Blamyr, John Nash's will).
89 Prob. 11/22 (P.C.C. 22 Porche, Thos. Tynmer's will), and see p. 117.
90 B.M. Add. Ch. 37522.
91 In 1518: Prob. 11/19 (P.C.C. 10 Ayloffe, Wm. Russell's will).
92 Waylen, *Chrons.* 312.
93 Prob. 11/14 (P.C.C. 39 Holgrave, Wm. Selfe's will).

Denis belonging to the hospital which disappeared after 1338.[94] It was originally a chapel within the parish of Bishop's Cannings and the peculiar jurisdiction of Salisbury chapter.[95] It possessed, however, its own graveyard by 1505,[96] maintained its own registers from 1572,[97] and was appointing its own wardens by 1571[98] and its own overseers of the poor by 1676–7.[99] A curate was 'admitted' to serve the cure in 1683.[1] The church became a perpetual curacy in 1832[2] comprising the tithings of Bedborough, Nursteed, Roundway, and Wick, the first three of which are now within the civil parish of Roundway.[3] The area of the ecclesiastical parish was reduced in 1867, when the consolidated chapelry of St. Peter's was created.[4] The patron was the vicar of Bishop's Cannings[5] until 1967 when he transferred his rights to Salisbury chapter.[6]

In 1831 the benefice was endowed with £39 yearly out of the tithes of Bishop's Cannings.[7] This was augmented by a capital grant of £200 from Queen Anne's Bounty in 1832, an annuity of £33 from the Ecclesiastical Commissioners in 1841, a share, amounting to £80 yearly, out of a rent-charge in 1858, a further annuity of £163 from the Ecclesiastical Commissioners in 1886, and c. £50 gross out of the benefices of the two Orchestons after their union in 1925.[8] At various times, however, the stipend of the vicar was reduced by abatement either of the capital or the annuities, notably in 1894 on the removal of the Rotherstone area to St. Peter's parish. Consequently it has been calculated that the net stipend totalled c. £260 from 1873 to 1894 and c. £500 in 1936. As an endowment for parochial needs some land behind Church Walk was bought in 1918,[9] four houses in Brickley Lane and a house in Church Walk in 1923, and two more in Church Walk in 1931.

94 V.C.H. Wilts. iii. 362.
95 Ibid. vii. 194; W.A.M. xxviii. 210.
96 Prob. 11/14 (P.C.C. 39 Holgrave, Wm. Selfe's will).
97 W.A.M. liii. 448.
98 Parker's Reg. (Cant. & York Soc.), ii. 611.
99 Cunnington, Annals, i (2nd pagin.), 163.
1 Sar. Dioc. R.O., Communar's Subscriptn. Bk.
2 Returns relating to New Parishes, H.C. 433, p. 52 (1870), liv.
3 V.C.H. Wilts. vii. 187, 194.
4 See p. 198.
5 V.C.H. Wilts. iii. 194.
6 Lond. Gaz. 31 Aug. 1967, p. 9546; ex inf. Ch. Commrs.
7 Unless otherwise stated this and the next paragraph are based on C.W. Pugh and C. A. Plaxton, Hist. of Southbroom (priv. print. 1936), and personal observations.
8 Lond. Gaz. 16 Oct. 1925, pp. 6682–4.
9 Benefice Bk. Southbroom.

Some of the incumbents have been locally notable. B. C. Dowding, 1838–70, largely helped to create St. Peter's parish and C. E. B. Barnwell, 1883–97, was remembered as an organizer and powerful preacher.[10] In 1864 there were morning and afternoon services on Sundays with average congregations of 400, daily prayers in Lent, and week-day services on litany and holy days. Holy Communion was celebrated once a month and on the great feasts, when attendance averaged 30–40. There were two assistant curates.[11] On the completion of the Le Marchant Barracks in Roundway parish in 1878,[12] St. James's became the garrison church of the Wiltshire Regiment.

The church of St. James, Southbroom, in 1803

The only ancient part of the church of *ST. JAMES* is the 15th-century tower, with stair-turret, panelled parapet, and traceried two-light bell-openings. The tower still bears the marks of its battering during the Rebellion, when a cannon ball, discovered in 1780, lodged itself in

10 *W.A.M.* xli. 305–6.
11 Sar. Dioc. R.O., Vis. Queries, 1864.
12 *V.C.H. Wilts.* vii. 188.

the belfry.[13] In 1831, just before rebuilding, the church had a chancel and nave with continuous aisles, south porch, and west tower.[14] Within was a north arcade of three bays with square stone piers and a south arcade of four bays with moulded piers. The north aisle had grouped lancet windows of 13th-century character and may have been the original chapel. If so, the site, adjacent to the road, may have made a new axis to the south necessary when enlargement took place. The steep gable and window tracery of the chancel suggest an earlier 15th-century date which may also be the period when the lower stages of the tower were built. The south aisle, porch, and upper stage of the tower are to a more elaborate design, reminiscent of the Beauchamp chapel at St. John's,[15] and were probably added towards the end of the 15th century. In 1789 there was a door at the east end of the south aisle but it had been blocked by 1831, as had another, visible in 1823, on the north-west side. A west gallery, there in 1831, was perhaps an 18th-century insertion.

In order to provide accommodation for a growing congregation the church, apart from the tower, was rebuilt in 1831–2 in a Perpendicular style to the designs of one Pennistone, presumably John Peniston. It has a chancel of one bay, aisled nave of three bays with west gallery, and the tower, the lower stage serving as a porch. Some materials from the old building were reused, possibly including some of the window tracery from the south aisle. Not long after the rebuilding the church was again closed but was reopened in 1849 after the 'embellishment' of the chancel.[16] Perhaps at this time the vestry was added on the south. The choir vestry on the north was built in 1934.[17] The gallery was rebuilt in 1939–40.[18]

The more notable monuments commemorate some Nicholases: Robert (d. 1722), Robert (d. 1725), and Oliffe Richmond (d. 1767); some Drews: Robert (d. 1671) and Robert (d. 1695); Robert Parry Nisbet (d. 1882); Bridget Keynes (d. 1752); Edward Colston (d. 1859), and several members of the Flower, Hayward, Paradise, and Read

13 Gillman, *Annals*, 20.
14 Unless otherwise stated this paragraph and the next are based on Pugh and Plaxton, op. cit. 13–14, corrected where necessary by (i) B.M. Add. MS. 36391, ff. 15B and 16 (1803, 1823) and (ii) Soc. Antiq. Lond. Incorp. Ch. Bldg. Soc. plans, B 1375, nos. 2 and 4. Pugh and Plaxton relied on Dore's plan and a print of 1807. See also illustration on p. 195.
15 See p. 185.
16 Gillman, *Annals*, 37.
17 Pugh and Plaxton, op. cit. 31.
18 Ex inf. the Revd. K. E. Brown, Vicar.

The Crammer, with St. James's church and churchyard, in the early 20th century

families (17th and 18th centuries) and Coward family (19th and 20th centuries). There are memorial windows to B. C. Dowding, the vicar, and his kin.[19]

A barrel organ was in use until 1841 when it was replaced by a pipe organ. Choir stalls were introduced in 1890 and new pews in 1897. A clock was placed in the tower in 1888.

In 1553 the king's commissioners found 11 oz. of plate of which they took 2½ oz. Among the plate in 1973 were a chalice and paten, and a pair of alms-dishes, hall-marked 1849, and a flagon given in 1855. Twentieth-century additions include two chalices, one with a paten, and a pyx.[20]

In 1553 there were three bells. By the 18th century there were four. They were rehung in 1909 and two new ones, (i) and (ii), cast by J. Taylor of Loughborough (Leics.), added; (iii), formerly the treble, cast by William and Roger Purdue was recast by Taylor at the same time and is dated 1663; (iv) is dated 1742, and (v) and (vi) 1612.[21] The registers date from 1572 and are complete.[22]

19 Mon. inscriptions are transcribed in vol. xviii of M.I.s in W.A.S. Libr., Devizes.
20 Nightingale, *Wilts. Plate*, 151; ex inf. the Revd. K. E. Brown, Vicar.
21 Walters, *Wilts. Bells*, 71–2.
22 In W.R.O. 594. Marriages 1572–1837 are printed in *Wilts. Par. Reg.* ed. W. P. W. Phillimore and J. Sadler, vi. 41–92.

The churchyard was enlarged c. 1844, at the expense of the Crammer, and was closed in 1876.[23] A parsonage-house stood on the Green in 1647, on the site of Heathcote House,[24] and with barn and glebe, amounting to a little over an acre, was still there in 1736–7.[25] By 1841 it had been rebuilt and was in lay ownership.[26] A new Vicarage, later enlarged, was built in 1846 on the north-west side of London Road.[27]

A hall-church in Eastleigh Road to serve the new housing estate was opened in 1957.[28] It was closed in 1966–7 and became the printing works of Messrs. Springfield and Rose.[29]

The church of St. Peter in Bath Road was built in 1866 through the efforts of B. C. Dowding, vicar of St. James's, to meet the spiritual needs of people living in the Nursery and Piccadilly.[30] A consolidated chapelry formed out of Rowde and Southbroom parishes was assigned in 1867 and enlarged in 1886.[31] The site was given by the county who foresaw that the church would serve the militiamen in the neighbouring barracks.[32] The church has had a ritualistic bias. In 1870 it was one of the few in the Wiltshire portion of the Salisbury diocese to have regular Communions on each Sunday and holy day,[33] and Canon F. Phipps, vicar 1901–34, was a high churchman. The bishop has the patronage.

The church of *ST. PETER* is of Bath and Ham stone and was designed by Messrs. Slater and Carpenter of London. It consisted at first of chancel with octagonal apse, nave of four bays with west bell-cote, and north porch.[34] A south aisle, now a Lady Chapel, and a vestry and organ-chamber were added in 1884.[35] The chancel screen was completed in 1902 in memory of A. C. Devas, vicar 1885–1901, and was crowned

23 *W.A.M.* liii. 450.
24 Pugh and Plaxton, op. cit. 21.
25 W.A.S. Libr., Devizes, Map, 1736–7.
26 W.R.O., Tithe Map, Southbroom.
27 W.A.S. Libr., Devizes, Revd. J. Wilkinson's par. hist. colls. (Southbroom); Pugh and Plaxton, op. cit. 21.
28 Wilts. Cuttings, xxi. 4.
29 Ex inf. the Revd. K. E. Brown, Vicar.
30 *Par. Ch. of St. Peter, Devizes* [1959], 4.
31 *Benefice Bk.* St. Peter's, Devizes.
32 Pugh and Plaxton, op. cit. 23.
33 *V.C.H. Wilts.* iii. 73.
34 Pugh and Plaxton, op. cit. 24; *Par. Ch. of St. Peter*, 3.
35 *Par. Ch. of St. Peter*, 7–8.

by three figures in 1938.[36] The glass in the west window, said to be one of the best examples of modern stained glass in Wiltshire, was inserted in 1934 in memory of the Dowdings.[37] In 1935 a new altar was erected in memory of Canon Phipps and the original one moved to the Lady Chapel.[38] There is one bell of 1865 by Warner & Sons.[39] A chalice (c. 1600 and foreign), paten, and spoon were presented by H. A. L. Grindle, the first vicar, in 1869–70. By c. 1890 there was also a plated chalice[40] and by the early 20th century a plated pyx.[41] In 1973 the plate consisted of two chalices, one of them the old one, two patens, the pyx, and three ciboria, one of which was given at the church's centenary. A First World War memorial in the churchyard was designed by (Sir) Ninian Comper.[42]

By will proved 1920 Martha Clark left £800 to be invested and a quarter of the income to be spent on church expenses. The residue was to be applied in thirds to the same purpose, to charities connected with the church, and to the maintenance of Anglican education.[43] In 1971 the income was divided into quarters, one spent on ordinary and one on extra-ordinary church expenses, one on St. Peter's school, and one on the poor. The fourth was not then being distributed.[44]

Belle Vue House was used as the Vicarage from 1889[45] until 1933.[46] Since 1939, if not before, the vicars have lived at a house to the west of the church.[47]

ROMAN CATHOLICISM. No Devizes papist is known before 1767. There were then three.[48] In 1780 there were four[49] and by 1861 about twenty, who worshipped at Chippenham.[50] The first Mass centre in

36 Ibid. 12, 13; *Benefice Bk.* St. Peter's, Devizes.
37 *Par. Ch. of St. Peter*, 10.
38 Ibid. 13.
39 Walters, *Wilts. Bells*, 74.
40 Nightingale, *Wilts. Plate*, 149.
41 *Benefice Bk.* St. Peter's, Devizes.
42 Ex inf. the Revd. R. H. E. Maude, Vicar.
43 Dept. of Educ. and Science, files.
44 Ex inf. the Revd. R. H. E. Maude, Vicar.
45 *Benefice Bk.* St. Peter's, Devizes.
46 Gillman, *Dirs.*
47 *Kelly's Dir. Wilts.* (1939).
48 J. A. Williams, *Cath. Recusancy in Wilts. 1660–1791*, 258.
49 Ibid.
50 St. Joseph's Convent, Llantarnam Abbey, Cwmbran (Mon.): 'Missionaries of St. Francis de Sales in England' (TS. Diary of Fr. Larive).

Devizes was established by Fr. Larive, a Salesian missionary, in a disused warehouse in Monday Market Street, whose site is now occupied by Stringer's garage.[51] C. G. Dowell, formerly an army officer and later a Jesuit lay brother, whom Larive had helped to convert, partially financed the project.[52] The mission was served from Chippenham until 1864, when the present church of Our Lady of the Immaculate Conception, in St. Joseph's Road, opened in 1865, was started.[53] At its restoration in 1887[54] it was an aisleless rectangle of five bays with 'Decorated' windows on the north and two lancets at the west end.[55] In 1909 an apsidal chancel and sacristy with bellcote were added.[56] About 1956 its priests were serving four chapels of ease in adjacent villages.[57]

The church of St. Francis de Sales, Brickley Lane, was opened in 1960.[58] It is a rectangle of ten bays, with seven windows on the north and six on the south.

PROTESTANT NONCONFORMITY. Devizes was early a place where unconventional religious opinions were professed. William Prior, a native, was executed for Lollardy in 1507 and there is other evidence of heresy in the neighbourhood before the Reformation.[59] During the Civil War a conventicle of doubtful legality was being held in the town[60] and Quakerism and Anabaptism began to flourish.[61] Bishop Henchman of Salisbury, after conducting a visitation of his diocese in 1661, found the people of Devizes 'not good', though owing to the excellence of the rector they were giving 'very little trouble'.[62] In 1662 41 parishioners of St. Mary's and 73 of St. John's were presented for not attending church, but the rector asked that no citation be issued against some of the latter who had repented and begun to conform.[63] After 1662, however, ejected

51 Larive's Diary (see above, n. 50). The diary shows that the warehouse was next to St. Mary's ch. The garage is the only possible site.
52 Larive's Diary; *W.A.M.* xliii. 171.
53 Larive's Diary.
54 *Kelly's Dir. Wilts.* (1895).
55 For its then appearance see Mate's *Guide.*
56 *Kelly's Dir. Wilts.* (1911).
57 *V.C.H. Wilts.* iii. 97.
58 *Wilts. News,* 20 May 1960.
59 *V.C.H. Wilts.* iii. 99; Waylen, *Hist.* 102–4.
60 *Wilts. Q. Sess. Rec.* ed. Cunnington, 161.
61 *V.C.H. Wilts.* iii. 102, 116.
62 S.P. 29/43 no. 78.
63 Sar. Dioc. R.O., Chwdns.' Pres. 1662.

ministers settled in the town and taught there,[64] and in 1670 Devizes enjoyed the reputation, perhaps not fully deserved, of being one of the two most notable seats in the diocese of 'great and outrageous meetings'.[65] By the end of the 17th century several leading Devizes families were nonconformist.[66]

Towards the end of that century the unorthodox began to group themselves into sects. The most ancient, perhaps, were the Baptists. As early as 1646 a community of Baptists was congregating in the house of John Freme, and in 1654 what appears to have been a baptismal service in progress beside the Crammer was broken up by a mob.[67] By 1669 the meeting in Freme's house had become Independent,[68] though it is thought eventually to have rejoined the Baptists.[69] Two other Baptist meetings are discernible at this time, one in Mary Fidsall's house, in St. Mary's parish, and the other, reckoned to be Fifth Monarchist, at the house of Thomas Okey, a woolbroker.[70] The second seems to have joined up with the first by 1672.[71] Thomas Hicks was a leading 'teacher' of the Fidsall meeting in the sixties and gathered round him a congregation of 60–80.[72] James Webb, a succeeding minister, took a leading part in the London General Assembly in 1689.[73]

Out of the followers of Hicks and Webb emerged the Old Baptist church or Strict and Particular Baptist church, as it has long been called. In its early days the congregation comprised a number of leading townsmen,[74] including Sir John Eyles, M.P. for the borough in 1679–81. The chapel consequently enjoyed a sober prosperity and attracted several benefactions in the earlier 18th century. These were mainly for the support of ministers, and, so far as can be learnt, there has been an almost unbroken succession of settled ministers from the time of John Filkes (c. 1709–

64 *V.C.H. Wilts.* iii. 105, 108.
65 *Cal. S.P. Dom.* 1670, 424, 448.
66 *V.C.H. Wilts.* iii. 109.
67 Ibid. 102.
68 See p. 207.
69 *V.C.H. Wilts.* iii. 108.
70 G. Lyon Turner, *Orig. Rec. of Early Nonconformity*, i. 117–18; Sar. Dioc. R.O., Chwdns.' Pres. 1662.
71 Okey then joined with another man to register Mrs. Fidsall's house: Lyon Turner, op. cit. ii. 1072–3.
72 Ibid. i. 117.
73 *V.C.H. Wilts.* iii. 108.
74 E. Waylen, 'Nonconformity in Devizes', no. v. A series of articles in *Devizes Advertiser*, May–Dec. 1877, mounted as book in W.A.S. Libr., Devizes.

23).[75] The congregation numbered 59 in 1704, 300 in 1717,[76] c. 50 in 1777, and 69 in 1797. During the 18th century the main events in its history were the erection of a proper chapel in 1780, the establishment of seven village stations between 1782 and 1797, and the secession of some worshippers to the Presbyterians c. 1796.[77] This secession led to a dispute over the title to the Merewether, Eyles, and Hancock charities, which the congregation at the New Baptist chapel claimed. The dispute was settled in Chancery in favour of the Old Baptists in 1816.

The chief subsequent events have been a secession in 1837 to found the Salem chapel,[78] the termination of that congregation in 1895, and the enlargement of the chapel in 1860 and 1928. Two notable pastors deserve a mention: C. H. Marston (1858–70), a physician renowned at the time for relieving cancer, who simultaneously conducted his spiritual and physical therapy, and J. P. Wiles (1907–27), author of *Half-Hours with Isaiah* (1915), an abridgement of Calvin's *Institutes* (1920), and other works, and a public denunciator of R. J. Campbell's 'new theology'. Just before the secession of 1837 the congregation numbered 109, probably in consequence of the zeal of Roger Hitchcock, minister 1830–3, a former Anglican clergyman who is said to have converted fifty. The numbers stood at 96 in 1842, but in 1851 the actual attendances were declared to be much higher.[79]

The congregation first met at no. 22 the Brittox.[80] The premises, two lower rooms and an upper one, appear to have been in two parts. One part was a converted factory leased by Samuel Fidsall in 1664. In 1673 the lease was bought by Sir John Eyles, who presented it to the church. It was renewed in 1772[81] and was still held in the church's name in 1834.[82] By her will dated 1712 Sarah Wright devised in trust a ground-

---

75 Unless otherwise stated the rest of this paragraph, and the three succeeding ones, are based upon 2 notebks. and an unpublished article ('Three Centuries of Christian Witness in Devizes', 1947) compiled by H. Tull and in 1960 *penes* the Minister, Strict Baptist chapel, Devizes. They in turn largely rely upon the records of the chapel, 1905–12, kept (1960) in the chapel safe, of which there is a list in W.R.O.
76 Dr. Williams's Libr., MS. 34. 4 (Evans MS.), f. 125. The figure seems very high but was supplied by Chauncey, the Presbyterian minister, who vouched for its accuracy. See p. 205, n. 91.   77 See p. 205.
78 See ibid.   79 H.O. 129/256/4/8.
80 Waylen, 'Nonconformity in Devizes', no. v, says the meeting-house stood behind no. 20 and was approached thence by a passage.
81 *W.A.M.* xlii. 105; *V.C.H. Wilts.* iii. 122.
82 *Endowed Char. Wilts.* (1908), lxxx, p. 420.

floor room, then used as a meeting-house, which formed part of her dwelling. The remains of the meeting-house could still be traced in 1970. There once appears to have been a graveyard close by.

In 1780 a new chapel, not conventionally orientated, was built in Maryport Street, a plain square box without porches or vestries. An east gallery was added in 1785 and in 1818 a vestry, schoolrooms, and side galleries were provided. In 1860–4 the chapel was furnished with new windows, two porches were added at the east end, and a pipe organ installed. After the closure of Salem chapel the Sunday schools were enlarged. In 1922 an apse was erected and the side galleries removed.

At an unknown date a Mrs. Read, of Devizes, left £100 for the benefit of the Baptist church, Southampton, or, if that should cease, of the church in Devizes. The Southampton church closed c. 1820. The capital was then paid to Devizes, and, with interest arising from some other charities, was invested in the purchase of land near the meeting-house, apparently to secure the approach to the chapel and to serve as a graveyard. By will dated 1699 John Rede left £100. This was lost c. 1720.

Joseph Wright, by will dated 1711, left £500, the interest on £200 of which was to be applied to the minister's stipend, on £100 to be distributed in six-monthly doles to poor worshippers, and on £200 in training a man for the ministry. In 1712 Sarah, Joseph's relict, left the same sum, the interest to be distributed in the same way. Elizabeth Filkes, by will proved 1789, left £950, £5 of the interest upon which was to be distributed to poor worshippers and the rest to the minister. She also made a bequest to the Congregationalists.[83] In 1825 the capital (£527) of these three funds, which in the case of the Filkes charities had been reduced by the fall in South Sea stock, was spent upon the purchase of 21 a. at Broughton Gifford. In 1834 this yielded £46 rent, of which two-thirds was appropriated to Filkes's charity and a third to Wrights'. The share of Filkes's charity was divided according to the terms of the foundress's will. Two-fifths of the share of the Wrights' went to the minister, two-fifths to education, and a fifth to the poor. The poor's doles amounted to 2s. 6d. to 5s. a head. In 1901 the land was let at £50 and the rent applied in the same way.

Hannah Merewether, by will dated 1730, left £500, to be invested in land, the proceeds to be paid to the minister. By will proved 1703 Sir

83 See p. 209.

John Eyles left £50 to be invested in land for the unspecified benefit of the congregation. The money was settled in trust in 1706. At an unknown date Sarah Hancock left £20 to be invested for the benefit of the minister. The money was paid over in 1747, in which year the capital of all three charities was sunk in the purchase of 30 a. at Seend, reduced in 1804 to 25 a. In 1834 the land was let at £60 and the rent paid to the minister.

John Cooper, by will proved 1805, left £200, subject to a life interest, for preaching the Gospel in Potterne. This seems to have been used by the Strict Baptist village station there so long as it lasted. Some time before 1907 the capital with accumulated interest (£252) was transferred to the Maryport Street chapel. T. B. Sloper, by will proved 1932, left in trust a house in Maryport Street. The land was sold as the Mortmain Act, 1891, required. With the £343 thus raised the house was apparently repurchased as a home for the chapelkeeper.

In 1901 the gross income of the six charities then existing was £98 10s., all of which was paid to the minister, apart from £7 to the poor and £5 13s. to the Sunday school. In 1973 the total income of the then eight charities was £321. Most was spent on the maintenance of the minister, the chapel building, and the manse. The poor doles and the charity for training a minister were devoted to missionary work.[84]

Salem chapel, New Park Street, was founded in 1837 by George Wessley, who had been appointed pastor of the Maryport Street chapel in 1836, but left because of divisions in the congregation. The schismatics first worshipped in an old tobacco factory, but built the present chapel in 1838. In 1851 the average congregation was 175.[85] The congregation rejoined the parent body in 1895.[86] After this their chapel was used by the 'open' Brethren,[87] and was sold to them in 1929.[88]

Another Baptist chapel is said to have been opened in High Street before 1815. It existed in 1851, when the average congregation was 120.[89]

---

84 *Endowed Char. Wilts.* (1908), lxxx, pp. 418–20, 472; Char. Com. G. file and 113601; H. Tull, MS. hist. of chapel *penes* the Revd. D. J. Knights, minister; other inf. from Mr. Knights. For the date of Eyles's will see Prob. 11/470 (P.C.C. 109 Degg).
85 H.O. 129/265/4/6.
86 Tull's 'Notes'. A place of worship was certified in 1837: G.R.O. Worship Returns, iv. no. 1563.
87 See p. 214.
88 Char. Com. file 23989.
89 H.O. 129/256/4/3.

The Presbyterian church seems to have originated in the congregation that adhered to William Gough, Timothy Sacheverell, and Benjamin Flower, all ejected ministers, who preached in Devizes in the 1670s and 1680s.[90] By c. 1717 there was a distinct Presbyterian meeting of 500, which followed Nathaniel Chauncey, who had been Flower's assistant.[91] Perhaps it was for them that Edward Pierce registered his house for worship in 1713.[92] They were presumably the 'paedobaptist' congregation of 1773, which, apart from the Friends and the Baptists, was then the only nonconformist congregation.[93] Their chapel, erected by 1734, stood behind some houses at the south end of Long Street.[94] It fell into decay and the worshippers moved to a site on the east side of High Street.[95] J. L. Fenner, minister of 1788 and also the principal of a school,[96] used c. 1788 to give a feast every Whit Monday to tradesmen, servants, and weavers, for which they paid, and to 'hold a club' every six weeks for poor townsmen.[97]

In 1791 a new chapel was opened in Sheep Street next to the present Baptist chapel.[98] Shortly after 1796, when James Biggs (d. 1830),[99] a Calvinistic Baptist, became pastor, the seceders from the Old Baptist chapel (q.v.) partially fused with the Presbyterians for worship.[1] It is from Biggs's pastorate that the establishment of the New Baptist chapel is conventionally dated.[2] About ten years after the partial fusion the two

90 V.C.H. Wilts. iii. 105, 108.
91 Ibid. 108; Dr. Williams's Libr., MS. 34. 4 (Evans MS.), f. 272. Chauncey himself provided the information for the accuracy of which he was prepared to vouch: the number of hearers, however, seems very high. Chauncey was perhaps the son of Ichabod Chauncey, a Congregational minister who d. Bristol 1601: *Calamy Revised*, ed. A. G. Matthews, 112.
92 W.R.O., Certs. Dissenters' Meeting-Houses.
93 *Trans. Cong. Hist. Soc.* v. 376.
94 W.R.O. 234/1, no. 6, deed declaring its use; W.A.S. Libr., Devizes, Map, 1737–8.
95 Gillman (*Dir.* 1859) calls the site 'White Swan Yard', then Mr. Macdonald's offices. So far as is known, there was never a White Swan in High St., only a Black Swan. Its yard, called 'Old Swan Yard' in 1900, lay close to no. 6, W. Budd's shop: Gillman, *Dir.* (1895); *Devizes and Wilts. Gaz.* 26 Apr. 1900.   96 See p. 231.
97 *N. & Q.* cxcii. 208–9. Fenner is there wrongly called an Independent.
98 Cunnington, *Annals*, ii. 268.
99 Tablet in the present chapel. For a pen picture see Waylen, 'Nonconformity in Devizes', no. xiii.
1   S. M. Loveridge and A. Whiting, *New Bapt. Ch. Devizes, Centenary Souvenir*, 4; J. S. Bunce, *Sermon occasioned by Death of late Rev. James Briggs* (1830).
2   *Kelly's Dir. Wilts.* (1848) gives 1792 as foundation date for the Presbyterian chapel. The vols. for 1851–1903 give 1851 as foundation date for the New Baptist chapel. The vols. for 1907 *et post* give 1796.

communities agreed to communicate together, and by 1823 the congregation had apparently assumed the name of the United Society[3] although its home continued to be called 'the Presbyterian Chapel' until the rebuilding of 1858.[4] During the pastorate of J. S. Bunce (sole pastor 1830–46),[5] new schoolrooms and vestries were added to the meeting-house and two galleries. In 1848 the two bodies formally united. Since the beginning of the century the Baptists had been gaining in numbers on the Presbyterians, and in 1851 they resolved to build a new chapel 'with the understanding that it is a Baptist Church' and to invite the Presbyterians to occupy it with them. That chapel, seating 700, was opened in 1852. The rebuilding was the chief event in the pastorate of Charles Stanford,[6] subsequently a national Baptist leader and 'the Chrysostom of this generation'. He drew large congregations, which included some prosperous and sophisticated worshippers, to his chapel, and he evangelized the neighbourhood by such devices as 'cottage preaching'. In 1851 the average congregation at the Sheep Street chapel was 260.[7] After 1852 it doubled in size, and two regular week-night services were conducted in the chapel. In 1858 the old meeting-house was sold and demolished and the site added to the burial ground. A new chapel was built southwards of the old. There are vestries at the north-east and south-east corners. Schoolrooms, enlarged in 1894, lie to the east. The church was restored in 1901 and 1926.[8]

The church enjoys several charities. The largest of these was founded by Thomas Bancroft, of Bristol, who, by will dated 1774, left £500 in trust. Half of the invested interest was to be distributed to 20 poor men of the congregation in cash in April, and the other half in blue coats in October. Bancroft also left £2 yearly to the minister for preaching two sermons, but how this was secured is not apparent. His educational charity is dealt with elsewhere.[9] In 1834 the clothing charity

> 3 What follows is drawn from Loveridge and Whiting, op. cit., from *Charles Stanford, Memories and Letters edited by his Wife*, 42–5, 47, and from personal observation. For Stanford see also *D.N.B.*
> 4 Waylen, 'Nonconformity in Devizes', no. xiii.
> 5 Ibid. for a pen picture.
> 6 Tablet in the present chapel.
> 7 H.O. 129/256/4/7.
> 8 A lithograph in one of the vestries shows the building as it was before the reconstruction of the schools, and a photograph in another shows the fittings *ut olim*.
> 9 See p. 221.

was distributed every second year to about 18 men. About 1777 the capital amounted to £589. William Temple, by will proved 1716, and Sarah Handcock or Hancock, by will dated 1740, left rent-charges of £2 and £3 respectively for the minister. Mary Russell (1756), Mrs. Waite or Wright (1759), Sarah George (1783), Mrs. Gough (at an unknown date), and Mrs. Maye or Mayo (at an unknown date) left £300, £100, £100, £20, and £20 respectively for the minister, and further small sums amounting to £21 had also been accumulated for his benefit by the mid 19th century. Of these small benefactors Betty Sloper, who is named in Schemes of 1925 and 1957, may have been one. In 1859 the trustees of the New Chapel applied to the Charity Commission for the transfer to them of these endowments. They claimed that, though the endowments were nominally for the benefit of Presbyterians, the worshippers at the New Baptist chapel were the Presbyterians' lineal successors. After prolonged argument the charities were adjudged to belong to the New Baptist chapel by Chancery order of 1871 and a Scheme was prepared. The effect of this was to divide the charities into Minister's, Poor, and School Funds and to leave in the first two £852 and £772 respectively, after deducting the costs of the Chancery suit. Since 1888 the figures have been £854 and £774. The rent-charges were still unredeemed in 1973. Herbert Sainsbury, by will proved 1939, left £250 and Rosalie Emily Guy in 1949 gave a house, both in trust for the chapel. The house was sold in 1955 and the capital valued at £274 in 1973. The revenue due from all charitable sources in 1972 was £55. Of this £19 was distributed to 20 poor men in doles of 95p, £21 to the minister, and £8 to the school fund.[10]

Congregationalism in Devizes goes back to 1669 when John Freme's house was registered and John Frayling licensed as minister. Frayling's congregation numbered about thirty. Freme's house was registered again in 1672, and the house of Edward Hope (or Hopes), the younger, added. Frayling, whose licence was then renewed, served both houses and Obadiah Wills was licensed as an additional teacher. Both Frayling and Wills were ejected ministers.[11] After this no more is heard

10 All inf. unless otherwise stated from *Endowed Char. Wilts.* (1908), lxxx, pp. 420, 467–70; Char. Com. files 32647, 122429 and accts. file; ex inf. Mrs. Ingerid Beaven. For Temple's will see W.R.O. 402/74.
11 V.C.H. Wilts. iii. 108; G. Lyon Turner, *Orig. Rec. Early Nonconformity*, i. 118, 303, 337, 344, 474; ii. 1069, 1070.

of Congregationalism for some time; as has been shown, the Freme meeting seems to have become Baptist.[12]

The present Congregational chapel in Northgate Street, often called St. Mary's chapel from the parish in which it lies or 'Bottom Town Chapel',[13] has an unusual origin. From 1763 a group of churchmen living in the town were in the habit of receiving pastoral epistles and visits from Richard Baddely, then rector of Hilperton. Baddely's efforts were supplemented, somewhat later, by other clergymen living in the neighbourhood who were tinged with Methodist ideas, and finally by Rowland Hill, who visited Devizes twice in 1771 and preached in the open air.[14] The second meeting was broken up by a 'mob' instigated thereto by Edward Innes, the assistant curate who some years before had stirred up opposition to Wesley.[15] In the same year in which these meetings occurred Baddely's followers came together as a congregation, allied neither with any branch of Methodism nor with any of the existing dissenting connexions, and certified a house for worship.[16] Other houses were certified in 1772[17] and 1773,[18] one in St. Mary's and the other in St. John's parish. It has been claimed that one or other of these early buildings was a house at the corner of New Park Street and Couch Lane, later used by the 'exclusive' Brethren.[19] In 1776 the nucleus of the present chapel was built.[20] By the foundation deed, to which the countess of Huntingdon, Rowland Hill, and Cornelius Winter were parties, the chapel, already called St. Mary's chapel, was assigned to Calvinistic Methodist worship. The trustees, however, might choose a minister of any denomination provided that he did not preach against such of the Articles as Independent ministers usually subscribed to. Both Anglican

12 See above, p. 201.
13 Ex inf. the late Miss C. M. Pugh (d. 1957).
14 Waylen, 'Nonconformity in Devizes', nos. xx–xxii. Several of Baddely's letters are there printed.
15 See below, p. 212.
16 The certification (G.R.O. Worship Returns, iv, no. 26) was made by Edw. Bayly, one of Baddely's original 'hearers' (Waylen, op. cit. no. xx). The house was said, unintelligibly, to be in 'Newport Street'.
17 G.R.O. Worship Returns, iv, no. 28. Since 1907 the foundation of the congregation seems to have been dated from this registration: *Kelly's Dirs. Wilts.* (1858, 1907).
18 G.R.O. Worship Returns, iv, no. 40.
19 By J. Oram, a former member of the congregation, in *Wilts. Gaz.* 1922: Wilts. Cuttings, ii. 72. See also p. 214.
20 Waylen, *Chrons.* 314.

and nonconformist ministers might administer the sacraments. The former might do so in surplices, and, when they celebrated Holy Communion, might withdraw behind a rail. At some later date, probably within the 18th century, the worshippers discarded their Anglican and Methodist affiliations and became Congregationalists.[21]

In its earlier years the chapel was served voluntarily by the Revd. Robert Sloper (d. 1818), whom the Revd. Richard Elliott (d. 1854) succeeded as the first settled minister.[22] Elliott raised the chapel to its peak of popularity and attracted many of the leading townsmen.[23] Towards the end of his pastorate congregations averaged 525 people.[24] Elliott was an important figure in Congregationalism, and for 28 years was secretary of the Wilts. and East Somerset Congregational Union. In his time Devizes became (1842) the head of a district in the Union and so remained for 50 years.[25] In youth vigorous and eloquent, Elliott later became a champion of the anti-slavery movement and an opponent of papal 'aggression'.[26] His successor, William Kingsland (1852–62), was less popular and during his time a secession to the New Baptist chapel took place. Robert Dawson, the next minister, restored its fortunes by increasing the attendances.[27]

The chapel enjoys four charitable endowments. John Filkes, by will dated 1780, left £100 in trust, the interest to be paid in doles to needy members of the congregation. Elizabeth Filkes, John's sister, by will proved 1789, settled about £969 in trust, £5 of the interest on which was to be paid to poor persons attending the sermons at the chapel and the rest to the minister. She also made a bequest to the Strict Baptists.[28] The capital was subsequently a little reduced but rose again, and in 1834 £1,058 stock was purchased. Thomas Chandler, by will proved 1879, left £100, the proceeds to be applied to the support of the Sunday school. W. A. Waylen, by will proved 1938, left £300 for chapel maintenance.

---

21 S. B. Stribling, *Hist. Wilts. and E. Somerset Congregational Union* (1897), 35.
22 Waylen, *Hist.* 574. There are engravings of both in the vestry.
23 C. Gillman (a member of the congregation) in *Wilts. Advertiser*, 28 July 1904.
24 H.O. 129/256/4/4.
25 A. Antrobus, *Hist. Wilts. and E. Somerset Congregational Union* (1947), 27, 29; Waylen, *Hist.* 574–5; Waylen, 'Nonconformity in Devizes', no. xxiii.
26 Waylen, *Hist.* 574–5.
27 C. Gillman, *Hist. St. Mary's Chapel*, 7.
28 See p. 203.

In 1834 the John Filkes charity was paid out in small doles. Of the Elizabeth Filkes charity £5 was then paid to the poor and the residue to the minister. By 1901 these two charities were being administered together. Their income amounted to £32 and they were similarly divided, except that the poor's share was then £7 14s. In 1973 about a quarter of the Filkes charities was paid to sick and needy worshippers and the residue to general chapel funds. The Chandler and Waylen charities were paid according to the foundation trusts.[29]

The original chapel was a small oblong building entered from the east. In 1790 it was enlarged and made square by an eastward extension.[30] A beam running through the chapel indicates the line of the old east wall. Later, probably in 1810–11, schoolrooms and an assembly room were added on the south.[31] Recertifications of 1835[32] and 1855[33] may represent other changes, and certain improvements were made in 1859.[34] In 1868–9 a lecture hall and schoolroom, designed by Benoni Mullens, were built on the north in 'Early English'.[35] Henceforth the chapel was entered from that side. Substantial internal improvements, designed by J. A. Randell, were carried out in 1876 and in 1892 the windows were remodelled.[36] Further changes were completed in 1925.[37]

The history of Quakerism in Devizes has been traced from 1647,[38] but it is doubtful whether a meeting could have existed so early. By the middle of the next decade, however, there were Quakers in the neighbourhood, and in 1658 Samuel Noyes, a leader of the town

29 *Endowed Char. Wilts.* (1908), lxxx, pp. 417, 471–2; Char. Com. files 93459, 121071; ex inf. Mr. F. Hards, Potterne. Chandler's charity is not reported on in the first source.
30 F. Broster-Temple [pseudonym for F. Hards], *Story of St. Mary's* (priv. print. 1971), 15, 17 (plan). A writer in 1925 (Wilts. Cuttings, x. 142) places these changes within Elliott's ministry. Elliott was joint minister from 1802 and sole minister from 1818 until his death in 1852: Broster-Temple, op. cit. 25.
31 Broster-Temple says that the work was done 'some two years' later and prints an account of 1792. That account, however, may be for work done on the 1790 extension only. It is clear that some enlargement did occur in 1810–11: Waylen, *Chrons.* 314; *Evang. Mag.* xix. 325.
32 G.R.O. Worship Returns, iv, no. 1503. That this was a certification for this chapel may be inferred from the fact that Robt. Waylen, a member of the congregation, was a certifier: *Endowed Char. Wilts.* (1908), lxxx, p. 417.
33 G.R.O. Worship Reg. no. 6657.
34 Gillman, *Hist. St. Mary's Chapel*, 7.
35 Broster-Temple, *Story of St. Mary's*, 38–9.
36 Ibid. 43, 48.
37 Wilts. Cuttings, x. 142.
38 Waylen, 'Nonconformity in Devizes', no. xv.

Quakers,[39] was prosecuted for brawling in church.[40] In 1669 the Devizes Friends were meeting in John May's house[41] and in 1682 in John Clark's, whence they were on one occasion ejected by the constables.[42] In 1702 the house of William Coole and John Bartlett was certified for worship and at the same time a house 'newly erected' by the Friends for their meetings.[43] The freehold of the second of these, no. 23 High Street, occupied in 1971 by the 'exclusive' Brethren,[44] had been acquired in 1701.[45] It became the sole Quaker place of worship. Anglicans and other Nonconformists 'assisted' in its erection. It remained in use until 1826. The meeting then lapsed,[46] and the meeting-house was sold in 1840.[47] Quakerism was revived in Devizes in 1853–4.[48] The old meeting-house was repurchased in 1858,[49] and was again in use for Quaker worship in 1872–3.[50] The meeting was discontinued in 1879.[51] In 1884 the Friends sold the building.[52] They reoccupied it in 1903–7,[53] but apparently not afterwards. The Devizes meeting numbered 80–100 in 1669,[54] about 30 in the 1790s,[55] and seven in 1904.[56] During the 18th century several members of leading local families were adherents, including John Beaven or Bevan, who helped to found the first Devizes bank in 1775, and William Powell of Nursteed Lodge, and on the eve of its first closure it was attended regularly by some non-Quakers, including Anglicans.[57] A

39 *V.C.H. Wilts.* iii. 116.
40 *W.N. & Q.* ii. 165.
41 G. Lyon Turner, *Orig. Rec. Early Nonconformity*, i. 118.
42 C. Gillman in *Wilts. Advertiser*, 30 June 1904.
43 W.R.O., Certs. Dissenters' Meeting-Houses.
44 See p. 214.
45 *Charitable Trusts, Bristol and Som. Qrly. Mtg.* 79.
46 Waylen, 'Nonconformity in Devizes', no. xv.
47 *Charitable Trusts, Bristol and Som. Qrly. Mtg.* 79.
48 *Friends Bk. of Meetings*, 1853–4. E. H. Milligan, 'Meetings Settled, Discontinued or United' (*Jnl. Friends Hist. Soc.* xlix. 99) gives 1854, but there was a week-day meeting in the previous year.
49 *Charitable Trusts, Bristol and Som. Qrly. Mtg.* 79.
50 Gillman, *Dirs.*
51 *Jnl. Friends Hist. Soc.* xlix. 102.
52 C. Gillman in *Wilts. Advertiser*, 30 June 1904.
53 *Procs. of London Yrly. Mtg.* 1904, 1908.
54 G. Lyon Turner, *Orig. Rec. Early Nonconformity*, i. 118.
55 Friends House, Euston Rd., London, Mins. Wilts. Monthly Mtg. ii.
56 *Friends Bk. of Meetings*, 1904.
57 Waylen, 'Nonconformity in Devizes', no. xv; C. Gillman in *Wilts. Advertiser*, 30 June 1904; and see p. 102.

burial ground was acquired in 1665,[58] probably the same as that which now (1973) forms part of Hillworth Park. A graveyard existed on that site by 1759, then accessible by a lane connecting Gallows Ditch (now Hillworth Road) with the Lavington road.[59]

John Wesley first visited Devizes in January 1747 to preach at the house of a Mr. Clark. Before his coming the inhabitants had been roused against him by Innes, the assistant curate.[60] The town was in an uproar 'as if the French were just entering' and Wesley heard an 'abundance of swelling words, oaths, curses and threatenings'. Many of the 'mob' came to Clark's house, at which Innes had announced that 'an obnubilative, pantomime entertainment' would be 'exhibited'. Once there, however, they 'listened a little and stood still'. On a return visit later in the month similar efforts were made to obstruct Wesley, but met with very little success; in fact he preached thrice.[61] Charles Wesley, however, coming in February next in his friend Meriton's company, was blockaded by the mob in a house west of St. Mary's church and barely escaped alive.[62] The reception meted out no doubt explains the reluctance of the Wesleys to revisit Devizes for some time to come. There was indeed no further visit from John until 1764[63] and there is no evidence that he preached again until 1772,[64] by which time the old prejudice had gone. Between that year and 1790 he paid thirteen visits and preached eleven times, in 1778 with Charles in a 'commodious room'.[65]

A house in St. Mary's parish, probably that in which Charles Wesley had stayed, was certified for Methodist worship in 1777.[66] In 1783 the rector thought its congregation was declining and that it included few 'of better rank'.[67] Other certifications were made by ministers in 1807[68] and 1809[69] and one or other of these was no doubt the weaving-room behind what was once no. 20 Sheep Street, occupied by the weaver and

58 *V.C.H. Wilts.* iii. 116 n.
59 Dore, Map, 1759.
60 See p. 208.
61 J. Wesley, *Jnl.* ed. N. Curnock, iii. 275–6.
62 Ibid. 275 n.; *Wesley Hist. Soc.* iii. 138.
63 Wesley, *Jnl.* ed. Curnock, v. 94.
64 Ibid. 447.
65 Ibid. v. 447, 485; vi. 79, 212, 256, 295, 337, 374, 452; vii. 24, 309, 424; viii. 98.
66 G.R.O. Worship Returns, iv, no. 55.
67 *W.R.S.* xxvii, p. 86.
68 G.R.O. Worship Returns, iv, no. 420.
69 Ibid. no. 441.

lay-preacher John Cheeter at the turn of the century.[70] Finally, in 1818, a Methodist chapel in New Park Street was certified, and apparently opened next year.[71] That building, which had 316 sittings,[72] lasted until 1898 when it was replaced by the present red-brick chapel in Long Street.[73] The old chapel was later taken over by the Salvation Army.[74] It was derelict in 1971 and had been pulled down by 1972.

Devizes, formerly a mission attached to Melksham, became the head of a circuit in 1828.[75] It so remained until 1894 when the Wiltshire Mission was formed.[76] Between 1832 and 1886 its own church membership averaged 42 rising to 54 in 1837 and falling to 31 in 1852.[77] The minister formerly derived part of his stipend from the charity (£10) of Amelia Holloway of Horton in Bishop's Cannings (will proved 1851).[78] In 1973 the interest was wholly paid to the Horton Methodist church.[79]

Other forms of Methodism have not flourished in the town. A building on the Green, occupied by George Franklin, was certified for Primitive Methodist worship in 1853.[80] Its certificate was cancelled in 1895 and it had probably been closed by 1882 at the latest.[81] A Wesleyan Reform chapel, in New Park Street, is mentioned between 1855 and 1865.[82]

The Church of Latter Day Saints certified a building in Bridewell Street in 1853. The certification had been cancelled by 1876.[83] A

70 Waylen, 'Nonconformity in Devizes', no. xix.
71 G.R.O. Worship Returns, iv, no. 754. The traditional date of foundation is 1819: *Kelly's Dirs. Wilts.* (1848 and later edns.).
72 *Returns of Wesleyan Chap. Accom.* (1873), *penes* Superintendent, Methodist Wilts. Mission.
73 *Kelly's Dir. Wilts.* (1899). Certified in 1899: G.R.O. Worship Reg. no. 37468.
74 See p. 214. 75 *V.C.H. Wilts.* iii. 142–3.
76 T. R. Jones, *The Departed Worthy*, 102; Wilts. Mission Superintendent's Notebk. *penes* Superintendent, Methodist Wilts. Mission.
77 Devizes Wesleyan Circuit Qrly. Schedules and Devizes Circuit Acct. Bk. 1829–52 *penes eundem*. A much higher average was returned in the 1851 census: H.O. 129/256/4/5.
78 *Endowed Char. Wilts.* (1908), lxxx, pp. 58, 473; *V.C.H. Wilts.* vii. 195.
79 Ex inf. the Revd. C. Cole, minister, Devizes.
80 G.R.O. Worship Reg. no. 830.
81 Not mentioned in *Return of Churches ... registered for Relig. Worship*, H.C. 401, p. 109 (1882), 1.
82 *Kelly's Dirs. Wilts.* It was possibly this chapel which was certified in 1854 (G.R.O. Worship Reg. no. 3175). On the other hand the certificate was cancelled in 1899, on the opening of the new Wesleyan Methodist chapel in Long St.
83 G.R.O. Worship Reg. no. 830.

congregation of 'exclusive' Brethren certified a room in Couch Lane in 1873.[84] In 1929 they removed to no. 23 High Street (High Street hall),[85] which since 1908 had been in secular use.[86] At no. 6 High Street a group of 'open' Brethren, sometimes described as Baptist Brethren, certified two rooms, in 1879 and 1890.[87] In 1895 they moved to Salem chapel, New Park Street,[88] where they still met in 1971. Since 1970 Salem has enjoyed the interest on the proceeds of the sale of the former Brethren's meeting-house in Urchfont and upon a fund established in 1896 for the maintenance of that building.[89] The Salvation Army opened fire in 1881,[90] and first met in the Warehouse Barracks, Couch Lane, where they certified a meeting-place in 1887.[91] They had removed to Commercial Road by 1894.[92] Thence they went to Monday Market Street in 1898[93] and in 1900 to their halls in New Park Street, formerly the Wesleyan Methodist chapel.[94] They left the halls in 1967 and after occupying temporary accommodation opened a centre in the former Civil Defence headquarters, Station Road, in 1971.[95] Between 1891 and 1908 High Street hall was used for undenominational worship by the Y.M.C.A.[96] An undenominational mission room behind Estcourt Street was certified in 1949.[97] 'Premises' in Back (presumably New Park) Street were certified by Thomas Billett in 1851,[98] and a building in St. Mary's parish by Maurice Britton, 'minister',[99] or alternatively by John Weston in the same year.[1] These buildings have defied identification.

84 G.R.O. Worship Reg. no. 21365; and see p. 211.
85 G.R.O. Worship Reg. no. 52097.
86 Gillman, *Dir.*
87 G.R.O. Worship Reg. nos. 24423, 32180.
88 G.R.O. Worship Reg. no. 35103. For the earlier history of Salem chap. see p. 204.
89 See *V.C.H. Wilts.* x. 189.
90 Gillman, *Annals*, 58.
91 G.R.O. Worship Reg. no. 30554; Gillman, *Annals*, 61.
92 Gillman, *Dir.* (1894).
93 G.R.O. Worship Reg. no. 36429.
94 Ibid. no. 37676 and see p. 213.
95 Ex inf. Capt. J. Jones, Devizes Salvation Army Centre.
96 Gillman, *Dir.*
97 G.R.O. Worship Reg. no. 62228.
98 Ibid. Worship Returns, iv, no. 1846.
99 Ibid. no. 1847. A Maurice Britton, stone mason, lived in New (now Snuff) Street in 1848: *Kelly's Dir. Wilts.*
1 W.R.O., Return of Regns. 1851.

SOCIAL AND CULTURAL ACTIVITIES. A theatre, designed by Messrs. Gamble and Whichcord, was erected on the Island on the Green c. 1792.[2] It hardly seems to have succeeded. A spectacle of George IV's coronation was staged in 1822,[3] and in 1833 there was a brief autumn season.[4] There are no other recorded uses. The building, much altered, was felled in 1957.[5] The Palace cinema in the Market Place was opened in 1912,[6] the Regal cinema, New Park Street, in 1939.[7] The latter was closed in 1960.[8]

A Literary and Scientific Institute was formed in 1833 and housed in no. 6 High Street. Capt. J. N. Tayler was a leading founder. In its first year the Institute arranged 34 lectures and had started a library and museum.[9] It moved soon after to premises near St. Mary's church. Those premises were burnt in 1843 and the society migrated to the Chequer and thence to the 'old' Town Hall.[10] In 1851 the society had over 200 members, a library of over 800 volumes, and between 12 and 14 lectures annually.[11] In 1863 it was reconstructed[12] and ten years later gave some of its scientific objects to Devizes museum.[13] By 1907 it had acquired the building of the former British School, Northgate Street, which still housed it in 1971. In 1907 it had about 350 members, a library of 6,000 books, and recreation rooms.[14] Its flourishing condition owed much to C. H. Lowe (d. 1909), a merchant trading to Brazil.[15]

The Devizes Church Library was founded in 1830. It consisted partly of Dr. Charles Bray's clerical library[16] of 200 volumes on loan from London, to which the neighbouring clergy had free access, and partly of church subscription and 'missionary' libraries. The last two, it

2 Wilts. Cuttings, iii. 9; Gillman, *Annals*, 21.
3 Gillman, *Annals*, 26.
4 Ibid. 32.
5 A. Hare, *Georgian Theatre in Wessex*, 148.
6 Gillman, *Dir.* (1912).
7 *Kelly's Dir. Wilts.* (1939).
8 Ex inf. Mr. Dennis Kingman, *Gaz.* reporter.
9 Wilts. Tracts, cxxxi, no. 21; Gillman, *Dir.* (1859); Waylen, *Chrons.* 321. For location of no. 6 see p. 104.
10 Gillman, *Dir.* (1859).
11 *Census*, 1851, *Educ. Eng. and Wales Rep. and Tables*, p. 229.
12 Gillman, *Annals*, 45.
13 *W.A.M.* xiv. 123; *W.A.S. Centenary Hist.* (1953), 8.
14 *Kelly's Dir. Wilts.* (1907).
15 *W.A.M.* xxxvi. 150–1.
16 For Bray see *D.N.B.*

seems, were open to both clergy and laymen. The library first occupied the building in which the Free School and Bear Club School were housed successively[17] and there remained until at least 1897; next it was in St. John's Street; and finally in Station Road, until it closed in 1915. It furnished a meeting-place for the clergy of the district but its usefulness for that purpose declined after Bishop Moberly had established the diocesan synod in Salisbury in 1871.[18]

A branch of the county library was opened in 1927–8 in co-operation with the Literary and Scientific Institute. It moved to St. John's Street in 1936 and thence in 1968 to purpose-built premises in Sheep Street.[19]

The Devizes Club existed by 1823[20] and was perhaps the same as the Brittox Club, which owned a cup and ladle now among the borough insignia.[21] By 1879 it had become the Devizes and North Wilts Club, no. 27 St. John's Street,[22] and had perhaps been reconstituted in 1868.[23] It was dissolved in 1931 and immediately resurrected as the Devizes and District Club.[24] The Liberal Club, no. 22 St. John's Street, was founded in 1890 and enlarged in 1898.[25] Both survive. The Bateson Reading Rooms, New Park Street, were founded in 1879 by Sir Thomas Bateson (cr. Baron Deramore, 1885), M.P. for the borough, for people of all creeds and opinions. The basement of the Rooms was used as a branch National infants' school until 1886, when the children were ejected and the building converted into a Conservative club.[26] In 1961 the club was called the Bateson Conservative Club and was moved to Wilsford House, Long Street. It has since been called the Devizes and District Conservative Club.[27]

---

17 See p. 223. Shown by the fact that the Bear Club School was *c.* 1875 housed in the Church Library: *Kelly's County Topographies, Wilts.* (1875), 132.
18 Wilts. Cuttings, xiv. 230; Wilts. Tracts, lxviii, no. 10; *Devizes Advertiser*, 20 May 1897. For the synod see *V.C.H. Wilts.* iii. 72 where the date of its establishment is wrongly given.
19 Wilts. Tracts, clxxiv, no. 13.
20 W.A.S. Libr., Devizes. Inscription on ballot box.
21 See p. 157.
22 Gillman, *Dir.* (1879).
23 *Whitaker's Almanack* (1920).
24 Ex inf. Mr. R. E. Sandell, Devizes.
25 *Kelly's Dir. Wilts.* (1911).
26 Wilts. Cuttings, iii. 90; Gillman, *Annals*, 61; Nat. Soc. files.
27 Wilts. Cuttings, xxi. 364.

A benefit society for Congregationalists existed in 1780.[28] The Independent lodge of the Odd Fellows was founded in 1820, followed in 1842 by the Providential Dolphin lodge.[29] In 1859 there were four friendly society lodges besides these.[30] In 1844 the Independent Odd Fellows met at the Rising Sun, and did so still in 1859. In the earlier year the Providential Dolphin met at the Castle inn.[31] In 1873 an Odd Fellows hall was opened in Maryport Street[32] and there both lodges met from at least 1886 until *c.* 1948, when the Dolphin, which continues, ingested the other lodge.[33] The hall, which was given up on fusion, had contained a concert room and orchestral gallery, and by 1882 was sheltering the Workingmen's Club,[34] founded in 1863[35] and occupying no. 6 High Street in 1866–9.[36] The club remained in Odd Fellows hall until 1900[37] if not longer.

T. Burroughs or Burrough, bookseller and printer, who occurs from 1734,[38] published or distributed a Devizes edition of the *Salisbury Journal*, known between 1752 and 1774 as the *Salisbury Journal and Devizes Mercury*.[39] Its connexion with Devizes was probably remote. The story of Devizes newspapers really begins in 1819[40] when George Simpson (d. 1871) transferred *Simpson's Salisbury Journal*, founded 1816, from Salisbury and renamed it the *Devizes and Wiltshire Gazette*. The title was changed to *The Wiltshire Gazette* in 1909 and so continued. It remained in the hands of George Simpson—founder, son, and grandson all bearing the same name. Until 1914 the Simpsons were also editors. A management company, Geo. Simpson & Co. Ltd., was then formed and by them the paper was sold in 1956 to Wiltshire Newspapers, Ltd., of

28 See p. 209.
29 *Odd Fellows List of Lodges*, 1886–7.
30 Gillman, *Dir.* (1859).
31 Ibid.; *Odd Fellows List* (1886–7).
32 Gillman, *Annals*, 54.
33 *Odd Fellows Lists of Lodges* and *Qrly. Rep.* 1948.
34 Gillman, *Dir.* (1882).
35 Gillman, *Annals*, 45.
36 Gillman, *Dirs.*
37 W.A.S. Libr., Devizes, sale cat. viii, no. 45.
38 *W.N. & Q.* ii. 35.
39 Ibid. viii. 415.
40 Unless otherwise stated the rest of this account is drawn from three articles on Wiltshire newspapers by J. J. Slade, editor of the *Gazette* from 1914 to 1935, in *W.A.M.* xl. 40–52, xlii. 231–41, 319–20.

Swindon, a member of the Westminster Press group.[41] The paper was then united with the *Wiltshire Herald and Advertiser* and subsequently published in Swindon as the *Wiltshire Gazette and Herald*. In 1836 it had become officially Conservative. In 1872 a cheaper version, designed for working men, was started under the name of *The Wiltshire Telegraph*. It continued until 1933 when it was amalgamated with the *Advertiser* and became *The Wiltshire Telegraph and Advertiser*. In 1942 it was absorbed by the *Gazette*. The *Gazette* offices have stood continuously in the Market Place though not always in the same position.

The *Wiltshire Independent*, mouthpiece of Liberalism in north Wiltshire, was founded in 1836. Edited by Charles Hooton (1836–9), William Burrows (1839–40), and J. R. Fox (1840–76), it was published in Wine Street until 1840, when it moved to no. 36 Market Place. In 1876 it fused with the *Wiltshire Times*, published by Henry Barrass at no. 39 Market Place. Four years later Barrass moved it to Trowbridge,[42] where it has since remained.

The *Devizes Advertiser* was founded by Charles Gillman (d. 1898) in 1858. It was likewise a paper of Liberal inclinations and was originally financed in part by Simon Watson-Taylor of Erlestoke, M.P. for Devizes. It became openly Liberal after 1877, probably upon the disappearance of the *Independent*. It changed its name to *The Devizes and Wilts Advertiser* in 1877 and to *The Devizes and Wiltshire Advertiser* in 1896. It was owned and edited by the Gillmans throughout its course: R. D. Gillman (1894–1910), his nephew W. H. Gillman (1910–14), and his niece Mrs. R. Rogers (1914–?17 *et post*). In 1933 it was incorporated with *The Wiltshire Telegraph*. The works were first at no. 28 the Brittox and a little later at no. 19 in the same street. In 1880 they were enlarged by the purchase of nos. 29–30 Maryport Street and in 1902 transferred wholly to that street. The printing press, purchased in 1877, was operated by a gas engine, one of the first in the district. A linotype machine was bought in 1915. Almost from the beginning the firm published annual almanacs, under titles slightly differing from period to period, and a street directory.

The *Bath Guardian*, a Liberal paper, was known as the *Bath and Devizes Guardian* in 1835–7. The *Devizes Herald and North Wilts Intelligencer*, a Conservative paper, existed in 1869–70.

41 *Newspaper Press Dir.* (1970).
42 Cf. *V.C.H. Wilts.* vii. 140.

EDUCATION. In 1619, in ambiguous circumstances, the corporation paid a Mr. Davis for allowing a schoolmaster to teach in the town[43] and at the same time paid rent for a school-house which they repaired and equipped.[44] Perhaps there had been a town schoolmaster for a long time, for a 'master of the schools' is mentioned in 1322.[45] Nothing, however, suggests that in the early 17th century there was any means of paying such a person a regular salary.

By will proved 1642 John Pierce left among other charities £50 in trust to the corporation the interest to be applied to a schoolmaster's salary until a school site could be bought or a 'right' schoolmaster found.[46] The old school building had, therefore, either been abandoned or was unfit. By 1649 Pierce was dead and the corporation decided to use the interest to pay the existing schoolmaster to teach four children of their own choosing.[47] References to a schoolmaster recur in 1658–9,[48] 1672–3,[49] 1682,[50] and 1689–90.[51] In the first year he was using Pierce's charity, in the second he was called 'schoolmaster of this borough', and in the third two men are named and there is mention of 'the free schools' in the plural. In 1678–80 the corporation was again maintaining a school house.[52] About 1664 William Woodruff devised a rent-charge of £5 to keep ten Devizes boys at school,[53] but there are no references to its use until 1696, when the income was three years in arrear.[54] The charity was eventually recovered but how soon is unknown. In 1697 the corporation arranged to pay £10 out of the chamber for the next seven years to a schoolmaster to keep a Latin school for five boys nominated by themselves. The interest (£3) on Pierce's charity was to be paid to the teacher as well.[55] No appointment, however, seems to have been made until 1699.[56]

43 Cunnington, *Annals*, i (2nd pagin.), 57.
44 Ibid. 58–9, 67.
45 Sar. Dioc. Regy., Reg. Martival, Ep. Sar. ii, f. 315v.
46 *Endowed Char. Wilts.* (1908), lxxx, p. 414. For his other charities see pp. 170, 240, 245, 248.
47 Cunnington, *Annals*, i (2nd pagin.), 116–17.
48 Ibid. ii. 151.
49 Ibid. i (2nd pagin.), 157.
50 Ibid. 167.
51 Ibid. 190.
52 W.R.O. 844, Entry Bk. vol. 'C'.
53 Phillipps, *Wilts. M.I.* 77.
54 Cunnington, *Annals*, i (2nd pagin.), 194–5.
55 Ibid. 195.
56 Ibid. 200.

In 1704 a rent of £8 charged on the Elm Tree, then the Salutation inn, was settled in trust by Mary Eyles, widow, for charitable purposes.[57] One of these was the teaching of six children, on whom £3 was to be spent annually. The residue of the charity (16s.) which was left to augment the foundress's other charities was also spent on teaching c. 1834.[58] It thus seems that by the early 18th century there was provision for a school building and a schoolmaster and that there were charitable exhibitions for children. A schoolmaster was actually being employed in 1719.[59]

Shortly after this there was a more important endowment. About 1725, by which year he had died, John Smith gave £300 for a new school building. With that sum a school was put up on corporation land in Maryport Street,[60] on a site later covered by the National schools. Under the name of the Free School it still existed in 1791[61] and for some time afterwards. The older school, however, seems to have remained open for a while. In 1725 the upper room of the New Alms-house was being occupied by 'the schoolmaster' who was ordered to pay his rent or else to quit.[62] No more is heard of it as a school and apparently by 1732 its former furniture was in a carpenter's hands.[63]

About 1733 a schoolmaster was occupying Smith's school and was receiving the interest on Pierce's and Wild's charities in return for teaching nine boys nominated by the corporation.[64] The second of these foundations was due to Thomas Wild who, apparently c. 1731, had given or bequeathed £100 for the education of five boys.[65] In 1737 the corporation appointed a schoolmaster, but whether to succeed or complement the man of 1733 is not clear. They also seem to have aimed at enlarging the school building.[66] After 1733 Pierce's teaching charity disappears, possibly confused with his other charities.

During the century and a half from James I's accession more had been done for primary, though not for secondary education in Devizes

57 For her other charities see pp. 242, 249.
58 *Endowed Char. Wilts.* (1908), lxxx, pp. 392, 445.
59 W.R.O. 632/89, Rate Bk. 26 Apr. 1719.
60 Cunnington, *Annals*, i (2nd pagin.), 206; Phillipps, *Wilts. M.I.* 77; *Endowed Char. Wilts.* (1908), lxxx, p. 415.
61 Cunnington, *Annals*, ii. 175.
62 Ibid. 152.
63 W.R.O., Con. Sar. Invent. of Ambrose Zealy.
64 Ibid. 844, Entry Bk. vol. 'D'.
65 *Endowed Char. Wilts.* (1908), lxxx, p. 416.
66 W.R.O. 844, Entry Bk. vol. 'D'.

than for many another town of comparable size and wealth. The satisfaction which the S.P.C.K. expressed in 1709 at the progress made was consequently not unjustified.[67] Nothing, however, had occurred to make the existence of a charity school for 70 boys, 50 of them clothed, such as Thomas Cox declares to have existed c. 1738, credible.[68]

Five further charitable provisions were made for primary education in the 18th century. First in 1756 the Bear Club, a social gathering at the inn of that name, was founded. Its rules imposed a fine on absentees, and these fines, supplemented later by subscriptions and donations, created a fund for teaching the elements to six boys and partially clothing them.[69] The number of boys rose to ten and by 1775 to sixteen, by which year some of the income was devoted to apprenticing.[70] The charity was augmented by the bequest of £100 from James Maynard (will proved 1786).[71] The later history of the charity is resumed below.[72]

The other educational charities of the 18th century were Powell's, Bancroft's, and Imber's. By will dated 1743 Eleanor Powell (*née* Phillips) left £500 the income on the bulk of which was to be used for clothing and educating six poor unrelieved girls. By 1790 the capital had risen to £600 and yielded £18 of which £17 was used for education and clothing. A schoolmistress then received a guinea for each girl and taught them reading, writing, and needlework.[73] Thomas Bancroft, by will dated 1774, bequeathed £500 the interest to be applied to teaching 20 boys of the two parishes and also of the Presbyterian congregation English and writing. The choice of pupils was to be made by the rector and Presbyterian minister and as far as possible the three congregations were to share equally. By 1783 the capital amounted to £731.[74] In 1788 Elizabeth Imber, of Winchester, had given money to purchase £1,333 stock, two-fifths of the interest to be applied to teaching reading and needlework to seven girls of St. John's parish and to clothe them. The

---

67 [S.P.C.K.], *An Acct. of Char. Schools* (1709), 19; cf. *Rep.* for 1710, 21, which states that £20 was yearly subscribed for a charity school.
68 Thomas Cox, *Magna Britannia* (1738), vi. 199.
69 *Endowed Char. Wilts.* (1908), lxxx, p. 433. The following account slightly modifies that given in *V.C.H. Wilts.* v. 350–1.
70 Wilts. Tracts, xxvii. 11A.
71 *Endowed Char. Wilts.* (1908), lxxx, p. 433.
72 See pp. 223–4, 228–9.
73 *Endowed Char. Wilts.* (1908), lxxx, pp. 405–6; for her other charities see above and below, pp. 178, 250.
74 *Endowed Char. Wilts.* (1908), lxxx, p. 416.

girls were to stay three years in school.[75] Finally, though he endowed no educational charity, Thomas Thurman (d. 1777), a notable Devizes benefactor, left £732 for clothing, teaching, and apprenticing 30 boys and £295 for the like benefit to 15 girls, each of whom was to stay three years in school.[76]

Thus by the end of the 18th century there was a town school and fairly abundant provision for exhibitions. The situation, if muddled, was favourable to education and it can well have been true, as was said in 1783, that 'most of the children of the town go to the schools'.[77]

With the opening of the 19th century Devizes began to acquire a complex of elementary schools of the usual type. A girls' school was founded in 1813 and united with the National Society next year.[78] From the outset it taught handicrafts[79] and in 1818 contained 80 girls.[80] It is not known where it stood but in 1819 John Pearse, a borough M.P., built a schoolroom, which since 1882 has been the Masonic Hall in Morris's Lane.[81] In 1822 a subscription was raised to provide other schools both for the town and Southbroom, though Southbroom later withdrew from the joint scheme, taking a share of the capital.[82] With the residue a town infants' school was built on the west side of Sheep Street in 1825.[83]

In 1833 the girls numbered 100 and the infants 60,[84] and Imber's charity was being spent upon them.[85] By 1846–7 there was a teacher for each school and a house provided for the girls' teacher.[86] In 1858 the girls were additionally benefiting from Powell's and 'Nicholas's' charities.[87] The second of these is puzzling; though different members of the Nicholas family had founded charities,[88] none was expressly educational. Soon

---

75 *Endowed Char. Wilts.* (1908), lxxx, p. 395. For her parallel benefaction to Winchester see *V.C.H. Hants*, v. 80.
76 Prob. 11/1033 (P.C.C. 333 Collier).
77 W.R.S. xxvii, p. 85.
78 *Nat. Soc. Reps.* 1815, 1828.   79 Ibid. 1815.
80 Ibid. 1818.
81 *Endowed Char. Wilts.* (1908), lxxx, p. 460.
82 Ed. 49/8170.
83 Nat. Soc. files, declar. of trust of 9 Nov. 1876; elsewhere the rector said that date of building was 1826: Ed. 7/130 no. 100. For the location see W.R.O. 844, Corp. Lease Bk., corp. lands, no. 105.
84 *Educ. Enquiry Abstract*, H.C. 62, p. 1035 (1835), xliii.
85 *Endowed Char. Wilts.* (1908), lxxx, p. 460. They should also have enjoyed Powell's char.   86 Nat. Soc. *Ch. Schs. Enquiry*, 1846–7.
87 *Acct. of Wilts. Schs.* H.C. 27, p. 20 (1859 Sess.1), xxi (2).
88 See p. 248.

after this the girls began to enjoy the charity of Sarah Wadsworth who, by will proved 1854, left £50 in trust for their benefit.[89]

The old Free School, called the Blue Coat School in 1844,[90] continued as the place where the boys were taught. It was said c. 1834 to be under the rector's management and to possess a dilapidated building and a 'large and lofty' school-house.[91] In 1838 the corporation as trustees of Smith's charity settled the building in trust as a place for teaching the elements.[92] The school enjoyed Wild's, Woodruff's, Mary Eyles's, and Bancroft's charities, and the master taught those boys who were financed by the Bear Club charities and also fee-payers.[93] In all there were then 106 boys[94] and 126 by 1846–7.[95] By 1848 the school seems to have moved out of Smith's old building into Sheep Street[96] and therefore into the same building as the National infants occupied, which was probably enlarged for the purpose. By the same year the Bear Club trustees had formed their own school and taken over for its use the Free School building thus vacated.[97]

From that time onwards there were three Anglican schools within the ancient borough known until closure as the Town Schools. It is not clear when the boys' school was united with the National Society but in 1854 a trust was declared which 'imported the provisions' of the society's trust deed.[98] In 1858 the teachers in the boys' and girls' schools were certificated and the mistress in the infants' school trained. All three schools were well reported on, especially the infants'.[99] The boys' school was enlarged in 1857 and acquired the 'Angel rent' as extra income in 1858.[1]

[89] *Endowed Char. Wilts.* (1908), lxxx, p. 458.
[90] Pigot, *Nat. Com. Dir.* (1844).
[91] *Endowed Char. Wilts.* (1908), lxxx, pp. 415–16.
[92] W.R.O. 844, Corp. Min. Bk. 1835–46, 28 Apr. 1838.
[93] *Endowed Char. Wilts.* (1908), lxxx, pp. 415–17.
[94] *Educ. Enquiry Abstract* (1835), xliii, p. 1035.
[95] Nat. Soc. *Ch. Schs. Enquiry*, 1846–7.
[96] Listed as in Sheep St. and under the tuition of J. Gerrish who later was master of the Bear Club Sch.: *Kelly's Dir. Wilts.* (1848, 1875). On the other hand there survives an order for placing the National boys in Sheep St. which is dated 1852: Wilts. Cuttings, iii. 105.
[97] See pp. 221, 228–9.
[98] Ed. 49/8171. A boys' sch. united with the diocesan board is found in *Nat. Soc. Rep.* 1838. The date of union of the infants' sch. is also obscure. In 1854 the rector surprisingly remarked that the girls' and infants' schs. were unconnected with any society: Ed. 7/130 no. 100.
[99] *Acct. of Wilts Schs.* (1859 Sess. 1), xxi (2), p. 19.
[1] *Endowed Char. Wilts.* (1908), lxxx, p. 432; Ed. 49/8167; see p. 247.

By the same year it had lost Wild's charity.[2] The building was again enlarged in 1876,[3] no doubt in part to provide space for the Bear Club boys, whose school had ceased.[4] In 1882 the girls moved into the boys' building and the boys were transferred to an entirely new one built on the site of the old Free School.[5] Meanwhile a branch infants' school was opened in 1879 in Bateson's Reading Rooms, New Park Street, but had to be given up in 1886.[6] Average attendance in the three schools was 230 in 1893, although nominally there was space for twice that number.[7]

The British School closed in 1893,[8] and church education at the primary level was given a sudden jolt. The Anglican managers were forced to find more accommodation quickly or else submit to the establishment of a school board. Bishop Wordsworth guaranteed £1,000 if the town would double it. The town did so and a 'Devizes Day Schools Association' was formed to foster the cause.[9] The boys' and infants' schools were under enlargement in the same year and so were the other schools.[10] But it was putting new wine into old bottles. The Town School buildings either were incorrigibly bad or the L.E.A. and the inspectors were determined to deem them so. In addition, unlike Southbroom parochial school, they do not seem to have been pedagogically efficient.[11] Plans for a single new church school for Devizes began to be formulated in 1914[12] but naturally could not then be realized. Meanwhile the accommodation figures had been reduced in 1908–9 from 546 to 471. The average attendance was then 351.[13]

Early in 1925 the county council began to cast longing eyes on Southbroom House,[14] which with much surrounding land had been bought by the firm of W. E. Chivers.[15] They felt that the house itself

2 See p. 220.
3 Nat. Soc. files.
4 See pp. 228–9.
5 *Endowed Char. Wilts.* (1908), lxxx, p. 460; plans and elevations in Ed. 21/18392.
6 Ed. 7/130 no. 100; Nat. Soc. files.
7 *Return of Schs. 1893* [C. 7529], p. 638, H.C. (1894), lxv.
8 See p. 227.
9 Nat. Soc. files; *Wilts. Gaz.* 13 Nov. 1913.
10 Nat. Soc. files; Ed. 21/18392.
11 Ibid.
12 Ed. 21/18390.
13 *Bd. of Educ., List 21* (H.M.S.O. 1910), 506.
14 See p. 72.
15 Unless otherwise stated this and the following two paragraphs are based on Ed. 21/42202.

with its park would serve as a base for a new council school and 'would give us a school of a novel and attractive type'. The property was bought the same year and had been adapted as a senior school by August 1926. In the interval it had been sententiously described as a 'new departure in Primary Schools'.[16] Thereupon all the old Town Schools were closed. Under a Scheme of 1928 the Maryport Street building was sold and under the name Maryport Street chambers used as offices. The Sheep Street building, however, was reserved for instruction.[17] The two buildings were demolished respectively in 1969[18] and 1958.[19]

The new Southbroom school rapidly won approval. By 1930 it had a 'housecraft centre' near by and a large school garden. In 1949 it became 'secondary modern' under the name Southbroom Secondary School and had an average attendance of 452 in 1950.[20] It was enlarged in 1956[21] and 1964.[22]

Southbroom National schools, north of the church, were built in 1833. A state building grant became payable in 1834. The school consisted of two rooms one above the other and was of stone with a thatched roof.[23] It was said to be capable of holding 128 boys and 105 girls.[24] Two teachers, male and female, existed by 1846–7 and there was a teacher's house.[25] In 1859, when both teachers were declared to be of 'high respectability', only 50 of each sex attended.[26] The school was enlarged in 1872 by the addition of an infants' school on a separate but adjacent site and two years later had an attendance of 238.[27] It was again enlarged in 1879 by providing room for more infants.[28] To meet Board of Education requirements it was substantially rebuilt in 1894–5[29] and thereafter had approved accommodation for 165 boys, 134 girls, and 168 infants.[30] In 1893, on the eve of the last enlargement, average

16 *The Times Educ. Sup.* 14 Nov. 1925.
17 Nat. Soc. files; W.A.S. Libr., Devizes, sale cat. xix, no. 23.
18 Demolition then in progress: *Wilts. Gaz.* 3 Apr. 1958.
19 Wilts. Cuttings, xxiii. 244.
20 Ex inf. Wilts. Educ. Cttee. and Scrap Bk.
21 Wilts. Educ. Cttee. Scrap Bk.
22 Wilts. Co. Council, *Education in Wilts. 1963–6*, 43.
23 *Acct. of Wilts. Schs.* (1859 Sess. 1), xxi (2), p. 13.
24 *Educ. Enquiry Abstract* (1835), xliii, p. 1035.
25 Nat. Soc. *Ch. Sch. Enquiry*, 1846–7.
26 *Acct. of Wilts. Schs.* (1859 Sess. 1), xxi (2), p. 13.
27 Ed. 2/461.
28 Ed. 21/18391.
29 See p. 224, n. 10.
30 *Kelly's Dir. Wilts.* (1895); Ed. 21/18391.

attendance had been 311.[31] It was 382 in 1908–9 and 304 in 1937–8.[32] On the reorganization of the Devizes schools in 1926 it became under the name of Southbroom Parochial School a school for standard I children and infants only and was enlarged in 1928.[33] It was granted controlled status in 1949 and in 1950 average attendance was 452.[34] In the earlier 20th century the school was much praised by the inspectors in three separate annual reports.[35]

Heathcote House, the former seat of a proprietary school,[36] became the home of the headmaster of Southbroom Senior School in 1926, and was still partly used as a school residence in 1972. In the 1930s it was also used for other purposes connected with teaching. In 1954 classrooms were there provided to rehouse a part of Southbroom Parochial school. In 1957 it was decided to split that school into two: Southbroom Church of England Controlled Infants' school to remain at Heathcote House and a Southbroom Church of England Controlled Junior school, to be purpose-built, in Nursteed Road.[37] The second of these was opened in 1961.[38] The first was afterwards enlarged. In January 1973 there were respectively 451 and 668 pupils on the roll.[39] In 1971 the old Southbroom parochial schoolrooms were being used as a youth centre.[40]

A British school for girls was built in 1822 in Northgate Street on land given by Robert Waylen. An evening school for boys was subsequently started, but by 1833 there was still no British day school for boys.[41] In 1834, however, a state building grant was received,[42] and by 1836 a boys' school had been opened. At the annual examination in that year it was stated that 'the interrogative system' had been 'fully developed'.[43] In 1869 an infants' school was being conducted in or near the Congregational chapel,[44] and in 1872 a new schoolroom for infants,

31 Return of Schs. 1893 (1894), lxv, p. 638.
32 Bd. of Educ., List 21 (H.M.S.O. 1910, 1938), 506, 422.
33 Ed. 21/42204; Bd. of Educ., List 21 (H.M.S.O. 1928), 359.
34 Ex inf. Wilts. Educ. Cttee. 1950.
35 Ed. 21/42204.
36 See p. 232.
37 Wilts. Educ. Cttee. Scrap Bks.
38 Wilts. Co. Council, Education in Wilts. 1960–1, 18.
39 Ex inf. Wilts. Educ. Cttee.
40 Ex inf. the Revd. K. E. Brown, vicar of Southbroom.
41 Wilts. Cuttings, iii. 109.
42 Mins. Educ. Cttee. 1848–50, i, p. ccxlvii.
43 32nd Rep. Brit. Schs. Soc. 59.
44 Weaver, Map, 1869.

presumably forming part of the main school buildings, was opened.[45] The schools were closed at very short notice in 1893, in the belief, which proved mistaken, that a board would soon be formed,[46] or, according to the Anglican contention, to force its formation.[47] The average attendance was then 422.[48] The children were fitted into other schools in the town or into parish rooms.[49] In 1895 the buildings were handed over to the borough for a technical school and sold in 1906.[50]

St. Peter's National school, with buildings south of the church, was opened in 1870[51] with the help of a state building grant.[52] Average attendance was 66 in 1893[53] but the school was then enlarged[54] so that by 1899 it had risen to nearly 200.[55] By 1910 the school had been organized in two departments, mixed and infants, with respective average attendances during 1908–9 of 129 and 88.[56] The buildings were again enlarged in 1911–12.[57] The departmental structure was the same in 1950 when average attendance was 208.[58] Aided status was granted in 1951.[59] After the closure of the former Grammar School in 1969 (see below) St. Peter's Church of England Aided School (its present designation) had used part of the buildings. In January 1973 there were 233 pupils on the roll.[60]

Sisters of the teaching order of St. Joseph of Annecy reached the town in 1864 and at once opened a Roman Catholic 'poor school' in the improvised Roman Catholic chapel in Monday Market Street.[61]

45 Gillman, *Annals*, 53.
46 Ibid. 64.
47 Nat. Soc. files, Devizes Town Schs., letter from rector, 21 July 1893.
48 *Return of Schs. 1893* (1894), lxv, p. 638.
49 Nat. Soc. files, Devizes Town Schs., letter from rector, 21 July 1893; *Wilts. Gaz.* 13 Nov. 1913.
50 W.A.S. Libr., Devizes, Min. Bk. of Trustees, 1891–1917. The lease was formally signed in 1897; *Endowed Char. Wilts.* (1908), lxxx, p. 462. Min. Bks. for 1847–91 are also at Devizes.
51 Gillman, *Annals*, 52.
52 *Sch. Building Grants* [Cd. 1336], p. 138, H.C. (1902), lxxviii.
53 *Return of Schs. 1893* (1894), lxv, p. 638.
54 *Kelly's Dir. Wilts.* (1907).
55 *Return of Schs. 1899* [Cd. 315], p. 856, H.C. (1900), lxv (2).
56 *Bd. of Educ., List 21* (H.M.S.O. 1910), 506.
57 Nat. Soc. files; Ed. 21/18389.
58 Ex inf. Wilts. Educ. Cttee.
59 Wilts. Educ. Cttee. Scrap Bk.
60 Ex inf. Wilts. Educ. Cttee.
61 St. Joseph's Convent, Llantarnam Abbey, Cwmbran (Mon.): 'Missionaries of St. Francis de Sales in England' (TS. Diary of Fr. Larive).

Early in 1865 the school, then numbering 14, was moved to the new church in St. Joseph's Road and conducted in that church until in 1868 it was provided with a one-room schoolroom, consecrated for worship, west of the church.[62] That building survives. The school has been called St. Joseph's School since at least 1886.[63] Average attendance was 96 in 1893.[64] In 1901 an infants' room was built,[65] and since 1904 there has been a separate infants' department under a separate head teacher.[66] In 1908–9 the respective average attendances were 101 and 59.[67] A new school building was put up in 1930 beside the existing one.[68] The accommodation was fixed at 240.[69] In 1950 average attendance for junior children was 183 and for infants 92.[70] Aided status was granted in 1952,[71] and the buildings again enlarged in 1970.[72] In January 1973 there were 122 children on the roll of the junior school and 96 on that of the infants' school.[73] The sisters of St. Joseph have for long lived close to the school.

About 1848 the Bear Club trustees acquired the old Free School building and with it the man who had hitherto taught the boys.[74] Henceforth under that master they carried on an independent boys' school.[75] By the same time the funds, originally meant for Devizes boys alone, were put at the disposal of all boys in Wiltshire.[76] In 1858 the school was being called the Bear Club School, and had acquired Wild's charity, formerly attached to the Free School, though the boys' Town School kept the other endowments. The master was then teaching 30 boys. The results of his labours, however, were said to bear 'no adequate proportion to the expenditure'.[77] By 1874 the school, which earlier in

62 Larive's Diary (see above, n. 61); Ed. 7/130 no. 97. For the ch. sites see p. 200.
63 *Rep. of Educ. Cttee. of Council, 1885–6* [C. 4849–I], H.C. (1886), xxiv.
64 *Return of Schs. 1893* (1894), lxv, p. 638.
65 Ed. 21/18388.
66 Log. Bk. *penes* St. Joseph's Infants' Sch.
67 *Bd. of Educ., List 21* (H.M.S.O. 1910), 506.
68 *Wilts. Gaz.* 19 June 1930.
69 Wilts. Educ. Cttee. Scrap Bk.
70 Ex inf. Wilts. Educ. Cttee.
71 Wilts. Educ. Cttee. Scrap Bk.
72 Ex inf. Sister Mary Thomas, St. Joseph's Convent.
73 Ex inf. Wilts. Educ. Cttee.
74 See p. 223. Probably he could not remain at the Town School because he was uncertificated.
75 'The Society's school': *Wilts. Times*, 8 Jan. 1910, quoting news item of 1848.
76 Wilts. Tracts, xxxvi. 2.
77 *Acct. of Wilts. Schools* (1859 Sess. 1), xxi (2), pp. 19–20; and see above, pp. 220–1.

the century had been deemed 'a very superior' one 'in the education and preparation of boys for the practical duties of an active life' and capable of providing a 'plain English education', had fallen in repute and numbers. It was closed in 1875 and the boys transferred to the Town School.[78] Thereafter the charity moneys seem to have been held for a while in suspense,[79] but in 1901, when the capital was £725, a scheme was framed for distributing the income in exhibitions payable to Wiltshire and preferably Devizes boys who sought professional, industrial, or pedagogic training. In 1922 Maynard's charity, then worth £253, was so regulated that the income should be applied to augment the substantive charity. In 1964 the trusts were further broadened to include university education and the purchase of books and educational equipment.[80]

In 1833 there were two private infant or dame schools with 56 children between them.[81] In 1859 there were five in the old town with 100 and one in Southbroom with 20–30 children.[82] In 1833 there were also five Sunday schools.[83] In 1869 there were five other schools besides those named above. They included St. Bartholomew's Home and Industrial School, facing the entrance to Old Park,[84] which in 1874 was a place for training girls for domestic service.[85]

Devizes Secondary (later Grammar) school, for both sexes, was opened in Bath Road in 1906.[86] The building, designed by R. E. Brinkworth, is of Bath stone faced with Newbury bricks. Initially it provided space for 120 children and was furnished with a laboratory and art room.[87] By 1919 the school had outgrown these premises and in 1920 a house on the opposite side of the road, renamed Braeside in 1921, was acquired as an extension. In this extension the headmaster lived until 1932, and a preparatory school was maintained until 1938. Congestion continued and minor enlargements were made to meet it. These proving insufficient, plans for a school in Southbroom Park had

78 Wilts. Cuttings, xiii. 190; Gillman, *Annals*, 55; *Endowed Char. Wilts.* (1908), lxxx, p. 434.
79 *Wilts. Gaz.* 23 Nov. 1893.
80 Dept. Educ. and Science char. files. Schemes of 1903 and 1910 made minor changes.
81 *Educ. Enquiry Abstract* (1835), xliii, p. 1035.
82 *Acct. of Wilts. Schs.* (1859 Sess. 1), xxi (2), pp. 13, 19.
83 *Educ. Enquiry Abstract* (1835), p. 1035.
84 Weaver, Map, 1869.
85 Ed. 2/461.
86 *V.C.H. Wilts.* v. 354.
87 *Devizes Gaz.* 6 Sept. 1906 contains a picture, plan, and full description.

been drawn by 1945.[88] In 1969 the school was fused with Southbroom Secondary school, the buildings of which were consequently enlarged. Together they have since formed a comprehensive school on the Southbroom site under the name of the Devizes School. In January 1973 there were 1,373 pupils on the roll.[89]

One new educational charity was founded in the later 19th century. Ann Sophia Slade, widow, of Bath, by will proved 1887, left £50, the surplus income of which was to be paid to the Town Schools.[90] The history of the older charities in that century and the next is as follows. One-third of Bancroft's until the Education Act, 1891, was applied to the week-day education of boys who were members of the New Baptist chapel Sunday school, all of whom in practice attended the British School. By Scheme of 1893 this third was applied to prizes for such children attending any of the Devizes schools[91] and was so used in 1971.[92] Between 1888 and 1896 three-sevenths of Mary Eyles's charity were applied to educating six children at the Town Schools.[93] After that its educational element seems temporarily to have ceased.[94] Eleanor Powell's charity, which until 1891 had been paid over to the Town Schools, was afterwards spent on clothing 13 girls.[95] In 1901 the income of the non-Baptist share of Bancroft's[96] charity and Imber's,[97] Wadsworth's,[98] Wild's,[99] and Woodruff's[1] charities and the Angel rent[2] were paid to the Town Schools. It is uncertain whether this was then true of Slade's. In 1949 all these eight charities, excluding Wild's but including the site of the old Sheep Street school and the profits on the sale of the Maryport Street school, were vested in the Salisbury Diocesan Council of Education,[3] who apply

88 Wilts. Educ. Cttee. Scrap Bks.; Olive Chivers, 'Reflections on . . . Education in Devizes' (1962) (MS. *penes* the author, 1973), f. 18. Braeside was formerly called Beltwood Dalling.
89 Ex inf. Wilts. Co. Co.
90 *Endowed Char. Wilts.* (1908), lxxx, p. 448.
91 Ibid. pp. 470–1.
92 Ex inf. Mr. G. E. Pearce, Devizes, and Dept. Educ. and Science.
93 *Endowed Char. Wilts.* (1908), lxxx, p. 445.
94 See p. 231.
95 *Endowed Char. Wilts.* (1908), lxxx, p. 457.
96 Ibid. pp. 444, 460.
97 Ibid. p. 447.
98 Ibid. p. 458.
99 Ibid. p. 442.
1 Ibid. p. 461.
2 Ibid. p. 460.
3 Scheme.

the income to the council's general purposes, mainly the provision of better church schools throughout the diocese.[4] The Angel rent was redeemed in 1972.[5] Wild's charity remained separate. In 1970 and for many years before it was distributed in rotation to the schools in the town.[6]

A part of Mary Eyles's charity seems to have been again put to school use by 1905 and was so applied in 1915.[7] In 1966 the managers of St. Peter's School were made trustees of what was then named the Mary Eyles educational charity[8] and were administering it in 1971, when it was of the approximate capital value of £334. The income was then distributed equally between St. Peter's, Southbroom junior, and Southbroom infants' schools.[9]

Devizes has had numerous private schools. 'Perhaps no town of its size', said a writer in 1920, 'has . . . been better provided for in this respect'. Fifty separate establishments could then be listed as well as sixteen houses in Long Street which had once been schools.[10]

The first schoolkeeper to be noticed is Timothy Sacheverell, an ejected Presbyterian and sometime vicar of Enford. After settling in Devizes in 1672 he conducted a girls' boarding school there until his death in 1680.[11] About 1770 the Revd. J. L. Fenner (d. 1795), Independent minister, set up a school at no. 40 Long Street. Among its pupils were Fenner's nephew, the diarist Crabb Robinson,[12] Robert Waylen, the cloth manufacturer, and possibly Sir Thomas Lawrence.[13] That school was replaced by one conducted by Richard Biggs[14] held in 1822–3 in High Street[15] and moved by 1830 to Lansdowne House, Long Street.[16]

    4 Ex inf. Salisbury Dioc. Counc. Educ. 1971.
    5 Ex inf. Town Clerk, Devizes.
    6 Ex inf. Mr. H. L. Smith, Clerk to the Devizes Municipal Chars.
    7 Ed. 49/8164.
    8 Ex inf. Dept. Educ. and Science.
    9 Ex inf. the Revd. R. H. E. Maude, vicar of St. Peter's.
  10 *Wilts. Gaz.* 6 May 1920.
  11 *Calamy Revised*, ed. A. G. Matthews, 422.
  12 *Diary . . . of Henry Crabb Robinson*, ed. T. Sadler, i. 11–12.
  13 Scrap Bk. of cuttings on Devizes Nonconformity, from *Wilts. Advertiser* 19 May–16 June 1904, *penes* the Revd. J. O. Dobson (*c.* 1960), art. v; *Wilts. Gaz.* 6 May 1920; *N. & Q.* cxcii. 182–6, 208–9; the second source describes life at the school.
  14 *Wilts. Gaz.* 6 May 1920.
  15 Pigot, *New Com. Dir.* (1822–3).
  16 Pigot, *Nat. Com. Dir.* (1830). For the location see *Devizes Gaz.* 4 Aug. 1910; *Wilts. Gaz.* 6 May 1920.

By 1839 Richard had been joined by his son R.W. Biggs (LL.D. Dublin, 1847), a Baptist.[17] The school later moved to Wilsford House, also in Long Street.[18] In the later 1840s it aimed to prepare boys for the universities and had an unusually wide curriculum and somewhat unorthodox disciplinary system.[19] Roughly contemporary were the school of the Hon. Charlotte Kerr for little children where fluency in French was a speciality, and that of George Evans held between 1839 and c. 1861 for 60–70 boys at Eastbourne House, Bridewell Street.[20]

In 1859 the Devizes Proprietary Grammar School Co. Ltd. was formed.[21] Soon afterwards it opened a school in a building in Long Street, later to become part of the museum.[22] It closed in 1871[23] and that year the Revd. S. S. Pugh (d. 1899),[24] minister of the New Baptist chapel, set up a school in his house, no. 3 Lansdowne Grove, providing 'advanced education for boys'. In 1874 the school moved to Heathcote House, the Green, and by 1879 had changed its name to Devizes Grammar School. It remained in the hands of the founder's sons until 1917 when it was transferred to J. Thurnham.[25] It was closed in 1920[26] and the buildings sold to the county council.[27]

A high-class girls' school was kept by Mrs. Elliott, wife of the Congregational minister, in the mid 19th century in no. 41 Long Street, the house taken over by the Proprietary Grammar School c. 1862 (see above). The girls then moved into no. 32 Long Street for a time.[28] From c. 1877 there was another girls' school at no. 40 Long Street transferred there by the Misses Farmer from Bridewell Street. It closed in 1905 but before then had moved, for in 1902 no. 40 Long Street was acquired as an extension to the museum.[29] A school drawing girls from all parts of the county was conducted by Miss Elizabeth Bidwell and her niece for

17   Ed. 49/8170; Robson, *Com. Dir.* (1839), ii. R.W. Biggs matriculated in 1832.
18   In 1844 father and son were no longer in partnership: Pigot, *Nat. Com. Dir.* (1844).
19   *Wilts. Gaz.* 4 Aug. 1910, 6 May 1920; *V.C.H. Wilts.* v. 350.
20   Ibid.
21   Wilts. Tracts, cxlix, no. 5A.
22   *W.A.S. Centenary Hist.* (1953), 8 and plan facing p. 33.
23   *V.C.H. Wilts.* v. 353.
24   Grandfather of the author of this article.
25   *Wilts. Gaz.* 6 May 1920; D.G.S. Jnl. *penes auctorem*.
26   *Wilts. Gaz.* 6 May 1920.
27   Wilts. Co. Co. Fin. Cttee. orig. mins. ix. 340.
28   *Wilts. Gaz.* 6 May 1920.
29   Ibid.; *W.A.S. Centenary Hist.* (1953), 9.

about 30 years until 1901. It had premises in no. 9 New Park Street, successively the home of John Tylee the brewer (d. 1812) and the former White Hart inn, and later in Brownston House.[30] Another girls' school founded in 1870 by Miss Davies lasted until 1937. It occupied four different sites, two in Long Street and two in the Market Place. After 1886 it was named Parnella House.[31] A Roman Catholic 'middle class' girls' school was carried on in St. Joseph's Convent from c. 1889 until 1969.[32]

A somewhat unusual school was that founded by the Misses Bennett and Miss Cole who came to Devizes in 1886. Ada Bennett opened a school at no. 19 Long Street, the other two at Meath Lodge, Potterne Road. Later the two schools moved to separate houses in St. John's Street, and later still Ada's school moved to no. 12 Market Place. The schools, which were financially independent of one another, were called 'Devizes College and High School'. Miss Bennett and Miss Cole sold their interest c. 1897–8 to a Miss Horne who renamed the establishment the High School.[33] Ada Cole continued to run her school for boys and girls until c. 1914.[34] Stephen Reynolds, an alumnus, described the headmistress as a 'genius among teachers'.[35]

By 1864 there was a 'successful' night school for men and boys in St. John's parish[36] and at about the same time there seems also to have been one for women.[37] By 1867 there was a Government School of Art held at the assize courts,[38] and by 1880 a 'branch' school in the Town Hall.[39] By 1889 these institutions were renamed the Government School of Science and Art.[40] The school was thereafter maintained by the borough technical committee, with county council support, under the Technical Instruction Acts, 1889 and 1891.[41] By 1895 it possessed 'workshops' in the former premises of the British School,[42] and in 1898 a chemical

---

30 *Wilts. Gaz.* 6 May 1920; W.A.S. Libr., Devizes, sale cat. ii, no. 23; Mate's *Guide*.
31 Gillman's *Dirs.*; *Wilts. Gaz.* 6 May 1920; Olive Chivers, 'Reflections', f. 20.
32 *Kelly's Dir. Wilts.* (1889); ex inf. Sister Mary Thomas, 1971.
33 *Wilts. Gaz.* 6 May 1920.   34 Ibid.; Gillman, *Annals*, advert.
35 *Letters of Stephen Reynolds*, ed. H. Wright, p. xiv.
36 Sar. Dioc. R.O., Vis. Queries, 1864 (St. John's).
37 W.A.S. Libr., Devizes, Revd. J. Wilkinson's par. hist. colls. (Devizes).
38 *Kelly's Dir. Wilts.* (1867).   39 Ibid. (1880).
40 Ibid. (1889).
41 Ibid. (1898); Wilts. Educ. Cttee. Scrap Bk.
42 *Kelly's Dir. Wilts.* (1895); W.R.O. 844, Corp. Min. Bk., 24 Nov. 1890, 5 Jan. 1891; Olive Chivers, 'Reflections', f. 31. The rooms were let to the borough technical cttee. in 1895: W.A.S. Libr., Devizes, Min. Bks. of Brit. Sch.

laboratory and art room.[43] The buildings were sold in 1906 and the proceeds surrendered to the county council towards the erection of the Secondary school in which the functions of the 'government' school were absorbed.[44] A Further Education Institute was maintained in the town between 1955 and 1960, when it moved to the Southbroom site and became the Devizes branch of the West Wilts. and Trowbridge College of Further Education. Since 1971 this has been called Trowbridge Technical College.[45]

CHARITIES FOR THE POOR AND HIGHWAYS. The ancient chantry lands of Devizes have a complicated and puzzling history. St. Mary's owned some land in the Middle Ages designed for church maintenance,[46] and land was attached to chantries in both churches.[47] There was also almshouse property. Over all the charitable lands the borough, itself a landowner, at times exercised a superiority as trustees, which makes it hard to determine the legal owner at any given time.[48]

Soon after the chantries were dissolved in 1548 some of their lands were granted away by the Crown. In 1549 a small part of the younger John Coventry's chantry in St. Mary's was given to John Berwick of Easton, one of Lord Seymour's servants,[49] and to Robert Freke,[50] and in 1555 most of the St. Mary's chantry lands went to William Allen, of Calne, and his son Roger.[51] Most of the Cardmaker lands in St. John's seem to have escaped confiscation,[52] though a small parcel was given in 1590 to William Tipper and Robert Dawe.[53] Some other lands, of uncertain connexion but probably obit lands, were given in 1575 to John Herbert and Andrew Palmer, a London goldsmith, contingent upon proof that they were concealed before 1570.[54] In 1586 the burgesses

43 *Kelly's Dir. Wilts.* (1898).
44 Ibid. (1907); W.A.S. Libr., Devizes, Min. Bks. of Brit. Sch.
45 Wilts. Educ. Cttee. Scrap Bk. and inf. supplied by Wilts. Educ. Cttee.
46 See p. 177.
47 See pp. 180–1.
48 For a very fair survey of the whole subject see *Reps. to Council [on] ... Chantry Property* (priv. print. 1909).
49 *W.A.M.* x. 71.
50 *Cal. Pat.* 1549–51, 139.
51 Ibid. 1555–7, 151–2.
52 *Chantry Report*, 8.
53 C 66/1340 m. 10.
54 L.R. 2/87 f. 81v.

began to acquire some of this alienated property. First they procured a Crown grant of some of the land to feoffees to hold to their use. They alleged, in some cases perhaps rightly, that the property was not chantry land at all but had been unlawfully 'plucked' from the borough.[55] Thenceforth they seem to have been the *de facto* owners,[56] and in 1610 they received the lands in fee. The lands were in just under 80 parcels, mainly in Devizes, more or less equally divided, where there is any indication, between the two Ports, but with a little in Bishop's Cannings, Rowde, and Marlborough.[57] In 1629 the burgesses secured 23 further parcels, all in the borough, which had gone to the Allens in 1555 and had subsequently passed through various hands. These were held for them by sixteen feoffees.[58]

Thus by the late 16th century the corporation had much old chantry land either in fee or in trust, and to it more trust properties were added. Like other corporations, however, they failed to keep the groups of trust lands distinct from one another or the trust lands as a whole from their own. The result was that when the borough charities came to be surveyed c. 1834 there was much uncertainty about the origins of the parcels. The more ancient trust lands were then grouped as follows: St. Mary's Church and Poor Lands, St. John's Church and Poor Lands, and the Old and New Alms-houses.[59]

St. Mary's Church and Poor Lands then consisted of 39 parcels, mostly in Devizes but with 7 in Bishop's Cannings and 3 in Rowde.[60] About two-thirds of the income, which averaged £307 10s. between 1822 and 1832, had been immemorially spent on repairing the church, the rest on the poor.[61] About 1812 some of the charity moneys were used to rehouse the poor, as shown elsewhere.[62] The income was similarly applied throughout the 19th century, though from 1881, without legal warrant, some of it was used for the conduct of church services. In 1901

55 *Constitutions*; C 66/1284 mm. 36–9.
56 e.g they were dealing with the Weavers' Hall in 1599 (Cunnington, *Annals*, i (2nd pagin.), 34), but were not granted it in fee until 1610.
57 *Chantry Report*, 3–5, where a translation of the patent is printed. The particulars are L.R. 2/87 ff. 47–50, 81–2. The lands were actually delivered in 1609 to Robt. Drew, a borough M.P.
58 B.M. Add. Chart. 37567.
59 *Endowed Char. Wilts.* (1908), lxxx, pp. 386–417.
60 Ibid. pp. 396–402.
61 Ibid. p. 403.
62 See p. 161.

it was c. £420 gross.⁶³ By Scheme of 1902 the endowments were consolidated, a single body of trustees appointed, and the charity divided into Church and Alms-house branches.⁶⁴ This partition continues. The administration of the two branches since 1902 is referred to elsewhere.⁶⁵

St. John's Church and Poor Lands consisted c. 1834 of 14 parcels in Devizes and 2 in Marlborough. The average annual income in 1815–33 was £28 10s., which was spent on church maintenance. The income of the Marlborough property was divided between that object and poor relief. By 1901, largely it seems through the conversion of quit-rents into rack-rents and the exchange of one parcel for stock, the income of the charity had risen to £129. Of this £15 was given to the inmates of the Old and New Alms-houses, £10 towards the general expenses of the Municipal Charities, and the rest to St. John's churchwardens.⁶⁶ Between 1903 and 1954 nearly 30 houses or plots in or near Devizes were sold and in 1913 and 1925 the Marlborough lands.⁶⁷ The present state of the charity is considered below with the other Municipal Charities.

Before 1451 Thomas Coventry had founded an alms-house in the town and by his will, dated that year, devised for life most of his Devizes lands to his relict on condition that she supported ten beds in the alms-house. Upon her death the land was to pass to the corporation with the same stipulation. Any surplus, subject to a yearly fee to the mayor, was to be applied to support the almspeople.⁶⁸ William Coventry, said to have been Thomas's brother,⁶⁹ by his will charged the lands of the chantry, which he founded in St. Mary's, with a payment of £1 13s. 4d., to four almswomen. That sum was being paid in 1548.⁷⁰ John Coventry, the younger (d. *ante* 1475), by his will charged the endowment of the chantry which he founded in St. Mary's with £4 to the alms-house poor.⁷¹

By 1552 there were two alms-houses in the town, the Old and the New.⁷² Which of these was Coventry's foundation is uncertain, but

63 *Endowed Char. Wilts.* (1908), lxxx, p. 450.
64 Char. Com. file 201342.
65 See p. 242.
66 *Endowed Char. Wilts.* (1908), lxxx, pp. 386–9, 428–9.
67 Char. Com. files 201444/2, /3, /6, /7.
68 Prob. 11/1 (P.C.C. 17 Rous).
69 *W.A.M.* ii. 255.
70 See p. 180.
71 *Cal. Pat.* 1555–7, 152.
72 A deed of that date in W.R.O. 212A/36/2 refers to the 'Old Alms-house'.

reasonably good authority suggests that it was the new one.[73] In 1488 one of the almshouses lay beside St. John's church.[74] In 1569 reference is made to two stewards of the Old Alms-house,[75] in 1573–6 to a warden, and in 1576 to two wardens of the new one.[76] In 1833 there were two wardens of each, all then common councillors.[77]

In 1614–15 new regulations for both alms-houses were promulgated by the corporation, and the Old Alms-house, formerly, it seems, of timber, was rebuilt in stone on a new site in 'the orchard'.[78] The salient points in the New Alms-house regulations were that the inmates, who might be of either sex, should be single, over 50, and have lived at least 20 years within the borough. They were to bring their own furniture which would remain the property of the house after their death. They were to attend church frequently, be of good behaviour, and clean their rooms. In the following year two London citizens contributed to the alms-house funds.[79]

When the Old Alms-house was investigated c. 1834 it stood in St. John's churchyard and was almost certainly the building of 1615 at the top of Estcourt Hill, which after 1896 became the sexton's house. Its four rooms were occupied by widows, two from each parish, who were without other relief. Two underground rooms were let by the overseers of St. John's to parish paupers.[80] A garden had existed since 1726.[81] The house was endowed with fifteen plots within the borough.[82] In 1896 seven cottages were bought in Sutton Place, which were converted into two-room alms-houses, and to them were transferred the inmates of the Old Alms-house.[83] In 1902 there were four widows receiving a weekly dole and fuel, and three men receiving nothing. The Municipal Trustees, who had meanwhile assumed the management,[84] no longer appointed a separate warden for each alms-house. After the paupers of St. John's

73 Edw. Kite: Soc. Antiq., Jackson MSS. v, f. 169.
74 B.M. Add. Ch. 37529.
75 In W.R.O. 212A/36/2.
76 Cunnington, *Annals*, i (1st pagin.), 66.
77 *Rep. Com. Munic. Corps.* (1835), xxiv, p. 1265.
78 Cunnington, *Annals*, i (2nd pagin.), 50–2, 64.
79 Ibid. 64.
80 *Endowed Char. Wilts.* (1908), lxxx, pp. 406–11.
81 In W.R.O. 844, town deeds, box 9, 17 Feb. 1736.
82 *Endowed Char. Wilts.* (1908), lxxx, pp. 407–9.
83 Plans and elevations in Char. Com. file 204453/2; *Endowed Char. Wilts.* (1908), lxxx, p. 437.
84 For these trustees see p. 252.

The Old Alms-house in St. John's churchyard in 1998

were removed from St. John's Buildings members of the Old Alms-house seem to have shared them with the Eyles almsmen of St. John's. Some of these almspeople, as vacancies occurred, were moved into the Sutton Place alms-houses nearby.[85] Mary Eyles's charity[86] was used to repair the building which was empty in 1973.

About 1834 the New Alms-houses stood where St. John's churchyard meets St. John's Court and consisted of a large common kitchen with 'sleeping places' on two sides of it. A lumber-room above was not then in use.[87] The house was endowed with three plots in the borough.[88] Not long before 1855 it was rebuilt, a process which revealed that it had been fashioned out of the stones of the Norman nave of St. John's.[89] Thereafter the whole house was open to the almspeople, who in 1901 were three women, chosen alternately from each parish, of no defined age and not necessarily drawn from the second poor. They

85 *Endowed Char. Wilts.* (1908), lxxx, p. 445.
86 See p. 242.
87 *Endowed Char. Wilts.* (1908), lxxx, p. 440.
88 Ibid. p. 412.
89 *W.A.M.* ii. 254.

received a weekly dole and coals.[90] In 1971 the building, which had been altered c. 1895,[91] formed two separate dwellings.[92]

By Scheme of 1904 the Old and the New Alms-houses were formed into a trust distinct from the other Municipal charities, though the same body of trustees remained. The houses themselves were administratively united to provide homes for eight almswomen of at least two years' residence within the borough and normally unrelieved. At least half were to be widows. They were to receive weekly stipends to which the trustees might add benefits in kind and services.[93] In 1913 the Old and New were united with the Eyleses' alms-house charities.[94] Powers were taken to move the almspeople to other alms-houses, provided the Eyles almspeople always had three sets of rooms secured for them and bore their founder's name. The almspeople might be of either sex, and must be unrelieved before appointment and resident within St. John's parish for the two preceding years.[95]

By Scheme of 1933 the alms-house trustees were authorized to spend not more than £5,600 of their considerable capital in building twelve alms-houses in Southbroom parish, so as to provide for 22 almspeople in all.[96] As soon as these were ready, houses in Commercial Road, built in 1828 by St. Mary's parish, were to be given up and let at rack-rents. In future there were to be three Eyles almspeople of either sex, four married couples or single people of either sex, and the rest women. All must have a two-year residence qualification in the borough. All but seven must have small means, and all were to receive stipends and might receive extra benefits. Land in Sedgefield Gardens had been already bought for this rehousing and nos. 1–12 Sedgefield Gardens began to be built upon it in 1932.[97]

In 1940 the trustees were empowered to spend money on the conversion of the former 'New' Alms-houses. Thereafter they received new benefactions. By will proved 1945 Henry Tratman left £1,000 for the erection and maintenance of new alms-houses, and by will proved

90 *Endowed Char. Wilts.* (1908), lxxx, p. 440.
91 Plans and elevations in Char. Com. file 204453/2.
92 Ex inf. Mr. H. G. Awdry.
93 Char. Com. file 204453.
94 See p. 242.
95 Char. Com. file 204453.
96 This and the following paragraphs are based on Char. Com. file 204453.
97 Date stone.

1955 Henry Tull left £10,000 for the erection of further alms-houses, preferably for pensioners. By Scheme of 1958 the trustees were authorized to build the Tull alms-houses which became nos. 13–18 Sedgefield Gardens. The occupants were to be pensioners and stipends became permissive. Finally under Scheme of 1970 the Sutton Place alms-houses were sold in 1971, qualification was reduced to mere residence in the borough, and the almspeople, who now ceased to receive stipends, might be required to contribute towards their own accommodation. In 1971 additional alms-houses were being built in Victoria Road.[98]

The stipends and other benefits enjoyed by the almspeople after the Reformation were in part drawn from the Church and Poor Lands of the two town parishes.[99] In addition the almspeople were entitled to some benefactions expressly provided for them. By 1614 William Boke had devised 6d. charged on lands in the town for six poor people in 'the alms-house'.[1] Though the money was long received it was not so applied but rested in the general poor account of St. Mary's. From 1834 to 1901 it was divided between the Old and New Alms-houses.[2] By will proved 1642 John Pierce[3] left £10 to each alms-house for fuel. The capital seems to have been held as part of the Alms-house funds and not to have been separately accounted for.[4] Before 1786 Mary Sellwood bequeathed £50 between the two alms-houses and in 1750 Thomas Sutton £20 to the New Alms-house. The total of £70 was invested and yielded a small income to each alms-house in 1834 and 1901, the New Alms-house enjoying the larger share.[5] Before 1627 Anthony Hart or Hort had provided a legacy which yielded £1 yearly to the poor of 'the alms-house', apparently the new one. It was still received in 1836 but seems to have been lost soon after.[6]

After 1904 the alms-house trustees blent all the alms-house endowments including those for supporting the inmates. Between 1919 and 1928 they sold 16 houses or plots.[7] In 1970 the property, apart from

---

98 Ex inf. Mr. H. G. Awdry.
99 See pp. 235–6.
1 W.R.O. 632/107, accts. of 18 Apr. 12 Jas. I and 1618–19. It is also described as a gift of £1 6s. to both almshouses: Phillipps, *Wilts. M.I.* 76.
2 *Endowed Char. Wilts.* (1908), lxxx, pp. 410, 439.
3 For his other charities see pp. 177, 219–20, 245, 248.
4 *Endowed Char. Wilts.* (1908), lxxx, pp. 410, 413, 439, 441.
5 Ibid. pp. 410, 413, 439.
6 Ibid. pp. 413, 441; Phillipps, *Wilts. M.I.* 76.
7 Char. Com. file 204453/1.

the alms-houses themselves, consisted of just over 20 houses or plots, 2 rent-charges, and cash and investments of the nominal value of £19,000.[8]

By 1668 Sir John Eyles (d. 1703) had founded an alms-house in Short Street in St. Mary's parish in or near a 'gatehouse' there.[9] By his will, proved 1703, he settled the house, then consisting of eight rooms, in trust upon the poor of St. John's parish. It was used by them until 1829 (see below). Eyles also left two houses in Short Street for the poor of St. Mary's.[10] The separate origins of the two benefactions were indistinct c. 1834 and the early 19th century is a period of uncertainty in their history.[11]

The St. Mary's houses were rebuilt by the vestry in 1812 but pulled down again in 1828.[12] Both parishes built new combined alms- and poor-houses 1828–9. St. John's Buildings, erected 1829 and so called by 1885, housed Eyles almspeople in 6 of its 24 rooms. They shared the building with parish paupers and, after the Union workhouse was built in 1836, apparently with members of the Old Alms-house.[13] Thenceforward the history of the Eyles almspeople of St. John's is traced with that of the Old and New Alms-houses.[14] In 1828 St. Mary's built premises on a site at New Town in Commercial Road.[15] They consisted of a two-storeyed brick building of two blocks, facing one another across a garden. Each block contained sixteen rooms. Two rooms were assigned to each inmate and four pairs of rooms, the first floor of the north block in 1901, represented Eyles's benefaction and the building was so inscribed. Both men and women, sometimes married couples, occupied it c. 1834, and then and in 1901 all were paupers.[16] In 1911 those not on the Eyles foundation were removed (see below) and the Eyles almspeople left in

8 Ibid. 204453, Scheme of 1970, which incorporates a schedule of property presumably made up to Dec. 1969.
9 The alms-house is mentioned in a deed of 1673, which refers back to a deed of that date, and also mentions a 'gatehouse': W.R.O. 212B/26/Dv.13A. A 'gatehouse or alms-house' is marked at the west end of Short St. on a plan of 1801: W.R.O. 844, Corp. Lease Bk., alms-ho. lands, nos. 7 and 8. Some kind of gate or barrier seems to have traversed Short St. in 1901: Char. Com. file 204453/1.
10 Prob. 11/470 (P.C.C. 109 Degg); *Endowed Char. Wilts.* (1908), lxxx, pp. 392, 405.
11 The confusion is best exhibited in *Endowed Char. Wilts.* (1908), lxxx, pp. 392, 403, 405.
12 Ibid. pp. 403, 405.
13 See pp. 160–1.
14 See pp. 238–9.
15 *Endowed Char. Wilts.* (1908), lxxx, p. 405.
16 Ibid.

sole possession of the site at New Town. By Scheme of 1913 the management of the Eyles alms-house was fused with that of the Old and New Alms-houses and by Scheme of 1933 the trustees were authorized to abandon the Commercial Road building and rack-rent it.[17] Thenceforth the story of the St. Mary's Eyles alms-house charity is absorbed in that of the Old and New Alms-houses.[18]

Mary Eyles, by deed of 1704, settled in trust a rent of £8 charged upon the Elm Tree inn. Of this rent £1 4s. was to be used to buy fuel for six poor women living in Sir John Eyles's alms-houses. The residue was for clothing[19] and teaching.[20] The inn was sold c. 1886, the rent-charge redeemed, and the proceeds invested in stock. From 1888 to 1896 four-sevenths of the income was applied in equal shares to poor women of the two town parishes, not necessarily almspeople. Thereafter until at least 1901 this share was used for repairing not these but the alms-houses in St. John's parish, which had been much neglected.[21] By Scheme of 1905 the trustees were authorized to spend the share on repairing the Eyles alms-house[22] and by Scheme of 1913 the whole charity was amalgamated with those of the Old and New Alms-houses and with Sir John Eyles's alms-house charity.[23]

When in 1902 the St. Mary's Church and Poor Lands charity was divided into two, the alms-house branch was set apart for the support of a block of alms-houses for the use of eight persons, four of whom might be married couples. All the inmates were to be unrelieved Devizes residents of not less than five years' standing, preferably from St. Mary's parish, and all were to receive stipends.[24] Between 1904 and 1913 the trustees sold some fifteen houses or plots.[25] By these complicated arrangements a new alms-house was founded out of lands which in part had been given not for an alms-house but for general eleemosynary purposes and the Eyles's charities were detached from the parish to which they originally belonged.

17 Char. Com. file 204453.
18 See pp. 239–40.
19 See p. 249.
20 See p. 220.
21 *Endowed Char. Wilts.* (1908), lxxx, p. 445.
22 Char. Com. file 201444/5.
23 Ibid. 204453, Scheme.
24 Ibid. 201342, Scheme.
25 Ibid. 201342/C/1.

The almspeople not on the Eyles foundation, who were removed from New Town in 1911, were housed in eight purpose-built almshouses lying beside the canal to the east of Victoria Road.[26] Thus were created St. Mary's Alms-houses. They were enlarged in 1925 by four additional sets,[27] and by 1948 had been renamed St. Mary's Gardens.[28] The branch was regulated by Schemes of 1961 and 1968, the second of which authorized the almspeople to contribute towards their own support.[29] The trustees of the charity continued to sell off their land. Between 1919 and 1970 nearly 50 dwellings or plots were sold.[30] By the second year the property had been reduced to barely a dozen plots, yielding £714 net in rent. Stock was held of the market value of £57,857 and yielded £2,900.[31]

By Scheme of 1902 the church branch income was to be paid to the rector and churchwardens for the maintenance, repair, and insurance of the church fabric and for churchyard maintenance. By Scheme of 1921 not more than £100 of the branch income might be paid to an assistant curate's fund. Schemes of 1949 and 1970 amended this provision so as to secure that not more than £200 and £300 respectively of the branch income might be used to augment the rector's stipend.[32] In 1970 this branch received five-eighths of the total income and the alms-house branch the rest.[33]

Between 1927 and 1930 William Richard Helms, farmer, of Frome Selwood (Som.), built four cottage homes in Commercial Road, facing the east end of St. Mary's church, for eight poor persons, resident in Devizes for at least five years, who might be either married couples, two sisters, or single persons aged 60. By declaration of trust of 1930 all were to receive weekly stipends. By Scheme of 1964 the land on which the homes were built was slightly reduced for the benefit of the charity.[34]

By Scheme of 1961 provision was made for homes for old people at as low a rent 'as is economically consistent with good management'. This Scheme regulated the bequest of Samuel Harry Ward (d. 1952),

26 *W.A.M.* xxxvii. 484.
27 *Wilts. Gaz.* 3 Mar. 1955.
28 Gillman, *Dirs.* (1947, 1948).
29 Char. Com. file 201342.
30 Ibid. 201342/C/4.
31 Ibid. 201342, accts.
32 Ibid. Schemes.
33 Ibid. accts.
34 Ibid. file 241446.

successively of Devizes and Bournemouth, who subject to a life interest left three-quarters of the residue of his estate for this purpose. The bequest, then £8,972, became available in 1957 and the trustees built the 'Ward Homes' in Church Row, opened in 1961.[35] By the terms of the trust they are to be occupied by married couples, two sisters, or single persons all over 60.[36]

The Lucas and Brown charities, devoted, as they have been, to the relief of the old and sick, are best treated at this point. In 1882 Frances Mary Lucas settled in trust the Grange, Bridewell Street,[37] which she had established as a day-nursery for working-class infants. By will proved 1886 she left £4,500 towards maintaining the nursery and pensioning, if need be, its existing or a future matron. Should the nursery be discontinued £2,000 was to be raised from the investments and applied equally to the cottage hospital and the dispensary.[38] The residue was to go to repairing the Grange and supporting aged women.[39] Under Schemes of 1909 and 1910 the nursery was closed and the building became a home for needy old women of the borough. From 1922 to c. 1956 it also housed, in conformity with the Scheme, a nurse attending the sick poor. She was partially supported out of the fund, which, since the dispensary had closed, could not be paid to it. By Scheme of 1952 £30 of the income was to be spent on medical supplies and comforts and domestic help for the sick poor, or generally for the relief of suffering. The building was vacated in 1971 and the almswomen moved to the Victoria Road alms-houses.[40] The trustees, however, still owned it and enjoyed an income of about £100, spent in doles to the alms-women, then numbering four, and the maintenance of the building.[41]

By will proved 1896 Charlotte Brown left to the trustees of the Grange £400 to provide a trained nurse for the borough poor. The benefaction was invested as £343 and the interest (£9) was at first paid to the Devizes Nursing Society, which the testatrix had founded. By 1910 the capital had been merged in the Lucas charity.[42]

35 *Wilts. Gaz.* 25 May 1961.
36 Char. Com. file 203928.
37 See p. 75.
38 See pp. 165–6.
39 *Endowed Char. Wilts.* (1908), lxxx, pp. 463–4.
40 See p. 243.
41 Char. Com. file 207052A; Gillman, *Dir.*; inf. from Mrs. M. M. Chivers, a trustee.
42 Char. Com. file 207052B; *Endowed Char. Wilts.* (1908), lxxx, pp. 464–5, where the date of probate is incorrectly stated.

Three highway charities have been known. William Salter, by will dated 1404, left a house in trust subject to life interests,[43] William Page, of Devizes, by will proved 1542, ewes and lambs, an optimistic endowment,[44] and John Pierce, by will proved 1642, £50.[45] Of the first two charities no more is heard. The third was being paid c. 1834 but had been lost by c. 1870, perhaps, as was suggested in 1901, because it lapsed when the corporation became the highway authority.[46]

There have also been at least eleven loan charities, but a like fate has overcome them all.[47] In 1587 Walter Keymes, rector of Compton Bassett, gave £20 for interest-free loans to 20 poor handicraftsmen each year. In 1594 Anne, relict of Sir Henry Sharington of Lacock, settled £40 to provide like loans of £2, payable in alternate years, to 20 clothworkers. At the same time she founded a sermon charity.[48] It was found in 1630 that interest on the loans was being charged and the practice was interdicted.[49] In 1603 Hugh Attwell, parson of St. Tew (Cornw.), left £1 6s. 8d. for yearly loans to poor artificers and handicraftsmen. Before 1614 John Archard or Orchard, a Lyneham clothier, gave £10 to be lent in moieties to poor tradesmen.[50] In 1616 Sir Henry Baynton, of Bromham, left £20 to be lent yearly in sums of 6s. 8d. to three artificers or tradesmen, and £10 to be lent in sums of £2 or £5 to five or two such persons. In 1620 the Virginia Company gave £40 to be spent in loans of £6 13s. 4d. of three years' duration for six artificers and tradesmen and for apprenticing. In 1622 Thomas Shepperd, of Seend, left £10 for loans, at ½ per cent, to poor artificers and tradesmen, which in practice was lent in sums of £5 to two persons. In 1623 Ralph Pierce, of Hilmarton, gave £5 to the poor, which was yearly lent at the same interest to an artificer or tradesman. In 1624 William Barrett, a London merchant, son of a Devizes man, gave £5 for interest-free loans.[51]

43 Waylen, *Chrons*. 285.
44 Prob. 11/29 (P.C.C. 4 Spert).
45 *Endowed Char. Wilts.* (1908), lxxx, p. 414. For Pierce's other charities see above and below, pp. 177, 219–20, 240, 248.
46 *Endowed Char. Wilts.* (1908), lxxx, pp. 442–3.
47 Except where otherwise stated this paragraph is based upon *Constitutions*.
48 See p. 178.
49 Cunnington, *Annals*, i (2nd pagin.), 86.
50 For proof that the charity was founded by 1614 see W.R.O. 844, Ct. Bk. 1583–1621.
51 He is probably the man who contributed to the rebuilding of the old Alms-house in 1615: see p. 237. For the date see Phillipps, *Wilts. M.I.* 76.

In 1631 Robert Hyde, of Hatch, gave £10 for like loans to leather-workers. It is said that in 1647 Edward Northey gave £24 for such loans.[52] The capital of all these charities, apart from Northey's, was intact in 1663[53] but is not heard of again. In 1614 36 people were drawing upon the Keymes, Sharington, Archard, and Attwell charities.[54] In 1622 22 people drew £1 apiece repayable in the following year.[55]

The charities paid in food, clothing, and doles are or have been numerous and have naturally survived longer than the foregoing. Richard Gobett's benefaction,[56] which became a bread charity, had been distributed for 150 years before c. 1834. The feast of St. Thomas, however, had replaced the Friday after Epiphany as dole-day.[57] In 1901 the charity was thought to have been merged in the stipends paid to the New Town almspeople.[58] An annual dole of 8s. 4d. on Good Friday, founded by Thomas Newman and Robert Paynter, was paid in 1525–6 and 1533–4,[59] but not afterwards. Newman may have been a chantry priest.[60]

Most highlighted among Devizes charities is Coventry's dole.[61] Tradition, as recorded in 1786, declares that a destitute vagrant of that name, passing through the town, was given a loaf by a baker. The vagrant, having made his fortune in London, directed that a loaf should be given yearly on a fixed day to everyone then present in the town. The funds, whatever they were, were administered by the corporation, who between 1586 and 1786 paid out varying sums to meet the alleged requirements of the charity. An attempt made in 1663 to limit the expenses and to exclude 'taxpayers' from the benefit proved abortive. In 1786 Archduke Ferdinand of Austria and his wife, passing through Devizes, were 'tickled' at receiving the dole. Next year the corporation abolished it, though it was decided during the 'scarcity' of 1802 that a payment in lieu might be made out of borough funds,[62] and even the chamberlains of 1835–6, in their austere report, budgeted for its resumption.[63]

52 Phillipps, op. cit. 76.
53 Cunnington, *Annals*, i (2nd pagin.), 137–8.
54 W.R.O. 844, Ct. Bk. 1583–1621.
55 Cunnington, *Annals*, i (2nd pagin.), 66.
56 See p. 180.
57 *Endowed Char. Wilts.* (1908), lxxx, p. 404.
58 Ibid. p. 459.
59 W.A.S. Libr., Devizes, Wilts. MSS. no. 3.
60 *W.A.M.* ii. 253 n.
61 The best accounts will be found ibid. ii. 256, l. 95–7. For the earliest payment see Cunnington, *Annals*, i (2nd pagin.), 12–13; cf. ibid. 238; ii. 251–2; and *Gent. Mag.* 1786 (2), 803, 903.
62 Cunnington, *Annals*, ii. 14.
63 Ibid. 230 and see above p. 145.

By will proved 1564 Robert Drew or Trew, of Southbroom, gave the poorest people of Devizes 20s. out of his lands in Devizes to be dispensed by his widow and after her death by the mayor.[64] No more is known of this, but by 1618 another Robert Drew was paying to the churchwardens of St. John's 9s. yearly left to the poor by his father John. This sum was being received c. 1834 and was applied to relieve the poor-rate. In 1900 it was still received and in St. John's parish was used on gifts of calico in lieu of the flannel formerly bought. In St. Mary's it was added to the Nicholas charities.[65] It survives.[66]

Henry Morris, by will proved 1573, gave £1 to the poor charged upon his Bromham lands. The rent was withheld until 1618 when it was recovered by Chancery suit.[67] About 1834 it was used to relieve the poor-rate in both parishes, in 1901 it formed part of the Thurman group of charities,[68] and consequently was subsequently administered by the Municipal Trustees. The rent was unredeemed in 1970.[69] In 1625 Thomas Poller, of Devizes, gave land in Bridewell Street, apparently in perpetuity, to repair St. John's church and relieve St. John's poor.[70] It is not heard of again. The Angel rent, presumably named after an inn,[71] was being received in 1618,[72] and in 1625, when it amounted to £4, was paid in doles and clothing.[73] About 1834, when it formed part of the Thurman group of charities, it was worth £4 and was payable to the poor of the two parishes in moieties.[74] From 1858 it was applied to the boys' Town School and remained educational.[75] Between 1630 and c. 1834 5s. was paid out of 'Read's house' to St. John's parish and in the latter year formed part of the Thurman group of charities.[76] It is not mentioned again. In 1634

64 Prob. 11/47 (P.C.C. 29 Stevenson).
65 *Endowed Char. Wilts.* (1908), lxxx, pp. 390, 406, 446–7, 459. For the date of the first receipt see W.R.O. 632/107, acct. of 1618–19.
66 Char. Com. file 204922.
67 *Endowed Char. Wilts.* (1908), lxxx, p. 389; Cunnington, *Annals*, ii. 140–2; *Constitutions*, which gives the correct date of probate.
68 *Endowed Char. Wilts.* (1908), lxxx, pp. 389–90, 404, 432.
69 Mun. Char. Accts. 1970.
70 Cunnington, *Annals*, i (2nd pagin.), 78.
71 First recorded 1598: ibid. 32.
72 Ibid. 56.
73 Ibid. 79.
74 *Endowed Char. Wilts.* (1908), lxxx, pp. 390, 403.
75 See p. 223.
76 *Endowed Char. Wilts.* (1908), lxxx, p. 391. Perhaps the donor was William Rede, a Devizes clothier: *W.A.M.* xxxvi. 161.

Elizabeth Strangwidge gave £40 in trust to the corporation, which, after deduction for a sermon, was to be spent on clothing the poor. About 1834, when it was administered with the Thurman group, the income of 38s. was divided equally between the two parishes.[77] Griffin Nicholas, by will dated 1634, gave £150 to St. Mary's, the interest on which (£9) had for many years before c. 1834 been used to clothe the poor.[78] He also gave £50 to the poor of St. John's parish.[79] In 1638 Michael Nicholas gave £5 divisible between the two parishes, which c. 1834 produced 6s. for each.[80]

Besides his other benefactions,[81] John Pierce, by will proved 1642, left £40 to St. John's parish for clothing and bedding for the needy.[82] By 1901 the charity was administered with the three Nicholas charities[83] and so remained in 1962.[84] About 1645 Samuel Martin had entrusted to the corporation £10 for the poor of both parishes. About 1834, as one of the Thurman group, it yielded 6s. for each.[85] In 1650 Robert Nicholas, judge of the Upper Bench and later borough recorder, gave £30 to the poor of both parishes. Of that total £20 was intended for St. Mary's to which parish the same donor added £10 in 1652. The corporation, however, admitted c. 1834 to having received only £20, which apparently yielded 6s. to St. John's and 12s. to St. Mary's.[86]

Before 1657 a Mrs. Grubbe had given £5 to St. John's which yielded 6s. By 1667 St. Mary's was administering the income on £25 which the same donor had left for clothing the poor. In 1669 the interest seems to have been spent on St. Mary's bells.[87] The charity then disappears.[88] About 1670 Robert Walter left £20, out of which 17s. 4d. was paid to the St. Mary's poor according to his will.[89] In 1670 Mary Collier left the same sum, yielding the same, to St. John's poor, together

77 *Endowed Char. Wilts.* (1908), lxxx, pp. 391, 404.
78 Ibid. p. 404.
79 Ibid. p. 391.
80 Ibid. pp. 390, 404; Phillipps, *Wilts. M.I.* 76.
81 See pp. 177, 219–20, 240, 245.
82 *Endowed Char. Wilts.* (1908), lxxx, p. 391.
83 Ibid. p. 432; and see below.
84 Char. Com. file 204920.
85 *Endowed Char. Wilts.* (1908), lxxx, pp. 390, 403.
86 Ibid. pp. 390, 403.
87 Ibid. pp. 392, 404.
88 Ibid. p. 459.
89 Ibid. p. 404.

with money for a sermon charity.[90] About 1834 these formed part of the Thurman group of charities.[91] Sir John Eyles, by will proved 1703, left two houses in St. Mary's parish for the parish poor and also three sums of £60 to the poor of the two town parishes and St. James's.[92] The money was to be invested in land, and, until it had been, Sarah, his relict, was to pay £3 to each parish out of the estate. The fate of the two houses is narrated elsewhere.[93] The other charity moneys seem never to have been sunk in land. At sundry times, however, up to 1776 Eyles's heirs seem to have paid sums of about £3 to St. Mary's and these were spent on cloth. Nothing was being received c. 1834 and the charity seems thereafter to have been lost.[94] The benefaction to St. John's, stated in 1724 to have been £80 yielding £4, was then applied to the church debt and in 1739 and 1746 to cloth. Thereafter it is lost.[95] It was thought c. 1834 that Eyles's bequest to St. James's had been used to rebuild some houses left to the chapelry by an unknown donor.[96]

By declaration of trust of 1704 Mary Eyles provided that £3 of the rent-charge which she had left for various purposes should be used to distribute annually linen shifts to 20 poor women of the borough not being beggars, and 16s. to augment other charities apart from her fuel charity. Shifts were still being distributed c. 1834 and the residue applied to teaching. When the property bearing the rent-charge was sold in 1888 four-sevenths were paid until 1896–7 equally to the two parishes to provide fuel or flannel for poor women. After 1896–7 the money was used for alms-house repair.[97] About 1705 John Rogers gave £10 to the poor of both parishes apparently to buy cloth. Payments, when stated, of 10s. seem to have been received by St. John's in 1705 and by St. Mary's until 1723. Both charities are then lost.[98]

By will proved c. 1696 Richard Hiller or Hillier left £20, the income to be distributed in cloth to the poor of both parishes on St. Andrew's day. St. John's was receiving 10s. yearly c. 1834; payments to St.

90 Ibid. p. 391; for her forename see Phillipps, *Wilts. M.I.* 76.
91 *Endowed Char. Wilts.* (1908), lxxx, pp. 391, 404.
92 Prob. 11/470 (P.C.C. 109 Degg).
93 See p. 241.
94 *Endowed Char. Wilts.* (1908), lxxx, p. 405.
95 Ibid. pp. 392–3.
96 Ibid. pp. 52–3; and see below, p. 253.
97 *Endowed Char. Wilts.* (1908), lxxx, pp. 392, 414, 445–6. For her other charities see pp. 220, 242.
98 *Endowed Char. Wilts.* (1908), lxxx, pp. 422–3.

Mary's seem to have ceased much earlier. The charity formed part of the Thurman group. About 1707 Edward Want left £10, the income to buy bread for the poor of St. John's on St. Thomas's day. Valued at 10s., it seems to have been so applied until 1749 and possibly thereafter. By c. 1834 it was lost.[99] In 1720 Eleanor Phillips gave a rent of 52s. charged on land in Rowde to purchase 2d. loaves for six poor unrelieved church-going women of St. Mary's parish on Sundays.[1] It survives.[2] In 1728 a Mrs. Kent left £20 for bread for the poor, apparently of St. John's parish, on Christmas Day. It was paid in doles between 1731 and 1745 and was thereafter lost.[3] In 1739 John Gifford, ironmonger, is said to have given £10 to the St. John's poor for 'bread on St. Thomas's day'. This never seems to have been paid.[4] James Miln, by will proved 1759, gave £100 to be invested for the purchase of 3d. loaves on Sunday to church-goers of St. John's parish. For a time in the 18th century the income was incorrectly paid to St. Mary's parish. About 1834 it was being distributed in loaves to poor widows of St. John's each Sunday with a bonus distribution at Easter. In 1901 it was given to poor church-going widows on Sundays.[5] By will dated 1770 Joan Bisse left the same sum to be distributed in bread to the poor of St. John's parish twelve months from her death. Since the parish would not accept the bequest, her niece, Ann Blagdon, by will dated 1773, left a rent of £4, charged on her lands in Steeple Ashton, for the distribution of 3d. loaves to the same beneficiaries. The income was so distributed c. 1834 and 1901 in conjunction with Miln's charity.[6] Both charities survive.[7] About 1760 Thomas Thurman[8] gave £200 to buy shirts or shifts for the unrelieved poor of both parishes. By c. 1834 it had become one of several charities which were administered together, the income whereon was paid to 49 men and 49 women of both parishes in clothing, bread, and rent doles. In 1888, after their then recent transfer from the Municipal Charity Trustees to the two parishes,

---

99 *Endowed Char. Wilts.* (1908), lxxx, pp. 393 (Want); 391, 423 (Hiller). For Hiller's will see W.R.O., Con. Sar.
1 *Endowed Char. Wilts.* (1908), lxxx, p. 405. She is the same as Eleanor Powell. For her other charities see pp. 178, 221. A Philip Phillips is said to have founded a like charity by will proved 1717, which was never paid: ibid. p. 423.
2 Char. Com. file 204924.
3 *Endowed Char. Wilts.* (1908), lxxx, p. 423; Phillipps, *Wilts. M.I.* 77.
4 *Endowed Char. Wilts.* (1908), lxxx, p. 423.   5 Ibid. pp. 393–4, 447.
6 Ibid. pp. 394, 447; Phillipps, *Wilts. M.I.* 77.
7 Char. Com. file 204921.
8 For his expendable gift for education see p. 222.

the various capital sums were reinvested as £188. The income, with that from Drew's charity, was spent in 1901 on calico.[9] Besides his educational and sermon charities, Thomas Bancroft of Bristol, by will proved 1774, left £500 for the benefit of 20 men of each parish. The capital was invested and the income used, as directed by the testator, to provide doles in April and blue cloth in October. Shortly before 1834 the two charities had been blent and were being spent wholly on cloth. The moneys were afterwards reinvested as £1,247, which became £1,260 upon further reinvestment in 1885–6. In 1901 the income was £33 and was divided equally between the parishes. It was used towards buying coats.[10] It survives and is valued at £25–£50 yearly.[11] Before 1786 one Taylor gave a rent charged on land in Rowde to provide bread for the unrelieved poor of St. Mary's parish. It was so used c. 1834 but in 1901 was in practice confined to Anglican widows, most of whom were relieved.[12] It survives.[13]

Sarah Wadsworth, besides her educational charity,[14] left, by will proved 1854, £100 for bread each Sunday for six poor church-going women of St. Mary's parish. The capital was eventually invested and used in 1901 together with Phillips's and Taylor's charities for bread to poor widows on Sundays.[15] It survives.[16] Ann Biggs, by will proved 1860, left £50 for poor church-goers of St. John's. In 1901 the income was £1 2s. and was spent on flannel and calico.[17] It survives.[18] By will proved 1881 Sarah Anne Williams Lucas, of Bristol, left £12,000 to provide pensions to poor women nominated in rotation by the representatives of five nonconformist churches, of whom the minister of the Devizes Strict Baptist chapel should be one. In 1971 it yielded £295.[19] Frank Simpson, successively of Devizes and Fulham (Mdx.), by will proved 1897, left the residue of his estate, subject to a life interest, for the poor. The funds were transferred in 1917 and in 1922 were represented by

9 *Endowed Char. Wilts.* (1908), lxxx, pp. 390–1, 403–4, 432–5, 456–7.
10 Ibid. pp. 394–5, 406, 443–4.
11 Char. Com. file 201833.
12 *Endowed Char. Wilts.* (1908), lxxx, pp. 406, 459.
13 Char. Com. file 204923.
14 See p. 223.
15 *Endowed Char. Wilts.* (1908), lxxx, p. 458.
16 Char. Com. file 201832.
17 *Endowed Char. Wilts.* (1908), lxxx, p. 447.
18 Char. Com. file 201831.
19 Ex inf. Riders, 8 New Square, Lincoln's Inn, London, W.C. 2.

£1,330. By Scheme of 1923 the income was to be used to assist sick or unfortunate people with medical or surgical attention. George Simpson, successively of Devizes and Forest Row (Suss.), by will proved 1945,[20] left £1,000 for the sick and needy of the borough, and in 1936 Dr. Leonard Raby, successively of Devizes and Southbourne (Hants), gave £300 to the poor of the borough, especially for comforts to children and old people. These three charities are regulated by Scheme of 1946.[21] Maud Edith Cunnington, by will proved 1951, left £200 towards feeding deserving vagrants passing through the town.[22] It survives.

A body of Municipal Charity Trustees was formed in 1836 to administer those charities which, before the Municipal Corporations Act prohibited such a practice, had been managed by the corporation.[23] These were the Church and Poor Lands of St. John's, Pierce's gifts for St. John's, Thurman's charity and others consolidated with it, the Old and New Alms-houses and their associated charities, and the charities of Morris, Maynard, Hort, Smith, and Wild. The trustees survive but have lost some of their original responsibilities and gained new ones. They no longer administer the Maynard and Smith charities, but have acquired the Ellinor Pitt charity. That charity appears to have been established by 1738 but nothing is known of it until it was regulated by Scheme of 1909. The capital was then £743, and the income (£19) was to provide pensions for unrelieved widows, each pension to be payable for not less than three and not more than six years. In 1970 one pensioner received the bulk of the income but in 1971 it was not being distributed.[24] In 1970 the trustees acquired the alms-houses, though they administer them as a distinct trust. In 1970 the non-alms-house charities held two or three houses and stock of the nominal capital value of £7,032. Of the income the largest share (£369) was paid to the churchwardens of St. John's in respect of St. John's Church lands. The rest, apart from the Wild and Pitt charities mentioned elsewhere,[25] was divided in shares of £13, £11, and £8 between the two poor funds and the rector respectively. All are spent on church maintenance, poor relief, and parochial care.[26]

20 Princ. Prob. Regy.
21 Char. Com. file 203927.
22 Ibid. 239193.
23 *Endowed Char. Wilts.* (1908), lxxx, p. 426.
24 Char. Com. file 201444; inf. from Mr. H. L. Smith, Clerk to the Devizes Municipal Chars.
25 See pp. 230–1 and above.
26 Accts. 1970; ex inf. Mr. H. L. Smith, Clerk to the chars.

Before their separation from Bishop's Cannings the people of Southbroom presumably benefited from all the charities of that parish. There is, however, evidence of two charities expressly assigned to Southbroom. By declaration of trust of 1757 Edward Rose and others assigned to the second poor of the chapelry a rent-charge grounded upon £20 formerly devised by unknown persons for the same purpose. The house whence the rent issued seems to have been demolished by c. 1834 and five houses to have been built upon the site possibly out of Sir John Eyles's charity to the chapelry.[27] The houses were then occupied by parish paupers and any income distributed in clothes to the second poor.[28] In 1901 the houses still existed and were let at low rents.[29] In 1910 any income was spent on a parish provident and children's clubs.[30]

It was stated in 1786 that 'Mr. Eyles', i.e. Sir John Eyles, had given £200 to the unrelieved poor of the chapelry, which yielded £8, and that Thomas Smith had given £10, yielding 10s. The former was said to be a rent-charge. No more is known of it. The second seems to have been immediately distributed and not to have constituted a perpetuity.[31] Some houses, other than those mentioned above, have been thought to have formed a charitable donation, but to have been sold to the Guardians in and after 1837.[32]

Annette Sarah Grindle, of Brighton, by will proved 1899, gave to the poor of St. Peter's parish £200 to be spent at the discretion of the vicar and churchwardens. In 1970 the income provided coal for six persons.[33]

---

27 See below.
28 *Endowed Char. Wilts.* (1908), lxxx, pp. 52–3.
29 Ibid. p. 58.
30 *Benefice Bk.* Southbroom.
31 *Endowed Char. Wilts.* (1908), lxxx, p. 52.
32 *Benefice Bk.* Southbroom.
33 Ex inf. the Revd. R. H. E. Maude, vicar.

HOSPITALS

THE HOSPITAL OF ST. JOHN THE BAPTIST

The first reference found to this hospital occurs in 1314, when John Wyt, of Potterne, priest, was presented to the 'Priory of the Hospital of St. John the Baptist' by the Mayor and Burgesses of Devizes.[1] Of the four remaining recorded presentations, two (in 1321 and 1513) were made by the mayor and burgesses,[2] one (in 1469) by the mayor alone,[3] and one (in 1336) by the queen,[4] who held the town in dower.[5] In 1399 the king granted the custody of the hospital to one Nicholas Coventry for life.[6]

About 1325 the Bishop of Salisbury, through his commissaries the Prior of Bradenstoke and the Abbot of Stanley, intervened in a dispute—which had reached the Holy See—between the Prior of St. John's Hospital and the Rector of 'the parish church' of Devizes. The rector, Thomas of Yorkfleet, had been presented in 1312 to the church of St. John the Baptist, Devizes,[7] which by 1398,[8] and probably much earlier, became annexed to the church of St. Mary, Devizes. The cause of the dispute of 1325 seems to have been encroachment by the prior of the hospital, which in the 16th century is expressly said to be within the parish of St. Mary,[9] upon the parochial rights of the Rector of Devizes. The award, confirmed in 1326 by the bishop, safeguarded the right of the rector to receive oblations, and the like, on those occasions when his parishioners were admitted to the hospital chapel, or when special services

1 *Reg. Simon de Gandavo* (Cant. & York Soc.), ii, 824.
2 Phillipps, *Wilts. Inst.* i, 18, 191.
3 J. Waylen, *Chronicles of the Devizes*, 240.
4 Phillipps, *Wilts. Inst.* i, 31.
5 *Cal. Pat.* 1330–4, 55, 332.
6 Ibid. 1399–1401, 141. Coventry was a well-known Devizes name.
7 Phillipps, *Wilts. Inst.* i, 11.
8 Ibid. 84.
9 E 301/56/44.

were held there. The right of the prior or the sick of his house to all bequests made to them was likewise safeguarded, provided the bequests did not deprive the rector of any income due to him. The prior and all the inmates of his house were, it was emphatically stated, parishioners of 'the parish church' of Devizes.[10]

William Salter, clothier of Devizes, left 2s. 6d. to the prior in 1404.[11] An indulgence of 40 days in favour of the hospital was granted by the bishop in 1503.[12]

The chantry commissioners of 1546 and 1548 made returns for the free chapel of St. John the Baptist, but make no mention of a hospital. In 1546 the free chapel had a clear income of £2 13s. 2d. after paying 8s. 2d. rent resolute to the queen.[13] In 1548 the commissioners reported that the free chapel had property in Bishop's Cannings, Stert, Rowde, and Poulshot worth £4 2s. 4d. a year, and still paid the rent of 8s. 2d.; it had goods and ornaments worth 14s. 8d., and a bell worth 6s. 8d.; the incumbent (who had been incumbent of Whaddon 1533-8)[14] was honest, of good report, with no other living.[15] In 1550 the late free chapel and its possessions (except bells, lead on roofs, and advowsons) was sold by the Crown to Richard Roberts of London.[16] The property appears to have come later into the hands of the Old and New Almshouses. This forms part of the story of Devizes town.

THE HOSPITAL OF ST. JAMES AND ST. DENIS, SOUTHBROOM

The date of the foundation of this leper hospital is unknown. It has been said that it was founded by a bishop of Salisbury,[17] and it was indeed situated within the fee of the bishop, since it lay at Southbroom in the ancient parish of Bishop's Cannings.

---

10 Sar. Reg. Mortival, ii, f. 191. A précis of the award is given by Waylen in *Chronicles of the Devizes*, 240–6.
11 Waylen, op. cit. 284.
12 Sar. Reg. Audley, f. 172.
13 E 301/56/44.
14 W.A.M. xli, 206.
15 E 301/58/73.
16 *Cal. Pat.* 1549–51, 6–7.
17 R. M. Clay, *Hospitals of Medieval Engl.* 262, 328.

King John, staying at Devizes in March 1208, granted to the lepers of Devizes a two-day fair at their house on the vigil and feast of St. Denis (8 and 9 Oct.), provided it did no harm to neighbouring fairs.[18] This fair seems to have been lost later in a fair granted in 1227 to the bishop to be held also at Southbroom on the vigil and feast of St. Denis and two following days.[19] In 1232 Henry III granted wood from Melksham Forest for the building of the lepers' chapel.[20] They had protection in 1231 and 1260,[21] and in 1336-8 for the purpose of collecting alms.[22] They then disappear from history, but a house near St. James's Church called until recently Spitalcroft, now The Croft, seems to preserve their memory.

Richard de Breton, 'hermit' of the hospital, is mentioned in 1337 and 1338,[23] when he was collecting alms for the house.

18 Rot. Litt. Claus. (Rec. Com.), i, 105b.
19 Cal. Chart. R. 1226–57, 51.
20 Close R. 1231–4, 43.
21 Pat. R. 1225–32, 426; Cal. Pat. 1258–66, 93.
22 Cal. Pat. 1334–8, 266, 404; 1338–40, 49.
23 Ibid., 1334–8, 404; 1338–40, 49.

INDEX

NOTE. A page number in italics refers to a map or illustration on that page. A number followed by *n* is a reference only to the footnotes on that page.

Abingdon (Berks.), 65
Abington, L. J., architect, 118
Addington, Hen.,Vct. Sidmouth, 12, 116, 118, 120, 142, 152
Adlam, Sam., 97
agricultural implements, manufacture of, 100
Aldbourne, 188, 193
Aldermaston (Berks.), atomic energy establishment, 101
Alexander, bp. of Lincoln, 37
Alexander:
  Hen., earl of Stirling, 61–2
  (or Zinzan), Hen., 61
  (or Zinzan), Jacoba, *see* Vanlore
  Judith, w. of Hen., earl of Stirling, 61
  Mary, *see* Vanlore
All Cannings, rector of, *see* Byng
Allen (Alleine):
  John, 134 *n*
  Jos., 11
  Mat., 156 *n*
  Rog., 234
  Wm., 234
Alvediston:
  Norrington, 62
Anabaptists, *see* Baptists
Andrews (Andrewes):
  Eliz., *see* Drew
  Sir Hen., 71
  Thos., 92 *n*
  ——, 150
Anne, queen of Richard II, 47, 55
Anne Boleyn, queen of Henry VIII, 50
Anne of Cleves, queen of Henry VIII, 50
Anstie:
  B.W., 66, 96 *n*
  E. & W., Ltd., 95
  F. E., 11
  G.W., and his w., 66
  J. O., 99
  John, s. of Ric. (fl. 1698), 95
  John (d. 1830), 67, 90, 92, 96
  Paul, 145 *n*
  Ric. (fl. 1698), 95
  Ric. (fl. 1728, ? the same), 90 *n*
  fam., 66
Ansty, Hospitallers of St. John of Jerusalem, property of, 73
Appleshaw (Hants), ch., 188
Aragon, Cath. of, *see* Catherine
Archard (or Orchard), John, 245
architects, *see* Abington; Baldwin; Brinkworth; Comper; Gamble & Whichcord; Goodridge; Hill,Wm.; Ingleman; Lawrence, Mr.; Mullens; Overton; Peniston; Pollard; Randell; Scott; Slater; Slater & Carpenter; Woodyer; Wyatt, Benj., Jas., *and* T. H.
Arundell:
  Anne, *see* Wyndham
  Jas. Everard, 62
  Jas. Everard, Ld. Arundell, 62
Ashlers Green, *see* Devizes
Ashton, Steeple, 250
Attwell, Hugh, rector of St. Tew (Cornw.), 245
Attwood, Ric., 88
Aumale, ctss. of, *see* Forz

257

Austria, Archduke Ferdinand of, 106, 246
  his w., 246
Axford, Hen., 102

Baddely, Ric., rector of Hilperton, 208
Badger, Thos., 191
Bailey (Baily):
  E. H., sculptor, 187
  Thos., 93 *n*
  and see Bayley
Baker, John, 83
Baldwin, Thos., architect, 152
Banaster, *see* Banister
Bancroft, Thos., 178, 206, 221, 223, 230, 251
Banister (Banaster):
  Ralph, 59 *n*, 110 *n*
  Mr., 70
Bank of England, 172
Baptists and Anabaptists, 145, 200–9
Barnwell, C. E. B., vicar of Southbroom, 195
Barrass, Hen., 218
Barrett, Wm., 245
Bartlett:
  Jas., bell-founder, 94
  John, 211
Basset:
  Gilb., 40, 44
  Phil., 41, 55
Bassingbourne, Alex. de, 40
Baster, ——, fell-monger, 93
Batelscombe, Rob. de, 46 *n*
Bateson, Sir Thos., Ld. Deramore, 157, 216
Bath (Som.), 8, 27, 64, 71–2, 152, 187, 198, 229
  gas supply, 167
  road to London, 7, 105
Bath Guardian, 218
Batt:
  John (d. 1600), 83
  John, s. of John (d. 1600), 86 *n*
  Ric. (d. *c.* 1569), 83, 87
  Ric. (d. 1612), 86 *n*
  fam., 86
Bayley (Bayly):
  Edw., 208 *n*

Revd. P. L., 69
Wal., 83
——, 67
and see Bailey
Baynton (Bayntun):
  Sir Edw. (d. 1544), 56, 60, 110 *n*
  Sir Edw. (d. 1656), 9, 134
  Sir Hen. (d. 1616), 245
  Hen. (fl. 1682), 142
  Revd. Hen. (fl. 1829), 69
Beal:
  Hen., 90 *n*
  Thos., 90 *n*
Beauchamp:
  Ric., bp. of Salisbury (d. 1481), 49, 56
  Sir Ric., Ld. St. Amand (d. 1508), 49
  Rog., Ld. Beauchamp, 46–7
  and see Devizes, ch. of St. John (Beauchamp chap.)
Beaven (Beavan):
  John, 102, 211
  Sam., 93 *n*
Bedborough, *see* Roundway
Bell, Steph., 93 *n*
bell-founders, *see* Bartlett, Jas.; Burrough, Jas.; Coney; Cor, Rob. *and* Wm.; Purdue; Taylor, J.; Wallis; Warner & Sons; Wells
Belvedere mill, *see* Roundway
Benger, Eliz. O., 11
Bennett:
  Ada, 233
  Wal., 92 *n*
  the Misses, 233
Berks. & Hants Extension Railway, 8
Berkshire, *see* Abingdon; Aldermaston; Harwell; Reading; Tilehurst
Berwick:
  Gilb. of, 46
  John, 234
Bidwell:
  Eliz., 232
  the Misses, 67
Biggs:
  Ann, 251
  Jas., 205
  R. W., 232
  Ric., 231–2

258

Billett, Thos., 214
Birmingham, 63
Bishop's Cannings, see Cannings
Bishop's Rowborough, see Rowborough
Bisse, Joan, 250
Blackborrow:
  Hen., 83
  Thos., 88
Blackwell, John, 27 n
Blagdon, Ann, 250
Blois, Chas. of, 128
  children of, 48, 128
Bluet:
  John, 46 n
  Ralph, 69
Boke, Wm., 240
Boleyn, Anne, see Anne
Bonner, G. D., 11
Boulton, V. C., & Co., 93
Bourman, Francis, 133
Bournemouth (Hants), 244
Bower, Joshua, 65–6
Bowman, Edw., 89
Box:
  Ric., 100
  Wm., 94, 100
Box, 55, 186
Brabant, R. H., 11
Brackenbury, Ric., 60
Bradenstoke Priory, 72
  prior, 254
Bradford-on-Avon, inns, 103
Bragg, Messrs. T. & J., 157
Brasyere, John, 81
Bratton, 42
Bray, Dr. Chas., 215
Brazil, 215
Breach, the, see Devizes
Brede, Cath., 83
Brethren, 204, 208, 211, 214
Breton, Ric. de, 256
Brewer, Wm., 39 n, 40
brewing, 97–9; and see malting
brick-making, 32, 101–2
Brighton (Suss.), 253
Brinkworth, R. E., architect, 229
Bristol, 10, 178, 192, 205 n, 206, 251

port, 82
Bristow:
  Wm., 93 n
  ——, 73
Brittany, Hervey of, 38
Britton:
  John, 113
  Maur., 214
Bromham, 69, 245, 247
  Bromham Ho., 9, 56
Brooks:
  Ric. (fl. 1716–19), 90 n
  Ric. (fl. 1743, ? the same), 92
Broughton Gifford, 42, 203
Brown (Browne):
  Charlotte, 244
  H., 63
  Thos., 67
  Wm., 69
Brown & May Ltd., 69, 100–1, 167
Browne, see Brown
Brownsmith, John, 82
Bruges, fam., 188
Buckingham, duke of, see Stafford, Hen.
Buckinghamshire, see Chequers
Budd, W., 205 n
building industry, 100–1
Bunce, J. S., 206
Bupton, see Clyffe Pypard
Burges, Dr. J. H., rector of Devizes, 183, 189
Burgh:
  Hubert de, 44–5, 183
  Wal. de, 41
Burleigh, John, 59 n, 110 n
Burney, Fanny, 106
Burrough (Burroughs, Burrows):
  Jas., bell-founder, 94, 188
  T., 217
  Wm., 218
Burt, H. and J., 94
Butcher:
  Gabriel, 93 n
  Hen., 157
Butler:
  Sir Reg., 65, 101
  fam., 65
Butterfield, Edm., 50 n

Byng, Rob., rector of Devizes and of All Cannings, 174, 182

Caen Hill, see Devizes
Caird, R. H., 72
Calne, 79, 234
　chant., 73
　hosp., 42 *n*
Calstone Wellington, 42
Cambridgeshire: Ely, bp. of, see Niel
Campbell, R. J., 202
canal, see Kennet & Avon
candle-making, 137
Cannings, All, rector of, see Byng
Cannings, Bishop's, 3, 58, 61, 73, 180, 235, 253, 255
　chap., 194
　Coate, 42
　Horton, 42, 213
　man., 36, 73
　Shepherd's Shore, 162–3
　tan-ho., 84
　tithes, 194
　vicar, 194
Cannings hundred, 1
Canterbury, abp. of, see Theobald
Capital and Counties Bank, 103
Cardiff, Wm. of, 39 *n*
Cardmaker:
　Ric., 179
　Thos., 180
Carpenter, Ric., 68; *and see* Slater & Carpenter
Carter, Thos., 100
Catherine of Aragon, queen of Henry VIII, 49, 114, 129
Catherine Howard, queen of Henry VIII, 50
Catherine Parr, queen of Henry VIII, 50
Central Wiltshire Bacon Co., 101
Chandler, Thos., 209–10
Chandler & Co., maltsters, 99
chantries, see Calne; Devizes (ch. of St. John; ch. of St. Mary)
Charles II, 10
Charlotte, queen of George III, 10, 106
Chartists, see Devizes

Chauncey:
　Ichabod, 205 *n*
　Nat., 202 *n*, 205
Cheeter, John, 213
Chequers (Bucks.), 61
Child, Sir Francis, 12
Chilmark, 186
Chilton Foliat, 172
Chippenham:
　forest, 39, 41, 45
　inns, 103
　mkt., 114
　road through, 7
　Rom. Cath., 199
　taxation, 89
Chivers, W. E., & Son, 100–1, 224
Chobham (Surr.), 35
church-house, see Devizes, ch. of St. Mary
Chute:
　Chaloner (d. 1659), 61
　Chaloner (d. 1666), 61
Cirencester (Glos.), 9
Civil War, see Devizes; Malmesbury
Clappen, R. J., 63
Clare, Wm., 68
Clark:
　Jacob, 66
　John (fl. 1682), 211
　John (fl. 1725), 90 *n*
　Martha, 199
　Mr., 212
Cleves, Anne of, see Anne
clock-making, 94
cloth industry, see Devizes, ind. and trade (textiles); wool-stapling
Clyffe Pypard:
　Bupton, 42
Coate, see Cannings, Bishop's
Cole, Miss, 233
Collier, Mary, 178, 248
Collins, John, 12
Colston, Edw., 196
Comper, Sir Ninian, architect, 199
Compton Bassett, rector of, see Keymes
Coney, Wm., bell-founder, 188
Congregationalists, 203, 207–10, 217, 232

260

INDEX

Conyger, Little and Upper, *see* Devizes
Coole:
  Peter, 92 *n*
  Wm., 211
Cooper, John, 204
Cor:
  Rob., bell-founder, 193
  Wm., bell-founder, 188, 193
Cornwall, *see* Launceston
  St. Tew, rector of, *see* Attwell
Corsham, 53, 55
county court, *see* Devizes; Wilton
Coventry:
  John, father of John (d. by 1475), 179
  John (d. by 1475), 180, 234, 236
  John (? another), and his w., 180
  Nic., 254
  Thos., 236
  Wm., 180, 236
  ——, 246
Coward, fam., 197
Cox, Thos., 221
Crammer, the, *see* Devizes
Croke:
  Sir Rob., 61–2
  Susan, *see* Vanlore
Cromwell, Oliver, Ld. Protector, 10, 57
Cross Manufacturing Co. Ltd., 101
Crowe, Mr., 70
Cunnington:
  Alf., 13
  Benj. Howard, 13, 93 *n*
  Edw., 93
  Hen., 13, 93
  Maud Edith, *see* Pegge
  Wm. (d. 1810), 12, 93
  Wm. (d. 1846), 12, 93
  Wm. (d. 1906), 12, 79, 93

dairy products, manufacture of, 101
Daniel:
  Edw., 180
  Joan, 180
Danvers:
  Chas., 138
  Sir John, 60
Daubeny, Phil., 40

Davis (Davies):
  Jas., 12
  Miss, 233
  Mr., 219
Dawe, Rob., 234
Dawson, Rob., 209
Deramore, Ld., *see* Bateson
Despenser:
  Hugh le (d. 1265), 41
  Hugh le (d. 1326), 45–6
Devas, Revd. A. C., vicar of St. Peter's, Devizes, 198
Devereux, Rob., earl of Essex, 60, 110
Devizes, Ric. of, 11
Devizes, *viii*, 2, *14–15*, 18
  agric., 109–12
  alms-hos., 145, 161, 234–44, 249, 252
  Eyles, 160–1, 241–2
  Grange, 74, 244
  Helm's, 243
  New, 220, 235–42, 252, 255
  New Town, 241–3, 246
  Old, 235–42, *238*, 252, 255
  St. Mary's Gdns., 243
  Sedgefield Gdns., 240
  Sutton Pl., 237–8, 240
  Tull's, 240
  Victoria Rd., 240, 244
  Ward Homes, 243–4
  and see Devizes, St. John's Bdgs.
  antiquaries, 12–13
  Ashlers Green, 21
  assize town, 77–8; *and see* Devizes, public bdgs. (assize cts.)
  Assoc. for preventing Felony, etc., 168
  banks, 30 *n*, 102–3, 105, 211
  Bateson Reading Rooms, 216, 224
  Bear Hotel, *see* Devizes, inns
  Bear monument, 106–7, *120*
  Belle Vue, 31–2, 36; *and see* Devizes, houses (Belle Vue Ho.)
  Belvedere, 164
  borough (corporation), 1–3, 38, 60, 87–8, 125–49, 245–6, 252
    aldermen (senior councillors), 138–9, 147; (policemen), 136, 168
    ale-taster, 136, 143, 148
    armour, 150

261

Devizes, borough (cont.)
arms, 155, *156*
assembly, ct. of, 131
bailiffs, 126–9, 135–6, 143
beadles, 127–8, 136–7, 143, 148
bellman, 134, 143
boundaries, 1, *2*, 3
burgesses: capital burgesses, 121, 130, 132, 137–42, 171; capital burgesses councillors, 130, 132–5, 137–42; free burgesses, 132, 137–9, 141–2, 171
by-laws, 132, 136–7, 141–2, 145, 148, 168
chamberlains, 135, 143, 145, 148, 246
charters, 126–8, 132–5, 138–40, 147 *n*, 158, 170
clerk (town clerk, common clerk), 132, 134–5, 138, 142–3, 146, 148–9, 155, 157
committees, 143–4, 148
common council, 130–2, 137–43, 151, 154
constables, 129, 135–6, 143, 148, 157, 168–9, 211
'constitutions', 135
coroners, 128, 135, 148, 157
cts., 129–31, 133–5, 137, 150, 154; clerk of, 135, 142, 148–9; ct. of record, 132, 137–9, 141, 143–4, 148; petty sessions, 142; quarter sessions, 132, 139, 141, 144, 148
crier, 136–7
franchises, 126–9, 131, 144, 147 *n*; parliamentary, 134, 138, 170–1; *and see* Devizes, constituency
insignia, 156–7
mayors, 83, 86–7, 128–35, 137–42, 144–9, 156, 170–1, 177, 236, 254; election, 132–3, 139–40; lists of, 158; seal, 155–6; *and see* Allen, Mat.; Baker; Batt, John (d. 1600) *and* Ric. (d. *c.* 1569); Cardmaker, Ric.; Erwood, Wm.; Flower, Ric. and Rob.; Hall, John; Haynes; Hull, Thos.; Maundrell; Morris, Hen.; Northey; Pugh, C. W.; Stephens, John; Tymmer; Willos

medical officer of health, 149
offices, 79, 155; *and see* (all s.v. Devizes) council ho.; guildhall; Town (Wool, or Old) Hall
politics, 149
property, 21, 103, 131–3, 144–5, 148, 234–5; eccl. patronage, 174–5, 181; pew, 187; *and see* (all s.v. Devizes) chantry lands; fairs; mkts.
rates, 144, 146, 148
recorders, 134–5, 138–9, 141, 144, 148, 157, 171, 248; deputy, 138, 141, 144
records, 128, 144, 146, 150, 152, 158
reeve, 129
regulation of industry and trade, 131–2, 137–8
seals, 155–6
stewards of the cts., 135, 142–3, 148
treasurers, 146, 148–9
'twelve', the, 130, 135
wards, 147
Breach, the, 35
bridewell, *see* Devizes, prisons
bridges, 5, 17, 27
burgages, 51, 67, 72
Caen Hill, 101
canal, 7–8, 27–8, 31, 164–5, 167
Canal Co., 162
locks, 8, 27 *n*, 162
wharves, 27–8; Wharf Co., 167
and see Devizes, bridges
castle, 1–2, 36–67, 74, 81, 115, 127, 173, 183
bdgs., 51–7, 62–5, 95
chaps., 54, 56, 173
chaplain, 42, 173
constable, 39, 42, 45–6, 48, 50–1, 109, 114, 122, 127, 170, 175
ditches, 15, 51–2, 61, 110–11
keepers, 39–42, 46, 128
porter, 48, 50
prison, 54
prisoners and distinguished occupants, 43–4, 46–8
water supply, 161–2
and see Devizes, Civil War *and* parks
castle-guard duty, 39, 42–3, 128
cemetery, 164

INDEX

chantry lands, 132, 180–1, 234–5
chaps., *see* (all s.v. Devizes) castle; hosps., St. John the Baptist; St. Thomas's
chars.:
  ch., 175–8, 199, 242–3
  educ., 219–24, 228–31
  highway, 245
  nonconf., 201, 203–4, 206–7, 209–10, 213
  poor, 234–6, 242–53; *and see* Devizes, alms-hos.
Chartists, 11, 108
chs., 172–99; *and see* Devizes, St. Thomas's chap.
ch. of St. James, *see* Southbroom, ch.
chs. of St. John and St. Mary:
  adv., 173–4
  glebe, 176
  peculiar, 174
  rectors, 42 *n*, 158, 173–7, 200, 212, 221, 223, 254–5; *and see* Burges; Byng; Johnson, Hen.; Phipps, E. J.; Prestwich; Shephard, John; Yorkfleet
  rectory, 174
  rectory-ho., 178
  tithes, 174–6
ch. of St. John, 44–5, 65, 158, *184*, 200, 247, 254
  archit., 183–8, 238
  Beauchamp chap., 179, 185, 196
  chantries etc., 179, 234; *and see* Devizes, chantry lands
  property, 177
  regs., 189
  and see (all s.v. Devizes), chs. of St. John and St. Mary; hosps., St. John the Baptist; parish of St. John
ch. of St. Mary, 82, *189*, 200, 254
  archit., 189–93
  chantries etc., 179–81, 234; *and see* Devizes, chantry lands
  ch.-ho., 193
  property, 22–3, 159, 177, 234
  regs., 193
  and see (both s.v. Devizes) chs. of St. John and St. Mary; parish of St. Mary

ch. of St. Peter, 194–5, 198–9
  adv., 198
  archit., 198–9
  vicars, 198–9; *and see* Devas; Phipps, F.
cinemas, 215
Civil Defence, H.Q., 214
Civil War, 9–10, 41, 56–7, 178, 183, 200
clubs, 216–17
  Bear, 221, 223–4, 228
  Brittox, 157, 216
  Conservative, 216
  Liberal, 216
  and see Devizes, workingmen's assoc.
constituency, the, 3, 142, 170–2; M.P.s, 12, 141–2, 145, 147, 170–2; *and see* Devizes, borough (franchises, parliamentary)
Conyger, Little and Upper, 111
Corn Exchange, 33, 106, 117, *117*, 124, 157; *and see* Devizes, mkt.-pls. (corn)
council ho., 150; *and see* (all s.v. Devizes) guildhall; Town (Wool, or Old) Hall; weavers' hall
county ct., 73–4
county constabulary, 169; *and see* Devizes, public bdgs.
county offices, *see* Wiltshire, county council
county quarter sessions, 56, 74, 150, 154
Crammer, the, 24, 198, 201
curfew, 188
ditches (town), 2, 9 *n*, 13, 16, 51–2, 179; *and see* Devizes, castle (ditches)
dom. archit., 17, 19, 21–2, 24–7, 29–36; *and see* Devizes, houses
drapers' hall, 154
Dunkirk, 3, 5, *6*, *31*, 32, 102
Estcourt Brewery, 99
fairs, 60, 122–6, 129, 131, 133, 136, 138, 144, 256
farms:
  Gillett's, 67, 111
  Lower (or Lower Park), 66, 111
  Old Park, 65, 111, 159
  Sunnyside, 66, 111

263

Devizes (cont.)
  fire brigade, see Devizes, public services
  friendly societies, 217
  gallows, 22, 155
  Gallows Ditch, 22–3, 33, 155, 160
  gasworks, see Devizes, public services
  gates, 16, 162
  Green, the, 4, 19, 21, 24, 103, 124–6, *125*, 193
  guildhall, 150–1, 154
  guilds, 80, 84–5, 87, 126, 129–30, 154
    arms, 85, *85*
  guildsmen ('yeldens'), 129–30
  Hare and Hounds Brewery, 99
  health, bd. of, 149, 165
  heralds' visitation (1565), 84
  Hillworth, 70; *and see* Devizes, houses (Hillworth Ho.)
  horticulture, 111–12
  Hospitallers, property of, *see* Ansty
  hosps., 165–6
    cottage (later Devizes) hosp., 165, 244
    St. James's (formerly Union Workho.), 161, 241
    St. John the Baptist, 20, 73, 254–5; adv., 254; chap., 20, 254–5; prior, 254–5
  house of correction, *see* Devizes, prisons
  houses: among those named:
    Ark, the, 22, 94, 97, 160
    Barford Ho., 169–70
    Belle Vue Ho., 31, 166, 199
    Bluet's Ct., 68–9
    Braeside, 6, 69, 229
    Brow, the (Browfort), 69–70
    Brow Cottage, 69–70
    Brownston Ho., 25–7, 67, *68*, 233
    Castle Ho., 57, 63–5, *64*
    Grange, the, 74, 244
    Great Porch, *17*, 19
    Greystone Ho., 24–5, *25*, 67–8
    Handel Ho., 30, 78
    Hartmoor Ho., 36
    Hazelands, 67
    Heathcote Ho., 198, 226, 232
    Hillworth Ho., 33 *n*, 70
    Knoll, the, 166

  Moorlands, 36
  Northgate Ho., 79, 155; *and see* Devizes, inns (King's Arms)
  Old Park, 65–6
  Parnella Ho., 26, 68, 233
  Prospect Ho., 70
  Southgate Ho., 13, 30, 93 *and see* Southbroom, Southbroom Ho.
  housing estates, 30–6
  Improvement Commissioners, 5, 29, 32, 106, 146–7, 149, 163–4, 166–9
  ind. and trade, 81–103
    agric. engineering, 100
    bell-founding, 94
    brewing, 97–9, *98*
    bricks, 32, 101–2
    building, 100–1
    candles, 137
    clocks, 94
    dairy products, 101
    leather, 81, 84, 87–9, 93–4, 246
    malting, 97, 99
    metal, 81–2, 84, 87; braziers, 81–2, 94
    metheglin, 100, 105
    snuff, 70, 95–6, *95, 96*
    textiles, 82–93, 205, 212, 245; broadcloth, 82–3, 88, 91; cassimeres, 90, 92; drugget, 90; factories, 90–2, 160, 162; felt, 88, 90; serge, 88–9; silk, 88, 92
    tobacco, 31, 95–6, 204
    and see (all s.v. Devizes) agric.; banks; drapers' hall; guilds; horticulture; mkt.-places; Town Hall; weavers' hall
  inns, 103–9; among those named:
    Angel, 105; Angel rent, 223, 231, 247
    Bear, 11, 105–7, 117–18, *117*, 221; *and see* (both s.v. Devizes) Bear monument; clubs (Bear)
    Black Swan, 26, 104–5, 205 *n*
    Castle, 108
    Crown, 104
    Curriers Arms, 93, 108
    Elm Tree, 21, 107, 220, 242
    Gun, 120

Hare and Hounds, 108
King's Arms (Northgate Ho.), 108
Lamb, 29 *n*
Queen's Head, 109
Swan, 100, 104–5
Three Crowns, 109
White Bear, 109, 115
White Swan, 104–5
Jews at, 80–1
judges' lodgings, 78–9
Jump, the, 9
Kennet Ho. (wareho.), 99
liberty, 39
  lordship, 38–51, 60–7, 174–5
  stewardship, 45, 50–1, 60, 110, 129
  and see Devizes, castle (constables, keepers)
Literary and Scientific Institute, 215
M.P.s, *see* Devizes, constituency
man., *see* Devizes, liberty (lordship)
mkt.-bell, 150
Market Cross, 115–19, *120*
Market Ho., 56, 115, 119–21, *120*, 152, 154
Market Place, 17, 20, 23, 25–6, 35, 57, 104–5, 116, 118–19, *118*, *120*, 122, 124, 147, 164; *and see* Devizes, mkt.-places
mkt.-places, 16–17, 20, 119–20
  butchers, 115–16; *and see* Devizes, mkt.-places (shambles)
  butter, 119–20
  cattle, 121–2
  cheese, 119–21, 150, 152
  corn, 115–17, 120, 137, 193; *and see* Devizes, Corn Exchange
  fish, 115, 120
  horses, 122
  hosiers, 88, 119–20
  New Port, 16–17, 115–16, 121
  Old Port, 16, 115–16
  poultry, 120, 152
  shambles, 104 *n*, 115–16, 120–2, 124, 162; *and see* Devizes, mkt.-places (butchers)
  shoemakers, 120
  tanners, 116, 119
  wool, 119, 121, 150; *and see* Devizes,

Town (Wool, or Old) Hall
mkts., 24, 51, 60, 80, 112–22, 127, 129, 131, 133, 136, 144–5
  Measuring Ho., 116–18
  tolls, 60, 113–15, 122
  weighing beams (ho.), 116, 121, 138
Masonic Hall, 222
Measuring Ho., *see* Devizes, mkts.
mills, 100
  windmills, 57, 63–4, 95
mint, 80
Moat Mead, 59
monastic property, 72–3
museum, 12–13, 118, 215, 232
Mutual Protection Soc., 168
New Hall, 119, 150–4
New Port, *see* Devizes, parish of St. John
New Town, 32, 241–3
newspapers, 217–18
nonconf., 139, 145, 200–1, 214, 231
  Baptists, 145, 201–9, 232; New Chap., 145 *n*, 202, 205–7, 230, 232; Old Chap., 201–5, 251; *and see* Devizes, nonconf. (Salem Chap.)
  Brethren, 204, 208, 211, 214
  Congregationalists, 203, 207–10, 217, 232; St. Mary's Chap., 208–10, 226
  Latter Day Saints, 213
  Methodists, 208–9, 212–14
  Presbyterians, 202, 205–7, 221, 231
  Quakers, 200, 205, 210–11; burial ground, 212
  Salem Chap., 202, 204, 214
  Salvation Army, 214
North Wilts. Dispensary, 165–6, 244
North Wilts. Foundry, 100
Northgate Brewery, *98*, 99
Nursery, the, 30–1, 36, 198
Nursing Soc., 244
Odd Fellows, 217
Old Hall, *see* Devizes, Town (Wool, or Old) Hall
Old Port, *see* Devizes, parish of St. Mary
parishes, 158–61
  boundaries, 2–3

265

Devizes

Devizes (*cont.*)
  parish of St. John (New Port), 1–2, 16–17, 27, 67, 144, 149, 179–80, 200
    mkt.-place, *see* Devizes, mkt.-places (New Port)
    officers, 158, 161, 236–7
    poor-relief, 158–60; *and see* Devizes, chars.
    records, 158, 161
    vestry, 158
  parish of St. Mary (Old Port), 1–3, 16–17, 27, 67, 144, 180, 200, 254
    mkt.-places, *see* Devizes, mkt.-places (Old Port)
    officers, 159, 161
    poor-relief, 159–61; *and see* Devizes, chars.
    records, 158, 161, 181, 193 *n*
    vestry, 159, 241
  parks, 51, 57–61, 127, 174–6
    new (or little) park, 58–62, 109–10; *and see* Roundway, New Park
    old (or great) park, 2, 34, 36, 58–62, 65–7, 82, 109–11, 161, 164, 176; *and see* Devizes, houses (Old Park)
    parkers, 59–60, 109–10
  pest house, 165; *and see* Devizes, hosps.
  Phoenix factory, 100
  Piccadilly, 24, 198
  pl.-name, 8, 36
  plague and other infectious diseases, 165
  police, 148, 168–9; *and see* Devizes, public bdgs.
  poor-law union, 161
    wkho., *see* Devizes, hosps. (St. James's)
  pop., 4–5, 81, 86
  prisons, 11
    castle, *see* Devizes, castle
    county (later state), New Bridewell, New Prison, 31, 35, 75–7, *76*, *77*
    house of correction, bridewell, Old Bridewell, 74–5, 86, 131, 155, 169
    town, 131, 154–5
  Proprietary Grammar Sch. Co. Ltd., 232
  Prosecution Soc., 168
  public bdgs., 145
  assize cts., 78, *78*, 169, 233
  county constabulary H.Q., 79
  govt. offices, 170
  militia stores, 79, 152
  police sta., 26, 169
  public meetings, 79–80; *and see* Devizes, riots
  public services, 161–70
    cleansing, 146, 163–4
    electricity, 167
    fire, 21–2, 147, 162, 167–8; brigade, 167; engine, 167
    gas, 166–7; works, 147, 149, 167
    lighting, 146, 166–7
    paving, 146–7, 163
    postal, 169–70
    sewerage, 164; sewage works, 111, 164
    watch, 147, 168–9
    water, 161–2, 164, 167
    weights and measures, 137–8, 143; *and see* (both s.v. Devizes, mkts.) Measuring Ho.; weighing beams
    and see (all s.v. Devizes) cemetery; hosps.; police; swimming pool
  rly., 8, 33, 162; Pans Lane Halt, 4, 8; sta., 8, 33
  riots, 10–11
  roads from, 5–7, 24
  Rom. Cath., 199–200
    chs., 33, 199–200, 227–8
    schs., 227–8, 233
  Rom. settlement, 4
  Rotherstone, 112, 194
  royal visits, 8, 10
  Rural District Council, offices, 69–70
  Rural Sanitary Authority, 164
  St. John the Baptist, hosp. of, *see* Devizes, hosps.
  St. John's Bdgs., 160, 238, 241
  St. Thomas's chap., 117, 193
  schs., 219–34
    Bear Club, 216, 221, 223–4, 228–9
    Blue Coat, *see* Devizes, schs., Free, later National Boys' (Town)
    British, 215, 224, 226–7, 230, 233
    Devizes (formerly Southbroom Senior) Sch., 72, 224–6, 230

Free, later National Boys' (Town), 216, 220, 223–5, 228–9
further educ., 234
Grammar (formerly secondary), 229–30
National Girls' (Town), 222–4
National Infants' (Town), 216, 222–4
private, 70, 231–3
St. Bartholomew's Industrial, 229
St. Peter's National, 199, 227, 231
and see Southbroom, schs.
sewage works, *see* Devizes, public services
shambles, *see* Devizes, mkt.-places
Southbroom, *q.v.*
Southgate (Upper Wick), 16, 32
streets, etc., 17–36, *18*; among those named:
Albion Terr., 30
Bath Rd., 24, 30–5, *31*
Big Lane, 6, 24
Brickley Lane, 35
Bridewell Sq., 75
Bridewell St., 17, 20, 22–4, 31, 74, 93
Brittox, the, 17, 20, 25, *28*, 29–30, 33, 52, 84
Castle Lane, 29
Castle St., 22–3
Chapel Corner, 20, 29 *n*
Chequer, the, 22, 29
Commercial Rd., 23, 32, 34
Couch Lane, 19
Dumb Post Passage, 27
Estcourt (Nestcot, Eastcroft) Hill, 22–3, 33, 176
Estcourt St., 21–2, 33
Exchange Pl., 33
Gains Lane, 23, 32–4
Half Moon Lane, 23
Hare and Hounds Ct., 3, 24
Hare and Hounds St., 2, 22, 24, 32
Hartmoor Rd., 7, 22
High St., 20, 22–3, 25, 27, 116, 119
Hillworth Rd., 6–7, 20–3, 33, 35–6; *and see* Devizes, Gallows Ditch
Keeper's Walk, 16
Lansdowne Grove (Terr.), 30
Little Brittox, 28–9
Little Lane, 6
London Rd., 33
Long St., 20, 22–3, 25–6, *26*, 30, 231
Longcroft Rd., 34
Maryport St., 2, 20, 22, 29, 93–4
Monday Market St., 18–20, 24, 94, 115, 124, 200
Morris's Lane, 2, 20
Mortimer's Ct., 24, 35
Nestcot Hill, *see* Devizes, streets, Estcourt Hill
New Park St., 17, 19–20, 36, 124
Northgate St., 19–20, 23
Nursteed Rd., 34–5
Pans Lane, 21, 23–4; *and see* Devizes, rly.
Perambulation (later Procession) Walk, 15–16
Potterne Rd., 6–7
Procession Walk, *see* Devizes, streets, Perambulation Walk
Quaker's Walk, 7
Roseland Ave., 34
St. John's Alley, 20–1, 24, 29
St. John's St., 19–20, 22–6, 120, *151*
St. Joseph's Rd. (formerly Pl.), 5, 33
Sedgefield Gdns., 35
Sheep St., 22, 36
Short St., 19–20, 116, 121
Sidmouth St., 16, 22, 29–30
Snuff St., 23
Southbroom Rd., 3, 21, 30
Southgate St., 22
Station Rd., 106
Trafalgar Pl., 30, *31*
Victoria Ct., 32
Victoria Rd., 36
Wick Lane, 21, 23
Wine St., 20, 22–3, 29–30, 116, 120, 152, 154
and see (all s.v. Devizes) Belle Vue; Gallows Ditch; Market Place; New Town; Nursery; Piccadilly; Rotherstone; Southgate
Stringer's garage, 200
subsidies, *see* Devizes, tax assessments

Devizes (*cont.*)
  swimming pool, 164–5
  tax assessments, 81, 85
  theatre, 215
  Three Crowns Brewery, 99
  Town (Wool, or Old) Hall, 29, 79, 106, 119, 121, 123, 145, 149–52, *151*, *153*, 154–5, 158, 169 and *n*, 215, 233
  urban district, 149
  watercourses, 1, 100, 161–2, 164
    town watering pl., 1, 23
  weavers' hall, 102 *n*, 153–4, 235 *n*
  Wick (Wick Green), *see* Southbroom
  Wiltshire Arch. and Nat. Hist. Soc., *q.v.*
  Wool Hall, *see* Devizes, Town Hall
  wkho., *see* Devizes, hosps. (St. James's)
  workingmen's assoc., 11; club, 217
  Worm Cliff, 23
  Y.M.C.A., 214
  yarn hall, 119, 150
Devizes Advertiser, 218
Devizes Church Library, 215–16
Devizes Club, *see* Devizes, clubs (Brittox Club)
Devizes Day Schools Assoc., 224
Devizes Herald and North Wilts. Intelligencer, 218
Devon, 70
Dinton, 62
Diva, Guy de, 40
Dorset, 41; *and see* Poole
Douglas, John, bp. of Salisbury, 182
Dover (Kent), ct. of castle gate, 51 *n*
Dowding:
  Revd. B. C., vicar of Southbroom, 195, 197–9
  Mrs., 199
Dowell, C. G., 200
Dredge:
  Jas. & Jos., 97
  Jos., & Co., 97
Drew:
  Eliz., w. of John (d. by 1664), m. 2 Sir Hen. Andrews, 71
  (or Trew), John (fl. 1501–2), 70–1
  John, father of Rob. (fl. 1618), 247
  John (d. 1614), 71
  John (d. by 1664), 71
  (or Trew), Rob. (d. *c.* 1564), 247
  Rob. (fl. 1609), 235 *n*
  Rob. (fl. 1618, ? the same), 247
  Rob. (d. 1645), and his w. Eliz., 71
  Rob. (d. 1671), 196
  Rob. (d. 1695), 196
  fam., 69, 71, 188
Drew's Pond, *see* Roundway
Dudley, Edm., 49
Dunkirk, *see* Devizes
Durand, Mrs. I. M., 63
Duras, Louis de, earl of Feversham, 10
Durham, Sir Phil. C. H., 12
Durnford, Jas., 112
Dyer, John, 59 *n*

Easton, 234
Edward I, 44–5
  as Prince Edward, 41
Edward IV, 49
Edward VI, 128 *n*
Edward VII, 166
  as prince of Wales, 10, 106
Edward, duke of York (d. 1415), 47
Effington, E., 105 *n*
Eldridge:
  John, 65
  Wm., 65
Eleanor, queen of Edward I, 45
Eliot, George (pseudonym), 11; *and see* Elliott
Elizabeth, queen of Edward IV, 49
Elizabeth, queen of Henry VII, 49
Elliott:
  Revd. Ric., 209, 232
  Mrs., 232
  and see Eliot
Ely, bp. of, *see* Niel
Enford, vicar of, *see* Sacheverell
Erlestoke, 218
Ernle, Sir Edw., 188
Erwood:
  John, 87 *n*
  Wm., 87
  fam., 87
Essex, earl of, *see* Devereux
Essex, *see* Pleshey

Estcourt:
  Jas. Bucknall, 12
  Thos. G. B., 28, 152
  T. H. S. Sotheron, 12, 79, 118, 172, 187
  fam., 4, 35
Estmonde, Wm., 180
Etchilhampton, 12, 42
Evans, Geo., 232
Everett, C. E., 66
Ewart, Wm., 112
Eyles:
  Edw., 71
  Sir John (d. 1703), 71, 201–4, 239, 241–2, 249, 253
  John (d. 1752), 187
  John (fl. 1757), 93 *n*
  Sir Jos., 150
  Mary, 220, 223, 230–1, 238, 242, 249
  Sarah, w. of Sir John (d. 1703), 249
  fam., 187

fairs, *see* Devizes
Farmer, the Misses, 232
Fennell, Wm., 93 *n*
Fenner, Revd. J. L., 205, 231
Ferdinand, Archduke, *see* Austria
Feversham, Ld., *see* Duras
Fidsall (Fidsell):
  Jas., 88
  Mary, 201
  Sam., 202
Field, John, 180
Figgins & Gent, brewers, 97–8
Filkes:
  Eliz., 202, 209–10
  John (fl. 1723), 201–2
  John (fl. 1780, ? the same), 209–10
  ——, 67
  fam., 191
Fisherton Anger, gaol, 77
FitzHubert, Rob., 38
Fitzwilliam, Brian, 129 *n*
Flavel, John, 46 *n*
Flower:
  Benj., 205
  Edw., 86 *n*
  Geo., 57, 62, 95 *n*
  Ric., 68, 86 *n*, 87

  Rob., 86 *n*, 87
  Rog., 86 *n*
  Thos., 86 *n*
  fam., 86, 196
Forest Row (Suss.), 252
Forman, John, 93 *n*
Forz, Aveline de, ctss. of Aumale, 43–4
Fox:
  J. J., & Co., 91
  J. R., 218
Foxhangers, *see* Rowde
France, 90; *and see* Gascony
franchises, *see* Devizes, borough (franchises); gallows
Franklin, Geo., 213
Frayling, John, 207
Freke, Rob., 234
Freme:
  John (fl. 1646), 201
  John (fl. 1669, ? another), 207–8
Friends, Society of, *see* Quakers
Frome (Som.), 121
Frome Selwood (Som.), 243
Fulham (Mdx.), 251

gallows, 22, 155
Gamble & Whichcord, architects, 215
Garlick (or Goulick), Thos., 93 *n*
Garrick, David, 106
Garth:
  Chas., 67
  John, 67, 191
Gascony, 48
Gent, Jas., 98
Gent & Tylee, *see* Tylee & Gent
George III, 10, 106
George IV, as Prince Regent, 11
George, Sarah, 207
Gerrish, J., 223 *n*
Gibbs, Geo., 102 *n*
Giddings, fam., 188
Gifford, John, 250
Gilbert, fam., 69
Giles, J. M., 66
Gillman:
  Chas., 218
  R. D., 218
  W. H., 218

Gloucester:
    duke of, see Humphrey
    earls of, see Robert; William
Gloucestershire, 254; and see Bristol;
    Cirencester
Gobett, Ric., 180, 246
Godalming (Surr.), man., 38, 179 n
Godbye, Ric., 88
Godfather, Phil., 88
Goodridge, H. E., architect, 64
Gore, Montagu, 12
Gough:
    Wm., 205
    Mrs., 207
Goulick, Thos., see Garlick
Grant Meek, see Meek
Gray, Ric. de, 40
Griffith, C. Darby, 117
Grindle:
    Annette Sarah, 253
    H. A. L., 199
Grubbe, Mrs., 248
Guy, Rosalie Emily, 207

Haggard, Rob., 93 n
Halcombe, Wm., 106, 108
Hall:
    John, 192 n
    Thos., 70
Hampshire, see Appleshaw; Bournemouth; Odiham; Southampton; Southbourne; Winchester
Hampshire militia, 10
Hampton, Joshua, 66
Hancock (Handcock), Sarah, 202, 204, 207
Hannes, Sir Edw., 11
Hardman, A. H., 65
Harrie, Thos., 92 n
Hart:
    (or Hort), Ant., 240, 252
    Hen., 59 n
Hartmoor, see Potterne
Harwell (Berks.), atomic energy establishment, 101
Harwood, John, 93 n
Hastings, Selina, ctss. of Huntingdon, 208

Hatch, West (in Tisbury), 246
Havering, John de, 41
Haynes, Edw., 83
Hayward:
    John, 69
    fam., 196
Hazeland, fam., 67
Hazelbury, quarry, 52, 55
Heathcote:
    Geo., 71
    Josiah Eyles, 71
    Maria, 187
    fam., 187
Helmes, Wm. Ric., 243
Henchman, Humfrey, bp. of Salisbury, 182, 200
Henry II, 126–7, 179 n
    as prince, 38
Henry III, 41, 43, 127, 256
Henry VI, 49
Henry VIII, 128 n
Henton, Chris., 67
Herbert:
    Hen., earl of Pembroke, 60, 110
    John, 234
    Phil., earl of Montgomery and earl of Pembroke, 61
    Wm., earl of Pembroke (d. 1570), 50, 60
    Wm., earl of Pembroke (d. 1630), 110
Herne, John, 93 n
Heydon, Sir John, 133
Heytesbury, 12
Hicks, Thos., 201
Hill:
    Rowland, 208
    Wm., architect, 117
Hiller (Hillier), Ric., 249
Hillman, Steph., 68, 91
Hilmarton, 245
Hilperton, rector of, see Baddeley
Hinchley Engineering Co., 101
Hitchcock, Rog., 202
Hoare:
    Prince, sculptor, 187
    Sir Ric. Colt, 12, 93
Holland, see Utrecht
Hollis, John, 97

Holloway:
　Amelia, 213
　——, 91
Holy Land, Edward I in, 41
Hooton, Chas., 218
Hope (Hopes):
　Edw., 207
　Mr., 94
Hopton, Sir Ralph, 9–10
Horne, Miss, 233
Hort, Ant., see Hart
horticulture, 111–12
Horton, fam., 191
Horton, see Cannings, Bishop's
Hospitallers, see Ansty
hospitals (medieval), see Calne, hosp.; Devizes, hosps. (St. John the Baptist); Southbroom, hosp. of St. James and St. Denis
house of correction, see Devizes, prisons
Howard:
　Cath., see Catherine
　John, 74, 155
Hugh the parker, 59 n
Hughes:
　Jas., 156
　Solomon, 102
　Wm., 102
Hull:
　Thos., 83
　fam., 191
Humby, J. F., 99
Humphrey, duke of Gloucester, 48, 173
Hungerford:
　Sir Edm., 48–50
　Sir Edw., 9
Huntingdon, Hen. of, 37
Huntingdon, ctss. of, see Hastings
Hunton, Phil., vicar of Westbury, 181 n
Hurst, see Worton
Hyde, Rob., 246

Imber, Eliz., 221, 230
Imperial Tobacco Co., 96
Independents, 139, 201, 208
industries, see agricultural implements; bell-founders; brewing; brick-making; building; candle-making; clock-making; dairy products; horticulture; leather trades; malting; metal trades; metheglin; snuff; tobacco; wool-stapling; *and see* Devizes, ind. and trade (textiles)
Ingleman, Ric., architect, 75
Innes, Edw., 208, 212
Isabel, queen of King John, 44
Isabel, queen of Edward II, 46

Jackson, fam., 188
James I, 8, 60–1
James II, 10, 138, 187
Jane Seymour, queen of Henry VIII, 50
Jefferies, R. H., 66
Jews, see Devizes; Marlborough; Wilton
Joan, queen of Henry IV, 47–8, 55
John, king, 43, 127, 256
　as count of Mortain, 173
John, chaplain, 173
John, Mat. s. of, see Matthew
Johnson:
　Geo., 192
　Hen., rector of Devizes, 174, 182, 191
Jordon's mill, see Potterne, mills
Jump, the, see Devizes

Keevil, 42
Kemp, E. B. M., 63
Kennet, riv., 7 n
Kennet & Avon Canal, 7–8; *and see* Devizes, canal
Kent:
　John, 187
　Mrs., 250
Kent, dchss. of, mother of Queen Victoria, see Mary Louisa Victoria
Kent, see Dover
Canterbury, abp. of, see Theobald
Kerr, Charlotte, 232
Keymes, Wal., rector of Compton Bassett, 245–6
Keynes, Bridget, 196
King, T., sculptor, 187
Kingsland, Wm., 209
Kite, Edw., 12

Lacock, 178
Lamb, Ric., 185
Lansdown (Som.), battle, 9
Larive, Father, 200
Latter Day Saints, 213
Launceston (Cornw.), 13
Lavington, Thos., 66
Lavington, Market, 42
　mkt., 112
Lavington, West, 42
　Littleton Pannell, 42
Lawrence:
　Thos. (father of Sir Thos., d. 1830), 105–6
　Sir Thos. (d. 1830), 11, 106, 108, 231
　Mr. (fl. c. 1734), architect, 150
Leach:
　Rob. Valentine, 63–5
　Valentine, 63
　Wm., 95, 102
leather trades, 81, 84, 87–9, 93–4, 246
Lee:
　Sir Geo., 176
　Sir Hen., 134
Leeds (Yorks. W.R.), 117
Leicestershire, see Loughborough
Leland, John, antiquary, 20, 56, 84, 113
Levingston, Thos. and his w. Anne, 61
Lewen, Thos., 97
Lewer, Rob., 46 n
Lewis:
　H. C., 67
　Rob., 93 n
Ley, Hen., earl of Marlborough, 134
Lincoln:
　bp. of, see Alexander
　castle, 37
Lindsey, Sir David, 48
Lisle, Sir Beauvoir de, 65
Littleton Pannell, see Lavington, West
Llewellin, John, 67, 192
Lloyd, Col. Chas., 10, 71
Lock, Hughes & Co.'s bank, 30 n, 103
Locke:
　John, 102
　Wadham (fl. 1744, 1755), 102
　Wadham (d. 1835), 67
　fam., 68

London, 7, 12, 38, 71, 82, 157, 186, 198, 215, 246, 255
　goldsmith, 234
　Ld. Mayor, see Eyles, Sir John (d. 1703)
　merchant, 245
　Tower of, 37
Long:
　Sir Rob., 12
　fam., 188
Lott, Tim., 90 n
Loughborough (Leics.), 197
Lovel, John, Ld. Lovel, 47
Lowe, C. H., 215
Lucas:
　Chas., 11
　Frances Mary, 244
　Sarah Anne W., 251
Ludgershall, 38, 55
Ludlow:
　Wm. (fl. c. 1680), 92
　Wm. (fl. 1784), 70, 95
Lyllebon, Wal., 42 n
Lyneham, 245

Macdonald, Mr., 205 n
McMahon, Sir Horace, 72
Malmesbury, 9
　Civil War at, 9
malting, 97, 99; and see brewing
Maple, Wm., 95
Margaret, queen of Edward I, 45–6
Margaret, queen of Hen., s. of Henry II, 44
Margaret, queen of Henry VI, 49
markets, see Devizes; Lavington, Market
Marlborough, earl of, see Ley
Marlborough, 73, 80, 235–6
　castle, 38, 41, 47
　ch., 84
　inns, 103
　Jews at, 80
　parliamentary representation, 170
　pop., 4–5
　privileges, 126–8
　taxation, 80, 85, 89
Marshal:
　John le (fl. 1140), 38
　John (fl. 1217–19), 40

Marston, C. H., 202
Martin, Sam., 248
Mary Louisa Victoria, dchss. of Kent, mother of Queen Victoria, 10, 106
Massey, Sir Edw., 10
Mathews, John, 97 *n*
Matthew son of John, 45
Maud, empress, 38, 126–7, 179 *n*
Mauley, Peter de, 40
Maundrell, Ric., 134
May (Maye):
  John, 211
  Messrs., 99
  Mrs., *see* Mayo
Maynard:
  Jas., 69, 221, 229, 252
  Jane, 69
Mayo:
  Revd. Jos., 69
  Jos., s. of Revd. Jos., 69
  (or Maye), Mrs., 207
  fam., 103
Medlam, W. B., 63
Meek:
  Alex., 70
  Alex. Grant, 166
  Mrs. Grant, 70 *n*
  fam., 70
Melksham, 66, 101
  forest, 39, 45, 51 *n*, 256
  nonconf., 213
  taxation, 80
Mere, 42
Merewether (Merryweather):
  Hannah, 202–3
  Thos., 88–9
  fam., 188
Meriton, John, 212
Merryweather, *see* Merewether
metal trades, 81–2, 84, 87, 94
metheglin, manufacture of, 100
Methodists, 208–9, 212–14
Methuen:
  John, 12
  Sir Paul, 142
Middlemarch, 11
Middlesex, *see* Fulham
Miles, John, 88

militia, *see* Hampshire militia; Wiltshire militia
mills, *see* Devizes; Potterne; Roundway
Milman, the Misses, 67
Miln, Jas., 250
mint, *see* Devizes
Mitcham (Surr.), 96
Moberly, Geo., bp. of Salisbury, 216
Monmouth's rebellion, 109
Montgomery, earl of, *see* Herbert, Phil.
Morris:
  Hen., 20, 83, 247, 252
  John, 86 *n*
  fam., 86
Mortain, count of, *see* John, king
Mortimer:
  Rog., 41
  Wm., 24
Mother Anthony's Well, *see* Roundway
Mountsorrell, John of, 46 *n*
Moxham, Edw., 93 *n*
Mullens, Benoni, architect, 210
Munham, Phil. de, 42 *n*

Naseby (Northants.), battle, 10
Neale, Wm., 93 *n*
Needham:
  Jos., 25, 102 *n*
  fam., 188
Neild, Jas., 75
Neville, Rob. de, 41
New, Jos., 66
New College, Oxford:
  warden, 104 *n*
New Model Army, 10
New Park, *see* Roundway
New Town, *see* Devizes
Newman, Thos., 246
Newsham, Ric., 167
Newsome, R. N., 63
Nicholas:
  Griffin, 222, 248
  John, 134 *n*
  Mic., 222, 248
  Oliffe Richmond, 196
  Rob. (d. 1667), 135, 222, 248
  Rob. (d. 1722), 196
  Rob. (d. 1725), 196

Nicholas (cont.)
  Rob. (d. 1826), 67
  fam., 222
Niel, bp. of Ely, 37
Nisbet, Rob. Parry, 72, 196
nonconformity, see Baptists; Brethren; Congregationalists; Independents; Latter Day Saints; Methodists; Presbyterians; Quakers; Salvation Army
Norfolk, Norwich, bp. elect of, see Pandulf
Normandy, Rob. of, see Robert
Norrington, see Alvediston
North Wilts. Dairy Co., see Wilts. United Dairies Ltd.
North Wilts. Dispensary, see Devizes
North Wilts. Foundry, see Devizes
Northamptonshire, see Naseby
Northey, Edw., 87, 246
Norwich, bp. elect of, see Pandulf
Nott, fam., 188
Noyes, Sam., 210
Nurse, W. M., 63 n
Nursery, the, see Devizes
Nursteed, see Roundway

Ocle (Okelegh), John, 180
Odiham (Hants), castle, 55
Okelegh, see Ocle
Okey, Thos., 201
Oldfield, T. B., 171
Oliphant, Mrs., 69
Oram, Jas., 99
Orchard, John, see Archard
Orchardsleigh (Som.), 42
Orcheston St. George, 194
Orcheston St. Mary, 194
Osmund, bp. of Salisbury, 36
Oswestry (Salop.), 164
Otto, cardinal-legate, 44
Overton, Thos. Collins, architect, 69
Oxford, 126; and see New College
Oyseleur:
  Hen. le, 39 n
  Rog. le, 39 n

Page:
  Mat., 69
  Wm. (d. c. 1542), 245
  Wm. (fl. 1570), 69
Painter, L. G., 112 n; and see Paynter
Palmer:
  And., 234
  Ric., 88
Pandulf, legate, bp. elect of Norwich, 40
Pannell, Edw., 92 n
Paradise (Paradice):
  Edw., 99 n
  Francis, 139
  Hen. (fl. 1722), 99 n
  Hen. (fl. 1726, ? the same), 91 n
  John, 91 n
  Thos., 87 n
  Wm. (fl. 1741–4), 99 n
  Wm. (fl. c. 1760), 91 n
  ——, 88, 91
  fam., 87, 91, 99, 196
parker:
  Hugh the, see Hugh
  William the, see William
Parr, Cath., see Catherine
Paynter, Rob., 246; and see Painter
Pead, Geo., 89
Pearse, John, 172, 222; and see Pierce
Peck, Jos., 90 n
Pegge, Maud Edith, m. Benj. Howard Cunnington, 13, 252
Pembroke, earls of, see Herbert
Peniston (Pennistone), John, architect, 196
Penruddocke, Chas., 62
Pewsham forest, 126
  yeoman ranger, 51 n
Philippa, queen of Edward III, 46, 254
Phillips:
  Edw. (fl. 1721), 90 n
  Edw. (fl. 1767, ? another), 91
  Edw. White, 91
  Eleanor, see Powell
  Geo., 90 n
  Phil., 250 n
  Sam., 90 n
  Thos., 166
  fam., 90
Phipp (Phip):
  J. F., 109

Nic., 90 *n*
Phipps:
　Revd. E. J., rector of Devizes, 176 *n*, 182
　Canon F., vicar of St. Peter's, Devizes, 198–9
Piccadilly, *see* Devizes
Pierce:
　Edw., 205
　John (fl. 1600), 105
　John (d. *c.* 1642, prob. another), 87, 177, 219–20, 240, 245, 248, 252
　Ralph, 245
　Ric., 9, 105, 140
　Ruth, 118
　Thos. (fl. *c.* 1690), 100, 105
　Thos. (d. 1691), dean of Salisbury, 11, 86 *n*
　fam., 86
　and see Pearse
Pitt:
　Ellinor, 252
　Wm., 10
Pleshey (Essex), 13
Plessis, John du, earl of Warwick, 40–1, 54–5
Pollard, ——, architect, 121
Poller, Thos., 247
Poole (Dors.), 113 *n*
Poor:
　Ric. le, bp. of Salisbury, 40
　Rog. le, 37
Porter, Rob., 48 *n*
Potter:
　Edm., 88
　Edw., 88
Potterne, 3, 7, 42, 112, 118, 254
　Hartmoor, 7, 24, 65
　mills:
　　Jordon's, 7
　　Whistley, 7
　nonconf., 204
　Wick, 4
Potterne and Cannings hundred, 1
Poulshot, 255
Powell:
　Sir Edw., 61
　(formerly Phillips), Eleanor, 178, 221–2, 230, 250
　Mary, *see* Vanlore
　Wm., 211
Presbyterians, 202, 205–7
Prestwich, John, rector of Devizes, 174
Price, Morgan, 90
Prior, Wm., 200
prisons, *see* Devizes; Fisherton Anger
Pugh:
　C. W., 139 *n*
　Revd. S. S., 232
Purdue, Wm. and Rog., bell-founders, 193, 197
Pyle, Wm., 90 *n*

Quakers, 200, 205, 210–11
Queen Anne's Bounty, 176, 178, 194

Rabeyn, Ellis, 41
Raby, Dr. Leonard, 252
railway station, *see* Devizes
railways, *see* Berks. & Hants Extension; Wilts., Somerset & Weymouth
Ralph, Wal. s. of, *see* Walter
Rameshalle, John de, 46 *n*
Ramsbury, Maud of, 37
Randell, J. A., architect, 64, 96, 99, 210
Read (Rede, Reed):
　E. C., 63
　John, 203
　Ric., 102
　Wm., 247 *n*
　Mrs., 203
　fam., 196
Reading (Berks.):
　abbot of, *see* Simon
　chs., 173
Rede (Reed), *see* Read
Reynolds:
　Geo., 84
　Rob., 94 *n*
　S., & Co., 94 *n*
　Steph., 11, 233
　fam., 93–4
Rich:
　Sir Chas., 63, 65
　Lady, 63
Richard II, 47

Richman, Wm., 90 *n*
Rievaux, Peter de, 40
Robbins, Revd. Mills, 35
Robert of Normandy, 36–7, 44
Robert, earl of Gloucester, 38
Roberts, Ric., 255
Robinson, Crabb, 29–30, 231
Roger, bp. of Salisbury, 37
Rogers:
  John (fl. 1654), 92 *n*
  John (fl. 1705), 249
  Mrs. R., 218
Romain, J., 28
Roman Catholics, *see* Chippenham; Devizes
Rose:
  Chas., 97
  Edw., 253
Roundway, 3, 21, 62, 67, 194
  Bedborough, 21, 69, 194
  Drew's Pond, 188
  Le Marchant Barracks, 195
  mills:
    Belvedere, 92
    Roundway, 7
  Mother Anthony's Well, 162
  New Park (later Roundway Ho.), 7, 58, 62, 90, 172; *and see* Devizes, parks (new park)
  Nursteed, 69, 194
  Roundway Down (Hill), 1, 16
    battle, 9
  Roundway hosp., 11, 166
Rowborough, Bishop's, hundred, 1
Rowde:
  Gillian of, 39 *n*
  Nic. of, 46 *n*
  Thos. of, 39 *n*
Rowde, 3, 6, 51 *n*, 198, 235, 250–1, 255
  Foxhangers, 8
  man., 39, 41, 45–7, 60
  Rowde Ford, 5, 163
  serjeanty, 43
  Wick, 4
Russell, Mary, 207
Russia, export to, 90
Rutter, I., & Co., 96

S.P.C.K., 221
Sacheverell, Tim., vicar of Enford, 192, 205, 231
Sainsbury:
  G. T., 102
  Herb., 207
Sainsbury Bros., brewers, 99
St. Amand, Ant., 49
St. Amand, Ld., *see* Beauchamp, Sir Ric.
St. Joseph of Annecy, teaching order, 227–8
St. Lo, John, 73
St. Tew (Cornw.), rector of, *see* Attwell
Ste. Mère Eglise, Wm. of, 39
Salisbury, 193
  assize town, 77–8
  bps., 45, 122, 174–5, 192–3, 198, 254–6; *and see* Beauchamp, Ric.; Douglas; Henchman; Moberly; Osmund; Poor, Ric. le; Roger; Wordsworth
  cathedral:
    dean, *see* Pierce, Thos.
    dean and chapter, 73, 194
  ch. of St. Edmund, 4
  diocese:
    council of education, 230
    synod, 216
  inns, 103
  parliamentary representation, 170
  pop., 4–5
  taxation, 80, 89
  textile ind., 82
Salisbury, Old:
  castle, 47
  taxation, 81
Salisbury Journal, 217
Salmon:
  Wm. (fl. 1404), 82
  Wm. (d. 1826), 62–3, 71–2, 143, 146–7, 187
  Wm. Wroughton, 63, 72
  fam., 143
Salter, Wm., 245, 255
Salvation Army, 214
Sandford:
  Ric. de, 39
  Thos. de, 39–40, 45
Sandwich, Ralph de, 41, 47, 55, 175

Savage Transformers Ltd., 101
Scott, Sir Gilb., architect, 186
sculptors, see Bailey, E. H.; Hoare, Prince; King; Westmacott, Ric. (d. 1808) and Ric. (d. 1856)
Seaton, Mrs., 70
Seend, 180, 204, 245
Sellwood, Mary, 240
Seymour:
  Sir Edw., duke of Somerset, 234
  Jane, see Jane
  Thos., Ld. Seymour of Sudeley, 50
Sharington, Sir Hen., and his w. Anne, 178, 245–6
Sharnesfield, Sir Nic. de, 47
Sheffield, Rog. de, 59 n
Shephard (Sheppard, Shepperd):
  John, rector of Devizes, 174
  R. P., 149
  Thos., 245
Shepherd's Shore, see Cannings, Bishop's
Sheppard, Shepperd, see Shephard
Showring:
  Hen., 94
  Rob., 88
Shropshire, see Oswestry
Sidmouth, Vct., see Addington
Simon, abbot of Reading, 40
Simpson:
  Frank, 251
  Geo. (d. 1871), 217
  Geo. (d. 1900), 217
  Geo., s. of Geo. (d. 1900), 217
  Geo. (d. c. 1945, ? the same), 252
  Geo., & Co. Ltd., 217
  fam., 188
Simpson's Salisbury Journal, 217
Skinner, Thos., 81
Slade:
  Ann Sophia, 230
  Sam., 93 n
Slater, W., architect, 186
Slater & Carpenter, architects, 198
Sloper:
  Betty, 207
  Geo., 112
  Revd. Rob., 209
  T. B., 204

Smith:
  Revd. A. C., rectory of Yatesbury, and his w., 65
  Alf., 65, 159
  John (fl. 1500), 192
  John (fl. 1709), 157
  John (d. by 1725, ? the same), 220, 223, 252
  Joshua, 120, 152
  Thos., s. of Wm., 180
  Thos. (unidentified Devizes benefactor), 253
  Wm., 82, 180, 190
snuff, manufacture of, 70, 95–6
Somerset, duke of, see Seymour, Sir Edw.
Somerset, see Bath; Frome; Frome Selwood; Lansdown; Orchardsleigh; Taunton; Wiltshire and E. Somerset Congregational Union
Sotheron Estcourt, see Estcourt, T. H. S. Sotheron
Southampton, 203
Southbourne (Hants), 252
Southbroom, 3–4, 33, 68, 73, 122, 198, 247, 255–6
  adv., 194
  Bedborough, see Roundway
  brewery, 99
  chapelry of St. James, 3–4, 89
  chars., 249, 253
  ch. (St. James's), 193–8, *195*, *197*
    curates (later vicars), 194–5, 197–8; and see Barnwell; Dowding, B. C.
  Green, the, see Devizes
  hosp. of St. James and St. Denis, 194, 255–6
    chap., 256
  inc., 112
  innkeepers, 103
  Nursteed, see Roundway
  officers, 194
  peculiar, 194
  pop., 5
  schs., 4, 222, 224–6, 231; and see Devizes, schs., Devizes (formerly Southboom Senior) sch.
  Southbroom Ho., 69–72, 224–5
  vicarage ho., 198

Southbroom (*cont.*)
vicars, *see* Southbroom, curates
weavers, 82, 89
Wick (Wick Green), 3–4, 19 *n*, 21, 23, 35, 68, 194
inc., 112
Rom. settlements, 4
Upper Wick, *see* Devizes, Southgate
Wick Farm, 36
Speed, John, 1
Springfield & Rose, Messrs., 198
Stafford:
Hen., duke of Buckingham, 49
Thos., 49
Standfield, John, 102 *n*
Stanford, Chas., 206
Stanley abbey, 72
abbot, 254
Steeple Ashton, *see* Ashton, Steeple
Stephen, king, 37–8, 80
Stephens, *see* Stevens
Stert, 42, 255
Stevens (Stephens):
John, 87
Phil., 11
Stirling:
ctss. of, *see* Vanlore, Mary
earl of, *see* Alexander, Hen.
Strachey, John, 57
Strangwidge, Eliz., 178, 248
Stukeley, Wm., 21, 57, 113, 162
Surrey, *see* Chobham; Godalming; Mitcham
Sussex, *see* Brighton; Forest Row
Sutton:
Jas. (fl. 1715), 68, 91
Jas., s. of Jas. (fl. 1715), 91
Jas. (d. 1788, another), 187
Jas. (d. 1801), 68, 102, 146, 162, 187
John, 91
Prince, 187
Thos., 240
fam., 25, 90, 187
Swanborough hundred, 1
Swindon, 218

Talbot, Sir John, 138
Taunton (Som.), 70

Taylor (Tayler):
Adam, 112
J., bell-founder, 197
Rear-Adm. J. N., 11, 30, 215
——, 251
fam., 188
Temple, Wm., 207
textile industry, *see* Devizes, ind. and trade (textiles); Salisbury; Wiltshire; wool-stapling
Theobald, abp. of Canterbury, 38
Thorer, John, 88
Thurman:
Thos., 176–7, 222, 247–9, 252
fam., 188
Thurnam, John, 11
Thurnham, J., 232
Tilehurst (Berks.), 61
Tipper, Wm., 234
Tisbury, *see* Hatch, West
tobacco, manufacture of, 31, 95–6, 204
Tocotes, Sir Rog., 49, 179
Tonnell, John, 93 *n*
Tratman, Hen., 239
Tregoze, John, 47
Trew, *see* Drew, John (fl. 1501–2) *and* Rob. (d. *c.* 1564)
Trinder, Chas., 67
Trollope, fam., 188
Trowbridge, 85, 158, 218
castle, 38
county town, 74
Technical Coll. (Devizes Branch), 234
Trueman, Ric., 166
Trymnell, Wal., 83
Tudor-Hart, Delia G. M., 63
Tull, Hen., 240
Twinney, Thos., 93 *n*
Tylee (Tyley, Tylye):
J. N., 63
John (fl. 1658), 92 *n*
John (d. 1812), 97, 99, 102–3, 233
Thos., 63, 142
Wm., 92 *n*
Tylee & Gent (later Gent & Tylee; J. & T. Tylee; Tylee & Co.), 97
Tymmer, Thos., 83
Tyndale, Rob., 59 *n*

United Dairies, Ltd., 101; *and see* Wilts.
United Dairies Ltd.
Urchfont:
nonconf., 214
Redhorn Hill, 163
Utrecht (Holland), 61

Vanlore:
Jacoba, m. Hen. Alexander (or Zinzan), 61
Mary, ctss. of Stirling, 61
Mary, m. Sir Edw. Powell, 61
Peter (d. 1627), 61
Peter, s. of Peter (d. 1627), 61
Susan, m. Sir Rob. Croke, 61
fam., 65
Victoria, queen, 187
as princess, 10, 106
Virginia Co., 245

Wadsworth, Sarah, 223, 230, 251
Wadworth, H. A., 99
Wadworth & Co. Ltd., 99
Waite (or Wright), Mrs., 207
Wales, prince of, *see* Edward VII
Walker:
Fred., 92
Peter, 92
Waller, Sir Wm., 9
Wallis, John, bell-founder, 193
Walter son of Ralph, 42 *n*
Walter, Rob., 177, 248
Want, Edw., 250
Ward, S. H., 67, 243–4
Wardour, Edw., 129 *n*
Warminster, 85
inns, 103
Warner & Sons, bell-founders, 199
Warwick, earl of, *see* Plessis
Warwickshire, *see* Birmingham
Watson-Taylor:
Geo., 72
Simon, 72, 218
fam., 69
Watton, Wm., 88
Waugh, T. G., 63
Waylen:
Jas., 12

John, 91
Rob. (d. 1841), 92, 210 *n*, 226, 231
Rob., s. of Rob. (d. 1841), 99
W. A., 209
Webb (Webbe):
Alex., 87 *n*
Jas. (d. *c.* 1559), 84
Jas. (fl. 1689), 201
Jeremy, 84
John, 59 *n*
Ric., 87 *n*
Thos. (fl. 1615), 87 *n*
Thos. (fl. 1701), 91 *n*
fam., 87, 91
Wells, Jas., bell-founder, 188
Wesley (Wessley):
Chas., 212
Geo., 204
John, 208, 212
Westbury, 93
vicar of, *see* Hunton
Westmacott:
Ric. (d. 1808), sculptor, 187
Sir Ric. (d. 1856), sculptor, 187
Westminster Press, 218
Weston, John, 214
Whaddon, 255
Whatley, Geo., 105, 107
Whistley mill, *see* Potterne, mills
White:
Geo., 100
T. H., 100
T. H., Ltd., 100
Thos., 92 *n*
and see Wyt
Wick (in Potterne), *see* Potterne
Wick (in Rowde), *see* Rowde
Wick *and* Wick Green (in Southbroom), *see* Southbroom
Wick, Upper, *see* Devizes, Southgate
Wild:
Thos., 220, 223–4, 230–1, 252
fam., 188
Wiles, J. P., 202
Wilington, Ralph de, 40, 44
William, earl of Gloucester, 38
William the parker, 127
Willos (or Willis), John, 83

Wills, Obadiah, 207
Willy, Geo., 116, 187
Wilton:
  county ct., 73
  Jews at, 80
  taxation, 80, 89
Wilts. and Dorset Bank, 105
Wilts., Somerset & Weymouth Railway, 8
Wilts. United Dairies Ltd. (formerly North Wilts. Dairy Co.), 101
Wiltshire:
  county constabulary, see Devizes
  county council, 66, 72, 74, 224–5, 232–4
  offices (Devizes), 8, 74
  county library, 216
  county (later state) prison, see Devizes, prisons
  county record office, 158
  fire station, 168
  quarter sessions, see Devizes, county quarter sessions
  sheriff, 39, 41, 73
  textile ind., 82, 84, 89; and see Devizes, ind. and trade (textiles); Salisbury
  and see Devizes, assize town, county ct., public bdgs.; Roundway, Roundway hosp.; Salisbury, assize town; Wilton, county ct.
Wiltshire and East Somerset Congregational Union, 209
Wiltshire Arch. and Nat. Hist. Soc., 12, 79; and see Devizes, museum
Wiltshire Friendly Soc., 79
Wiltshire Gazette and Herald, 218
Wiltshire Herald and Advertiser, 218
Wiltshire Independent, 218
Wiltshire Methodist Mission, 213
Wiltshire militia, 9–10, 105–6, 198
Wiltshire Newspapers Ltd., 217
Wiltshire Regiment, 195
Wiltshire Savings Bank, 108
Wiltshire Telegraph, 218
Wiltshire Times, 218
Wiltshire Yeomanry, 11

Winchester, 38, 126, 221
Winter, Cornelius, 208
Woodruff, Wm., 219, 223, 230
Woodward, C. H., Ltd., 96
Woodyer, Hen., architect, 118
wool-stapling, 92–3; and see textile industry
Worcester:
  castle, 37
Wordsworth, John, bp. of Salisbury, 224
workhouse, see Devizes, hosps. (St. James's)
Worm Cliff, see Devizes
Worton:
  Hurst, 42
Wright:
  Jos., 203
  Sarah, 203
  Mrs., see Waite
Wyatt:
  Benj., architect, 118
  Jas., architect, 152
  T. H., architect, 79
Wyndham:
  Anne, m. Jas. Everard Arundell, 62
  Hen., 62
  Hen. Penruddocke (d. 1819), 62
  John, 62
  Sir Wadham (d. 1668), 62
  Wadham (d. 1736), 62, 111
  Wm., 62, 65–6
  fam., 62, 176
Wyt, John, 254; and see White

Yatesbury, rector of, see Smith, Revd. A. C.
York, duke of, see Edward
Yorkfleet, Thos. of, rector of Devizes, 254
Yorkshire, see Leeds

Zinzan:
  Hen., see Alexander
  Jacoba, see Vanlore
Zouche:
  Eleanor la, 48
  John, 73